Breaking the Wave

Breaking the Wave is the first anthology of original essays by both younger and established scholars that takes a long view of feminist activism by systematically examining the dynamics of movement persistence during moments of reaction and backlash. Ranging from the "civic feminism" of white middle-class organizers and the "womanism" of Harlem consumers in the immediate postwar period, to the utopian feminism of Massachusetts lesbian softball league founders and environmentally minded feminists in the 1970s and 1980s, *Breaking the Wave* documents a continuity of activism in both national and local organizing that creates a new discussion, and a new paradigm, for twentieth century women's history.

Contributors: Jacqueline L. Castledine, Susan K. Freeman, Julie A. Gallagher, Marcia Gallo, Susan M. Hartmann, Sally J. Kenney, Rebecca M. Kluchin, Kathleen A. Laughlin, A. Lanethea Mathews-Gardner, Catherine E. Rymph, Julia Sandy-Bailey, Jennifer A. Stevens, Janet Weaver, and Leandra Zarnow.

Kathleen A. Laughlin is Professor of History at Metropolitan State University in Minneapolis/St. Paul, MN. She is the author of *Women's Work and Public Policy: A History of the Women's Bureau, US Department of Labor, 1945–1970.*

Jacqueline L. Castledine is a core faculty member of the University Without Walls program, University of Massachusetts, Amherst, where she teaches interdisciplinary studies.

NEW DIRECTIONS IN AMERICAN HISTORY

SCIENCE AND EMPIRE IN THE ATLANTIC WORLD
Edited by James Delbourgo and Nicholas Dew

NATURAL PROTEST: ESSAYS ON THE HISTORY OF AMERICAN
ENVIRONMENTALISM
Edited by Michael Egan and Jeff Crane

BREAKING THE WAVE: WOMEN, THEIR ORGANIZATIONS,
AND FEMINISM, 1945–1985
Edited by Kathleen A. Laughlin and Jacqueline L. Castledine

Breaking the Wave

Women, Their Organizations, and Feminism, 1945–1985

Edited by
Kathleen A. Laughlin and Jacqueline L. Castledine

Routledge
Taylor & Francis Group

NEW YORK AND LONDON

First published 2011
by Routledge
270 Madison Avenue, New York, NY 10016

Simultaneously published in the UK
by Routledge
2 Park Square, Milton Park, Abingdon, Oxon OX14 4RN

Routledge is an imprint of the Taylor & Francis Group, an informa business

© 2011 Taylor & Francis

The right of Kathleen A. Laughlin and Jacqueline L. Castledine to be identified as the authors of the editorial material, and of the authors for their individual chapters has been asserted by them in accordance with sections 77 and 78 of the Copyright, Designs and Patents Act 1988.

Typeset in Minion by EvS Communication Networx, Inc.
Printed and bound in the United States of America on acid-free paper by Walsworth Publishing Company, Inc., MO

Library of Congress Cataloging-in-Publication Data
Breaking the wave : women, their organizations and feminism, 1945-1985 / edited by Kathleen A. Laughlin and Jacqueline L. Castledine.
p. cm. — (New directions in American history)
Includes bibliographical references and index.
1. Feminism—United States—History—20th century. 2. Second-wave feminism—United States. 3. Women—Political activity—United States—History—20th century. I. Laughlin, Kathleen A. II. Castledine, Jacqueline L.
HQ1426.B728 2010
305.420973'09045—dc22
2010011469

ISBN 13: 978-0-415-87397-0 (hbk)
ISBN 13: 978-0-415-87400-7 (pbk)
ISBN 13: 978-0-203-84293-5 (ebk)

To our Friends and Mentors in Women's History,
Eileen Boris, Dorothy Sue Cobble, Susan M. Hartmann,
and Nancy Hewitt

Contents

Acknowledgements   ix

Foreword   xi
SUSAN M. HARTMANN

Introduction: The Long History of Feminism   1
KATHLEEN A. LAUGHLIN

Part I Mainstream, Leftist, and Sexual Politics   **9**

1 Civic Feminists: The Politics of the Minnesota Federation of
Business and Professional Women's Clubs, 1942—1965   11
KATHLEEN A. LAUGHLIN

2 The Legal Origin of "The Personal Is Political": Bella Abzug and
Sexual Politics in Cold War America   28
LEANDRA ZARNOW

3 "I'm Glad as Heck That You Exist": Feminist Lesbian
Organizing in the 1950s   47
MARCIA GALLO

Part II Women's Global Visions   **63**

4 Exporting Civic Womanhood: Gender and Nation Building   65
CATHERINE E. RYMPH

5 The National Council of Negro Women, Human Rights, and
the Cold War   80
JULIE A. GALLAGHER

6 From Ladies Aid to NGO: Transformations in Methodist
   Women's Organizing in Postwar America   99
   A. LANETHEA MATHEWS-GARDNER

Part III The Politics of Location   113

7 The Consumers' Protective Committee: Women's Activism in
   Postwar Harlem   115
   JULIA SANDY-BAILEY

8 "Pregnant? Need Help? Call Jane": Service as Radical Action in
   the Abortion Underground in Chicago   136
   REBECCA M. KLUCHIN

9 Feminizing Portland, Oregon: A History of the League of
   Women Voters in the Postwar Era, 1950–1975   155
   JENNIFER A. STEVENS

10 Barrio Women: Community and Coalition in the Heartland   173
    JANET WEAVER

Part IV Feminist Consciousness and Movement Persistence   189

11 "Stop That Rambo Shit. . . This Is Feminist Softball":
    Reconsidering Women's Organizing in the Reagan Era and
    Beyond   191
    JACQUELINE L. CASTLEDINE AND JULIA SANDY-BAILEY

12 "It Would Be Stupendous for Us Girls": Campaigning for
    Women Judges Without Waving   209
    SALLY J. KENNEY

13 Building Lesbian Studies in the 1970s and 1980s   229
    SUSAN K. FREEMAN

    Conclusion: Looking Backward, Looking Forward   246
    JACQUELINE L. CASTLEDINE

    Selected Bibliography   252
    Contributor Biographies   257
    Index   261

Acknowledgments

Kathleen A. Laughlin
I wish to thank Shulamit Reinhartz, founding director, and the staff and scholars at the Women's Studies Resource Center, Brandeis University, where this project started during my sabbatical year in 2007–2008. I thank the people I met during Hillary Rodham Clinton's presidential campaign in New England who continue to sustain feminist activism: Christine Samuelson, Emelia Encanllado, Ines Schulz, Ziva Paley, Mansi Saboori, John Doggett, Jenny Doggett, Myra Tattenbaum, Diane Balser, Janna Kaplan, Martina Jackson, and especially Massachusetts state representatives Ruth Balser and Kay Khan for their commitment to advancing the cause of women in politics. I also want to thank Christa Kelleher, Research Director, Center for Women in Politics and Public Policy, University of Massachusetts-Boston, Judith Roy, Coordinator of Women's and Gender Studies, Century College, and my colleagues in the History Department at Metropolitan State University, Doug Rossinow, Sumiko Otsubo, and Jeanne Grant for their ongoing support.

Jacqueline L. Castledine
It is always wonderful to have the opportunity to publicly acknowledge those who inspire one's scholarship, and I am happy to thank a number of people for the support that made this project possible. I am grateful to mentors Steven Lawson and Nancy Hewitt for their wisdom and their friendship. I am also indebted to Sue Cobble, Temma Kaplan, Laura Lovett, Joyce Berkman and Kathleen Laughlin, among many others, for nurturing my enthusiasm for women's history. Special thanks go to my parents Jim and Gail Lilley for reminding me that there is a world outside the academy. Above all, thanks to Bobby for being Bobby.

Foreword

Journalists often write the first draft of history, but so too do historical actors. Feminists who participated in the momentous changes that have transformed gender policy and practice since the 1960s shaped historical understanding of their movement as surely as did the reporters who covered them. Their adoption of the term "second wave" perhaps more than anything else influenced initial impressions of the women's movement, shaping our conceptions of who comprised it, for whom it spoke, and what changes it sought to remedy women's disadvantages.

The typically young and radical activists in the 1960s who portrayed their movement as second-wave feminism had good reasons to do so. In assuming that label, they summoned up historical legitimacy by recalling, if only vaguely, earlier movements for education, the vote, and other goals that most people in the 1960s would have considered women's self-evident rights. Yet, caught up in the surge of 1960s social movements and enthralled with the novelty of their insights, feminists also meant the term second wave to strike a break with the past, to clarify what was new about their movement, and to lend urgency to their demands. Their long list of practices and institutions that disadvantaged women demonstrated how far beyond their foremothers the new movement would have to go for women to gain genuine equality.

As the essays in this book so beautifully establish, in marking both their links to an older feminism that they assumed had died in the 1920s and the originality of their own movement, self-identified second-wavers elided what had come in between and what had laid critical foundations for their own projects.

These foundations were built in the 1940s and 1950s by women in traditional women's organizations, women of color, lesbians, religiously oriented women, radical women lawyers, and women who worked across national boundaries. The groundwork of 1960s protest was constructed by women written out of the definition of feminism both by their own reluctance to wear the label and by the new feminists' unawareness of what had immediately preceded their awakening. In addition, we see clearly in the essays on women's activism in the 1940s and 1950s the limitations of these efforts, whether constrained by the political climate or cramped by the inability of many women to reach out across the lines of color and class. These essays not only reveal currents in those years that flowed into the mass women's movements of the 1960s and 1970s, but they also cause us to rethink generalizations about the post-World War II era that stress conservatism, nationalism, and women's complacency.

Written, for the most part, by a new generation of women's historians, this book establishes not only continuities with the past but also the persistence of feminism beyond the 1970s in sites diverse as the federal judiciary, the softball field, and the college classroom. When seen through the lens of women's history, both the 1950s and the 1980s contained progressive impulses and feminist projects that have lain hidden behind the label of conservatism applied to those eras by "mainstream" historians. Moreover, these younger scholars make a compelling case for a more expansive definition of feminism and for examining it at the local level in various locations. They persuade us that service projects could have a radical feminist edge, they provide testimony of women who worked along side men and combated the disadvantages of both color and gender, and they show that lesbian activism led into the 1960s women's movement as much as it grew out of it.

The staying power of the wave metaphor is not hard to understand. Giving the 1960s and 1970s activism a short-hand label is certainly a matter of convenience. "Second wave" also demarcates the time when women's quest for justice mobilized a mass movement and claimed attention from all of society's major institutions. And, it tacitly acknowledges the absolutely crucial push that the black freedom struggle gave to women's activism of the 1960s and 1970s. Yet, whether the wave metaphor succumbs to the arguments of this book and other critics of its appropriateness is finally beside the point. Thanks to these scholars, we have a much richer, more complex, and more complete conception of American women's activism in the second half of the twentieth century.

Susan M. Hartmann
Ohio State University

Introduction
The Long History of Feminism[1]

KATHLEEN A. LAUGHLIN

"The Club Election" episode of the *I Love Lucy Show* (1953) satirizes women's affiliations with clubs and societies and interest in politics. Lucy is involved in the Wednesday Art club, which sometimes met on Tuesdays and Fridays. Disappointed that fellow club members nominated her best friend Ethel Mertz to be president of the club instead of her, Lucy insists on a caucus, which she learned about by watching presidential nominating conventions on television. Lucy's version of caucusing involved promising Caroline Appleby a darling sweater and purse set if Caroline would nominate Lucy to run against Ethel. Lucy and Ethel's husbands, Ricky and Fred, fearing nights eating alone if their wives are elected to office, try to ensure the defeat of both candidates by taking a swing voter out to Ricky Ricardo's club for an evening of dining and dancing. In this episode clubwomen, hardly committed to exercising citizenship, are easily swayed by bribes related to women's true interests: fashion and romance. Lucy does not learn about caucusing from her club but through the media, and then she employs the tactic with a feminine twist. Her club involvement comes from a need for attention rather than from a sense of civic duty—Lucy does not seek office in order to serve the public good but rather to challenge her friend Ethel. Popular culture in the 1950s routinely denigrated women's interests in anything outside of the home and emphasized competition between women for male attention. Even though the conflict in each episode of *I Love Lucy* stems from Lucy and Ethel's desire to do almost anything to avoid staying at home, their efforts to shape their own lives are treated as silly distractions from their true identities as wives and mothers.

Even in feminist history women's various expressions of autonomy in particular (or peculiar if we consider the fictional world of Lucy and Ethel) contexts and circumstances has not always been considered significant. Another powerful image that continues to endure despite research that complicates our understanding of women's lives and status in American society over time is the waves metaphor used to chart the history of women's rights activism. The standard and widely accepted waves chronology identifies the first wave as a movement for civil and political rights, such as property ownership and suffrage, dating from the first women's rights convention in the United States, the 1848 meeting in Seneca Falls, New York, to the ratification of the Nineteenth Amendment to the U.S. Constitution in 1920 granting women the vote. The second wave began in the mid-1960s, which is described in many sources as a resurgence of activism that broadened the notion of equality to include a re-examination of men's and women's social roles, which ends in the mid-1980s amid criticism, most notably from women of color and lesbians, that privileged, white, heterosexual women determined its goals, ideologies, and strategies. The third wave refers to efforts by younger women and men to take feminism from what they perceived as an exclusive concern with dichotomous notions of gender toward consideration of the multiple identities of age, class, race, sexual orientation. As Astrid Henry suggests, the notion that younger women of the third wave rebelled against their mother's feminism has shaped contemporary feminism.[2] In this typology feminists speak with the same voice and exercise authority in the same ways so that feminism becomes a singular notion rather than defined broadly to encompass all of the strategies women used to assert themselves in public life.

Despite historian Joan W. Scott's warning twenty years ago that a focus on feminist generations with its implied unity of purpose masks ideological differences between women, and that over the past decade historians, women's studies scholars, sociologists, and political scientists have recognized the diversity of feminisms in the ways Scott implied, the waves metaphor continues to shape our understanding of feminist organizing.[3] The titles of recent synthetic works on the history of modern feminism suggest the dramatic break from the past the waves metaphor embodies: *Tidal Wave: How Women Changed America at Century's End* (2003) by Sara Evans, Estelle B. Freedman's *No Turning Back: The History of Feminism and the Future of Women* (2002), and Ruth Rosen's *The World Split Open: How the Modern Women's Movement Changed America* (2000).[4] These important and widely read works have focused on the transformative and transgressive aspects of second-wave feminism to argue that the movement's ideas, ideals, and accomplishments have persisted into the twenty-first century. Many books on the modern women's movement have been published recently, as participants in that movement, either as professional historians or activists, look back on the experience that shaped their lives. Recent histories and personal narratives have entrenched further the notion that social change occurs in waves of activism representing a profound break from the past. Consequently, the activism of young, primarily white and middle class, "liberationists" willing to critique gender relations remains at the center of feminist history. Popular feminist history continues to marginalize diverse communities and burnish Lucy and Ethel as the image of women's concerns in the 1950s.

This anthology is precisely the intervention that a new generation of scholars wishes to make. This volume takes a longer view of feminist activism by systematically examining how women expressed their autonomy through collective action during moments of reaction and backlash from 1945 to 1985. The contributors, scholars committed to examining women's activism at different times in various locations, consider women's public activism both before and after the so-called second wave in the mid-1960s and 1970. The case studies of the various forms of women's collective action as it evolved within liberal and conservative establishments, in marginalized communities, and within progressive movements presented here explicitly end the "tyranny of the waves metaphor" in describing the trajectory of women's rights in the United States.[5]

Although the women in our studies of the period before the second wave did not use the term "feminist" to define themselves or their work, they sought to promote women's interests in multifaceted and complex ways, as did women who confronted changing political and social contexts during the so-called post-feminist era of the 1980s and 1990s. The various forms of civic and political engagement and institution-building employed by groups and individuals to improve women's lives deserve more recognition as essential to movement persistence in conservative and reactionary times. The many endeavors to engage in collective action against a backdrop of reaction have not been sufficiently recognized as an important exercise of autonomy.

We have attempted to broaden our understanding of who gets to be a feminist by suggesting that feminist practice has occurred and persisted in various social, political, and cultural contexts, taking many different forms such as direct action protest, mainstream civic engagement, and community service.[6] The politics of some of the women studied in this collection was resolutely in the mainstream; their activism was confined to and shaped by women's clubs, religious groups, professional practices, and local activism and neighborhood politics. In the 1950s they often adhered to gender norms and, with the exception of activism informed by leftist politics and racial identity, did not question the prerogatives and race and class privilege. The singular focus of the African American women in Harlem to lower food prices; the civic engagement of the Portland Oregon League of Women Voters; the religious purpose of Methodist women; the neighborhood organizing of Mexican American women in Iowa; and the lonely leftist politics of Bella Abzug are recognized here as equally important as second-wave feminism with its more radical politics. New research also reveals women's quest for autonomy and social change during the post-feminist years in locations as disparate as softball diamonds and academia. Through studies of local activism and singular groups and institutions we not only explain how woman-centered politics evolved over time, from at times ignoring class, race, and sexual identities to confronting the injuries of homophobia and racism, but we also consider when, why, and how differences between women stymied efforts to organize for a common cause.

In some ways, as it was a decade later, sisterhood was powerful in the 1950s, as women developed meaningful and significant relationships with other women in the context of a backlash against women in public life. World War II and the postwar period was a watershed for national women's organizations. Not only did the war contribute to increasing memberships of women's organizations as locations for service on the home front, it raised expectations among women that opportunities for public engagement and employment would continue to be available. When meaningful social change did not occur, meetings, social activities, and public protests organized by groups, clubs, and societies facilitated this nascent gender solidarity.

The first section of this book explores how women's personal awareness and collective action generated distinct challenges to the repressive culture and conservative politics of the 1950s. As Kathleen A. Laughlin shows in her case study of the Minnesota Federation of Business and Professional Women's Clubs, clubwomen defied popular assumptions about women's attitudes and desires in the 1950s by unabashedly promoting the Equal Rights Amendment. Local clubs nurtured women's aspirations and ended their isolation. Esther Tomljanovich, the third woman to serve on the Minnesota Supreme Court from 1990 until her retirement in 1998, recalled that during the 1950s "we were not only ignored, we were absolutely invisible," and that the Minnesota Federation of Business and Professional Women's Clubs in the 1950s was "a place where women were valued."[7]

Marcia Gallo reveals that the Daughters of Bilitis (DOB) combined personal and political awareness in organizing lesbians, a truly isolated group during the 1950s, setting the stage of lesbian feminism. Founding members were cognizant of their place as women in society and were just as committed to providing support for women as a group as the Business and Professional Women's Clubs. Just as women's clubs, DOB branches in U.S. cities were fully committed to maintaining a shared identity and common purpose through activities, meetings, and distribution of the national monthly magazine, *The Ladder*. The DOB's national publication, in contrast to the publications of mainstream women's clubs and organizations, provided a forum for personal expressiveness. Leandra Zarnow suggests that Bella Abzug's defense of Willie McGee, a Mississippi black man charged with the rape of a white woman epitomized the "personal is political" before the social revolution of the 1960s and 1970s. Abzug and other leftist lawyers exposed the structures of power during the 1950s in ways that anticipated New Left politics and radical feminism. Abzug was ahead of her time in using her training as a lawyer to confront sexual politics and racial injustice.

The formation of the United Nations in 1945 enabled women's organizations to critically evaluate the status of women in the United States using the rhetoric of global human rights, as Catherine E. Rymph, A. Lanethea Mathews, and Julie Gallagher explain in the second section of the book on women's distinctive global vision. Both black and white women's clubs used the backdrop of national security concerns in the United States during the Cold War era to present compelling arguments for human rights. Rymph's chapter on the international outreach efforts of the League of Women Voters indicates that clubwomen sought to both influence U.S. foreign policy and shape impressions of the U.S. abroad by forming relationships with women throughout the world. As Mathews explains in her chapter on Methodist women's engagement in international politics in the 1950s to the 1980s, the formation of the U.N. in 1945 altered the purpose of the Women's Division of Christian Services, from a commitment to missionary work to advocacy of human rights and the eradication of gender, race, and class inequality. Mathews argues that religious identity has not been recognized fully as providing a powerful reason for women's activist impulses in the mid-twentieth century.

The National Council of Negro Women (NCNW) also used the U.N. to advocate for equality throughout the world. Julie Gallagher's study of the internationalism of the NCNW demonstrates that organized African American women sought active participation in postwar planning with other powerful national women's organizations and repudiated the notion that men should be the architects of postwar foreign policy. While the NCNW was just as eager as prominent white women's organizations to enter discussions about the direction of U.S. foreign policy and the U.N., Gallagher suggests that it was not readily accepted by largely segregated white organizations such as the General Federation of Women's Clubs and the American Association of University Women. Research on mainstream organizations heretofore unrecognized as important subjects of study deepens our understanding of how racial, class, and ideological differences compartmentalized public activism to the detriment of a unified women's rights agenda. The first two sections of this volume suggest that sisterhood was powerful but had its limits. Women sought solidarity often within the confines of their own organizations.

The essays in the section on the politics of location provide a nuanced assessment of the disparate forms of women's public engagement only possible through local case studies. Jennifer A. Stevens, Rebecca M. Kluchin, Julia Sandy-Bailey, and Janet Weaver provide a sampler of regional politics and organizing in the 1950s to the 1970s. Stevens's local study of the Portland, Oregon League of Women Voters examines how the League, even though it was strictly nonpartisan, preferred to gently inform citizens about local elections, and did not seek common cause with communities of color, determined the direction of urban planning in Portland as the city confronted the aftereffects of dislocation caused by World War II and a postwar population explosion.

Weaver's study of Mexican American women in Davenport, Iowa, and Sandy-Bailey's examination of consumer rights activism in Harlem reveals how communities of color organized on the margins of mainstream suburban culture. Mexican American women, unlike the clubwomen in Stevens' study, did not form sex-segregated organizations but focused on economic issues and integration of neighborhoods in partnership with men. The American G.I. Forum and the League of Latin American Citizens, groups formed to support Mexican American World War II veterans, also became locations for women's organizing. Thus, when the landmark 1964 Civil Rights Act was passed by Congress, they were poised to further civil rights in Iowa. Similarly, black women in Harlem confronted economic inequality. Sandy-Bailey's chapter on the Consumers' Protective Committee in Harlem charts the long history of female-led direct action protest. CPC members linked race, location, and consumer practices by publicizing and protesting against high prices in black neighborhoods.

A distinct approach to community organizing informed by the civil rights movement and the New Left emerged in Chicago. Community organizers joined with housewives, teachers, students, and secretaries to form an underground service that performed illegal abortions from 1969 until the historic *Roe v. Wade* Supreme Court decision in 1973. Rebecca Kluchin contends that community-based service has not been recognized as equally important as direct action protest in accounts of the genesis of radical feminism. Service activism such as work with Freedom Schools in the South was an important conduit for women's engagement in radical politics.

The final section of this anthology considering feminism from the 1970s to the 1990s makes clear that feminist consciousness did not begin and end within one generation. Exploring women's activism during what is commonly referred to as a period of backlash, these chapters argue that continuity, as much as the better chronicled issue of discontinuity, characterizes recent feminist activism. Sally J. Kenney, Susan K. Freeman, Jacqueline Castledine, and Julia Sandy-Bailey challenge the notion of conflicting generations of the second and third waves by revealing ideological continuity into the so-called post-feminist era. In doing this, they suggest that the notion of post-feminism may be overstated. The chapters in this section stress the importance of visibility in sustaining feminist values, ideologies, and goals.

Visibility within institutions was an important function of feminism in the 1980s and 1990s. Susan Freeman's study of the origins and growth of lesbian studies programs emphasizes the tremendous significance of the locations of the classroom and the academic department as places where lesbian feminist identities and agendas could evolve. With a focus on the educational practices rather than scholarship in the field of gay and lesbian studies, Freeman considers the significance of collaboration across generations. Exchanges of ideas refined feminist critiques of gender relations and sexual identities over time. Women's political visibility was equally important, as Sally Kenney explores in her case studies of the judicial careers of Florence Allen and Rosalie E. Wahl. The courts have been neglected locations of feminist agency in analyses of women's political participation. Her study provides another view of feminists' strategic engagement with mainstream institutions over time. Jacqueline Castledine and Julia Sandy-Bailey display how softball players used sport as another way to expand their feminist activism and to explore a shared outlook on gender and sexual orientation. In their local study of the politics of recreation, Castledine and Sandy-Bailey suggest that consciousness-raising occurred in a variety of contexts and locations.

The historians, political scientists, and women's studies scholars in this collection have recognized and documented adjustments to highly charged and altered political environments that often demanded different rhetorical and strategic methods promoting the interests of women as a group, which often became more mainstream and institutionalized during times of conservatism—and far less dramatic than either the first wave or the second wave. Scholarship on feminism informed by the case studies that can follow individuals and groups across the waves can more effectively consider how and why methods of organizing and feminist ideologies changed over time. Leandra Zarnow, by considering Bella Abzug's ideological commitments in the 1940s and 1950s, charts ideological continuity. Rosalie Wahl was one of only two women in her law class, but, in 1978, with the backing of organized feminist groups in Minnesota, including the women's legal fraternity Phi Delta Delta where she met Esther Tomljanovich who had been a practicing attorney since the mid-1950s, she was appointed to the Minnesota Supreme Court in 1978. Laughlin's and Kenney's case studies of Minnesota draws attention to the political life cycles of women, charting their earliest engagement in public life to alliances with feminist organizations and eventual success within mainstream institutions, where they sustained a feminist ethic into the 1990s.

All of the women profiled in this collection were committed to woman-centered politics over a long period of time. It is in writing this history where scholars have become acutely aware of the limitations of the waves metaphor. Our purpose here is not to reject extant historical accounts of feminism that accurately assess the significance of momentous social change but to bring to the forefront scholarship that has also evaluated and charted how feminists' have adjusted during periods of reaction. Feminism has survived sharp political and cultural divisions following women's increased autonomy both after World War II and the women's movement's successes in the 1970s; feminists have persisted in the midst of a return to domesticity in 1950s and with the ascendancy of the New Right in the 1980s.

Notes

1. The term "long history" has been used to describe civil rights activism. See Jacqueline Dowd Hall, "The Long Civil Rights Movement and the Political Uses of the Past," *Journal of American History* 91, no. 4 (March 2005): 1233–1263.
2. Astrid Henry, *Not My Mother's Sister: Generational Conflict and Third-Wave Feminism* (Bloomington: Indiana University Press, 2004), 4.
3. Joan W. Scott, "Conference Call," *differences* 2, no. 3 (1990): 52–108. Astrid Henry explains Scott's arguments in *Not My Mother's Sister*, 6.
4. Sara Evans, *Tidal Wave: How Women Changed America at Century's End* (New York: The Free Press, 2003); Estelle Freedman, *No Turning Back: The History of Feminism and the Future of Women* (New York: Ballantine Books, 2004); Ruth Rosen, *The World Spit Open: How the Modern Women's Movement Changed America* (New York: Viking, 2000).
5. Kathleen A. Laughlin et al., "Is it Time to Jump Ship? Historians Rethink the Waves Metaphor, *Feminist Formation* (Vol. 22) Spring 2010: 81.
6. Ibid., 92. Eilene Boris raises the issue of who gets to be a feminist in her discussion of "what's in a name."
7. Esther Tomljanovich, phone conversation with the author, 8 December 2009.

PART I

Mainstream, Leftist, and Sexual Politics

CHAPTER **1**

Civic Feminists
The Politics of the Minnesota Federation of Business and Professional Women's Clubs, 1942–1965

KATHLEEN A. LAUGHLIN

In 1947 the *New York Times Magazine* published a feature article by Margaret Culkin Banning on the burgeoning women's club movement in the United States. She knew this milieu well. As the National Federation of Business and Professional Women's Clubs' (BPW) national program chair in 1946, Culkin Banning was one of the architects of an intensive lobbying effort to persuade Congress to pass the Equal Rights Amendment (ERA) while there was favorable public opinion about women's contributions on the home front during World War II.[1] An estimated twelve million women were members of gender-segregated social, religious, or civic voluntary associations in the 1940s, and an impatient Culkin Banning used her platform in the *New York Times* to assail organized women for failing to transform mainstream politics: "Why, after women have had organizations for twenty-five years which have made it their concern to give women political education, is a woman mayor in some remote small town still national news?"[2] Enid C. Pierce, a former state president of the Vermont Federation of Women's Clubs, complained about this public scolding of clubwomen in a letter to the Editor: "But when the clubs do fold their tents, a vast amount of village improvement will steal away with them—such homely but desirable activities as libraries, improvement in schools, establishment of youth canteens, and even garbage disposal."[3] These competing visions of the purpose of women's public activism—modest or transformative—that played out in the *New York Times* reveal the difficulties in assessing clubwomen's contributions to history.

Were clubwomen little more than well-meaning dilettantes, or were they committed community leaders and shapers of public policy—even feminists? The culture and politics of the Minnesota Federation of Business and Professional Women's Clubs (MFBPW) during and after World War II was decidedly proactive, pro-woman, and feminist. MFBPW members asserted themselves politically in local communities, addressed negative stereotypes of women in the media, and achieved policy victories on the state level that were far more significant than the modest goals Culkin Banning dismissed and Pierce praised in the *New York Times*. Neither commentator could truly appreciate the implications of women's full civic participation and what various forms of political engagement would mean on the local and state level. With hindsight, though, historians can reassess the significance of state and local politics and the transformative potential of women's exercises of autonomy within the repressive climate of the 1950s, especially if we look beyond the waves metaphor. However fierce they were in their politics and identities as women, though, they did not refer to themselves as feminists or to their activities as feminist. Thus, as other women's historians writing about postwar America, I have modified the term feminist to describe this generation of activists.[4] Clubwomen were civic feminists: They believed that women's equality was essential to democracy and national security and considered all forms of public engagement, no matter how modest, as significant exercises in authority and autonomy. Civic feminists linked the suffrage movement and the modern women's movement, the so-called first and second waves; they continued the rhetorical legacy of the suffrage movement by making claims for women's rights as essential to the public interest, yet they anticipated a mass-based women's rights movement in the 1960s and 1970s by unapologetically claiming power and authority in public life in great numbers.

Continuity between first and second wave feminism is not a new idea. For two decades women's historians have examined how and why women asserted themselves in public life during the 1940s and 1950s.[5] Yet, the waves metaphor remains the dominant conceptual framework used to determine the importance of women's activism during and after World War II. "Second wave" feminism is a durable metaphor because it is a picturesque way to describe the tumultuous decade of the 1960s. The transformative politics of 1960s and 1970s feminism is indisputable. Unfortunately, though, the notion of movement resurgence in the 1960s implies that women's sustained civic pursuits during the interregnum between the suffrage movement and modern feminism was unremarkable, even unmemorable.

Consequently, clubwomen have not been recognized fully in recent books on the history of feminism in the United States as agents of social change.[6] The waves metaphor cannot possibly capture the political life cycle of these women, which evolved from conventional voluntarism to bolder feminist activism that was evident in the 1950s and flourished during the 1960s and 1970s. The BPW and its state branches kept the waves moving over time. It is about time the long history of women's public engagement replace the chronicle of tides of resurgence.

World War II revitalized a moribund club movement that had lost direction after the passage of the Nineteenth Amendment to the U.S. Constitution in 1920 granting women the right to vote. Clubs drew members eager to participate in the war effort through volunteer work and community leadership. By the 1950s women's clubs had become large, modern bureaucratic organizations that anticipated contemporary feminist interest groups. The large number of disparate, active women's clubs that Culkin Banning dissected in the *New York Times* reflected a desire for affiliation among women who embraced domesticity but also believed in responsible citizenship. We will see in the case of the Minnesota Federation of Business and Professional Women's Clubs that civic engagement in the 1940s and 1950s was an important precondition for grassroots feminism.

From its inception in 1919 in the midst of a vibrant suffrage movement, the BPW championed full engagement in mainstream politics. However, in the 1920s and 1930s forays into politics were either educational to prepare women for the newly acquired franchise or defensive efforts to repel discriminatory employment policies and practices during the Great Depression. The group endorsed the Equal Rights Amendment in 1937 but did not launch a national lobbying campaign toward its passage until 1946 under Margaret Culkin Banning's leadership.[7] Women's expanded political and economic roles during World War II offered the BPW and other women's organizations a proactive platform to make wartime gains permanent.

Although politically ineffectual and programmatically adrift during the Great Depression because of dwindling memberships and shrinking resources, BPW clubs were nevertheless established and well-known institutions in local communities that federal and state agencies relied upon to recruit women for the war effort. A significant number of BPW members in Minnesota, especially teachers, attorneys, home demonstration agents in rural communities, and public relations and human resources experts, formulated policies and executed programs for national defense. The War Production Board invited Minneapolis club member Sally Woodward, in charge of public relations at General Mills, and ten other businesswomen to Washington, D.C., for two months to help organize the Women's Division for Salvage. Woodward wrote two U.S. government publications designed to enlist both male and female voluntary associations in the war effort, "Organizing Your Defense" and "War Work."[8] Other MFBPW members worked in regional offices of the War Production Board. State international affairs chair Frances Sains set policies in the Division of Priorities in Minneapolis.[9] Republican Governor Harold E. Stassen appointed fellow state federation officers to help direct Minnesota's defense effort on the War Manpower, War Finance, and Consumer's Interests Committees.[10]

It is likely that civilian and military recruitment was a MFBPW project in 1942–43 because Maud Whitacre, as the womanpower supervisor for the Minnesota War Manpower agency, and State of Minnesota Civil Defense Coordinator Frances Schneider enlisted fellow members to meet employment shortages and to assume responsibilities for civil defense. A quarter of the 1,300 members in the state federation eschewed more conventional voluntary pursuits such as war bond drives and service with the Red Cross for leadership positions on community selective service, civil defense, and rationing boards. The Stillwater, Winona, and Northfield clubs claimed to administer the food and gasoline rationing policies of their towns. Fifty-seven members reported heading volunteer recruitment efforts in their communities.[11]

Successive Republican governors from 1939 to 1951, known for their progressive politics and interest in administrative reform, Stassen, Edward J. Thye, and Luther W. Youndahl considered MFBPW members for appointments. Led by Stassen, governor from 1939 to 1943, who embraced the ideals of Progressive era reform, the Republican Party was able to defeat the Farmer-Labor Party in 1939 by offering an alternative to liberal and moderate voters alienated from the Democratic Party organization dominated by conservative German and Irish Catholics and increasingly distrustful of the economic radicalism of farmer-laborism.[12] Progressive Republicans ended nine years of Farmer-Labor rule during the Great Depression by embracing moderate policies, emphasizing active citizen involvement, and eschewing centralized authority.[13] Daniel J. Elazar has suggested that "Republicans gave Minnesota a succession of organizationally independent governors."[14] Encouraging citizen involvement was not only politically advantageous in the context of third-party politics, but necessary in a state where centralized authority was limited. Until the 1960s, Minnesota governors served two-year terms and functioned with a very small number of staff assistants. Governor Thye had only three assistants to help him with the transition from wartime to peacetime in 1945.[15] The MFBPW took full advantage of this political culture to claim power in state politics. There is little evidence that the MFBPW actively supported the Republican Party, however. Rather, the group was more opportunistic than ideological in state politics. As we will see, when the Democratic Farmer Labor Party

(DFL), a product of a merger between the Democratic Party and farmer-laborism, was on the rise in the mid-1950s, MFBPW officers did not hesitate to work with party members on women's issues.

An unprecedented commitment to civic leadership during and after World War II engendered a re-evaluation not only of club goals but of women's place in society. Joanne Meyerowitz has shown how the BPW crafted a "language of reform" from an increasing public awareness of national security during World War II and the Cold War: "By deploying arguments articulated during World War II, the Federation linked enhanced national security to women's greater participation in government and business."[16] A resolution adopted at the 23rd Annual Convention of the MFBPW in 1942 supports Meyerowitz's thesis that national security was employed as a rationale for equal rights:

> Because women are called upon to come out of their homes in increasing numbers in order to release men for combat service and help win the war; and because so many will be unable to resume their former jobs after the war is over and because we realize that women have a tremendous stake in the future of our country and the world; and because we know that there is no security for any group unless there is security for all...we believe that the BPW should devote considerable and real thought and effort to securing a world in which there shall be work for all.[17]

The state program for 1942, "Mobilize for Democracy," included a recommendation that each club convene a panel for the first program meeting of the year to reflect upon the purpose of club work and to reconsider the "objectives and accomplishments of women."[18] Suggested panel questions such as "What has been accomplished?" and " Is the Business and Professional Women's Club an effective organization?" from the state program chair Frieda Monger encouraged a critical evaluation of programs and goals.[19] Monger reminded members that they should use club programs to assume positions of public of authority: "As clubs which have spent years in study we have a valuable contribution to make to the thinking of our community and nation and that we take a real part along that line."[20]

Members took umbrage at the persistent denigration of women's public service in the media. Incoming state president Viola Sheffer impressed upon her board of directors that the MFBPW was an educational and civic organization, not a social club.[21] A letter from a member of the Owatonna club, read aloud at a board of directors meeting in 1942, complaining that Fred Allen's radio program ridiculed women's contributions to the war effort, prompted state-wide action to "denounce the outrage."[22] The public affairs committee lodged a formal protest with the National Broadcasting Corporation (NBC). Perhaps as a result of state organizing to promote positive images of women workers and volunteers on NBC radio programs in 1942 and 1943, the state convention in 1944 adopted a resolution exhorting the National Federation to find new ways to answer media stereotypes against women workers and other forms of discrimination against women.[23]

Minnesota Business Women openly denounced another source of perceived discrimination against women, the "knight errant" economics of protective labor legislation.[24] Several convention resolutions adopted during and immediately after World War II referred to home front activities as proof that legislation establishing maximum hours requirements and minimum wages for women as a group was based on antiquated notions about their capabilities. A resolution proposed by former state federation presidents and adopted at the convention in 1946 opposed any effort of the Minnesota legislature to reinstitute protective labor legislation that was suspended during the war emergency because "women have made an outstanding and valuable contribution to the war and entered all fields of labor and management without serious effects on their health."[25]

The MFBPW collaborated with the equal rights feminist organization the National Woman's Party (NWP) to lobby for passage of the Equal Rights Amendment (ERA). Encouraged by a favorable report on the ERA from the U.S. Senate Judiciary Committee in 1942, the MFBPW passed a resolution commending the NWP for its work on ERA and pledging active collaboration with the group, which included joining the NWP in opposition to increased appropriations from Congress for the Women's Bureau, U.S. Department of Labor, until it reversed its opposition on the ERA in defiance of national BPW policy.[26] The *St. Paul Business Woman* published "Legislative Letters" from NWP executive director Caroline Lexow Babcock outlining the political action necessary to bring a vote on the ERA to the floor of Congress.[27]

Differences of opinion about the implications of protective labor legislation between women's organizations sometimes stymied efforts to organize nationally and locally on women's issues. Social and labor feminists rejected the NWP's purist stance on equal rights.[28] Working-class women and their middle-class allies believed that protective labor legislation as a means to improve labor conditions was sacrosanct. ERA politics to some extent created barriers between women's organizations, but on the national and local level the BPW tended to be pragmatic. Members viewed protective labor legislation in the narrowest of terms as legislation that limited employment opportunities for women rather than from a class-based perspective. They were far from laissez-faire ideologues.[29] Indeed, their approach to government was informed more by a concern with employment discrimination than by a desire to protect business. In essence, government regulatory power was fine if it was used to protect women from discrimination rather than from working conditions. There were more workers in the BPW than business owners. A requirement for membership was full time work, and clubs drew a fair share of clerical and other white collar workers as well as teachers and attorneys.[30] Consequently, the National Federation was far less doctrinaire than the equal rights feminists in the NWP and often joined broad-based coalitions with labor feminists under the auspices of the Women's Bureau, U.S. Department of Labor to support equal pay for equal work legislation and other policies on women's issues.[31]

MFBPW activists were ardently committed to defending women's rights in the workplace during reconversion from wartime mobilization. An executive committee on reconversion organized club projects to oppose and prevent discrimination against working women after the war. In 1944 these initiatives included efforts to encourage members to join community postwar planning boards and survey postwar employment needs in each community. Twenty members comprised a speakers' bureau to promote the case for fair play when the war was over. State president Viola Sheffer, an attorney from St. Paul, drafted a plank opposing discrimination against women in postwar employment for inclusion in the platforms for both the Democratic and Republican parties, and she formed "convention group" to organize support for the plank among convention delegates.[32]

During the postwar years, the MFBPW's ambitious reconversion agenda was bolstered by a powerful national BPW organization with a new headquarters in Washington, D.C., and a full-time lobbyist. High-profile leaders, effective community organizing, and the formation of "swing-shifters" clubs to take advantage of the influx of women workers in defense industries increased national club membership throughout the 1940s, from the static membership of 47,000 in the 1930s to 160,000 by 1949.[33] In the postwar years, the BPW and many women's clubs functioned as effective national organizations with permanent staff who created highly organized communication networks. Dues paid by state branches and local clubs subsidized national programs organized by professional lobbyists and public relations personnel, such as Margaret Culkin Banning and the BPW's first lobbyist, former Women's Army Corps Lieutenant Colonel Geneva McQuartters, who, in turn, trained the rank and file how to be community leaders. Professional staff wrote guidelines for civic engagement and articles on the status of pending legislation before Congress in the national publication, *Independent Woman*.[34] Staffed by unmarried and married "career" women, who were more aware of and more vulnerable to discriminatory practices, the BPW pursued equal rights legislation, actively campaigned for the appointment of more women to public office, and recruited women to run for elective office. Staff members employed current events study programs, community visits by national officers, and national conventions to mobilize state and local branches. Consequently, for the first time in its history, the BPW had the resources and the political wherewithal to recommit to the passage of the ERA and federal equal pay for equal work legislation. Women's contributions to civilian defense emboldened the group to more forcefully promote the principle of equality.

A watershed national biennial convention in 1946 approved several resolutions recommended by state federation presidents, club presidents, and state committee chairs that refocused the national program from education to social action. Most notably, an approved convention resolution abandoned a policy of strict nonpartisanship so as not to discourage members from entering mainstream politics. Other resolutions initiated campaigns for the immediate passage of the ERA and called for the election of qualified women for local, state, and national offices. The subsequent national program, "Is Today's Woman Ready for Her Tomorrow?" made passage of the ERA before the 100th anniversary of the Seneca Falls Women's Rights Convention the foremost political goal of the BPW because of "a lively awareness of the obligation which rests upon us to preserve the hard-won gains of the war years."[35] Program suggestions for local and state club projects in 1947 included at least one program meeting on equal rights, establishment of a bipartisan equal rights committee headed by two chairpersons, one from each political party, and lobbying the state legislature. The new "Political Alertness Project" gave clubs citations for meeting five requirements for effective civic engagement: "All members are enrolled in the political party of her choice; every club member has volunteered to do tasks at her party election district; every member is identified with a local political party club; every member is informed of state and local election laws; and every member votes in primaries."[36] Incoming national president Sally Butler linked national security to women's position in society: "Isn't it ridiculous to talk about keeping women from their full rights as citizens in a world where civilians are as much in danger from war as the men who fly the planes, or dispatch the rocket bombs?"[37]

The MFBPW executed the national program by forming subcommittees to coordinate efforts on ERA, to draft state equal pay and ERA bills, and to seek the appointment of qualified women to boards and commissions in the state. During the 1947–48 club year attorneys on the subcommittees on equal pay and the ERA drafted legislation for consideration by the Legislative Research Council, a body composed of members of the Minnesota House and Senate. Reserve war bonds and money shifted from other programs funded the lobbying effort for the ERA and equal pay resolutions, and members accepted a dues increase to employ a field worker to expand the Minnesota Federation's program throughout the state.[38]

Legislative action also attempted to forestall a postwar backlash against working women. Proposed bills in the Minnesota House Committee on Employees' Compensation Committee and the Senate Labor Committee promised to not only reinstate protective labor legislation suspended during the war emergency but to deny married women the right to file unemployment claims if dismissals were due to marital status. These legislative proposals confirmed the worst fears of activists that a backlash against married women would occur after the war. Precious resources were spent to defeat proposed legislation into the 1950s.[39]

The subcommittee created to place more women in policy-making posts was more immediately successful with Republican governors dependent upon active citizens. The special advisory committee appraising the qualifications of women collected resumes of qualified women to send to Republican Governor Youngdahl, who needed high levels of civic engagement to support his ambitious program to improve the administrative functions of state government during the postwar period.[40] The Minnesota Federation threatened to withdraw support for the Youngdahl administration unless more women were placed on boards and commissions and in state agencies. Youngdahl responded by placing of several members on bodies charged to administer social welfare and education policies.[41]

Political goals were executed on the state level by an increasingly large and politically engaged membership. Clubs remained prominent in local communities, and state membership increased by 50 percent, from 1,200 members before World War II to over 2,000 members by 1947.[42] Several members active on wartime planning boards became involved in postwar planning committees or civil defense boards in Austin, Crookston, Madison, Stillwater, and Worthington, and twenty out of twenty-eight clubs reported legislative meetings featuring equal pay and the ERA and meetings to organize opposition to the reinstitution of protective labor legislation.[43] It was also a busy year for clubs committed to supporting legislation to improve secondary and primary education in Minnesota, a priority for clubs with a large contingent of teachers. Several clubs reported concerted efforts to pass this legislation, even at the expense of undertaking broader programmatic goals. One club petitioned a local school board to eliminate wage differentials between male and female teachers.[44] State legislation chair Maud Whitacre encouraged these efforts and other forms of "grass-roots" advocacy consistent with the goals of the BPW's "Political Alertness Project."[45] Whitacre also attempted to enlist other women's organizations in political activism. The state legislation program in 1950 included a dinner with representatives from the American Association of University Women, the League of Women Voters, and the General Federation of Women's Clubs to "stress the mutuality of interest rather than differences."[46]

Political activism within state branches and local clubs became even more important after feminists failed in their efforts to pass the ERA in Congress following World War II. National BPW president Dr. Frances Scott, a professor at Smith College, reiterated Culkin Banning's criticism that women lacked political clout in her 1950 executive report: "It is time we realized that voting power, not reason or persuasion, sways our legislators. Unless we can fully mobilize the voting power of all women behind the amendment it is unlikely it will pass in its original form."[47] Toward this end, Scott revitalized the "Political Alertness Project" and inaugurated another concerted lobbying effort to pass the ERA, "Operation Buttonhole"; Scott's initiatives endeavored to link civic education and engagement with coordinated lobbying for the ERA. The "Yardstick for Political Citizenship" and "Operation Buttonhole" guidelines, published in the group's publication *Independent Woman* "measured" members' political alertness, commitment to "home town" issues, and civic knowledge.[48] Program goals for clubs included civic schools for young women voting for the first time and briefings by county Democratic and Republican committeewomen on requirements for public office and state election procedures.

The defeat of proposed protective labor legislation bills in Minnesota reflected the growing effectiveness of local clubs and the state federation in the arena of mainstream politics. When protective labor legislation bills were introduced in the Minnesota Legislature again in the early 1950s, the MFBPW sought alliances with the Democratic Farmer Labor Party on women's issues and met with Republican leaders. The Democratic Party merged with the Farmer-Labor Party in 1944 to form the Democratic Farmer Labor Party in an effort to challenge Republican power in the state when national politics was dominated by the Democratic Party.[49] The DFL slowly began to run successful campaigns for state and national office, an ascent that began with the election of Hubert H. Humphrey to the U.S. Senate in 1948.[50] Viola Sheffer, Maud Whitacre, Agnes Anderson, and Stella Olsen met with the only female state representatives in the Minnesota legislature, Sally Luther and Coya Knutson from the DFL, co-sponsors of House File No. 89: A Bill for an Act Regulating the Hours of Labor for Women, in 1951 to explain their ongoing opposition to any form of protective labor legislation. Knutson made a commitment to "try to get the legislation re-written" to exempt office workers, whereas Luther remained unconvinced that protective labor legislation did more harm than good for women in the workplace.[51] In addition to meeting with DFL women, the MFBPW contingent met with Governor Youngdahl and the Republican leadership, including Speaker of the House John A. Hartle.[52]

When hearings on the legislation were convened by Republican Alf L. Bergerud, chairman of Employees' Compensation Committee, MFBPW members presented arguments that associated women's rights with national security, explaining that restrictive hours legislation would create another labor shortage during a "national emergency" (the Korean War).[53] Letters and telegrams sent to state representatives and senators raised fears about a labor shortage but also made claims for equal rights. St. Paul resident Clara Villar's letter to her state representative, Republican Joseph Priferl, emphasized that Minnesota businesswomen "were perfectly able to protect ourselves" and that the proposed restriction was "discriminatory against women."[54] During the 1951 legislative session, members sent fifty-two letters, twenty-eight telegrams, and seventeen special delivery letters to members of the Senate Labor Committee and House Employees' Compensation Committee decrying protective labor legislation.[55] State legislation chair Stella Olsen claimed credit for the defeat of the House bill to regulate the hours of women and made no mention of support from other women's organizations in her report to the national legislation chair, Cecelia P. Galey.[56]

State legislative platforms during the 1950s included proactive advocacy for antidiscrimination policies. The MFBPW zealously promoted "Operation Buttonhole," beginning with action to oppose the Hayden rider on the U.S. Senate version of the ERA allowing exemptions for protective labor legislation. Members wrote letters and sent wires to members of Congress opposing any rider to the ERA. Olivia Johnson wrote to Minnesota Republican Senator and former governor Edward Thye that she was "damn mad" that the Hayden rider was attached to the bill, and, referring to the United Nations Charter declaring equality for women, suggested that "we will be the laughing stock of the world if the original Equal Rights Amendment is not passed."[57] In the 1950s activists used Cold War rhetoric to make a case for the ERA. Dr. Janet McGregor of the Crookston, Minnesota Club circulated a paper, "Equal Rights—A World Issue," in which she suggested that the adoption of the ERA would "answer communist propaganda."[58] She believed that women in the United States were the targets of and more susceptible to communist propaganda because they did not have full citizenship rights. In an interview with Senator Hubert H. Humphrey, though, MFBPW leaders emphasized fairness and rebuffed Humphrey's belief that the law should recognize biological differences.[59]

While the Hayden rider stalled the national lobbying effort, Minnesotans refocused attention on state legislation to guarantee full citizenship rights. Draft legislation, with the title "Equal Pay for Equal Rights," proposed in the 1950s combined ERA-like language with a prohibition on unequal wage rates: "legislation ensuring the right of all women to work for compensation and to full recognition in all legal, economic, and human rights; and opposition to discrimination against women on the basis of age, sex, race, creed or marital status in the exercise of their rights and responsibilities as full citizens."[60] Since the Minnesota Federation had stronger ties to the state Republican Party due to its work with a succession of Republican governors, it may have lost clout when the DFL won the governorship with the election of Orville Freeman and the majority in the House in 1954.[61] In any case, the following year the state legislation committee refocused its efforts on documenting wage inequality. A graduate student supported by a BPW fellowship supervised the collection of data breaking down wages by occupation in Minnesota collected by legislation chairwomen charged to evaluate employment conditions in their local communities.[62] Community-based research enabled members to focus attention on sex discrimination in employment in their communities when legislative change stalled on both the state and federal levels.

By 1960 draft legislation language emphasizing equal rights and human rights was abandoned in favor of a bill for equal pay for comparable work. In 1961, just as President John F. Kennedy's Commission on the Status of Women (PCSW) was meeting to develop national policies on women's issues, the Equal Pay for Comparable Work bill lost by one vote in Minnesota Senate Labor Committee; it was the closest the Minnesota Federation had come to getting a bill to a floor vote. State legislative chair Eleanor Krohn blamed "farmers in the legislature" and a "dastardly editorial in the *Minneapolis Morning Tribune*" for the set back.[63] The editorial expressed doubts that comparable work could be quantified.[64] Krohn's letter to the editor dismissed this concern, declaring that "The Equal Pay bill asks no favors—simply that discrimination based on sex be eliminated."[65]

Even though the PCSW did not recommend the passage of the ERA, recommendations included equal pay for equal work and other suggestions to create employment and educational opportunities for women that the BPW could embrace.[66] The BPW had a long history of collaboration with the Women's Bureau, U.S. Department of Labor, despite differences over the ERA. Virginia Allan, the BPW's national program chair, explored the idea of establishing state commissions on the status of women with Esther Peterson, director of the Women's Bureau. Allan prepared guidelines for organizing commissions for state federation presidents.[67]

The MFBPW was the impetus behind Minnesota Governor Karl Rolvaag's (DFL) creation of a Governor's Commission on the Status of Women (MNCSW) by executive order in 1964. Edna Schwartz, former president of the Minnesota Federation and active campaigner for a state equal pay bill in the early 1960s, recalled that she did not worry about implementing Allan's mandate that state federations focus on organizing state commissions because "we knew we could do it here."[68] St. Paul club member Esther Tomljanovich knew Governor Rolvaag from her work in state government in the office of Revisor of Statutes, the service arm of the Minnesota legislature, and "could run in and out of the governor's office."[69] Such access surely made a difference. Rolvaag even went as far as sending a telegram to Schwarz while she was attending a national BPW biennial convention in Dallas in 1964 to let her know that he had established a commission.[70]

The Minnesota Commission on the Status of Women brought together a body of forty-five members from associations, unions, and organizations sympathetic to the progressivism of the Democratic Farmer Labor Party. Business leaders and medical and legal professionals served with educators and politicians, four women's clubs officers, five representatives from labor unions, and two civil rights leaders. Of the four members from women's clubs, two represented the MFBPW, Schwartz and Tomljanovich, with Schwartz serving as MNCSW secretary and chair of the employment committee. Former national president of the National Council of Jewish Women and PCSW member Viola Hoffman Hymes chaired the Commission.[71] Tomljanovich does not believe that Rolvaag applied a DFL litmus test to appointments but simply "appointed people he knew."[72] Whatever political orientation, the Minnesota Commission was an important turning point in organized activism on women's issues according to Tomljanovich: "Women's organizations did not work together but all of sudden we found these people who were like-minded. We found union members. We found people across the state. We formed a more effective political group."[73]

The first state-sanctioned body to address gender inequality included MFBPW activists with longstanding commitments to women's rights and civic engagement. Consequently, the Minnesota Commission on the Status of Women offered the MFBPW a more effective location to advocate for equal rights. One of the recommendations of the MNCSW to Governor Rolvagg was the passage of a state equal pay bill, which finally passed in 1969. Schwartz represented the Commission at hearings on equal pay for equal work in the state legislature.[74] Ironically, Minnesota's Equal Pay Act, "relating to the abolishment of discriminatory wage rates based on sex, and providing for penalties and violations," was a pale imitation of the language of full citizenship rights proposed by the Minnesota Federation in the 1940s and 1950s.[75]

This study of one organization's persistent effort to stop a backlash against working women and promote equal rights legislation in Minnesota changes our understanding of the preconditions for the rise of the modern women's movement and complicates the waves metaphor. Revisionist histories that consider continuity from the first to the second wave have either charted nascent feminist activism in single national organizations and labor unions or have analyzed moribund campaigns for federal equal pay legislation and the Equal Rights Amendment. Attention to national groups and policies cannot document the flurry of political activity occurring in states and local communities. Local studies can illustrate the creation of a new feminist mainstream characterized by the diversity of feminisms that began to emerge in the 1940s. Edna Schwartz's political life cycle is a case in point. She was a former employee of a labor union, longstanding MFBPW member, and appointee to the Minnesota Commission on the Status of Women. The latter association led to her attendance at the third national conference for state commissions on the status of women convened by the Women's Bureau, U.S. Department of Labor, in 1966, where she joined Betty Friedan to form the National Organization for Women. She quickly signed up fifteen women to join, all members of the Minnesota Federation of Business and Professional Women's Clubs.[76]

Notes

1. Margaret Culkin Banning was a public relations executive and a frequent contributor to the national BPW's publication *Independent Woman*. She outlined the BPW's national program for 1947–48 in *Independent Woman* (June 1947): 153.
2. Margaret Culkin Banning, "Inquiry Into Women's Clubs," *New York Times Magazine*, September 15, 1947.
3. *New York Times*, September 22, 1947.
4. Historians have used the terms "social feminism," "labor feminism," and "equal rights feminism" to distinguish the forms of women's public activism from the suffrage movement to the rise of the modern women's movement. Leila Rupp and Verta Taylor define the members of the National Woman's Party as equal rights feminists. See Leila Rupp and Verta Taylor, *Survival in the Doldrums: The American Women's Movement in America, 1945 to the 1960s* (New York: Oxford University Press, 1987). Other groups and individuals that were committed to improving the status of women but not at the expense of social welfare legislation predicated on the assumption of female difference have been described as labor or social feminists. See Dorothy Sue Cobble, *The Other Women's Movement: Workplace Justice and Social Rights in Modern America* (Princeton, NJ: Princeton University Press, 2004) for a discussion of how social class affected the mission and goals of women's organizations and labor union women. While the BPW shared the NWP's commitment to the ERA, it is important to make a distinction between the two organizations. Unlike the NWP, the BPW did not embrace the notion that women were the same as men to the extent that coalitions with labor and social feminists were impossible to forge.
5. Still, research considering continuity of feminist activism ignores women's clubs. For studies of working-class feminism in postwar America, see Cobble, *The Other Women's Movement*; Nancy Gabin, *Feminism in the Labor Movement: Women in the United Auto Workers Union, 1935–1975* (Ithaca, NY: Cornell University Press, 1990); and Dennis A. Deslippe, *'Rights Not Roses': Unions and the Rise of Working-Class Feminism, 1945–1980* (Urbana: University of Illinois Press, 2000). Several books focus on discrete women's organizations: Rupp and Taylor, *Survival in the Doldrums*; Susan A. Levine, *Degrees of Equality:*

The American Association of University Women and the Challenge of American Feminism (Philadelphia: Temple University Press, 1995); Susan Lynn, *Progressive Women in Conservative Times: Racial Justice, Peace, and Feminism, 1945 to the 1960s* (New Brunswick, NJ: Rutgers University Press, 1993). Susan Ware's work on the League of Women Voters recasts voluntarism as political activism, but she does not consider the role of the LWV in various state-wide political coalitions. See Susan Ware, "American Women in the 1950s: Nonpartisan Politics and Women's Politicalization," in *Women, Politics and Change*, Louise A. Tilly and Patricia Gurin, eds. (New York: Russell Sage Foundation, second edition, 1992), 281–299. Cynthia Harrison considers how the divisive politics related to the Equal Rights Amendment compromised broader policy networks among women's organizations in *On Account of Sex: Public Policies on Women's Issues, 1945–1970* (Berkeley: University of California Press, 1989); Anna L. Harvey, *Votes Without Leverage: Women in American Electoral Politics, 1920–1970* (New York: Cambridge University Press, 1998), argues that women's organizations failed to influence electoral politics until the 1970s. Carol M. Mueller makes a similar argument in "The Empowerment of Women: Polling and the Women's Voting Bloc," in *The Politics of the Gender Gap: The Social Construction of Political Influence*, Carol M. Mueller, ed. (Beverly Hills, CA: Sage Publications, 1988), 16–36.

6. While many monographs and articles have demonstrated the continuity of feminist activism from the post-suffrage victory to the rise of the modern women's movement, recent popular books on the history of modern feminism in the U.S. written by women's historians continue to uncritically rely on the waves metaphor. See Ruth Rosen, *The World Split Open: How the Women's Movement Changed America* (New York: Viking, 2000) and Sara Evans, *Tidal Wave: How Women Changed America at Century's End* (New York: Free Press, 2004).

7. *Independent Woman* (April 1947): 199. See also Rupp and Taylor, *Survival in the Doldrums*, 59–60 for a discussion of the BPW's commitment to equal rights activism after World War II.

8. World War II Activities Report, Box 7, Minnesota Federation of Business and Professional Women's Clubs Papers, Minnesota Historical Society, St. Paul, Minnesota (hereafter cited as MFBPW Papers).

9. *The St. Paul Business Woman* (July 1942): 8, Minnesota Historical Society, St. Paul.

10. World War II Activities Report, Box 7, MFBPW Papers.

11. Ibid.

12. Millard L Gieske, "Minnesota in Midpassage: A Century of Transition in Political Culture," in *Perspectives on Minnesota Government and Politics* (Dubuque, IA: Kendall Hunt Publishing, 1977), 6.

13. Millard L. Gieske, *Minnesota Farmer-Laborism: The Third Party Alternative* (Minneapolis: University of Minnesota Press, 1979), 294–95.

14. Daniel J. Elazar, "Epitome of the Moralistic Political Culture," in *Minnesota Politics and Government*, eds. Daniel J. Elazar, Virginia Gray, and Wyman Spano (Lincoln: University of Nebraska Press, 1999), 21.

15. Homer Williamson, "The Minnesota Governor: Potential for Power," in *Perspectives on Minnesota Government and Politics*, 4th edition, ed. Steve Hoffman, et al. (Edina, MN: Burgess Publishing, 1998), 33.

16. Joanne Meyerowitz, "Sex, Gender, and the Cold War Language of Reform," in *Rethinking Cold War Culture*, eds. Peter J. Kuznick and James Gilbert (Washington, DC: Smithsonian Institution Press, 2001), 107–09.

17. Minutes 23rd Annual Convention of the Minnesota Federation of Business and Professional Women's Clubs, May, 24, 1942, Box 1, MFBPW Papers.

18. *The St .Paul Business Woman* (September 1942): 3–4.

19. Ibid.

20. Minutes Board Meeting, August 17, 1942, Box 1, MFBPW Papers.

21. Minutes of the Mid-winter Board Meeting, January 25, 1942, Box 1, MFBPW Papers.
22. Ibid.
23. Minutes August 17, 1944 Board Meeting, Box 1, MFBPW Papers.
24. *The St. Paul Business Woman* (January 1942): 3.
25. Minutes 26th Annual State Convention, May 17, Box 1, MFBPW Papers.
26. Minutes 23rd Annual Convention of the Minnesota Federation of Business and Professional Women's Clubs, May, 24, 1942, MFBPW Papers. See also Report Resolutions Committee, 1947 State Convention, Box 1, MFBPW Papers.
27. *St. Paul Businesswoman*, Minnesota Historical Society, St. Paul.
28. Cobble, *The Other Women's Movement*, 60–66.
29. A content analysis of the National Federation's publication, *Independent Woman*, in the late 1940s and 1950s reveals surprisingly little rhetoric about the role of government or labor unions, and the publication was not used to promote Republican Party policies. Protective labor legislation is considered narrowly as an obstacle to social change. Even though the BPW abandoned a policy of strict nonpartisanship after World War II, there is no evidence that the organization embraced or was embraced by the Republican Party.
30. Esther Tomjanlovich, phone conversation with the author, December 8, 2009. My extensive research on BPW state federations in Massachusetts, Minnesota, Wisconsin, New Hampshire, Maine, and Ohio indicates that the group was dominated by white collar workers, but not necessarily only from the ranks of professionals and business owners.
31. For a discussion of women's rights coalitions under the auspices of the Women's Bureau, see Kathleen A. Laughlin, *Women's Work and Public Policy: A History of the Women's Bureau, U.S. Department of Labor, 1945–1970* (Boston: Northeastern University Press, 2000). For an overview of the politics of ERA and women's organizing, see *Account of Sex: Public Policies on Women's Issues, 1945–1970*.
32. Minutes Winter Board Meeting, January 23, 1944, Box 1, MFBPW Papers.
33. *Independent Woman* (September 1950): 270.
34. Laughlin, *Women's Work and Public Policy*, 34
35. *Independent Woman* (April 1947): 102
36. Ibid., 199.
37. Ibid., 216.
38. Minutes Pre-Convention Board Meeting, May 20, 1948, Box 1, MFBPW Papers.
39. Bulletin No. 3 Minnesota Federation of Business and Professional Women's Clubs, Box 9, MFBPW Papers.
40. Williamson, "The Minnesota Governor: Potential for Power," 44–47.
41. Minutes Advisory Board Meeting January 29, 1950, Box 1, MFBPW Papers.
42. Report of State President for Club Year 1946-47, Box 1, MFBPW Papers.
43 Ibid.
44 Ibid.
45 Minutes Pre-Convention Board Meeting, May 20, 1948, Box 1, MFBPW Papers.
46. Maud Whitacre to Stella Olsen, December 15, 1950, Box 9, MFBPW Papers.
47. *Independent Woman* (September 1950): 268.
48. Ibid.
49. Gieske, *Minnesota Farmer-Laborism*, 294. See also Joseph A. Kunkel, III, "Political Parties in Minnesota," in *Perspectives on Minnesota Government and Politics*, 161–87.
50. Kunkel, "Political Parties in Minnesota," 166.
51. Stella Olsen to Clara Villars, February 11, 1951, Box 9, MFBPW Papers.
52. Stella Olsen to Mabel Bischoff, February 11, 1951, Box 9, MFBPW Papers.
53. Stella Olsen to Alf L. Bergerud, March 11, 1951, Box 9, MFBPW Papers.
54. Clara Villars to Joseph Priferl, February 6, 1951, Box 9, MFBPW Papers.
55. Concise Report of the Legislation Committee, 1950-51, Box 9, MFBPW Papers.
56. Stella Olsen to Cecelia P. Galey, April 20, 1951, Box 9, MFBPW Papers.

57. Olive Johnson to Edward J. Thye, February 24, 1950, Box 9, MFBPW Papers.
58. Janet McGregor, "ERA: A World Issue," Box 9, MFBPW Papers.
59. Natalie B. Nelson to Board of Directors, Sept 19, 1953, Box 9, MFBPW Papers.
60. Legislative Recommendations Report, Box 9, MFBPW Papers.
61. Gieske, "Minnesota at Midpassage," 26.
62. Nellie Miner to Committee Members, March 15, 1955, Box 9, MFBPW Papers.
63. Eleanor Krohn to Agnes Merritt, March 30, 1961, Box 9, MFBPW Papers.
64. "Equal Pay Bill," *Minneapolis Morning Tribune*, March 30, 1961.
65. Eleanor Krohn to Mailbag, *Minneapolis Morning Tribune*, April 7, 1961.
66. Margaret Mead and Frances B. Kaplan, eds., *American Woman: The Report of the President's Commission on the Status of Women* (New York: Charles Scribner's Sons, 1965).
67. Laughlin, Women's Work and Public Policy, 100.
68. Bonnie Watkins and Nina Rothchild, *In the Company of Women: Voices from the Women's Movement* (St. Paul: Minnesota Historical Society Press, 1996), 9.
69. Esther Tomljanovich, telephone conversation with author, December 8, 2009.
70. Watkins and Rothchild, *In the Company of Women*, 11.
71. Minnesota Commission on the Status of Women, Annual Report, 1966, Box 54, Viola Hoffman Hymes Papers, Minnesota Historical Society, St. Paul. For a discussion of Edna Schwartz's life and career, see *In the Company of Women*. Esther Tomljanovich's professional and political career is described in Paul H. Anderson, "A Tribute to Justice Esther M Tomljanovich," *William Mitchell Law Review* 32 (2006):1737–50.
72. Esther Tomljanovich, telephone conversation with author, December 8, 2009.
73. Ibid.
74. Watkins and Rothchild, *In the Company of Women*, 11.
75 H.F. No 332, Box 9, MFBPW Papers.
76. Watkins and Rothchild, *In the Company of Women*, 12.

CHAPTER 2

The Legal Origins of "The Personal Is Political"

Bella Abzug and Sexual Politics in Cold War America

LEANDRA ZARNOW*

In the early 1970s, New York Representative Bella Abzug positioned herself as the ring leader of feminist legislative action. "We put sex discrimination provisions into everything," she boasted, "There was no opposition."[1] Yet, she never defined feminism as solely about achieving gender equality. Nor did she believe that the "personal is political" was a concept first practiced by supporters of women's liberation, who coined the term in the 1960s. Rather, Abzug's conceptualization of sexual politics and intersectional understanding of oppression remained rooted in an earlier period—her Left feminist past. At the height of McCarthyism, she worked tirelessly as a "cause" lawyer to combat sexism, white supremacy, economic inequity, and political repression.[2] In so doing, she joined a renegade group of feminist lawyers engaged in the legal Left who braved anti-Communist attacks to work toward their broad vision of gender justice.

This chapter considers one representative strand of Bella Abzug's multi-issue organizing during the early Cold War—her legal challenge of the sexual color line at the heart of the Jim Crow system. In 1948, Abzug joined the Willie McGee defense team, and led the appeal of this Mississippi black-on-white rape case. For this ambitious young radical lawyer, this American Left cause celebré was a career case. Yet, more than professional notoriety motivated Abzug as she attempted to save her client from execution, the sentence delivered to African American men convicted of raping a white woman in Mississippi. Most centrally, she sought to bring into the legal record a crucial element McGee's previous trial lawyers had shied away from between 1945 and 1948. In the final stage of appeal, she boldly introduced McGee's claim that he had engaged in a consensual inter-racial sexual relationship with plaintiff Wiletta Hawkins. As Abzug saw it, the case was tainted "by the distorted mores of the State of Mississippi which makes sex relations voluntarily entered into between a Negro man and a white woman a greater offense than the crime of rape itself."[3] Significantly, she understood that the McGee case was about sexual freedom as much as it was about racial equality. Seeing the multiple layers of oppression preserved in southern rape law, she demonstrated how the law functioned as a mechanism to control the social mobility *and* physical bodies of white women and African American men and women. By misusing rape law to police racial boundaries, she argued, Mississippi officials diminished the law's primary intent: the protection of women.

The multifaceted legal argument Abzug introduced in the McGee defense exemplifies Left feminist legal thought. An ideologically diverse group, Left feminists were Communists, socialists, and independent leftists who engaged in coalition work to build a progressive social order more just and equitable than the U.S. quasi-democratic, capitalist system. These radical women also shared, as Ellen DuBois put it, the common "recognition of the systematic oppression of women with an appreciation of other structures of power underlying American society."[4] Though small in numbers, Left feminist lawyers played a crucial role during the 1940s and 1950s in exposing how law served as a function of power. They crafted an important legal critique of the double bind of race and gender oppression, what lawyer Pauli Murray called "Jane Crow."[5]

Abzug's innovative legal argument has been overlooked in the historical record because it was not successful; Willie McGee could not be saved. Nevertheless, her attempt to radically reframe southern rape law is significant for three central reasons. First, her decision to foreground "the inner citadel of the color line" demonstrates how far women lawyers believed civil rights law should go.[6] Before *Brown v. Board of Education* (1954), lawyers pushed for legal changes that would not only dismantle public segregation, but also the sexual color line. Thus, this study requires historians to consider more centrally links between sexuality and civil rights claims, as well as how sexual politics governed Jim Crow.[7]

Second, it is now known that Cold War containment policy did not entirely equate to dry years for feminism.[8] Yet, first histories documenting Left feminist politics after World War II have largely overlooked the law as a site of activism.[9] Left feminist lawyers' defense work during the

McCarthy era is an important precursor to the more known activities of organizations such as NOW Legal Defense and Education Fund and the American Civil Liberties Union's Women's Rights Project in the 1970s.[10] These radical lawyers engaged in gender conscious antiracist work despite the toll of anti-Communism, threat of disbarment, loss of clients, and sexism in the profession. These great odds make their story all the more important.

Last, Abzug's legal campaign to dismantle the sexual color line encourages historians to take a longer view of the axiom "the personal is political." Certainly, she had a more complex, intersectional understanding of rape culture than presented by some women engaged in women's liberation. Left feminist lawyers used cases, such as *McGee v. State,* to articulate how essential it was for people of color and all women to have the right to control their own bodies. Thus, personal politics were not the sole domain of feminists organizing in the 1960s and 1970s.

Driving alone to Laurel, Mississippi, in early 1948, Bella Abzug took in the dire poverty of the rural landscape, where brushfires burned unattended. The languid countryside sharply contrasted with the hustle and bustle of her familiar New York City streets. This was "a whole other world from the one I had been raised in," observed Abzug years later. Her southern education continued at her first stop, a meeting with Laurel's District Attorney Albert Easterling. "Do you really think anybody here is going to pay any attention to you?," she remembered he asked, while he took aim at the spittoon behind her.[11] Abzug failed at her first task in the McGee case. She was sent to Mississippi by the Civil Rights Congress (CRC)—a New York headquartered Left legal defense organization—to convince the district attorney to delay McGee's final re-trial, which he quickly rejected.[12] Unfazed, she set out to complete her second assignment. She was instructed to find McGee new local counsel after his last lawyers, fearing mob violence, abandoned the case just short of trial. Drawing on her Jewish ties, she called a friend of her brother-in-law's at the Jewish Welfare Board to get a list of Jewish attorneys in Jackson. She then "literally went from building to building where lawyers were housed" in search of counsel.[13] Finally, one Jewish Welfare Board contact, A. N. London, suggested a trial attorney who might just be brave enough to take on the case. With John Poole on board, Abzug found a rough "southern kind of personality" she believed equipped to challenge southern vigilantes inside and outside the court.[14] With her mission fulfilled, she returned to a more familiar world of the New York legal Left.

At first glance, it seems remarkable that lawyers entrusted twenty-eight-year-old Bella Abzug with a case that would become an internationally renowned cause celebré. Yet, in 1948 senior Left lawyers had their hands full resisting anti-Communist attacks. The previous year, the House Un-American Activities Committee characterized the CRC as a Communist front, marking the organization as un-American.[15] Likewise, the 1947 Taft-Hartley Act forced a Left-liberal divide within the labor movement, leaving both radical unions and their lawyers scrambling.[16] Meanwhile, radical lawyers were preoccupied with preparation for *United States v. Dennis* (1948), the Smith Act trial of eleven Communist Party leaders.[17] This multi-front legal campaign against Cold War repression provided young lawyers with an opening to engage in national cases early in their careers.

Abzug was poised for the task. She recalled joining the labor law firm Witt & Cammer in 1946, shortly after graduating from Columbia Law School, because they "didn't ask me if I could type."[18] Yet, her choice to begin her career at this leftist firm was more intentional than this account suggests. She was well aware of the reputation of its partners, Nathan Witt, Harold Cammer, and Lee Pressman, all notable New Dealers and superstars in Left legal circles. She knew these labor lawyers worked with progressive unions, many in the Communist orbit, just as she knew that they were in the leadership of the National Lawyers Guild. During the Cold War, the Guild's obstinate choice not to purge its organization of Communists set this professional organization apart from its counterpart, the American Bar Association. And its commitment to labor, civil rights, civil liberties, and peace, made the Guild a natural home for cause lawyers such as Abzug.[19] In this center of Left legal activity, she found an optimal place to practice the leading principle she learned in law school—the legal realist tenet that law was "the social instrument for change."[20] She also recognized the Guild would enable her to remain active in the "Left-feminist scene," a milieu of Communist and independent Left women activists she engaged in since her 1930s Hunter College days.[21]

During the early Cold War, the Guild served as the central gathering place for Left feminist lawyers. In this period, sex discrimination was a secondary focus for members preoccupied with questions of race, class, and political freedom. Nonetheless, the Guild was known to be one of the only places welcoming to women in the profession. They were not only a strong presence in the rank-and-file of the organization, but also in its leadership.[22] As professional women, these Guild members defied proscribed notions of domesticity, purposely challenging what Abzug later described as the "cocoon approach to living" of the 1950s.[23] And as radical thinkers, they shared her interest in steering the Guild's political direction in the area of civil rights and civil liberties.

When considering how best to defeat Jim Crow and McCarthyism, Left women lawyers did not lose focus of the "woman question." Rather, they tapped into a wider Left feminist discourse that recognized what

Landon Storrs characterizes as a "sensibility of linkages" between male chauvinism, white supremacy, and economic hegemony.[24] They applied this multi-layered understanding of oppression—what critical race theorists would later term intersectionality—to their legal thinking.[25] Thus, the women-only, equal rights focus of the National Woman's Party was not the approach Left feminist lawyers chose to take.[26] Nor did they opt to engage heavily in women's volunteer organizations such as the Young Women's Christian Association.[27] Instead, Left feminist lawyers favored mixed-sex, multi-issue organizing that focused on gender as one of many central issues. They also emphasized their professional role in their activism. Their social justice work focused on remaking the legal frameworks that preserved elite power structures, what Abzug called "the status quo."[28]

Taking on the status quo and sexism in the law was doubly risky for women lawyers. To be a Left feminist lawyer meant to go against the grain in their profession. Liberal defense organizations such as the National Association for the Advancement of Colored People and the American Civil Liberties Union purged known and suspected Communist members left and right. And the Guild saw a mass exodus of members concerned to be affiliated with this organization that resisted anti-Communist forces.[29] Consequently, radical women attorneys were marked as outsiders and Reds, ostracized within a profession not wholly welcoming to women in the first place. The small number of Left feminist lawyers who, as Catherine Fosl put it, "wore the label 'subversive' as a badge of honor," did so because their faith in justice reigned supreme.[30] Unbending in their principled work, the Left feminist legal vanguard remained resilient and highly visible during the Cold War.[31]

Abzug did not hesitate to begin her career as an outlier civil rights lawyer, undeterred by the "un-American" label that came with this choice. Engaged in labor law initially, she soon became drawn into New York's hotbed of civil rights activity.[32] Civil rights law provided young radical lawyers with a chance to develop a reputation in this relatively untapped field. Cold War politics necessitated the shift away from labor law as well. Loyalty programs and Communist purges left the labor movement weak by the late 1940s, causing this once lucrative client base to be virtually nonexistent.[33] As a result, Left lawyers broadened their portfolios to include a wider range of issues than had occupied attention during the New Deal. Abzug rode this wave of change, becoming a rising star in the Committee on Constitutional Liberties of the Guild's New York Chapter. As the center of Guild civil rights activity, this committee worked closely with CRC, supplying manpower for their defense teams. It was only a matter of time before senior Guild and CRC lawyers called upon Abzug to join the Willie McGee case.

When they asked Abzug to go to Mississippi to find McGee local counsel, she had expressed initial reservations.[34] She had never been to the South, she would be paid only travel expenses, and McGee's prior lawyers faced threats of violence and disbarment. Moreover, she was in the early stages of her first pregnancy, and her husband Martin pled with her not to take the case.[35] Yet, after her initial trip to find McGee new counsel, there was no turning back. With the strong possibility that McGee's third trial would be futile, Abzug likely familiarized herself with the case history, gearing up for the impending appeal.

McGee's three jury trials held between 1945 and 1948 were highly staged performances of justice. Concerning the first trial held December 6–7, 1945, *Laurel Leader-Call* reported the "orderly" jury "prudently" weighed evidence and testimony, unhindered by "quiet…serious-faced spectators" that crowded the courtroom.[36] The prosecution produced police witnesses, Wiletta Hawkins's testimony, and McGee's coerced confession. While court-appointed defense attorney Forrest Jackson dared not call McGee or any witnesses to the stand, nor present a concluding argument. This thin veneer of impartiality and civility masked the underlying predetermined end: legal lynching. Thus, in less than two and a half minutes, the jury returned with the expected guilty verdict, which in Mississippi meant death by electric chair.

McGee's life could easily have stopped here, had CRC not been interested in expanding their civil rights legal defense in the South.[37] They believed the McGee case could be a significant test case because it exposed Jim Crow's most brutal elements: racism, corruption, intolerance, and mob violence. Despite CRC representation, McGee's re-trial in February of 1948 followed the same pattern as his first trial.[38] McGee's new trial team, local white labor lawyers Dixon Pyles and Dan Breland, won a change of venue to nearby Hattiesburg. However, this town's jury proved no more impartial. McGee's lawyers questioned Hawkins on the stand, poking holes in her testimony. The prosecution countered by introducing a signed confession, as well as multiple witnesses questioning McGee's sanity and character. Pyles and Breland also failed to give a closing argument, fearing the 3000 onlookers outside the courthouse.[39] This time the jury announced a guilty verdict after eleven minutes. But the Mississippi Supreme Court could not deny the U.S. Supreme Court ruling in *Patton v. Mississippi* (1947) that blacks had been excluded from the jury; the Justices conceded a reversal of McGee's sentence and granted retrial for the final time.[40] Breland and Pyles opted out of this third trial, disinterested in facing vigilantes in the courtroom another time.

Abzug had a stake in the third trial proceedings, beginning March 3, 1948, after hiring A.N. London and John Poole to fill their place. Back in New York, she learned that Poole and London proved more forceful in the courtroom, but no more effective in gaining a not guilty verdict. They questioned Hawkins more pointedly during the cross-examination, compelling her to concede, "No, I don't know Willie McGee."[41] McGee also testified for the first time. He confirmed that District Attorney Easterling and Deputy Sheriff Royals "beat me...threatened to put me in the gallows" and "take me back to Laurel and turn me over to the mob" if he did not sign a confession.[42] Poole did not, however, question his client regarding the alleged affair. He told McGee to remain silent on this issue, fearing that doing otherwise would get them both killed.[43] As it was, menacing bystanders patrolled the courthouse, compelling Poole to make a quick getaway from the courthouse without delivering closing remarks.

Hearing of McGee's guilty verdict over the phone, Poole and Abzug stalled the execution through an appeal to the Mississippi Supreme Court.[44] This Court, however, denied the appeal in April of 1949, arguing that the voluminous trial records alone offered a "physical picture of how completely the case was covered."[45] If the Mississippi Supreme Court could not exhibit the "freedom of consciousness and judicial calm needed" to adjudicate fairly, Abzug hoped the U.S. Supreme Court would intervene.[46]

Senior CRC and Guild lawyers did not entrust Abzug with drafting McGee's first U.S. Supreme Court certiorari (request for oral hearing) in 1949.[47] However, when the Supreme Court denied certiorari in October, they called on her to draft McGee's second Supreme Court brief, a "Petition for Rehearing."[48] When preparing this document, Abzug poured over recent case law and the Mississippi Constitution, but she also monitored developments in civil rights defense strategies. Still close to her law school friend Constance Baker Motley, a staff attorney at the NAACP, Abzug kept abreast of her work for this liberal civil rights organization.[49] Motley and Abzug's continued interaction demonstrates that personal relationships bridged the Left-liberal divide that formed among civil rights groups during the Cold War. From conversations with Motley, Abzug knew that the NAACP was making headway in black-on-white rape cases by emphasizing violations of equal protection in jury selection and criminal sentencing.[50] Initially in the McGee appeals, she opted to do the same. She argued that precedent set in other rape cases showed a bias engrained in the Mississippi legal system that excluded blacks from juries.[51]

Even this race-based argument was deemed too radical for the time. The U.S. Supreme Court passed on the case for a second time in May, 1950.[52] As a result, Mississippi state officials and local citizens prepared to execute their "criminal" on July 27, 1950. Meanwhile, CRC organizers orchestrated a grandiose "Save Willie McGee" campaign, using pressure tactics such as mass letter writing, celebrity endorsements, defense fundraising, and

White House pickets. The fourteen thousand telegrams and cables sent from places as far away as the People's Republic of China enraged Governor Fielding Wright. He told CRC leaders, "We will not tolerate a wild-eyed, howling mob of Communists and sympathizers, gathered by the Civil Rights Congress to stage a demonstration in Mississippi."[53] Wright proved every bit inhospitable. He remained unmoved from his position that McGee's trials were models of justice and his sentence reasonable.[54] Equally troubling, he refused to protect McGee's lawyers while in Jackson. To this inaction, Abzug reprimanded, if "harm comes to anyone, we will hold you personally responsible."[55] She had better luck on her first trip to the U.S. Supreme Court chambers. Justice Harold Burton granted a temporary stay just twenty-four hours before McGee's scheduled execution, after she compelled him to await their brief featuring new evidence.[56] In so doing, the U.S. Supreme Court enabled Abzug to boldly reframe the McGee defense. She determined that it was high time to foreground the sexual color line in her legal argument. With the clock ticking, she had nothing to lose.

At home, Martin Abzug continued to plead with Bella to leave the case. Her first daughter, Eve, was still an infant, and she was pregnant once again. Martin could hear the mobs outside the Jackson courthouse chanting angrily, "Get that Commie lawyer," each time she phoned. Nevertheless, Bella could not be swayed. Instead, she geared up to do "all the things you have to try to do in a case where the world is against you."[57] For Abzug, this meant pushing against convention as much as conservative forces pulled back. As a Left feminist, she instinctively recognized that this meant exposing the taboo issue of inter-racial sex at the heart of the McGee case. Moving beyond procedural claims, she determined that an argument connecting race and sex would be the most effective means to dismantle both public and private segregation.

Joined by senior Florida civil rights lawyer John Coe, Bella Abzug revamped the McGee defense in March, 1951.[58] On racial grounds, they argued more boldly that Mississippi rape law historically applied the death penalty solely to African Americans because they were black—"and for that reason alone."[59] Additionally, they secured McGee an alibi. Previously dissuaded by counsel, Willie's former neighbor Hattie Johnson testified that he had been playing cards at her house during the time of the alleged assault.[60] However, these two points paled in importance to new testimony of Willie and Rosalee McGee.[61] Speaking openly about the alleged consensual relationship between McGee and Hawkins, their testimony brought the issue of inter-racial sex into the legal record.

Abzug's determined choice to foreground the sexual color line in 1951 *McGee* briefs is her greatest civil rights contribution. In so doing, she updated the critique of rape law and southern lynching culture first theorized at the turn of the century by Ida B. Wells-Barnett and Jesse Daniel Ames.[62] Like her forbearers, Abzug realized that prior legal arguments were inadequate in their treatment of inter-racial sex. As a Left feminist, she recognized the multiple layers of control that functioned in southern rape law. White male elites maintained both political and sexual power by using rape law to monitor the sexual practices of both African Americans and white women. Thus, rape law was not being used for its original intent: to reprimand rape assailants.

Though Abzug disclosed the issue of inter-racial sex at play in *McGee*, she did not target Hawkins. She continued to believe—as she suggested first in a 1950 appeal to the Mississippi Supreme Court—that Hawkins's fumbles during cross-examination served as a "permissible inference that a relationship had existed between them."[63] Yet, Abzug determined in 1951 not to build on this line of argument. To frame her case around a question of Hawkins's character, as attorneys had done in Scottsboro, would not respect the limited choices she had within a repressive and misogynistic Southern culture.[64] If Hawkins had an affair with McGee, then she had asserted sexual agency not afforded to a white woman, especially one who was working-class and married.[65] Instead, Abzug focused on McGee, asserting in a Supreme Court brief that he "had an intimate sexual relationship with the prosecutrix, not only with her consent, but upon her insistence over a long period of time."[66] She zeroed in on how Mississippi rape law devalued McGee's claim to citizenship rights: the court not only convicted Willie unlawfully, but refused to recognize Rosalee's womanhood. Encouraging Rosalee and Willie McGee to tell their story, she afforded them limited agency within a system that denied them liberty and will.[67] However, the McGees took great personal risk in sharing their stories. Once Rosalee spoke publicly of Wiletta's liaisons with her husband, she and her children were forced to flee Mississippi.[68]

What compelled Abzug to address the sexual color line? When she sat down to revamp McGee's legal defense in early 1951, she had a few bones to pick regarding the treatment of women in the legal profession. Considering she later scolded constituents who began their letters with, "Dear Congressman Abzug," she was likely incensed when she received her first correspondence in May of 1950 from U.S. Supreme Court clerk Charles Elmore Cropley addressed "Dear Sir."[69] Pregnant off and on throughout the case, she was frustrated with the slight "menstruating lawyer" that she heard male colleagues whisper under their breath when she entered the courtroom.[70] And she still seethed from chauvinism exhibited by Witt & Cammer partner Lee Pressman, who required her to carry his briefcase when she accompanied him to court.[71]

The 1950 National Lawyers Guild convention confirmed she was not alone. Here, Cleveland lawyer Ann Fagan Ginger introduced a resolution on discrimination against women in the legal profession, much to the chagrin of her male colleagues on the resolution committee. Citing sex bias in the law, Ginger called for a reevaluation of all "statutes, regulations, rules and governmental practices which discriminate unfairly on the basis of sex."[72] Familiar with rights discourse that dominated Guild meetings, women members such as Ginger began to assess their own liminal status alongside that of their clients. Minorities in their profession, Left feminist lawyers intuitively understood that their efforts to remake civil rights law could include a refashioning of their own rights as well. Therefore, it is more than likely that Abzug reconsidered the issues in McGee's defense with her own sex discrimination experiences in mind. Attuned to Left feminist discourse, she believed it important to link sexual autonomy to racial equality. The personal, she already understood in 1950, was in fact political.

In fact, Abzug's legal notes and draft briefs suggest she wanted to foreground the sexual politics at play in *McGee* more so than fellow Guild members. Colleague Abraham Unger, who helped edit and draft McGee briefs, eliminated quite a few of Abzug's most bold assertions in the 1951 "Memorandum of Relator." One method of enforcing segregation, she argued in this draft brief, is to prevent inter-racial sexual relations. "The consequences of that enforced policy is to create in every Negro male the knowledge that should he be discovered," she asserted, "either in the act or to have had relations with a white woman, he faces the prospect of death to be meted out in one form or another."[73] She explained to Unger in an accompanying memo that it was "not legal judgment, but personal prejudice" that led Mississippi judges and lawyers to "very specifically deny" the issue of the voluntary inter-racial sexual relationship.[74]

Only federal judge Sydney Mize of the Southern Mississippi District Court considered a hearing on this new argument.[75] Mississippi officials and the public were clearly losing patience, annoyed that McGee's attorneys continued to disrupt their peace. Reflecting this sentiment, *Jackson Daily News* editor Frederick Sullens cautioned angrily,

> If Mrs. Abzug ever again appears in Mississippi, either as a lawyer or as an individual, it will be one time too often. She's the sort of person for whose company we care less than nothing at all....Too bad the courts don't have authority to send some lawyers to the electric chair along with their clients.[76]

Despite these threats, Abzug traveled to Jackson the following day, on March 8, 1951. Set on delivering her oral argument, she reassured herself that no one would harm a woman eight months pregnant.

The locals had other plans. At her hotel, she was refused a room, and the same thing occurred at every hotel at which she tried to register.[77] Finding herself without safe shelter as the evening hours approached, she decided to sit up all night in the local bus station. She soon realized, however, that even there she was being closely watched. "They paged me," she recalled, "so then I knew I was right; they had been trying to—I don't know, do something—scare me. Maybe they were going to do more."[78] Alarmed, she did not answer the page, and spent the night awake sitting in a stall in the women's restroom.

Shaken by this sleepless night, she nevertheless remained composed when it was time to deliver her lengthy argument. "Well, I'm here," she recalled announcing to the surprised Mississippi Attorney General, J. P. Coleman, "and I want you to know I'm going to be here, and if this happens again I am going to report you to the US Attorney General. You are depriving not only my client but me of my civil rights."[79] With the threat upon her own body in mind, she forcefully argued, "A class of people, namely, negroes [sic], have been subjected to the death penalty for a crime, whereas no white man has ever been subjected to death for that crime."[80] In closing, she urged Judge Mize to seize the "full and complete opportunity to see to it that [McGee] will get the maximum justice before his life is taken away."[81] While Abzug characterized Judge Mize as "the most enlightened but not very" of all the judges she argued before, she believed he simply could not "accept the idea" that her client had a consensual relationship with a white woman.[82] Regrettably, Mize dismissed Abzug and Coe's oral argument on the spot, decreeing, "There must be an end to litigation and when a person has had every opportunity of a full, fair, complete and honest hearing, then the case ends. This defendant had that opportunity."[83] No doubt Governor Wright, in the audience for this hearing, took Judge Mize's dismissal as consent for execution.

In the eleventh hour of the McGee case, Abzug and fellow lawyers exhausted every legal mechanism available to keep Willie McGee alive. Some temporary victories were realized. For instance, after bombarding civil libertarian Justice Hugo Black with thousands of telegrams, McGee's lawyers gained a hearing with the Justice in Washington, D.C.[84] When Justice Black granted a stay of execution, moving the execution date from March 25 to May 8, 1951, Abzug was so elated that she danced with *Daily Worker* reporter Mel Fiske down the halls of the Supreme Court.[85] Even though lawyers won more time, all final court maneuvers proved unsuccessful.[86] Meanwhile, the CRC orchestrated an elaborate international direct action campaign to pressure the governor to provide McGee clemency. Most notably, the CRC's white women's delegation and Sojourners for Truth, led by African American Left women, mobilized in Jackson and in Washington, D.C.[87]

As the McGee case wound to a close, Abzug did not abandon her client even though she had good reason to do so. She had just lost her baby one month prior to her due date. Years later, she and Martin would attribute her miscarriage to the stress of the harrowing night she spent at the Jackson bus station. At the time, she did not speak openly about this personal loss from which she never quite recovered.[88] Instead, she focused all of her attention on saving McGee. Recognizing her commitment, McGee determined, "I don't make no statement to no lady but Mrs. Abzug [sic]. She is the only one I talk to."[89]

On May 8, running on empty, Abzug raced to the court to file one last appeal as McGee was transported from Jackson to Laurel, where the electric chair sat in the courtroom of his original trial. Her frantic efforts proved futile when the clock struck midnight. Just prior to this last ditch effort, she sat down with McGee to write his wife one final letter. "You know I am innocent," he wrote, "tell the people again and again that I never did commit this crime tell them that the real reason that they are going to take my life is to keep the Negro down in the south they cant do this if you and the children keep on fighting."[90]

Abzug was not among the hundreds that turned out to witness Willie McGee's final moment. Still in Jackson, she listened over the phone in her hotel room to the "bloodcurdling screams of the [n]ight when he was executed." Upon hearing the crowd's jubilant reaction to his death, she sat down and cried. Then and there, "I realized that there was something so terribly, terribly wrong with our democracy..." she recalled years later, "... that a state and its apparatus could get away with killing people because of their race, their color."[91]

The McGee case left a profound imprint on Bella Abzug as a political activist, lawyer, and politician. She returned to the case with a heavy heart each time she re-read McGee's final letter to staff members.[92] Retrospectively, she acknowledged the personal toll of the case. She had braved death threats, suffered multiple miscarriages, and endured parenting, marriage, and professional pressures. Engagement in radical civil rights work during the Red Scare also left a professional toll. Upon representing McGee, Abzug's FBI file grew exponentially, and *Life* magazine's 1951 portrayal of her as McGee's "imported" lawyer cost her future clients.[93] Achieving few legal victories in the 1950s, Abzug's faith in the courts diminished as a result. She increasingly saw grassroots political organizing and national policy-making as more effective instruments for social change.

Although Abzug moved on from the McGee case, she did not move away from the Left feminist political framework she applied in her 1951 legal argument. Rather, she continued to think in intersectional terms as a legislator and feminist in the 1970s. She still believed, as she once had, that "one method employed to enforce segregation between Negro and white citizens is to prevent, at all costs, normal relations between Negro males and white females."[94] And she still understood that if feminists wanted to add teeth to rape law, both race and sex must be addressed.

Unfortunately, younger feminists theorizing about rape culture in the 1970s did not recognize the Left feminist sensibilities of women engaged in the McGee case. While completing research for *Against Our Will: Men, Women, and Rape,* Susan Brownmiller interviewed Abzug in 1973. She came to the interview with the preconceived notion that Abzug had not come to grips with "a lot of new thinking" on the issue of rape. Most centrally, she did not see how the women's liberation viewpoint that "the personal is political" was applied in *McGee.* Instead, she focused on what she believed to be the unfair treatment of the accuser, Wiletta Hawkins. Brownmiller attempted to corner the congresswoman with the question, did she think "then and…now that white women 'cry rape'?"[95] After some contemplation, Abzug responded, "I believe that the white woman was *always* the pivot, the excuse. The black man was played off against the white woman and the white woman was played off against the black man, to keep *both* oppressed groups down." Unsatisfied, Brownmiller rationalized unfairly, "the ambiguities [of the case] are too far in the past for her to want to sort out." As she saw it, the McGee case "had vilified and excoriated the hapless white woman."[96]

Brownmiller overlooked Abzug's Left feminist intervention in Cold War civil rights law largely because she centered her study on the subject position of white women. Likewise, she incorrectly assumed that white men mainly shaped the direction of civil rights doctrine in the 1940s and 1950s. Most problematic, Brownmiller missed Abzug's feminist critique of the sexual color line. Left legal feminists had overtly challenged the racist *and* sexist underpinnings of southern rape law. Yet, ironically, Brownmiller did not fully recognize or acknowledge this theoretical legacy. In *Against Our Will,* she argued, as Abzug had over twenty years before, that rape "must be understood as a control mechanism against the freedom, mobility and aspirations of all women, white and black."[97]

During the early Cold War, Left feminist lawyers thought in intersectional terms. They anticipated late twentieth century feminist theorizing about the links between gender, race, and class. Yet, because Left women chose not to associate with organized elite feminism, their expansive gender justice work is not greatly known. Bella Abzug's role in the McGee case demonstrates the importance of writing Left feminist lawyers into the narrative of feminist history. Indeed, radical women lawyers helped sustain feminism through their courtroom challenge of Cold War consensus, disrupting notions of sex alongside race.

Notes

* Portions of this work appeared first in, "Braving Jim Crow to Save Willie McGee: Bella Abzug, the Legal Left, and Civil Rights Innovation, 1948–1951," *Law & Social Inquiry* 33, issue 4 (Fall 2008): 1003–41.

1. Bella Abzug quoted in Sara Evans, *Tidal Wave: How Women Changed America at Century's End* (New York: Free Press, 2003), 67.

2. On cause lawyering, Thomas Hilbink, "You Know the Type…: Categories of Cause Law-yering," *Law and Social Inquiry* 29, no. 3 (2004): 657–98; and *Cause Lawyers and Social Movements*, eds. Austin Sarat and Stuart B. Scheingold (Stanford, CA: Stanford University Press, 2006).

3. Abzug, Draft Memorandum of Relator, 8, Box 2, Abraham Unger Papers (hereafter: AU), Tamiment Library, New York University, New York.

4. Ellen Carol DuBois, "Eleanor Flexner and the History of American Feminism," *Gender and History* 3 (Spring 1991): 81–90, 84.

5. Pauli Murray, "Why Negro Girls Stay Single," *Negro Digest* (July 1947), 4–8.

6. Herbert Blumer, "The Future of the Color Line," in *The South in Continuity and Change*, eds. John C. McKinney and Edgar T. Thompson (Durham, NC: Duke University Press, 1965): 322–26, 331. See also Earl Black and Merle Black, *Politics and Society in the South* (Cambridge, MA: Harvard University Press, 1987).

7. Here I join recent works considering Cold War era women's civil rights organizing atten-tive to issues of sexuality including, Erik S. McDuffie, "A 'New Freedom Movement of Negro Women': Sojourning for Truth, Justice, and Human Rights during the Early Cold War," *Radical History Review* 101 (Spring 2008): 81–106; Jacqueline Castledine, "'In a Solid Bond of Unity': Anticolonial Feminism in the Cold War Era," *Journal of Women's History* 20, no. 4 (2009): 57–81; and Danielle McGuire, "'It Was Like All of Us Had Been Raped': Sexual Violence, Community Mobilization, and the African American Freedom Struggle," *Journal of American History* 91, no. 3 (2004): 906–31.

8. For revisionist works illuminating Left and progressive women's political organizing of the 1940s to early 1960s, Daniel Horowitz, *Betty Friedan and the Making of the Feminine Mys-tique* (Amherst: University of Massachusetts Press, 1998); Kate Weigand, *Red Feminism: American Communism and the Making of Women's Liberation* (Baltimore: Johns Hopkins University Press, 2001); Catherine Fosl, *Subversive Southerner: Anne Braden and the Strug-gle for Racial Justice in the Cold War South* (New York: Palgrave Macmillan, 2002); Landon Storrs, "Red Scare Politics and the Suppression of Popular Front Feminism: The Loyalty Investigation of Mary Dublin Keyserling," *Journal of American History* 90, no. 2 (2003): 491–524; and Barbara Ransby, *Ella Baker and the Black Freedom Movement: A Radical Democratic Vision* (Chapel Hill: University of North Carolina Press, 2003).

9. For the few studies attentive to Left legal feminism, Daniel Horowitz and Kate Weigand, "Dorothy Kenyon: Feminist Organizing, 1919–1963," *Journal of Women's History* 14, no. 2 (Summer 2002): 126–31; and Kathleen Banks Nutter, "Jessie Lloyd O'Connor and Mary Metlay Kaufman: Professional Women Fighting for Social Justice," ibid.: 132–35.

10. For 1960s and 1970s legal feminism, Serena Mayeri, "A Common Fate of Discrimination": Race-Gender Analogies in Legal and Historical Perspective," *Yale Law Journal* 110 (Apr., 2001): 1045–87; Mayeri, "Constitutional Choices: Legal Feminism and the Historical Dynamics of Change," *California Law Review* 92 (May, 2004): 755–839; Martha F. Davis, "Welfare Rights and Women's Rights in the 1960s," *Journal of Policy History* 8, no. 1 (1996): 144–65; and Susan Hartmann, *The Other Feminists: Activists in the Liberal Establishment* (New Haven, CT: Yale University Press, 1998), 53–91.

11. Remembrances of Bella Abzug, Oral History Research Office, Columbia University (here-after: OHRO interview), 133. Note that transcriptions include interviews with: Ronald J. Grele (2 and 11 Nov. 1995); Ronald J. Grele and Amy Swerdlow (30 Nov. 1995); and Amy

Swerdlow and Mary Marshall Clark (1 and 11 Dec. 1995, 9 and 23 Jan. 1996, and 20 Feb. 1996); all interviews are paginated as one continuous transcript.

12. Founded in 1946, the Civil Rights Congress (CRC) carried on the mass legal defense tradition of the International Labor Defense, a Communist-linked organization most notable for representing the "Scottsboro Boys" in their 1930s Alabama rape case. Charles H. Martin, "The Civil Rights Congress and Southern Black Defendants," *Georgia Historical Quarterly* 71 (Spring 1987): 25–52; and Gerald Horne, *Communist Front?: The Civil Rights Congress, 1946–1956* (Rutherford, NJ: Dickinson University Press, 1988).

13. Abzug, OHRO Interview, 132.

14. Ibid.

15. House Un-American Activities Committee, *Report on Civil Rights Congress as a Communist Front Organization* (Washington, DC: Government Printing Office, 1947).

16. Nelson Lichtenstein, *State of the Union: A Century of American Labor* (Princeton, NJ: Princeton University Press, 2002), 115–22.

17. Stanley I. Kutler, *The American Inquisition: Justice and Injustice in the Cold War* (New York: Hill & Wang, 1983); and Michal R. Belknap, *Cold War Political Justice: The Smith Act, the Communist Party, and American Civil Liberties* (Westport, CT: Greenwood Press, 1977).

18. Abzug, OHRO interview, 83.

19. *The Proud Tradition* (New York: National Lawyers Guild, 1960), 5; available in National Lawyers Guild Papers (NLG), Tamiment Library, New York University; and Percival Roberts Bailey, "The Case of the National Lawyers Guild, 1939–1958," in *Beyond the Hiss Case: The FBI, Congress, and the Cold War*, ed. Athan G. Theoharis (Philadelphia: Temple University Press, 1982), 129–75.

20. Abzug, OHRO interview, 144.

21. Storrs, "Red Scare Politics and the Suppression of Popular Front Feminism," 494. Bella Abzug's Hunter College friend (and later speechwriter) Mim Kelber served as Betty Friedan's editor at the *Federated Press* when she wrote the 1952 United Electric pamphlet, the source Daniel Horowitz suggests revealed Friedan's Popular Front feminist ties. Moving in similar circles to Friedan and Kelber, Abzug joined others in the Left feminist legal vanguard who actively "conceptualiz[ed] the dynamics of women's oppression and liberation within a framework that made race and class central," Weigand, *Red Feminism*, 3; see also Horowitz, *Betty Friedan and the Making of the Feminine Mystique*, 127.

22. On women's experience in the Guild, Ann Fagan Ginger interview with author, 28 Apr. 2008, Berkeley, California; and Doris Brin Walker interview with author, 2 May 2008, San Francisco (transcripts in author's possession).

23. Abzug, OHRO Interview, 283. On challenges to Cold War domesticity, see generally *Not June Cleaver: Women and Gender in the Postwar America, 1945—1960*, ed. by Joanne Meyerowitz (Philadelphia: Temple University Press, 2002).

24. Storrs, "Red Scare Politics and the Suppression of Popular Front Feminism," 511.

25. On intersectionality, see Kimberlé Crenshaw, "Mapping the Margins: Intersectionality, Identity Politics, and Violence against Women of Color," *Stanford Law Review* 43 (July, 1991): 1241–99; and Patricia Hill Collins, *Black Feminist Thought: Knowledge Consciousness, and the Politics of Empowerment* (New York: Routledge, 1991).

26. Leila Rupp and Verta Taylor argue that the feminist movement was "elite sustained" by a small cadre of suffragist holdovers. Women on the Left defined themselves in opposition to these conservative women, Rupp and Taylor, *Survival in the Doldrums: The American Women's Rights Movement, 1945 to the 1960s* (New York: Oxford University Press, 1987).

27. Studies of women's progressive volunteerism in the postwar period include Susan Lynn, *Progressive Women in Conservative Times: Racial Justice, Peace, and Feminism, 1945-1960s* (New Brunswick, NJ: 1992); and Sylvie Murray, *The Progressive Housewife: Community*

Activism in Suburban Queens, 1945–1965 (Philadelphia: University of Pennsylvania Press, 2003).

28. Abzug later defined her legal philosophy as, "law...represents the status quo, and it never changes until you get changes in the status quo," OHRO interview, 148.

29. Jerold S. Auerbach, *Unequal Justice: Lawyers and Social Change in Cold War United States* (London: Oxford University Press, 1976), 231–62.

30. Fosl, *Subversive Southerner*, 120.

31. Joshua B. Freeman correctly notes, "Nowhere did left-wing and left-leaning ex-Communists have more influence than in New York. Those in the know. . . . could find them holding positions in the most likely and unlikely places." The Guild served as one key place for women leftists, *Working-Class New York: Life and Labor Since World War II* (New York: The New Press, 2000), 94.

32. Martha Biondi, To Stand and Fight: The Struggle for Civil Rights in Postwar New York City (Cambridge, MA: Harvard University Press, 2003).

33. A friend and Guild colleague of Abzug, Victor Rabinowitz notes this drop in clientele during the Cold War in *Unrepentant Leftist: A Lawyer's Memoir* (Chicago: University of Illinois Press, 1996).

34. Abzug, OHRO interview, 128.

35. bid., at 259; see also Liz Abzug, interviewed by Author, 2 Aug. 2005, New York City (transcript in author's possession).

36. "Willie McGee Declared Sane After Hearing and is On Trial for Life for Rape," *Laurel Leader-Call* (6 Dec. 1945), 1. See also "Another Negro is Jailed in Assault Case Investigation," ibid. (4 Nov. 1945), 1; and "Negro to Pay with Life is Court Edict," ibid. (7 Dec. 1945), 1. For a general account of the *McGee* trial proceedings, Craig Zaim, "Trial by Ordeal: The Willie McGee Case," *Journal of Mississippi History* 65, no. 3 (2003): 215–47. For the case record, U.S. Supreme Court Appellate Record, *McGee v. State,* 238 OT 1949, Appellate Case Files, Supreme Court Records (SC), National Archives, Washington. DC. See also *McGee v. State,* 26 So. (2d) 680 (Miss., 1946); *McGee v. State,* 33 So. (2d) 843 (Miss., 1948); and *McGee v. State,* 40 So. 2(d) 160 (1949).

37. Horne, *Communist Front?,* 74.

38. "Negro McGee Waives Sanity Trial," *Laurel Leader-Call* (7 Nov. 1946), 1; Willie McGee's Victim on Witness Stand," ibid. (12 Nov. 1946), 1; "Willie M'Gee in Hub Court," ibid. (13 Nov. 1946), 1; and "Willie McGee Again is Sentenced to Death," ibid. (14 Nov. 1946), 1.

39. Dixon Pyles interview with Emilye Crosby, 31 July 1992, interview 34, Mississippi Oral History Program, University of Southern Mississippi, Hattiesburg.

40. *McGee v. State* (1948).

41. U.S. Supreme Court Appellate Record, 657.

42. Ibid., at 996, 998.

43. Testimony of Willie McGee, 5 Mar. 1951, 4 (transcribed by Abzug), 417 Misc. OT 1950, 6562, entry 17, SC.

44. Supreme Court Appellate Record, 114-18; *McGee v. State* (1949).

45. Mississippi Supreme Court Opinion, 11 Apr. 1949, 17, 655 O.T. 1948, 5832 Misc., entry 21, SC.

46. Abzug, Draft Memorandum of Relator, 1951, 7, 1, 2, AU.

47. Samuel Rosenwein and Arthur G. Silverman, Certiorari, 8 Aug. 1949, 238 OT 1949, 42, entry 21, SC.

48. Abzug, Petition for Rehearing, 24 Oct. 1949, 2, Supreme Court Appellate Record.

49. On Abzug's exchange with Constance Baker Motley, Abzug, OHRO Interview, 312; and Suzanne Braun Levine and Mary Thom, Bella Abzug: *How One Tough Broad from the Bronx Fought Jim Crow and Joe McCarthy, Pissed Off Jimmy Carter, Battled for the Rights of Women and Workers, Rallied Against War and for the Planet, and Shook Up Politics Along the Way* (New York: Farrar, Straus, and Giroux, 2007), 47.

50. For the development of legal strategies in 1950s civil rights rape cases, Eric W. Rise, *The Martinsville Seven: Race, Rape, and Capital Punishment* (Charlottesville: University Press of Virginia, 1995); and Lisa Lindquist Dorr, *White Women, Rape, and the Power of Race in Virginia, 1900-1960* (Chapel Hill: University of North Carolina Press, 2004).

51. Recognizing that the Supreme Court avoided the issue of rape, Abzug noted instances when the Court overturned rape cases on procedural grounds: *Smith v. Texas* (1940), *Hill v. Texas* (1942), *Chambers v. Florida* (1940)—which extended *Brown v. Mississippi* (1936)— *Patton v. Mississippi* (1947). Michael Klarman notes the U.S. Supreme Court was unwilling to acknowledge "the discriminatory administration of the death penalty.... in the context of rape" until the 1970s, *From Jim Crow to Civil Rights: The Supreme Court and the Struggle for Racial Equality* (New York: Oxford University Press, 2004), 283.

52. Handwritten note with Justices' signature to deny oral hearing, 2 June 1949, 648 OT 1948-656 OT 1948, 5832 Misc., entry 21, SC; and Petition Denying Rehearing, 15 May 1950, 238 OT 1949, 42, ibid.

53. "Communists Coming Here," *Jackson Daily News*, 19 July 1950, 1.

54. Letter from Fielding C. Wright to CRC, 7 Nov. 1949, reel 10: 575, CRC Papers, Schomburg Center, New York.

55. Abzug quoted in, "Governor Warns Civil Righters to Mind Their Own Business," *Jackson Daily News*, 20 July 1950, 1.

56. Abzug, Petition for Stay of Execution, 25 July 1950, 254 Misc. OT 1950, 6539, entry 21, SC.

57. Abzug, OHRO interview, 133.

58. On John Coe, Sarah Hart Brown, *Standing against Dragons: Three Southern Lawyers in an Era of Fear* (Baton Rouge: Louisiana State University Press, 1998). Briefs filed using the new defense strategy, Abzug and Coe, Writ of Habeas Corpus and/or Writs of Certiorari Briefs, 20 Mar. 1951 and Writ of Error Coram Nobis, *McGee v. Jones*, 6 Mar. 1951 417 Misc. OT 1950, 6562, entry 17, SC; and Relator's Memorandum of Law, *McGee v. Jones*, 10 Mar. 1951, 5, 36, John Coe Papers (JC), Emory University, Atlanta, Georgia.

59. Writ of Habeas Corpus And/Or Writs of Certiorari Briefs, 3. Abzug knew that the NAACP legal team argued in the *Martinsville Seven* case in June, 1950 that Virginia courts had applied the death penalty only to African American men, denying their clients' equal protection under the Fourteenth Amendment. Her research revealed a similar trend: between 1930 and 1948, ninety African Americans had been executed for rape convictions in Mississippi as compared to eighteen whites. Affidavit of Abzug, 5 Mar. 1951, 417 Misc. OT 1950, 417 Misc., 6562, entry 17, SC. See also Rise, 99-132; and Dorr, 206.

60. Affidavit of Johnson, 5 Mar. 1951, 1, 417 Misc. OT 1950, 6562, entry 17, SC. See also letter from Oakley C. Johnson to Coe, 25 Feb. 1951, folder unknown, 56, JC.

61. Testimony of Willie McGee; and Testimony of Rosalee McGee, 5 Mar. 1951, 417 Misc. OT 1950, 6562, entry 17, SC. Note that Willie McGee has two lines of descendents from two separate wives, Rosalee McGee of Mississippi and Eliza Payton-McGee of California; CRC emphasized only Rosalee's role as Willie McGee's wife. Email from Bridgette McGee-Robinson to the author, 4 May 2009 (in author's possession).

62. Patricia Schechter, *Ida B. Wells-Barnett and American Reform, 1880-1930* (Chapel Hill: University of North Carolina Press, 2001); and Jacqueline Dowd Hall, *Revolt Against Chivalry: Jessie Daniel Ames and the Women's Campaign Against Lynching* (New York: Columbia University Press, 1993). On the historical misuse of rape law, Hall, "'The Mind That Burns in Each Body': Women, Rape, and Racial Violence" in *Powers of Desire: The Politics of Sexuality*, eds. Ann Snitow, Christine Stansell, and Sharon Thompson (New York: Monthly Review Press, 1983), 328–49.

63. Abzug quoted in, Abzug, Aubrey Grossman, and Emmanuel Bloch, Petition for Writ of Certiorari to Mississippi Supreme Court, 21 Nov. 1950, 15, 254 Misc. OT 1950, 6539, entry 2, SC. The historical record does not reveal more than rumors regarding McGee's and Hawkins's affair. Abzug believed her client's story, but also later conceded that McGee

was a known philanderer, Susan Brownmiller, Questions for Bella and Interview Notes, 27 Dec. 1973, 1, 12, 11, Susan Brownmiller Papers, Schlesinger Library, Harvard University, Cambridge, Massachusetts. Journalist Carl T. Rowan reported that "it was pretty much whispered around among Negroes since 1942 that McGee was going to get in trouble with that woman," *South of Freedom* (New York: Knopf, 1952), 178. Hattie Johnson's sister coincidently named Rosalee McGee (distant relation to Willie's wife), who worked for Hawkins's sister, later recalled, "[she] told me it was—he didn't rape her, said they had been lovers from growing up," R. McGee, interviewer unknown, n.d., 5, 1156, 139, Jessica Mitford Papers, Ohio State University, Columbus, Ohio.

64. Dan T. Carter, *Scottsboro: A Tragedy of the American South* (Baton Rouge: Louisiana State University Press, 1969), 92.

65. Glenda Gilmore, *Defying Dixie: The Radical Roots of Civil Rights, 1919–1950* (New York: W.W. Norton & Company, 2008), 1009.

66. Abzug and Coe, Writ of Error Coram Nobis, 4, 417 Misc. OT 1950, 6562, entry 17, SC.

67. Patricia J. Williams, "On Being the Object of Property," *Signs* 14, no. 1 (1988): 5–25. For African American women's use of rape law to demand public recognition, Ruth Feldstein, *Motherhood in Black and White: Race and Sex in American Liberalism, 1930–1965* (Ithaca, NY: Cornell University Press, 2000), 86–110; and Dawn Rae Flood, "They Didn't Treat Me Good': African American Rape Victims and Chicago Courtroom Strategies During the 1950s," *Journal of Women's History* 17, no. 1 (2005): 38–61.

68. Letter from R. McGee to William Patterson, n.d., 10: 549, CRC.

69. Letter from Charles Elmore Cropley to Abzug, 18 Oct. 1950, 254 Misc. OT 1950, 6539, entry 21, SC; and letter from Abzug to Ellen I. Perry, 1971, Correspondence—Incoming-General, 1971—January—March, 1, Bella Abzug Papers, Rare Book and Manuscript Library, Columbia University.

70. Abzug quoted in Levine and Thom, 55.

71. Abzug, OHRO interview, 389.

72. Ann Fagan Ginger, "The National Lawyers Guild versus Sexism," *National Lawyers Guild Practitioner* 34 (Summer 1977): 3–4, 3.

73. Abzug, Draft Memorandum of Relator, 6–7. For final brief, Abzug and Coe, Relator's Memorandum of Law, *McGee v. Jones*, 10 Mar. 1951, 5, 36, JC.

74. Memo from Abzug to Unger, 1951, 2, 2, 2, AU.

75. The Circuit Court denied hearing of the Writ of *Error Coram Nobis*, filed 28 Feb. 1951, as did Chief Justice Harvey McGehee of the Mississippi Supreme Court, leading Abzug to file a Writ of Habeas Corpus in the United States District Court. Abzug and Coe also filed an appeal unsuccessfully in the Fifth Circuit Court of Appeals.

76. Frederick Sullens, "The Low Down on the Higher Ups," *Jackson Daily News*, 7 Mar. 1951.

77. There is considerable discrepancy in the historical record over the exact time of the Jackson bus station incident; Abzug's recollection most accurately matches the court record, Abzug, OHRO interview, 137–38; Joyce Antler, *The Journey Home: Jewish Women and the American Century* (New York: Schocken, 1997), 267–79; Doris Faber, *Bella Abzug* (New York: Lothrop, Lee, & Shepard Company, 1976), 53–55; Debra Schultz, *Going South: Jewish Women in the Civil Rights Movement*. New York: New York University, 2001), xiii; and Judith Neis, *Nine Women* (Berkeley: University of California Press, 2002), 254.

78. Abzug, OHRO interview, 138.

79. Ibid.

80. Argument of Counsel, 9 Mar. 1951, 35, 417 Misc. OT 1950, 6562, entry 17, SC.

81. Ibid., 41.

82. Abzug, OHRO interview, 314, 321.

83. Charles M. Hills, "Stay of Execution Denied Willie McGee by US Judge," *Clarion-Ledger* (6 Mar. 1951), 1.

84. Zaim, "Trial by Ordeal: The Willie McGee Case," 234.

85. Email from Mel Fiske to Harry and Mim Kelber, 1 Apr. 1998, box 5, Mim Kelber Papers (unprocessed), Columbia University.

86. In the last three days before execution, McGee defense filed a federal suit against Mississippi state officials, *McGee v. Coleman* (1951), petitioned Justice Black unsuccessfully for another stay of execution, and argued the new suit unsuccessfully before Judge Mize. John M. Popham, "Mississippi Arrests 41 at Capitol as Willie McGee Plea is Studied," *New York Times*, 6 May 1951, 1; and Abzug, James T. Wright, Vito Marcantonio, and Ralph Powe, Petition and Denial for Writ of Habeas Corpus, *McGee v. Coleman*, 7 May 1951, OT 1950 Can-Z, 14, entry 30, SC.

87. On CRC's white women's delegation, Letters from Grossman to Mary Kalb, 2 May 1951, 10: 262–63, 355, CRC; and Jessica Mitford, *A Fine Old Conflict* (New York: Alfred A. Knopf, 1977), 160–94. On Abzug and Coe bailing out arrested delegates from jail, Anne Braden interviewed by Lenore Hogan, July 1979 (transcription available at OHRO). On Sojourners for Truth's role in the McGee case, McDuffie, "A 'New Freedom Movement of Negro Women'."

88. Liz Abzug interview.

89. Letter from W. McGee to Patterson, 27 Apr. 1951, 10: 524–30, CRC.

90. Letter from W. to R. McGee (wife), 8 May 1951, 10: 380, CRC.

91. Abzug, OHRO interview, 142, 315.

92. Martha Baker interview with author, 15 Nov. 2007, New York City (transcript in author's possession).

93. For surveillance of Abzug during the McGee case, Virginia Rafferty, Summary of File References—Abzug: 100-102413, Federal Bureau of Investigations, 17 Dec. 1951, 12, 148, NLG.

94. Abzug, Draft Memorandum of Relator, 6.

95. "Questions for Bella," 1.

96. Susan Brownmiller, *Against Our Will: Men, Women and Rape* (New York: Simon Schuster, 1975), 261, 269–70. Brownmiller recently reasserted her position, suggesting that Left lawyers alleged in black-on-white rape cases either the white woman "was hysterical and having a fantasy or she'd been having a long affair with the person," quoted in Levine and Thom, 48.

97. Brownmiller, *Against Our Will*, 282.

CHAPTER 3

"I'm Glad as Heck That You Exist"

Feminist Lesbian Organizing in the 1950s

MARCIA GALLO

In November 1956, Del Martin wrote an editorial in the Daughters of Bilitis (DOB) newsletter *The Ladder* entitled "The Positive Approach." She began by analyzing the impact of a recent police raid on a bar popular with women in San Francisco. "A paralyzing fear has been heaped upon an ever-present dread of detection. The persecuted are seeking cover yet again." As she had done in the first issue of *The Ladder* one month earlier, Martin went on to detail her understanding of gay women's place in society. She started with gender rather than sexuality: "The Lesbian is a woman endowed with all the attributes of any other woman. As an individual she has her own particular quota of intelligence and physical charm. She has equal opportunity for education, employment, intellectual and cultural pursuits. Her only difference lies in her choice of a love partner."[1]

Martin's words capture the essence of the founding Daughters' views on lesbians: they saw themselves as female first, homosexual second. They believed that they had it within their personal power to create a life worth living despite social and political restrictions on both and insisted that liberal ideals of "equal opportunity for education, employment, intellectual and cultural pursuits" applied not only to women but also to gay women. This was radical doctrine in 1956: in no other place could a lesbian find not only affirmation of her same-sex desires but a "we can do it" refrain harkening back to wartime mobilizations that had mostly faded from popularity.[2]

By organizing women-only groups focusing on issues of gender and sexuality in the mid-1950s, DOB by the mid-1960s had established activist networks for women who loved women in key American cities. In the private sphere, they effectively utilized personal discussions in members' homes to break through the isolation so identified with lesbianism at that time. In the public sphere, the gendered educational and advocacy programs organized by their chapters in San Francisco, Los Angeles, and New York opened up traditional civic spaces and public accommodations to women. The availability of publicized, regularly scheduled gatherings that highlighted important issues to women in general and lesbians in particular helped to facilitate an independent female presence in downtown auditoriums, hotels, and meeting rooms as well as parks and other recreational facilities. DOB leaders in chapter cities also brought women together for biennial conventions from 1960 to 1970. Each convention was preceded by press releases and outreach, and the Daughters were increasingly successful with local and national media coverage as the years went on, thus increasing the visibility of the organization and its supporters.

In addition, DOB's monthly magazine *The Ladder* provided a virtual transnational meeting space for its readers. For more than a decade *The Ladder* was the only regularly published cultural and intellectual source on female same-sex love and relationships that was produced by lesbians. It represented gay women as strong, independent, and equal (if not superior) to men, gay and straight; at the same time, in advance of women's liberation, *The Ladder* was among a handful of publications that regularly commented critically on women's status in society. Readers throughout the country applauded its debut in 1956; the staunch pro-woman message was a large part of the positive response for many of them. As playwright and civil rights activist Lorraine Hansberry wrote from New York months after she received the first few issues, "I'm glad as heck that you exist—Women, like other oppressed groups of one kind or another, have particularly had to pay a price for the intellectual impoverishment that the second class status imposed on us for centuries created and sustained. Thus, I feel that THE LADDER is a fine, elementary step in a rewarding direction."[3]

In this essay, I argue that DOB infused its efforts on behalf of lesbians with a commitment to women as a social and political group and thus reflected an unabashed if unnamed feminist perspective. The Daughters' strategic use of separatism provided small groups of lesbians in major U.S. cities with accessible sites as well as organizational skills for personal and political education and advocacy. Their woman-centered programming and organizing was framed by their dual activism as women and as members of a sexual minority; it meant that, within the new homophile (love of same) movement, issues of gender were ever-present, if less than adequately addressed by their male comrades. The Daughters' refusal to be subsumed under a male-dominated group further underscored their independence and telegraphed their strength as women.

To claim feminism for DOB a decade before women's liberation is to face squarely the challenge of how best to characterize women's social and political action on their own behalf during decades when "feminism" is viewed either as old-fashioned or irrelevant. In the 1950s, it was personified by Alice Paul and the National Woman's Party (NWP), whose sole focus in the years since winning federal women's suffrage in 1920 was passage of the Equal Rights Amendment to the U.S. Constitution (a goal still unachieved at the beginning of the second decade of the twenty-first century). Many politically active women rejected the feminist label for progressive political reasons: Paul and NWP eschewed political alliances with activists in labor unions as well as civil rights and civil liberties groups, and many of them shared U.S. Senator Joseph McCarthy's extreme anti-Communism. These may be among the reasons why, when DOB founders Phyllis Lyon and Del Martin were asked whether they considered themselves feminists in the mid-1950s, Lyon replied, "No—we didn't use the word then."[4]

Regardless of whether they used "the word" to describe themselves or their politics, however, DOB's organizing and outreach strategies provide potent examples both of feminist ideals as well as organizational feminist political potential.[5] The founding Daughters emphasized women's individual and collective strengths and capabilities; at the same time, they recognized the importance of personal support for women who wanted to accept themselves and their non-normative same-sex desires while taking their place in the world. Their belief in gender equality—at work and at home—was the foundation that secured all of their efforts on behalf of lesbians. They also believed in social reform. Lyon and Martin, as well as other early DOB activists, claimed Eleanor Roosevelt as an important role model. "ER" was the most famous and influential of the Roosevelt administration's Women's Bureau network in the U.S. Department of Labor, that formed the social feminist wing of the women's movement after 1930 and reconceptualized ways to define and fight sex and wage discrimination through the 1940s and into the 1950s.[6]

Further, DOB's focus on organizing in San Francisco, Los Angeles, and New York in the late 1950s and early 1960s helped them evolve from potential to actual feminist lesbian activism at a time when cities "offered the possibility of a life lived outside the romantic plot line of heterosexuality..." as Victoria Hesford asserts in her analysis of Patricia Highsmith's lesbian love story *The Price of Salt*.[7] Published in 1952 by Claire Morgan (Highsmith's pseudonym), the novel was hailed by lesbian readers as one of the first of the genre in which the female protagonists, despite the high prices they pay for their relationship, are not killed, imprisoned, or doomed to marriage with men after they return to New York from a road trip through small-town, postwar America. The city itself became a refuge for them and for other women like them. However, despite significant advances for women after the war, especially in terms of their continuing involvement in the workforce, real access to public space was limited. Women who went out alone or with one another without the protection of a male escort were fair game for harassment or assault at night as well as during the day.[8] DOB advanced the possibilities of women moving freely in public sites independent of men by opening up spaces for lesbians and their allies to congregate in its chapter cities.

In addition, the specific activities of the Daughters also helped define a feminist lesbian perspective. While their membership numbers may have been small, the range of projects they took on in their chapters was not: DOBers not only recruited members, answered mail and phone calls, and offered informal peer counseling, they also produced literature, maintained mailing lists and bank accounts, raised funds, created and promoted public programs, joined coalitions, organized protests, and engaged the media, locally and nationally. The skills learned by these early Daughters transformed many of them into self-aware lesbian leaders and provided examples of proud gay women engaged in social and political work. Their personal and organizational strengths would provide material support for DOB and for the lesbian feminist groups that developed in the next decade.

"From the City of Many Moods…"

As many historians have detailed, the military installations of the San Francisco area during World War II brought in tens of thousands of women and men who served in same-sex regiments or took advantage of plentiful employment opportunities in war-related industries. Postwar, many of those who had enjoyed the gay nightlife and cheap apartments in North Beach or the Mission district decided to stay.[9] Downtown San Francisco was bustling, part of the great American urban society that reached its zenith in the 1950s. It was a time when American cities still contained industry as well as entertainment; there were shopping districts and self-defined neighborhoods. All forms of urbanity—dress, manners, music, even drinks (like the "Manhattan")—were celebrated as exciting and sophisticated.[10] By 1955, however, the bars and nightclubs in San Francisco that welcomed lesbians and gay men experienced yet another round of police raids and arrests timed to coincide with city elections and media-driven "clean up" campaigns. The risks of unwanted public exposure due to a night out were, for some, not worth the possible cost. Private at-home parties were a popular alternative.

The first Daughters—an interracial, cross-class grouping of four female couples in their 20s and 30s—met over drinks and snacks in one another's homes in San Francisco in the fall of 1955 and carefully invited two or three friends to join them each time. Even the name they chose for themselves—after a book of erotic poetry published by Pierre Louÿs in the late nineteenth century and purportedly written by Bilitis, a female lover of Sappho—signaled that a woman would have to be, in the slang of the day, "on the *qui vive*," or "in the know" to understand its implications. Despite their shared initial desires to form a secret social club, however, disagreements soon surfaced among the founders over the rules and regulations they should follow, who could participate, even the dress code they should enforce. By the next summer, co-founders Del Martin and Phyllis Lyon had traveled south to attend homophile meetings in Los Angeles and brought back ideas for public discussions focusing on lesbians. The group's membership had dwindled to a hardy few but, unwilling to call it quits, they reorganized. The revitalized DOB decided that to recruit new members, they would hold public meetings on a regular basis and publicize them by starting a monthly newsletter, named after the image on their first cover, a pen-and-ink drawing of women at the base of a ladder extending into the sky. The words "From the city of many moods..." decorated the back cover.[11]

The artwork revealed their organizing strategy. For DOB, reaching women where they were, both spatially and emotionally, was a critical first step. Any woman concerned about "the problems of the female variant" could join; she did not have to declare a sexual or affectional attachment, or even attraction, to women to become a member. Again reflecting a feminist perspective, the Daughters' rhetoric and program emphasized personal discovery as well as political awareness to women, born in the 1920s and 1930s, who came of age in the ferment of World War II. Postwar, most of DOB's members actively resisted the era's fabled resurgence of domesticity. College-educated and accustomed to earning decent wages at jobs with increasing levels of responsibility before, during, and after the war, they lived in major metropolitan areas with lovers, roommates, or on their own. Their work lives were very important to them, as they provided for both economic survival and self-esteem; their private lives were women-centered. By consciously focusing on issues of gender in their publications and programs, these small groups of Daughters addressed the importance of women's independence and advocated for gender equality at the same time that they challenged social strictures on female sexuality. That they did so in the midst of a conformist Cold War culture that viewed collective action with suspicion, and made women justifiably concerned about losing families, jobs, and homes should their involvement in a lesbian organization become public, is all the more remarkable.

From the beginning, the Daughters saw the necessity of balancing visibility with the protection of members' privacy. For example, the notices DOB published within a year of the group's founding—"Your Name Is Safe!" was the headline they used—came after the arrests of three dozen women at a popular lesbian nightspot in San Francisco. Also in the headlines in the mid-1950s was the federal government's high-profile dismissal of thousands of employees merely on suspicion of homosexuality. In order for many lesbians to consider joining an organization, especially one formed to address "the female variant," it was necessary to assure them that their participation would not endanger them in any way.[12]

DOB fused gendered education and organizing with the integrationist philosophy of the tiny, male-led homophile movement based in southern California. Although the homophile activists were strongly influenced by postwar black civil rights advocacy as expressed by the reform agenda of the NAACP (National Association for the Advancement of Colored People), the DOB opted for a women-only membership and saw itself as more like the BPW (National Federation of Business and Professional Women's Clubs). In other respects, however, the group followed the structural model provided by the Mattachine Foundation, begun in 1950 and later renamed the Mattachine Society. Mattachine founder Harry Hay, a progressive activist shaped by his experiences with the Communist Party in Los Angeles, and Donald Webster Cory (Edward Sagarin's pseudonym), author of the 1951 first-person account *The Homosexual in America* and called "the 'father' of the homophile movement," were among the first to argue that gay people were a distinct minority group deserving recognition and equal rights. They insisted that homosexuals needed to reject the definition of themselves as "deviants" and begin to organize. A group of Mattachine members split off in 1953 and formed ONE, also in Los Angeles, to focus on education and outreach through seminars and publications. DOB was welcomed into the homophile fold, due in part to the recognition by some activists in the pre-existing groups that they had been unable to retain many lesbian members. Their emphasis on, and leadership by, gay men had made it difficult to keep women involved.[13]

DOB founders recognized that in order to be viable, they had to be seen as legitimate to potential new recruits. They quickly professionalized by subletting a room within Mattachine's local chapter offices in downtown San Francisco at 693 Mission Street. They also established telephone service and engaged a lawyer to draw up state incorporation papers for them. Historian Martin Meeker identified this "somewhat contradictory

strategy" as meaning that "the organization would regularly cross the defi-
nitional lines separating the activities characteristic of a private and even
secret organization from the actions typical of a public group looking to
advertise its message and gain new members."[14]

At the time that DOB was establishing its bona fides, San Francisco's
downtown was a vibrant center of activity. It is no coincidence that DOB
and Mattachine located their offices there; it meant that they were easily accessible to the gay men and women—especially the women—who
helped to fill the offices, department stores, warehouses, and restaurants
in the area. San Francisco author Margot Patterson Doss described the
city's downtown then as a female-dominated scene, at least during the day.
She wrote in 1964, "Convoys of secretaries break cover for coffee. Clerks
flit by hastily. Buyers stroll in pairs. The men are few." Within a year of its
first sublet, DOB moved on to several different locations, all within walking distance or a short streetcar ride from each other in downtown San
Francisco. The nitty-gritty work of the organization took place there, after
the end of the workday or on Saturdays. One of the organization's earliest recruits, Helen Sandoz (aka Helen Sanders), worked nearby in Macy's
print shop in the heart of the city. She not only attended DOB business
and social gatherings but also was featured as a speaker at one of their first
public meetings in 1956: a three-part series on the topic "What Are You
Afraid Of?"[15]

To encourage attendance and provide a safe environment, the Daughters
consciously anchored their public activities downtown, renting or borrow-
ing space in offices, hotels, or halls. A woman entering one of these spaces
did not have to worry about exposure or having to explain her presence
to passersby who might recognize her; she could simply say that she was
attending a lecture sponsored by a local women's group. The Daughters'
postwar feminism, as reflected in their program of lectures and discussions, aided the creation of lesbian community. In addition, DOB regularly organized women-only picnics in Bay area parks as well as parties at
bowling alleys, bars, and restaurants. The Daughters made visible female
independence and a nascent feminist group consciousness.

DOB also made good use of private space. Almost every week, women
crowded into one another's living rooms for parties or female-only "bull
sessions" dubbed "Gab 'n Javas" due to the quantities of talk and coffee
consumed. Finding and entering such personal sites proved challenging
for most newcomers, as it required them to make a mental and emotional
leap from attending a lecture to coming face-to-face with other lesbians in
the intimacy of a stranger's home. However, the private gatherings satisfied
many lesbians' desires for friendship, romance, and accessible community
beyond the bars. In this way, as the organization grew, slowly, through

the end of the 1950s and into the 1960s, they would provide a variety of portals for women to enter a new, previously unimagined, lesbian world—one located downtown as well as in the neighborhoods.

"About That Chapter in Your Area..."

Like San Francisco, Los Angeles also was the beneficiary of a great influx of people due to World War II. One estimate cites 250,000 "war migrants" to the area during the 1940s. Further, more of them—both straight and gay—returned to Los Angeles than to any other city after their tours of duty were over.[16]

DOB's emphasis on personal interaction meant creating an organizational structure that included groups beyond the San Francisco Bay area, and it was logical that their first glances would be southward. "A chapter in Los Angeles will be the first of many we hope to charter throughout the country," an unsigned report in the February 1957 issue of *The Ladder* stated. Assuming that their San Francisco activities would provide a blueprint for organizing in other areas, in January 1957 the Daughters held an organizing meeting in L.A. But in December 1957, Del Martin published an update entitled "About That Chapter in Your Area..." acknowledging the stalled status of DOB's efforts. She admitted that local organizing "takes time, strong leadership, thorough indoctrination of the principles and aims of the organization, imagination, hard work, planning. You name it—we need it!" Perhaps most hopeful, however, was the report that "Helen Sanders, publications director of the DOB, will be moving to Los Angeles next year. And after a suitable time for getting settled in her new home, she will be available to help organize a Los Angeles Chapter."[17]

More than politics or personal growth, it was romance that motivated the founding of Los Angeles DOB: Sandoz and Stella Rush met at the ONE conference in Los Angeles in 1957; after a few months of long-distance dating, they decided Sandoz would move there. A few months after they began living together, they held the first meeting of the new L.A. chapter at a friend's home. Thereafter, L.A. DOB meetings were held at the Rush/Sandoz house on Waterloo Street in the Silver Lake neighborhood; both women were mainstays of the group for the next several years.

Through the late 1950s and early 1960s, the local membership stayed small; it wasn't easy to convince women in the far-flung southland to travel to a meeting, especially if there were welcoming places closer to home. No downtown DOB office was established and geographic location did not aid their organizing as it did in San Francisco. Further, some scholars have speculated that Los Angeles lesbians in the late 1950s did not need to form a group: DOB's stated goal of integration of the lesbian into society was unnecessary and somewhat insulting to women who had already success-fully navigated business and professional worlds.

Despite this assessment, however, the self-revelatory nature of DOB dis-cussions could provide some women with a source of connection and con-fidence building. Like the San Francisco group, L.A. DOB's "Gab 'n Java" sessions brought together small groups of lesbians in one another's homes to discuss issues of importance to them many years before the notion that "the personal is political" was articulated by women's liberation activ-ists. Ann Bannon, the author of the wildly popular lesbian-themed Beebo Brinker books of the 1950s and 1960s, was a young (and closeted) house-wife living in the Los Angeles area; she attended DOB meetings there and found them inspiring but "scary." "In Greenwich Village I'd met people mainly in smoky bars. In L.A. everything seemed so expansive and beau-tiful. It seemed to spill over into the gay community," she explained. "We sat in a real home—a bottle of wine, a plate of cookies, all those attrac-tive women, talking about real things, like how do we counteract society's refusal to know we drink orange juice and eat cereal in the morning, just like them." Bannon acknowledged that, in DOB meetings, it was much more difficult to remain invisible and unknown.[18]

As a group, the Los Angeles Daughters took a big step out of the shad-ows and into public awareness when it agreed to host the organization's second national conference. In 1960, the DOB in San Francisco had begun to organize biennial conventions, open to the public and announced to the press, which brought together members and supporters at downtown hotels with "experts" on homosexuality. In June 1962, L.A. DOB proudly welcomed one hundred women and men to the Hollywood Inn to attend "POTENTIALS: The Lesbian in Society." The conference featured recent research on homosexuality by some of the biggest names in homophile cir-cles, including journalist Jess Stearn, author of the recently published book *The Sixth Man*. Stearn had produced one of the first fairly evenhanded nonfiction portrayals of gay men's lives. The DOB convention in Los Ange-les provided him with entre to the Daughters, who would prove crucial to the success of his next book, published in 1964.

Stearn's *The Grapevine* relied heavily on DOB leaders. It also character-ized them as feminist, although he never explicitly used the term: when Stearns reported on their 1962 convention, he described DOB as "a militant women's group." The use of the words "militant women's group" in 1964 would have conjured up images of early twentieth-century suffragists and other strong pro-female activists: in other words, feminism. *The Grapevine* highlighted DOB's particular brand of gender-centered homophile orga-nizing—and brought hundreds of inquiries from women who read it—but also caused divisions among the local chapters. In discussing DOB, Stearn had established a lesbian geography that was heavily weighted in favor of San Francisco; he emphasized the pathos of Los Angeles, especially Hollywood, and the debilitating bar culture of New York. In a small organization still struggling to establish a national network of lesbians, rooted in local communities but governed by a shared mission and strategies, such favoritism in a bestselling book could derail their organizing efforts. Tensions among West and East Coast Daughters were already surfacing by the early 1960s after the establishment of the New York chapter.

New York had been the city most identified with lesbian social life in the 1950s due to the popularity of lesbian novels like *The Price of Salt* as well as those written by Bannon and Ann Aldrich (Marijane Meaker's pseudonym). In their bestsellers, New York in general and Greenwich Village in particular became a leading character: it was a mecca for the fictional Beebo Brinker's friends and lovers, created by Bannon, and for the groups of "gay girls" described by Aldrich. There were enough lesbians in the New York area interested in the Daughters and *The Ladder* for a third chapter to be established in 1958.[19] New York DOB founders Barbara Gittings and Marion Glass (aka Meredith Grey) initially followed the DOB blueprint, organizing public meetings and events. Like DOB in San Francisco, DOB New York initially shared space with the Mattachine chapter, opening up their first office as a sublet at 1133 Broadway; future locations—especially the ones on 28th Street in Chelsea and on Charlton Street in Greenwich Village—would place them in the midst of late 1950s and early 1960s art, politics, and activism in the city.

The New York chapter soon carved out its own place in the homophile movement: by 1963, it was known for its independence within DOB and for its alliances with other East Coast gay groups despite the organization's ban on joining coalitions, a holdover from the paranoid 1950s. In the early 1960s, new recruits Kay Tobin Lahusen and Shirley Willer found New York DOB as well as new love interests. Lahusen became Gittings' life partner as well as one of the homophile movement's first activist photographers; Willer, who quickly paired up with Glass, led New York DOB in 1963 as well as National DOB in 1966. She also became a key player in the homophile coalitions of the mid-1960s, which the New York chapter helped to create.[20] DOB activists in New York utilized both private and public spaces to good advantage; however, when the editorship of *The Ladder* moved to New York in 1963, their energies shifted as well.

With Barbara Gittings at the helm of the organization's publication, which was by now a professionally printed magazine, the New York Daughters assumed a much more active role in constructing not only lesbian community but control over the ways in which the members of that community were viewed. Changing popular images of "the lesbian" had always been a crucial issue for DOB; it was one of the reasons why so much of their time and creativity went into *The Ladder*. For the Daughters who resided in New York—at the crossroads of American publishing networks—the challenge of engaging with the print media was greater than ever. Gittings, who with Lahusen created *The Ladder*'s content and cover portraits from 1963–66, continually urged DOB to use its resources toward greater lesbian visibility.

As the Los Angeles group had done two years earlier, the New York Daughters seized the opportunity to host the DOB's third biennial convention in June 1964, which coincided with the World's Fair. Held just off Central Park, at the Barbizon-Plaza Hotel, they not only brought together nearly 200 women and men but also were able to attract the New York media. As they reported in *The Ladder*, "reporters from both the *New York Times* and the *Herald Tribune* covered the event, taking reams of notes from the speeches and cornering various speakers and DOB representatives for statements." The *Times* article—a breakthrough in coverage of lesbianism in general and the Daughters in particular—was a five-paragraph report headlined "Homosexual Women Hear Experts." The story emphasized the then-prevalent opinions of psychologists and psychiatrists about causes and possible cures of homosexuality, provided contact information for DOB, and gave details on the rest of the weekend conference program. Shortly thereafter, a headline screaming "World's First Lesbian League!" appeared in *Confidential* magazine, a New York-based scandal sheet famous for its often-dubious "exposés." Its hysterical warnings about "the girls who would be boys" wreaking havoc on the streets of Manhattan and throughout society was motivated by the brief report on the DOB convention in the *New York Times*.[21] Although by today's standards the media attention given the 1964 convention was slight, as well as inaccurate and offensive, it nonetheless meant that the New York Daughters had engineered at least a partial crack in the wall of public indifference towards lesbians in the mid-1960s.

But *The Ladder* still was the only source for consistent, sometimes incendiary, feminist lesbian analysis. One New York *Ladder* contributor urged radical action in 1965. "Why this blackout on female homosexuality?" "L.E.E." asked in 1965. "The reason is that the lesbian is a dangerous subversive rebelling against the deepest injustices of our social order. Her existence brings up questions so uncomfortable that most people can't even bear to admit her existence." She went on to urge unequivocal rejection of the status quo in clear feminist language: "A lesbian living in a patriarchal male-dominated society like ours, who goes to a psychotherapist to be told she must be 'cured' and force herself into the straitjacket of the Feminine Role, is like a Mississippi Negro who might be told by a

therapist that he has to adjust himself into the 'Nigger' role society has cut
out for him." Calling for rejection of one of the DOB's longstanding goals,
she insisted, "There are times when revolt, not 'adjustment to society,' is
the only 'mature' and self-respecting course. And you can't depend on the
authorities-in-power to tell you when that time is."[22]

By June, 1966, New York chapter vice-president Ernestine Eckstein,
who had joined other gay picketers at federal sites in Washington, D.C.,
as well as Independence Hall in Philadelphia, also urged DOB to greater
militancy. "Any movement needs a certain number of courageous people,
there's no getting around it. They have to come out on behalf of the cause
and accept whatever consequences come," she asserted. As someone with
experience in black civil rights activism, Eckstein was asked about parallels between the NAACP and the homophile groups. Her sophisticated
response highlights the debates raging within the homophile movement
at the time. "Demonstrations, as far as I'm concerned, are one of the very
first steps toward changing society," she said. "The NAACP never reached
this stage—or at least not until it was pushed into at least giving lip-service
to demonstrations by other Negro organizations. And I think that in the
homophile movement, some segments will have to be so vocal and so progressive, until they eventually push the ultra-conservative segments into a
more progressive line of thinking and action."[23]

The Ladder, by 1966, was much more than the Daughters' organizational
digest. It had become an important networking tool as well as a forum for
debates over homophile activism; it also was the site for showdowns over
the importance of gender politics versus gay politics that developed within
DOB. For Gittings, by the mid-1960s the leading lesbian organizer on the
East Coast, the overarching cause was gay rights. As she has described it,
although she was certainly pro-woman, she had not felt discrimination due
to her gender but rather because of her sexuality. She and Lahusen left DOB
in 1966 to devote their energies to the growing gay rights movement. For
other Daughters, however, a resurgence of explicitly feminist activism starting with the founding of the National Organization for Women (NOW)
that same year would soon have many rethinking their organizational
priorities.

Some Daughters felt caught between the rhetoric of hostile straight feminists and the behavior of sexist homosexuals and, like Helen Sanders and
Stella Rush in L.A., dropped out of activism altogether, tired of shoring up
an increasingly weak local DOB. For others, it seemed that the only viable
choice was breaking with their gay brothers to join an (at best) wary NOW,
as Martin and Lyon did. They had decided that there would be no mini-
mizing of their relationship in order to participate in the new group: in

1966 they signed up as lesbian partners under the organization's "couples" category, which raised eyebrows (and caused the temporary elimination of the category) among some national NOW leaders three years before Betty Friedan's infamous "lavender menace" comment ruptured lesbian participation in the organization.

In 1969 Friedan claimed that the presence of open lesbians in NOW could derail the organization. The uproar led to some gay women dropping out or being asked to leave, as happened in the New York chapter. In Los Angeles, however, the NOW chapter developed and successfully passed a resolution equating lesbian rights with women's rights which then was overwhelming passed at NOW's 1971 national meeting. Although by this time they had greatly minimized their involvement in DOB, neither Martin nor Lyon left NOW; they helped move the L.A. lesbian rights resolution forward. Martin would go on to be elected as the first open lesbian to sit on NOW's national board.[24]

From Feminist Lesbians to Lesbian Feminists

Ironically, DOB officially disbanded in 1970 after then-editor Barbara Grier and DOB president Rita Laporte took *The Ladder* away from the organization and began to publish it independently. They claimed that they did so to devote the magazine and its resources—like the nearly 2,000 names on its mailing list—to the growing feminist movement. They promoted it as "the only women's magazine openly supporting Lesbians, a forceful minority within the women's liberation movement." Whether feminist or not, many Daughters denounced their action as theft, including Lyon and Martin. However, among the first articles published in the new *Ladder* was Del Martin's notorious essay, "If That's All There Is," in which she detailed her breaking point with the gay rights movement. On August 26, 1970, the day of the first National Women's Strike, Martin and other Daughters, including Shirley Willer, were joined by two new gay women's groups in confronting the closing session of the North American Conference of Homophile Organizations (NACHO), a group that New York DOB had been instrumental in creating. NACHO delegates passed a resolution in support of women's liberation but "decried the segregationist organizations which we represented." Martin was especially incensed that NACHO "would not address themselves to the underlying reason for the existence of separate women's organizations—that the female homosexual faces sex discrimination not only in the heterosexual world, but within the homophile community." Martin angrily bid "goodbye" to the "male chauvinists of the homophile movement;" the "co-ed organizations" where "women are invisible"; the "defense of washroom sex and pornographic movies;" the "gay bars that discriminate against women;" the "bastions of male privilege" including "male evangelists from two disparate worlds." Her goodbyes, she claimed, had no hate in them—"only the bitter sting of disappointment...and love, too, in this farewell—just as there has always been." The Editor's Note penned by Barbara Grier and accompanying the essay read, "it is heartening to note that Del Martin, founding daughter, has recognized where the action really is, in the unity of all women in the struggle for human rights for all human beings."[25] It was a clarion call for many former feminist lesbians—now was the time to remake their identity and their movement, from pro-woman homophiles and female gay rights activists to proud lesbian feminists.

In the late 1960s and early 1970s, some lesbians used DOB and *The Ladder* as a springboard for activism into new groups and publications; younger women—like Nina Kaiser in San Francisco, Jeanne Cordova in Los Angeles and Martha Shelley in New York—took the reins of the chapters in their cities and steered them into increased feminist, and then lesbian feminist, activism. A number of new DOB groups began and thrived for short periods of time, most of them in large cities. In 1969, a chapter was started in Melbourne as the first openly gay organization in Australia. DOB Boston, also founded in 1969, would outlast all other groups of Daughters; it remained active for the next twenty-five years primarily by providing safe, social space for lesbians, thus linking the program of DOB's last chapter to that of its first.

In the mid-1950s, DOB's intrinsic feminism flew under the radar of contemporary political discourse yet was complicated by their emphasis on same-sex sexuality: like female labor activists, the Daughters also wanted to eliminate sex-based disadvantages but they did so on behalf of some of the most culturally marginalized people of their era: women who loved women. They provided the first positive post-World War II iterations of American lesbian identity and community; over the next ten years, the Daughters also helped construct local as well as national networks for women's social and political action. Moreover, *The Ladder* was a monthly harbinger of possibilities: in its pages and on its covers from 1956 to 1972, women could find validation of their lives and inspiration for their futures—futures that soon would include a revitalized mass feminist movement. At the moment when women's liberation was entering mainstream political consciousness, some Daughters were able to utilize the organizational and oratorical lessons they had learned in DOB to help define a new woman-centered movement: lesbian feminism.

Notes

1. Del Martin, "The Positive Approach," *The Ladder,* November 1956, 8–9.
2. "We Can Do It!" was used as a slogan on posters promoting female factory work drawn by J. Howard Miller and produced by the Westinghouse Corporation in 1942.
3. Letter signed "L.H.N.," *The Ladder,* May 1957, 26.
4. See Leila J. Rupp and Verta A. Taylor, *Survival in the Doldrums: The American Women's Rights Movement, 1945 to the 1960s* (Columbus: Ohio State University Press, 1990); unpublished interview with Phyllis Lyon, San Francisco, September 2002; author's personal files.
5. See Estelle Freedman, "Separatism as a Strategy: Female Institution Building and American Feminism," *Feminist Studies* 5.3 (Fall 1979): 512–528 and *No Turning Back: The History of Feminism and the Future of Women* (New York: Random House, 2002).
6. See Dorothy Sue Cobble, *The Other Women's Movement: Workplace Justice and Social Rights in Modern America* (Princeton, NJ: Princeton University Press, 2004). See also Blanche Wiesen Cook, *Eleanor Roosevelt, Volume 2: 1933–1938* (New York: Viking, 1992).
7. Victoria Hesford, "Patriotic Perversions: Patricia Highsmith's Queer Vision of Cold War America in *The Price of Salt, The Blunderer, and Deep Water,*" *Women Studies Quarterly* Vol. 33 Nos. 3 & 4 (Fall/Winter 2005): 229.
8. See Anne Enke, *Finding the Movement: Sexuality, Contested Space, and Feminist Activism* (Durham, NC: Duke University Press, 2007).
9. See John D'Emilio, *Sexual Politics, Sexual Communities: The Making of a Homosexual Minority in the United States, 1940–1970* (Chicago: University of Chicago Press, 1983). See also Allan Berube, *Coming Out Under Fire: The History of Gay Men and Women in World War Two* (New York: The Free Press, 1990); Nan Alamilla Boyd, *Wide Open Town: A History of Queer San Francisco to 1965* (Berkeley: University of California Press, 2003); Martin Meeker, *Contacts Desired: Gay and Lesbian Communications and Community, 1940s–1970s* (Chicago: University of Chicago Press, 2006).
10. Michael Johns, *Moment of Grace: The American City in the 1950s* (Berkeley: University of California Press, 2003), 7.
11. See Marcia M. Gallo, *Different Daughters: A History of the Daughters of Bilitis and the Rise of the Lesbian Rights Movement* (New York: Carroll & Graf, 2006).
12. "San Francisco Police Raid Reveals Lack of Knowledge of Citizen's Rights" and "Your Name Is Safe," *The Ladder,* November 1956, 5; 10–12; see also David Johnson, *The Lavender Scare: The Cold War Persecution of Gays and Lesbians in Federal Government* (Chicago: University of Chicago Press, 2004).
13. Martin Duberman, "The 'Father' of the Homophile Movement" in *Left Out: The Politics of Exclusion* (Boston: South End Press, 2002), 59–94; Donald Webster Cory, *The Homosexual in America: A Subjective Approach* (New York: Greenberg, 1951).
14. Martin Meeker, *Contacts Desired,* 78.
15. Margot Patterson Doss, *San Francisco at Your Feet* (New York: Grove Press, 1964), 33; Calendar of Events, *The Ladder,* December 1956, 4.
16. Lillian Faderman and Stuart Timmons, *Gay L.A.: A History of Sexual Outlaws, Power Politics, and Lipstick Lesbians* (New York: Basic Books, 2006), 73.
17. *The Ladder,* February 1957, 10; Del Martin, "About That Chapter in Your Area," *The Ladder,* December 1957, 4–5.
18. Lillian Faderman and Stuart Timmons, *Gay L.A.,* 128–131.
19. See www.annbannon.com; see also www.mekerr.com.
20. Del Martin & Phyllis Lyon, "Shirley Willer (1922–1999)" in *Before Stonewall: Activists for Gay and Lesbian Rights in Historical Context,* ed. Vern Bullough (New York: Haworth Press, 2002).

21. "Postscript," *The Ladder*, November 1964; "World First Lesbian League!" *Confidential*, December 1964.
22. L.E.E., "The Invisible Woman: Some Notes on Subversion," *The Ladder*, June 1965, 4–8.
23. Kay Tobin and Barbara Gittings, "Interview with Ernestine," *The Ladder*, June 1966, 4–11.
24. Stephanie Gilmore, "Bridging the Waves: Sex and Sexuality in a Second Wave Organization" in *Different Wavelengths: Studies of the Contemporary Women's Movement*, ed. Jo Reger (New York: Routledge, 2005), 103–105.
25. Del Martin, "If That's All There Is," *The Ladder*, Vol. 15 No. 3 & 4 (December/January 1970–71): 4–6.

PART II

Women's Global Visions

CHAPTER 4

Exporting Civic Womanhood
Gender and Nation Building

CATHERINE E. RYMPH

In February 1949, seven German women arrived in New York for a two-month tour of the United States. In addition to meeting with Eleanor Roosevelt, the women visited local PTA and League of Women Voters meetings, school classrooms, and farm potlucks in order to see first-hand "the way citizens, particularly women, cooperate and solve their problems" in the United States.[1] A year later, in February 1950, ten Japanese women embarked from San Francisco on their three-month visit, making similar stops. These visits were one part of the larger post-war American effort to stabilize regions of the world recently ravaged by war and to promote U.S.-friendly, democratic societies among the peoples of former enemy nations. These travelers were the first of what would be hundreds of women from around the world who came to the United States in this period specifically to learn about women's participation in American democracy. The visits were officially sponsored by the American military governments in Japan and West Germany, and later the U.S. State Department. But American women's organizations, especially the League of Women Voters, were instrumental in seeing the projects through.[2]

While intended to assist foreign women, these projects also played a role in instructing post-war Americans themselves about women's roles in sustaining democratic society. In publicizing and promoting its work with international visitors, the League celebrated women's civic engagement and attention to foreign affairs as normative in a period often remembered more for the ways in which popular domestic ideology discouraged American women's interest in matters outside the small circle of home and neighborhood. The League was not alone in having done work that challenges this view. As historians have recently suggested, World War II and the early Cold War actually created opportunities for white, middle class women to assert their importance to national security through their contributions to home front preparedness, civil defense programs, and—in the case of the League's democratization projects—nation building.[3] The post-war years were a time when American women's organizations were flourishing. During World War II, millions of women had volunteered on behalf of the war effort through channels set up by the government or through existing women's organizations.[4] Capitalizing on the rhetoric of home front mobilization, women's organizations, including the League of Women Voters, were able to use this nationwide mobilization of women as an opportunity to build their organizations after the war. By the late 1940s, the League had a domestic and international reputation that enabled it to credibly assert that it could take on some of the important foreign policy work of democratizing former enemies.

The League's citizenship work with German and Japanese women can be seen as part of a long trajectory of one form of women's rights activism—one that the League embodied. The League of Women Voters' evolution over the twentieth century is often described in ways that exemplify the "waves metaphor." The League grew out of one of the most important suffrage organizations (the National American Woman Suffrage Association) and developed an ambitious agenda for further advancing female citizenship in the 1920s. But by the post-World War II period it had shied away from talk of equal rights and, like many other liberal women's organizations at the time, opposed the Equal Rights Amendment. Indeed, when Betty Friedan was looking for allies in 1966 to help convince the newly formed Equal Employment Opportunity Commission to take complaints of sex discrimination seriously, the League of Women Voters was one of the traditional women's organizations that would disappoint her.

This conventional telling of the League dovetails nicely with the idea of feminist activity rushing in on one wave, then subsiding into an inactive calm before the crash of the next. Yet, it overlooks the critical role of organizations like the League in sustaining interest in public life and international affairs for women during the mid-twentieth century. While less concerned with the *rights* of citizenship than it had once been, the League's commitment to promoting the *responsibilities* of female citizenship, as its leaders understood them, were significant. This included the responsibility to inform oneself (and subsequently educate the public) about critical issues as a means of nurturing the democratic process. An examination of the League's international work in the late 1940s and early 1950s shows an organization committed to expanding women's democratic participation in the United States and abroad. Although its work deserves a critical gaze, the League did important work on behalf of women, often in a context of reaction and backlash.

Founded in 1920 by Carrie Chapman Catt, the League had been one of the key organizations to continue to pursue a women's agenda after suffrage and to socialize enfranchised women into political life. Like many other women's organizations concerned with social justice for women, the League opposed the proposed ERA (introduced in 1923) on the grounds that it would abolish laws designed to protect women workers from the hazards of the workplace. Instead, the League, in the 1920s, lobbied for legal reforms to bring women into full citizenship; it educated women about such mysteries of formal politics as polling places, voting booths, the marking of ballots, the structure of parties; and it promoted the idea of the "educated voter." The League helped introduce new features to the political system such as "meet-the-candidate" nights, pre-election debates, and other events to encourage all voters—not just women—to reflect upon the issues at hand. By the 1940s, such events had become staples of American political life and were among the ways that enfranchised women subtly transformed American politics from its earlier emphasis on "party enthusiasm and unity" to a focus on candidates and issues.[5] While Catt herself had urged women to join the parties and hoped the League would be one path to do so, the League, as an organization, eschewed partisan politics, arguing that its members should consider issues only in terms of the "public interest." In the 1940s and 1950s, members of League chapters studied problems facing the country, such as United Nations membership, taxes, and school desegregation, evaluated various proposed solutions, and made recommendations that were gathered every two years into the League's "Program."

By the 1940s, the League had also largely dropped its emphasis on empowering women. Although many of its positions were on matters related to women, the League was not concerned only with "women's issues." As one scholar has put it, the "most distinctive" feature of the post-war League was its "disinterested commitment to the general welfare"— not any kind of commitment to women's issues per se.[6] The League model did not focus on sexual equality or on women's emancipation. But in the post-war period, organizations like the League, as Susan Ware argues, should not be under-estimated for their success in "creat[ing] public roles for women denied access to usual sources of power" and making those roles available "at the local level."[7]

The League of Women Voters had, by the late 1940s, earned an international reputation for its work in educating women about politics and advancing women's status. Indeed, many women in other countries looked to the League as a model of women's democratic citizenship. After World War II, the League received numerous requests from countries where women had only recently been enfranchised for assistance in training women to exercise their new responsibilities as citizens. To handle these requests (and to honor its founder, who had recently passed away), the League formed the Carrie Chapman Catt Memorial Fund in 1947 for the purpose of sharing American women's "practical experience as citizens" around the world. By 1950, the Catt Fund had opened its own office in Washington D.C.[8] Long committed to internationalism, the League in the late 1940s hoped it could share what it had learned about democratic citizenship with women around the world.

The foreign policy context of the moment would open doors to do just that. In the wake of World War II and at the onset of the Cold War, the U.S. State Department was keen to promote democratization among former enemies. A pro-Western, democratic Germany would play a key role in the security politics of Cold War Europe; and while the idea of Asia as a Cold War battleground was slower to emerge, the U.S. military was also committed to restructuring Japan's political institutions. The World War II and early Cold War years meant funds would be available (through the U.S. military and State Department) for programs promising to help put those goals into practice. Exposing citizens of Germany and Japan to American political values was part of that project. Yet, it was not immediately clear to State Department officials that it needed to work specifically with *women* in those countries.

American women journalists, politicians, and internationally minded women's organizations helped persuade U.S. officials that German women were critical to furthering American interests and that special programs for them were needed. Anne McCormick of the *New York Times* argued that women would "bear the major part in creating whatever Germany emerges from the war being waged over the wreckage," if for no other reason than that women currently constituted more than 60 percent of the adult population. And she expressed concern about the resources Communists were devoting to women's organizations in Berlin.[9] Rep. Chase Going Woodhouse (D-CT), after three months touring the British and American Sectors in 1948, reported something similar to the U.S. military. Her account was covered in the American press and, together with the "prodding" of the League of Women Voters, helped convince the nation to work with the League to develop exchange programs for German women.[10] In Japan, it was the lobbying of an American woman named Ethel Weed that proved crucial to establishing similar programs for Japanese women. Weed, as the Women's Information Officer in the Civil Information and Education Section of the Allied Occupation, was assigned to formulate policy and develop programs relevant to the "reorientation and democratization" of Japanese women. She surrounded herself with Japanese women leaders who had been involved with the suffrage movement before the war, immersing herself in the concerns of Japanese women activists.[11] Upon learning of the Catt Fund's project with German women, she wrote the Fund's Chair, Lucille Heming about the possibility of a similar program for Japanese women.[12]

Already by 1949, the United States was acting on the calls of McCormick, Woodhouse, Weed, and others, ostensibly agreeing that the new democratic nations it hoped to see emerge after World War II required the substantive participation of women. Uncertainty about whether women could really develop democratic values, however, stemmed from what both participants and organizers saw as problems particular to each nation's past. German women's negative experiences with National Socialist women's groups and rallies seemed to have left many, particularly younger women, skeptical about joining any kind of organization or attending any kind of meeting.[13] German women were said to be only now "emerging from their recently passive roles."[14] Observers of Japan, like Ethel Weed, emphasized the longer-term traditions of social and familial organization in that country.[15] And Nobuko Tomita, who visited America in 1950, described Japanese women as particularly difficult to bring into democratic public life because of the deeply rooted family system in which women held the "lowest positions in their families." Therefore they had "less education, less self-respect and less responsibility" than American women, making organization difficult.[16]

Those concerned about the implications of the history and culture of German and Japan shared a sense that female citizens of both countries were passive, repressed, and brand-new to politics and organizational life. Although these views were not entirely wrong, they did not reveal the whole picture. Both Germany and Japan, after all, had (like the U.S.) experienced important women's movements in the early twentieth century. German women had held the franchise during the Weimar period. And in Japan's post-war election of 1946, the first in which women could vote, Japanese women went to the polls in surprisingly large numbers. In addition, the war itself had required women to take on new roles and to re-think their place in society. In short, Japanese and West German women were not thoroughly isolated from public life.

The "solution" endorsed by the League to the obstacles nonetheless involved in "democratizing" both German and Japanese women was to encourage the organization of ordinary women into non-partisan civic groups along the lines of the League of Women Voters. Yet, the West German and Japanese women who visited the United States were hardly "ordinary women." All were active in political life in their respective countries as governmental officials, as non-Communist party members, as attorneys, as labor union representatives, or as journalists.[17] Many had been active in political life before the 1930s, some on behalf of women's rights. One of the German visitors, a leader in her local Social Democratic Party (SPD), had been imprisoned after the Nazis came to power. And among the first group of women to visit from Japan after the war were two attorneys who had recently helped rewrite Japan's civil code granting equal status to women under a variety of the nation's laws.

Visitors might have been exercising their citizenship in their home countries through service as elected officials or in their work rewriting their nation's laws. However, what American women most wanted to show these visitors about women's citizenship was the vitality of American women's middle class non-governmental organizations. In its efforts to nurture democracy abroad, the League promoted itself and its members as examples. The League model was not one of women's political empowerment, but, rather, was a model of women's citizenship that was rooted in the League's particular experiences with women's suffrage. The League's philosophy was based on a "belief in the responsibility of individual citizens to be active and informed participants in the democratic process."[18] Above all, it emphasized informed, active participation by its members. Only after a period of careful study—culminating in a consensus decision by members—was a local chapter to take a stand on any particular issue.[19] In this picture of a thriving civil society as the foundation of democracy, middle-class women played a critical role in educating voters and training citizens.

It was just such a model of an engaged, informed, female citizenry at the local level that the League wanted to show to foreign visitors. Local hostesses were instructed to plan programs allowing visitors not only to meet with area League of Women Voters chapters, but also to observe city council or school board meetings, to witness the proceedings of other local women's clubs, and to visit schools to see how democratic classrooms in the United States functioned.[20] For League-minded American women, joining organizations and attending meetings was the essence of political activity and a key part of middle-class womanhood. Indeed, more than one third of League members in the 1950s belonged to five or more organizations.[21]

Catt Fund leaders advised hostesses to bring visitors to meetings where they could really observe democracy in action. "Avoid large teas," was the message. It was necessary to let visitors talk with a few women at a time where the power of discussion would allow foreign women to see that "we are not perfect; we learn through mistakes sometimes." Hostesses were also encouraged to offer each visitor the opportunity to explore on her own so that she would have a sense that she was seeing "all of America—not just the parts we want her to see."[22] But the visits also gave American women themselves opportunities to reflect upon their own political roles. A visit by Annemarie Huthmann to Rapid City, South Dakota, involved the efforts of around 200 local citizens who were inspired by the "thought provoking" call to demonstrate how "Democracy work[ed] in [their] town."[23]

One could imagine that attending meetings of local middle-class women's clubs may not have been what prominent, international women visitors most wanted from their travels throughout the United States. Nonetheless, visitors routinely expressed admiration for the myriad of activities and organizations that American women took on. And in interviews with the press and in subsequent correspondence with tour organizers, international visitors commented enthusiastically on the confident way American women expressed themselves in public and seemed to find their own countrywomen lacking.

At a reception hosted by the Soroptimist Club in Washington, D.C., Tsuneko Akamatsu explained that, after the war, Japanese women learned that they could think for themselves. "We must look like children to you who have been thinking for yourselves for so long," she said humbly.[24] Akamatsu's statement was undeniably gracious, but it begs the question of whether this fifty-one-year-old member of Japan's House of Councilors really felt like a child in comparison to American clubwomen. Her reactions, though, seem to have been fairly typical. In 1952, after attending the League's 20th biennial convention in Cincinnati, attorney Michiko Watanabe remarked wistfully about how far Japanese women seemed to be from forming similar kinds of organizations. Women's organizations in Japan, she explained, were "weak and undemocratic." By contrast, Watanabe noted that at the League convention [m]any of the delegates expressed their opinions fully." This may have been a natural thing to Americans, she continued, "[b]ut in comparison with the situation at almost all of the conventions of women's organizations in Japan, it seemed to me a splendid sight."[25] Long-time SPD member Anna Haag of Stuttgart put it this way: "What would it mean to Germany, if her women could be taught to be really active, to forget their hampering self-consciousness, and to exercise the wonderful art of speaking to the point, expressing in a concise and sympathetic manner what they think!"[26]

Indeed, several of the Japanese and German visitors did take some of these ideas back home, forming women's organizations in their towns and cities, and encouraging other women to participate. Over the years, they would continue to correspond with the League about those activities. Back in Germany, Anna Haag worked with women's groups, giving over 100 speeches to their organizations by 1950; upon returning to Japan, Nobuko Tomita, of the Women's and Minors Bureau, put together a three-month program of weekly broadcasts on American women's organizations; and Satoko Togana, member of Parliament, delivered speeches on street corners from the back of a truck on the importance of political education for women.[27]

Overall, visitors' public comments about the United States and the League of Women Voters, were very favorable.[28] Hildegard Brücher (who would go on to become one of Germany's best-known female politicians) noted in Die Neue Zeitung, that she was "constantly surprised by the important role played by the League in American political life."[29] It was not only female visitors who expressed such enthusiasm. Konrad Mommsen, like Brücher an editor with Die Neue Zeitung, was "so sold" on the League that he asked to become a member, and he went on to maintain a correspondence with the League's Zella Leonard.[30] Yet, for all their enthusiasm, foreign observers did occasionally remark on the ironies of being "students" of women's political participation in a country where, in fact, so few women held elected office. In 1951, four German women visited Birmingham Alabama—three were members of the Bundestag (Federal Parliament). They expressed to the local paper their "dismay" on having come to the United States to study the participation of women in political life and finding that the percentage of American women holding political office to be much smaller than in their own country. This was in spite of the fact that American women had enjoyed the suffrage longer.[31] In the decade after the war, American women held less than 5 percent of all public offices, including those at the local level. In Germany, by comparison, women were 7.1 percent of the representatives in the West German Bundestag alone in 1949. By 1957 that figure had climbed to 9.2 percent. (Numbers for Japanese women in national office were not as impressive).[32] But, significantly, office-holding was not part of the model of women's citizenship the League was promoting.

The League's own model of women's citizenship was reinforced by local and national press coverage that typically invited American women to look appreciatively at their own situation. The visits offered plenty of opportunities for journalists to draw positive conclusions about women's role in American democracy and about their value as role models for other women. Newspaper headlines further encouraged readers to feel gratified that foreign women were coming to visit, observe, and learn from them: A sampling of such headlines read: "German Women to see U.S Democracy Work;" "Earnest German Women learn Valued Lessons in America,'" "Jap[anese] Visitors See...Democracy in Action."[33]

At times, the language of press reports seems riddled with clichés. One article described a group of visitors as "almost incredulous" when told that the "YWCA considered its strength to be in having people of all races and religions represented in the community participating in its activities, and yet that these people of different backgrounds and beliefs could come together in agreement on policy and program."[34] This idealized picture of America may have been one that many wanted to believe, but it masked a more complicated reality. League leaders were aware of this. They urged hostesses to not only show visitors the good things in America but to point out difficulties as well ("difficulties" was often a euphemism for racial discrimination). In fact, the humility and willingness to acknowledge existing problems was one aspect of American life that visitors frequently commented on favorably.[35]

This was not a generic celebration of American democracy, however, but rather an exploration of *women's* citizenship, featuring visions that were at times in tension. Although the backgrounds in leadership of the female visitors were noted in press releases and news coverage, journalists typically placed these foreign women of accomplishment into another framework of women's citizenship that Americans were familiar and comfortable with—as the mothers of future citizens. A *Washington Post* editorial, for example, praised the decision to bring German women leaders to the United States—not because these women were part of West Germany's new government, but because German women were "mothers who will shape the Germany of tomorrow."[36] This slippage between "women" and "mothers" was typical and did not simply reflect contemporary American views of women's place in society. It also reflected long-held ideas about American women and politics, and the ways in which the very nature of politics and citizenship has been gendered in the history of the United States.[37]

Along these lines, reporters (who were usually women themselves, covering the visits in the women's pages of their newspapers) stressed domestic themes, often at the expense of the picture of American women's citizenship promoted by the League. *Bloomington* [Indiana] *Daily Herald* reporter Nellie Winslow hardly emphasized female civic engagement in her coverage of German women's attendance at a local Home Economics Potluck. Instead she highlighted the allegedly universal female bonds of family and housework as most salient. Bloomington women could bond with the German women, Winslow argued, because they were all wives and mothers. "What could be more natural than an exchange of anecdotes about husbands and children?" Germans and Hoosiers also found common interests, she insisted, in the "long table loaded with food, from chicken to salads, to pies and cakes."[38] The lessons about women's essential place in democracy may not have been immediately obvious from this event, but such coverage did mean a Bloomington woman could look in her local paper and, reading between the lines, see other women holding indirect roles in U.S. foreign affairs, being informed about issues, and taking public roles.

Reporting on foreign visitors also offered journalists an opportunity to proscribe their own version of the visits, insisting, for example, that visitors, saw "beyond the apparent ease and comfort of American life and recognize[d] the steady, determined struggle by the vast mixture of people that make up America, to maintain that priceless possession known as individual freedom."[39] Such platitudes, in fact, were not entirely accurate. Certainly visitors did express great enthusiasm for the function of civil society in America, especially among women. However, the "ease and comfort" of American women's lives did, in fact, affect them. How could it not? Their own countries, after all, were still in the process of emerging physically and economically from a devastating war.

Matsuyo Yamamoto, for example, noted during a press conference that her work with the Japanese Agriculture and Forestry Ministry required teaching rural women to "put stove pipes on their primitive wood stoves" and that the homes of these women were "full of smoke." The problems of Japanese women, especially rural women, were very different from those of Americans, Yamamoto noted. "Your standard of living is so high."[40] German visitors repeatedly remarked on the size of American farms and homes in comparison with those in their home country. Above all they marveled over and over at the modern kitchens (including running water, gas and electric stoves, and modern refrigerators).[41] To many German observers, household conveniences were not merely sources of envy. Rather, they explained in and of themselves the great participation of American women in organizational and community life. Susi Windisch, who visited Lansing, Michigan, in 1951, reported that she and her party had been much impressed by the "time-saving devices and equipment" in American homes. "These facts as well as some others," Windisch suggested, "seem to explain to me why American women can spend more time for club activities."[42]

Windisch's analysis alarmed Betsy Knapp of the Catt Fund. Perhaps, Knapp feared, local League women in Lansing had not planned an appropriate visit. Windisch was surely focusing on the wrong things if she had concluded that the participation of American women in the community was "primarily related to household conveniences." Knapp stressed that it was important "for our foreign visitors to know that there was a tradition of participation in the community long before the gadgets and time-saving devices became so plentiful."[43] Knapp was both right and wrong. Indeed, associational life among American women did date from before the wide-spread ownership of vacuum cleaners and deep freezes. Organizational activity was part of a long-held definition of American middle class womanhood—a definition that post-suffrage organizations like the League of Women Voters had tried to fuse with political citizenship. Certainly, however, such conveniences made a difference. And for women from post-war Germany and Japan, they were difficult to ignore.

In their reaction to American middle-class domestic prosperity, visitors were developing their own understandings about what made America women's political participation possible—theories typically grounded in their own perspectives as outsiders. For many visitors, American prosperity and class privilege were an essential part of the equation, as the examples above suggest. For women coming from societies with more traditional gender arrangements in the household, another feature of American life stood out—its relative gender equality. Taki Fujita, who visited in 1949, suspected that part of the secret of female civic life in the United States was to be found in what she described as the "'League husband,'" without whose "understanding" her Oregon hostess would not have been able to participate in her many civic activities.[44] And Michiko Watanabe noted that Japanese women leaders were too stiff, formal, and serious, perhaps because they had to struggle so much with disapproval.[45]

Foreign women may have had their own theories, but in these discussions about democracy and women's status, the exchanges were hardly reciprocal. Although the League declared its educational programs to be a two-way street, what American women learned from these experiences concerned their own "heritage of freedom."[46] As the Catt Fund put it, "Seeing our democracy through the eyes of others has made us more aware of our good fortune, our power and our responsibility."[47] There was little sense that American women had something to learn about alternative models of women's citizenship or women's rights from the women they were "teaching."[48] Yet, there were developments in both post-war Germany and Japan that might have been of interest.

German and Japanese women were at a unique moment in their histories in the post-war period. In West Germany and Japan, the nature of women's roles in society were being re-negotiated at the same time that new political systems were being erected in close consultation with the United States. As Robert Moeller has argued, a "reassessment of gender relations [was] a crucial part of rebuilding Germany after 1945."[49] Something similar could be said of Japan. A shortage of adult men in both countries intensified the dislocations of the post-war period making it necessary to rethink the status of women, the nature of the family, and relations between men and women. Women in both countries were enfranchised after the war. And the new constitutions of Japan (1946) and the Federal Republic of Germany (1949) ostensibly required the equal treatment of men and women.[50] It was not yet clear, though, what that constitutional equality would mean in practice for the majority of Japanese and West German women. The Japanese and German women who visited the United States in the post-war period would be among those who helped shape the meanings of gender equality in the post-war period. Yet, on such subjects, American women involved in foreign exchanges seem to have been silent.

War had caused disruptions and dislocations in the United States, as well. And while these were certainly not as profound as what occurred in Japan or Germany, the country also experienced a reassessment of gender relations that fueled contradictory ideas about American women's roles as workers, as mothers, and as citizens. It seems the League had little help to offer its international "students" or American women themselves in articulating their own interests or in negotiating the meaning of women's rights in the debates over post-war gender relations. The publicity surrounding the League's work with international women helped to reinforce the idea that its model of female citizenship—of women as neutral political educators—represented the international standard, that the model was exportable, and that American women should be proud of, endorse, and live up to that model. The League's success in promoting that model affected American proposals for assisting foreign women. It was a palatable model to American military and State Department officials who sponsored these tours perhaps precisely because it acknowledged women's importance to democracy without challenging men's central roles as policymakers.

The League model of female citizenship sounds conservative, yet it needs to be understood within the context in which it thrived. The League's positions in the late 1940s and early 1950s were liberal and worldly during a period of intense anti-radicalism. And in an era imprinted with a contradictory domestic ideology, the League, by insisting on the centrality of women's civic organizations to a functioning democracy, helped lay the groundwork for at least some Japanese, West German, and American women to participate in the political debates that would shape post-war society.

In the United States, the League built institutions and networks of informed women, who—however imperfectly—were concerned about the political process and about women of other cultures. They were part of the broader network of organized women that the State Commissions on the Status of Women would reach out to in the mid-1960s and that would produce female candidates for office. The State Commissions, as well as female state legislators, have received much less attention from historians of feminism than have NOW and the radical feminist groups. But their ongoing commitment to the slog of research and legislative process, which reflected the League model of women's citizenship, would lead to significant feminist change.

A 1958 Catt Fund promotional pamphlet insisted that many foreign visitors, expecting all American women to be rich, instead "discover[ed]" that League members were able to do what they did "not because they [had] servants" but because they were "good administrators and organizers" because of the community of women that facilitated carpooling and potlucks, and "because of husbands who, when it comes to drying dishes or changing diapers, [were] neither aloof nor unskilled."[51] Women's civil society, according to this view, required leadership training, sisterhood, and some move toward gender equality in the home. In other words, the League's model of women's citizenship—which it tried to export abroad and reinforce at home through foreign exchange programs—contained ingredients that would be found in the middle-class, liberal feminism that gained mass appeal in the 1970s.

Notes

1. "7 German Women Due Here Saturday," *Bloomington* [Indiana] *Herald*, 15 March 1949.
2. The most thorough analysis of the role of women and gender in American post-WWII democratization projects is Helen Laville, *Cold War Women: The International Activities of American Women's Organizations* (New York: Palgrave, 2002). Laville's work gives special attention to Germany, though not Japan. On Germany, see also Hermann-Josef Rupieper, "Bringing Democracy to the Frauleins: Frauen als Zielgruppe der amerikanischen Demokratiserungspolitik in Deutschland, 1945–1952," *Geschichte und Gesellschaft* 17 (1991), 61–91. On Japan, see Susan J. Pharr "Soldiers as Feminists: Debate within U.S. Occupation Ranks over Women's Rights Policy in Japan," *Proceedings of the Tokyo Symposium on Women* (Tokyo: International Group for the Study of Women, 1978), 25–35.
3. Laura McEnaney, *Civil Defense Begins at Home: Militarization Meets Everyday Life in the Fifties* (Princeton, NJ: Princeton University Press, 2000); Joanne Meyerowitz, "Sex, Gender, and the Cold War Language of Reform," in Peter J. Kuznick and James Gilbert, eds., *Rethinking Cold War Culture* (Washington, D.C.: Smithsonian Institution Press, 2001), 106–123.
4. D'Ann Campbell, *Women at War with America: Private Live in a Patriotic Era* (Cambridge, MA.: Harvard University Press, 1984), 65–66.
5. Kristi Anderson, *After Suffrage: Women in Partisan and Electoral Politics before the New Deal* (Chicago: University of Chicago Press, 1996), 12.
6. Naomi Black, *Social Feminism* (Ithaca, NY: Cornell University Press, 1989), 273.
7. Susan Ware, "American Women in the 1950s: Nonpartisan Politics and Women's Politicization," in Louise A. Tilly and Patricia Gurin, eds.," *Women Politics and Change* (New York: Russell Sage Foundation, 1990), 291.
8. Helen Hill Miller, "Carrie Chapman Catt: The Power of an Idea," 1958 [pamphlet of the Carrie Chapman Catt Memorial Fund], Carrie Chapman Catt Memorial Fund, Box 13, League of Women Voters Records, Iowa Women's Archives, Iowa City. In 1952 alone, the Catt Fund would coordinate the programs of ninety-six visitors from twelve countries. By that point, seventy-one local Leagues in twenty-seven states had participated. Address by Percy Lee to the 20th Annual Convention of the League of Women Voters, April 28–May

2, 1952, reprinted in Barbara Stuhler, ed., *For the Public Record: A Documentary History of the League of Women Voters* (Westport, CT: Greenwood Press, 2000), 253. Little has been written on the Carrie Chapman Catt Memorial Fund. In addition to Laville, see Louise M. Young, *In the Public Interest: The League of Women Voters, 1920–1970* (Westport, CT: Greenwood Press, 1989), 63, 168; Jacqueline Van Voris, *Carrie Chapman Catt: A Public Life* (New York: Feminist Press at the City University of New York, 1987), 255 n. 12. The name of the Catt Fund was later changed to the Overseas Education Fund.

9. Anne O'Hare McCormick, "The Women's Vital Role in the War Amid the Rubble," *New York Times*, 14 February 1948, p. 14.

10. Rupieper, "Bringing Democracy to the Frauleins," 61–63; Anna Strauss to Mrs. Walter T. Fisher, 18 March 1949, CCCMF 1948–1954, Box III: 636, League of Women Voters Records, Library of Congress Manuscripts Division, Washington, D.C. See also Miller, "Carrie Chapman Catt: The Power of an Idea."

11. On Weed, see Susan J. Pharr, entry for Ethel Berenice Weed, *Notable American Women: The Modern Period* (Cambridge, MA: Belknap Press, 1980), 721–723.

12. Ethel Weed to Lucille Heming, 4 May 1949, Japan, CCCMF, 1948–1954, Box III: 636, LWV Records; Dorothy Robins-Mowry, *The Hidden Sun: Women of Modern Japan* (Boulder, CO: Westview Press, 1983), 111.

13. "German Women See U.S. Democracy Work," *Monitor*, 21 February 1949; Report by Mrs. Harold D. Dyke, U.S. Women's Panel No. 7, 18 May 1951, German, Box III: 284; Comments of Dr. Dorothy B. Ferebee, U.S. Women's Panel No. 9, 11 June 1951, German, Box III: 284; Report on German Project, 1949, CCCMF, 1948–1954, Box III: 636, LWV Records.

14. Press Release, 10 February 1949, CCCMF 1948–1954, Box III: 636 LWV Records.

15. See Civil Information and Education Section of the GHQ-SCAP, Monthly Summary, 15 May 1951, Japan, Box III; Ethel Weed to Lucille Heming, 4 May 1949, CCCMF, 1948–1954, Box III: 636; Ethel Weed to Zella Leonard, 10 October 1951, Japan, Box III, LWV Records.

16. Nobuko Tomita, typed copy of Questionnaire for Visitors, ca. 1950, CCCMF 1948–1954, Box III:636, LWV Records. The traditional system had obligated women to the "three obediences," obedience to father, then to husband, then to son." Robins-Mowry, *Hidden Sun*, 98–99.

17. Civilian Administrative Division, Frankfurt to Civil Affairs Division, Department of Army [copy], 6 January 1949, CCCMF 1948–1954, Box III: 636, LWV Records; "Seven German Women Here to Study Us," *New York Times*, 20 February 1949; "Japanese Visitors," *San Francisco Chronicle*, 16 February 1950.

18. Ware, "American Women in the 1950s," 282.

19. Ibid.

20. Carrie Chapman Catt Memorial Fund, "Sponsoring a Foreign Visitor," CCCMF 1948–1954, Box III: 636, LWV Records.

21. Ware, "American Women in the 1950s," 284.

22. Carrie Chapman Catt Memorial Fund, "Sponsoring a Foreign Visitor," CCCMF 1948–1954, Box III: 636, LWV Records.

23. Jo-Marie Ruddell, Report on Local Sponsor [probably 1953], Germany Box III: 284, LWV Records.

24. "Jap Visitors See 'Cake of Democracy" in Action," *Washington Post*, 2 March 1950, p. 4B.

25. Michiko Watanabe, "My Impression on the Convention of the League of Women Voters," u.d., ca. 1952, CCCMF 1948–1954, Box IIII: 636, LWV Records.

26. Mrs. Haag Describes Impressions Received on Sponsored Study Tour in United States," *Christian Science Monitor*, 28 March 1949.

27. "The Marshall Plan in Action," October 20, quoted in Zella Leonard to Lucille Heming, 5 December 1950, CCCMF, 1948–1954, Box III: 636; Ethel Weed, "New Notes on Japanese Women Leaders," CIES Monthly Summary, 15 August 1950, attached to Lt. Col. D. R. Nugent to Mrs. Lee, 16 August 1950, Japan, Box III, LWV Records.

28. Rupieper found this as well. Rupieper, "Bringing Democracy to the Frauleins," 84.
29. Hildegard Brücher, "Conscience of American Democracy," *Die Neue Zeitung*, 2 June 1950 [translation], CCCMF 1948–1954, Box III: 636, LWV Records.
30. Zella Leonard to Lucille Heming, 5 December 1950, CCCMF, 1948–1954, Box III: 636, LWV Records. *Die Neue Zeitung* was one of the better-known newspapers produced in the American occupation zone after the war.
31. "Four German Women Visit Our City to Learn How U.S. People Live," *Birmingham* [Alabama] *News*, 11 June 1951, German, Box 111: 284, LWV Records.
32. Sara M. Evans, *Born For Liberty: A History of Women in America* (New York: The Free Press, 1989), 247; Tabelle 4: Weibliche Abgeordnete im Deutschen Bundestag 1949–1990, Waltraud Cornelissen, "Politische Partizipation von Frauen in der alten Bundesrepublik und im vereinten Deutschland," in Gisela Helwig und Hildegard Maria Nickel, eds., *Frauen in Deutschland 1945–1992* (Bonn, 1993), 342; Robins-Mowry, *Hidden Sun*, 319; Paul J. Bailey, *Postwar Japan: 1945 to the Present* (Cambridge, MA: Blackwell, 1996), 40.
33. German Women See U.S. Democracy Work," *Christian Science Monitor*, 21 February 1949; "Earnest German Women Learn Valued Lessons in America with Visit to Serious and Good-Humored Town Meeting," *Christian Science Monitor*, 24 March 1949; "Jap Visitors See 'Cake of Democracy" in Action," *Washington Post*, 2 March 1950.
34. "US Amity 'Wins' German Women," *Christian Science Monitor* 23 February 1949, p. 6.
35. "US Amity 'Wins' German Women," *Christian Science Monitor*, 23 February 1949; "Earnest German Women Learn Valued Lessons in America," *Christian Science Monitor*, 24 March 1949.
36. "German Visitors," *The Washington Post*, 19 February 1949, p. 8.
37. See Linda K. Kerber's discussion of "Republican Motherhood" in *Women of the Republic: Intellect and Ideology in Revolutionary America* (Norton: New York, 1986; Chapel Hill: University of North Carolina Press, 1980).
38. "Visitors from Germany Enjoy Home Economics Potluck," *Bloomington Daily Herald*, [ca. March 1949], p. 4.
39. "Earnest German Women Learn Valued Lessons in America," *Christian Science Monitor*, 24 March 1949, p. 6.
40. "Japanese Visitors," *San Francisco Chronicle*, 16 February 1950.
41. See for example, "German Women See U.S. Democracy Work," *Christian Science Monitor*, 21 February 1947, p. 6; "Mrs. Haag Describes Impressions Received on Sponsored Study Tour in United States," *Christian Science Monitor*, 28 March 1949, p. 6; US Women's Panel No. 13, ca. May/June 1951, German, Box III: 284, LWV Records.
42. Susi Windisch to Betsy Knapp, 19 December 1951 [excerpts], German, Box III: 284, LWV Records.
43. Betsy Knapp to Mary Cannon, ca. Dec. 1951, German, Box III: 284, LVW Records.
44. Taki Fujita to Mrs. Charles Hemming, 5 August 1949, CCCMF 1948–1954, Box 111: 636, LWV Records.
45. Michiko Watanabe, "My Impression on the Convention of the League of Women Voters," u.d., ca. 1952, CCCMF 1948–1954, Box IIII: 636, LWV Records.
46. Speech by Lucille Heming, 30 November 1954, CCCMF 1948–1954, Box III: 636, LWV Records.
47. "Report on German Project," 1949, CCCMF, 1948–1954, Box III: 36, LWV Records.
48. Laville, *Cold War Women*, 80.
49. Robert G. Moeller, *Protecting Motherhood: Women and the Family in the Politics of Postwar West Germany* (Berkeley and Los Angeles: University of California Press, 1993), 1–3.
50. Article 14 of the Japanese Constitution (1947) states that "all people are equal under the law" and forbids discrimination on a number of grounds, including sex. Article three of the of (West) German Basic Law (1949) states that "men and women have equal rights."
51. Miller, "Carrie Chapman Catt: The Power of an Idea," p. 20.

CHAPTER 5

The National Council of Negro Women, Human Rights, and the Cold War

JULIE A. GALLAGHER

In May 1945 Mary McLeod Bethune, founder and president of the National Council of Negro Women (NCNW), wrote to Council members from San Francisco where she was attending the landmark conference called to establish the United Nations. When, in the course of her lengthy and informative letter Bethune remarked that, "I have been wonderfully received as the only Negro woman consultant to the International Conference," she spoke volumes about the way the international community and the United States valued women of color in planning the post-war world.[1] The reality behind the comment, that the world's leaders did not think these women's voices mattered, served as the basis for one of the NCNW's most significant goals in the post-war era. They endeavored through a variety of approaches to ensure that African American women and women of color from around the world, especially those living under the yoke of colonial oppression, had a say in shaping the new world order and had an opportunity to experience the full flowering of human rights that had been promised in the United Nations Charter. The NCNW, founded just ten years earlier to advocate for African American women's economic and social concerns within the United States, was now determined to serve an integral role in building a new global order grounded in the principles of economic and social justice, racial and gender equality, and respect for human rights. Leaders of the organization did this by advocating for black women's inclusion, and where appropriate, leadership in discussions about peace and justice taking place in international women's organizations, in the U.S. State Department, and the United Nations.

The NCNW's internationalist efforts and their contributions to post-war conferences and policy debates in the late 1940s and 1950s have received little coverage in women's history or civil rights history, but they deserve to be included in both. This rich story of African American women's endeavors for human rights is further evidence that the standard framework for analyzing women's history, namely the waves metaphor, is inadequate to accommodate the breadth of women's activism in the Cold War era. Similarly, historians of the political Left, especially of the African American political Left, have effectively charted the trajectory of activists like Shirley Graham DuBois, Claudia Jones, Eslanda Goode Robeson, and organizations like the Council of African Affairs (CAA), the National Negro Congress (NNC), the Civil Rights Congress (CRC), the Sojourners for Truth, and the Congress of American Women (CAW) from radical and creative activism to a virtual silencing.[2] But they have paid little attention to the efforts of NCNW leaders including Mary McLeod Bethune, Eunice Hunton Carter, Victoria Carter Mason, and Dorothy Height. These African American women, outside the familiar circle of black Left feminists, were very much engaged in debates about colonialism and its connections to U.S. racial inequality too and they should be included in the expanding evaluation of the civil rights movement in a global, Cold War context.

The NCNW's story in this period shares some noteworthy similarities with politically Left organizations and individuals, but it was not the same. Labels like "liberal," "progressive," and "radical" do not fit easily around the Council women, at least in the early Cold War years. A number of NCNW leaders held strong anti-colonial positions and were ardent Pan-Africanists. They circulated among Communists, Socialists, and Progressive Party activists. Their activism brought them into frequent contact with luminaries of the Popular Front, a broad-based leftist movement in the 1930s and 1940s that was not only opposed to fascism, but which venerated ideals about America's laboring classes, ethnic diversity, and racial equality.[3] At the same time, they formed alliances with mainstream organizations like the NAACP, the Urban League, and the YWCA. This chapter of NCNW's history enriches our understanding of the Cold War, race relations, and gender dynamics, and it also destabilizes, at least somewhat, the frameworks of analysis historians have often employed.

In 1947, less than two short years after the guns of war fell silent, President Harry Truman declared that the United States would defend "freedom-loving peoples of the world" under the auspices of the Truman Doctrine. At the same time, his State Department sought to restore Western Europe's infrastructure and win its loyalties through the Marshall Plan, and, to insure that the nation was internally secure, the president instituted the Federal Employees Loyalty and Security Program. This one-two-three-punch was devastating to politically progressive forces that had flourished in the United States for well over a decade. Truman's policies coupled with the growing influence of isolationists, who were not only hostile to the idea of the United Nations, but powerful enough to gut much of its potential for real change, marked the boundaries within which human rights advocates like the NCNW ultimately had to work.

When Bethune dispatched Edith Sampson on a pro-U.S. international speaking tour in 1949, the NCNW took an unmistakable step to the right. By the mid-1950s, the organization had parted ways with political leftists and took up the charge to defend the nation against hostilities emanating from the black Left and from anti-American forces including, but not only, the Soviets. Yet, even though the Cold War context limited the kinds of activism they engaged in and the cross-cultural conversations they could have about strategies for resistance to oppression, African American women nonetheless persisted in advocating for women's access to leadership positions and they pursued ways to use international relationships, especially those fostered through women's organizations, and the United Nations to advance ideals of freedom and equality all the way through the 1950s. The NCNW's various alliances, their aspirations, and the compromises they ultimately had to make to survive, tell us about the kinds of changes that were and were not possible in the post-war era; and how race, gender and the structure of such international bodies as the United Nations shaped outcomes.

African American Women's Participation in Post-War Planning

Between 1942 and 1947, women in the NCNW, an umbrella organization that represented over 800,000 African American women, joined with various other visionary women in New York, Washington, D.C., San Francisco, and Paris to stake a claim in post-war planning. Whereas a number of prominent U.S. women's organizations including the American Association of University Women (AAUW), the National Federation of Business and Professional Women's Clubs (BPW), the General Federation of Women's Clubs (GFWC), and the National Woman's Party (NWP) were largely segregated into the 1950s, many new women's groups that were forged in the midst and immediate aftermath of the war worked to embody egalitarian ideals by ensuring that African American and white women worked in greater partnership than ever before.[4] As a result, the NCNW was an early and active member of the Committee on Women in World

Affairs (CWWA), and members attended conferences like "How Women May Share in Post-War Policy-Making," in Washington, D.C., in 1944, the International Congress of Women in Paris in 1945, and the International Assembly of Women in New York in 1946, and in Paris in 1947.[5]

In late 1942, Mary Woolley and Emily Hickman, white, long-standing peace activists and leaders in women's higher education, formed the Committee on Women in Post War Planning (renamed the Committee on Women in World Affairs (CWWA) after the war) to make certain that qualified American women secured positions in the State Department, in inter-governmental bodies like the United Nations, and on U.S. delegations to international conferences.[6] Determined to have African American women included at all levels, Bethune maintained frequent contact with Hickman and committed the NCNW to the CWWA's undertaking. By design, her position as the organization's president carried with it great influence and allowed her to set the path of the organization. Bethune also, as part of the same effort, attended a conference called by First Lady Eleanor Roosevelt in June 1944 on "How Women May Share in Post-War Policy-Making." Chief among their priorities, the participants compiled a roster of qualified women who could be appointed to international conferences delegations, the State Department, and to policy positions, which the CWWA then persistently circulated to government officials.[7]

The NCNW used its attendance at the meeting and in the CWWA to lobby the State Department and President Truman for appointments to conference delegations on peace and security, labor rights, and world health issues. For example, Bethune proposed NCNW member Merze Tate, a government professor from Morgan State who had studied international relations in Geneva, Switzerland, and international law at Oxford University, to serve as a U.S. representative to the Inter-American Conference on Peace and Security in Rio de Janeiro. She also suggested to Hickman, chairman of the CWWA, that NCNW member Maida Springer, a trade union activist, would make an excellent appointee to meetings of organizations like the International Labour Organization (ILO) because she was the "first Negro woman to be designated by the trade union movement to be a representative on an international mission."[8]

Hickman cautioned Bethune that getting women appointed to the UN councils and commissions was an uphill battle, particularly when the United States was only given one or two slots on each. Despite their timely and vigorous efforts, women were all but excluded from some of the most significant planning sessions, including the Bretton Woods Conference in July 1944, which created the global economic order and the Dumbarton Oaks meetings held in Washington, D.C., in the late summer of 1944, which laid the ground work for the United Nations.[9] Gendered assumptions about who got to negotiate foreign policy refused to give easily but the CWWA persisted as did Bethune, who routinely submitted names of qualified NCNW members for all potential opportunities. While white women contended with gender discrimination, however, African American women were confronted with a further set of challenges. Historically, black women were socially positioned by the intersections of racial, gender and often times class oppression; yet this marginalization sparked continuous and at times notably successful resistance. This was the case for the NCNW leadership in the spring of 1945.

When the State Department compiled the list of forty-two organizations, including five women's organizations, that would serve as observer/consultants during the largest post-war planning meeting of all, the San Francisco conference called to establish the United Nations Organization, no African American women or black women's organizations were included on the list of invitees.[10] The NCNW leaders wrote to Secretary of State Edward Stettinius, urging him to appoint a black woman to one of the observer delegations. Claiming a place at the conference on the grounds that as women of color they had a distinct and valuable perspective to offer, the NCNW argued that, "It is imperative that along with other women's organizations Negro women be given the opportunity to get first hand information. None of the women's organizations named represent Negro women."[11] Stettinius declined the NCNW's request but then approved Bethune's appointment to the NAACP delegation. Although they were not official participants, the NCNW sent Dorothy Ferebee and Edith Sampson to San Francisco with Bethune.[12]

While the NCNW was often welcome among new post-war women's organizations, there is no evidence that leaders of the predominantly white women's organizations fought for black women's inclusion at the San Francisco conference. Not only that, the NCNW was excluded from strategy sessions conducted by the AAUW and the BPW. Bethune, a civil rights activist who had fought against racialized gender discrimination throughout her life, was undeterred, and when she learned about the meetings she urged NCNW members to find out how they could participate.[13] Hers and the other NCNW women's fortitude would be tested repeatedly by some of these white female leaders. As a case in point, they had to wage a similar struggle in 1946 when the UN Economic and Social Council established the Commission on the Status of Women (CSW).

Under the direction of Frieda Miller, the Women's Bureau held a series of consultative conferences with national women's organizations in 1946 to generate recommendations for the structure of the Commission on the Status of Women. Bethune attended these meetings.[14] At the initial gathering, she reminded the group of mostly white women that black women had been left out of the planning for San Francisco until she went to the State Department to insure their participation. She warned that this kind of exclusion could not be allowed to persist. "Six and one half million Negro women in America," she argued, "must be represented at all meetings."[15] In discussions about who would represent the United States on the CSW, however, Bethune was all but alone in pushing for racial diversity. She argued that the membership of the CSW should have "brains but also soul," and that "technical ability must be balanced by social consciousness."[16] She effectively held a mirror up to the planning committee and exposed as a lie the notion of universal womanhood. Just as they had found it necessary to do during the turn-of-the-century U.S. women's suffrage struggle, and at the preparatory meetings for the founding of the UN, black women had to remind white women that they too were included in the category of "woman" and they had vital insights to contribute to these planning discussions.

It was not just with the State Department or among mainstream white women's organizations that the NCNW had to fight for recognition. They also struggled to gain non-governmental organization (NGO) consultative status at the United Nations. In filing their paperwork, they again based their appeal on their social position as women of color. They contended that:

> The darker women, not only in the U.S. but all over the world have added handicaps which are not the concern of other women... Since our organization is the only one in the world of its kind and character—devoted not only to the study of the problems of women in general, but of the darker minorities, we feel we have a definitive stake in and a definite contribution to make to the deliberations of the Social and Economic Council and its various organizations.[17]

The observer status was ultimately granted and the NCNW created a permanent position so that the women in their organization could be kept abreast of the situations under negotiation at the UN and coordinate lobbying efforts as they saw necessary.

As the war drew to a close, there were signs of change among some white female leaders regarding racial discrimination.[18] Woolley and Hickman of the CWWA had been eager for the NCNW's participation. That was also the case with some key international women's conferences, where the NCNW was not only welcomed in their own right, but they were also understood to have privileged access to and valuable connections with women in Africa and the Caribbean. In the fall of 1945, for example, Bethune received a letter from French Resistance leader Nicole DeBarry of the Comité D'Initiative International, inviting the NCNW to attend the International Congress of Women in Paris. Upon receiving word that Vivian Carter Mason and Charlotte Hawkins Brown would attend the Congress on the organization's behalf, DeBarry telegrammed Bethune expressing evident appreciation for the NCNW's participation.[19] African American labor leader, Thelma Dale and left-wing white political activists, Gene Weltfish and Muriel Draper were also among the thirteen U.S. delegates to the Congress.[20] The conference brought together eight hundred women from forty-one countries. At the conclusion of the six-day meeting, the Congress formed the Women's International Democratic Federation (WIDF) which in its political orientation was vigorously anti-fascist and pro-Soviet communist. Upon their return to the states, a number of participants including Mason joined with other politically progressive women to form the WIDF's American affiliate, the Congress of American Women (CAW).

In this moment of geo-political realignments, the NCNW also formed alliances with other leftist women and organizations in the United States and overseas. For example, in addition to Mason serving as an officer in CAW, Bethune supported the National Council of American-Soviet Friendship's outreach efforts to the Soviet Women's Anti-Fascist Committee, and the NCNW lobbied President Truman to intercede on behalf of "three outstanding anti-fascist Spanish women" who were scheduled for execution in Madrid.[21] The NCNW would not be inclined or able to forge such connections for much longer, however, because the liberal-left coalitions of the Popular Front period were soon to become not just suspect, but illegal in the United States.

Before the Cold War's oppressive effects settled in on the NCNW, they pursued more opportunities to work with women around the world. As a case in point, in January 1946 Bethune wrote to Alice McLean, chairman of the International Assembly of Women, an American-based effort sponsored by Eleanor Roosevelt to bring women from around the world together to address economic, social, and political issues. McLean was keen to have the NCNW participate in the planning of the October 1946 Assembly and Bethune likewise thought it was essential for the NCNW to be there so she dispatched Mason to represent the Council in this more mainstream endeavor even as she was helping plan for CAW's inaugural event.

For her part, Mason had taken some important lessons from the Paris Congress and wanted to make sure that future international meetings addressed them. Of particular concern to her was the absence of women from the Caribbean, Central America, and Africa in Paris. Seeking names of potential representatives, Mason reached out to labor activist Dorothy Bellanca asking specifically for "women who have been active in progressive movements" in these regions. She also hoped to build new networks so that women "might know each other better by exchanging publications, newsletters and bulletins and exchanging visits."[22] Eager to solicit more names for the International Assembly and at the same time build deeper connections between the NCNW and women from Africa, Mason also wrote to Ollie Okala, a Harlem-based nurse who had married James Okala of Nigeria. Explaining her goal, she noted that "We regretted so much, for instance that at the recent Congress of Women, there were only three Negro women, and they were all from the United States. We are very anxious to have women from Africa, including Nigeria, and other countries." Okala obliged by sending her contacts in South Africa and Nigeria.[23] At the same time, Josephine Schain, a white woman and chair of the attendance committee, turned to the NCNW for contacts in "Ethiopia, Liberia, Haiti and from the colonial and mandated sections of Africa who they could invite to the International Assembly."[24] In these gatherings organized primarily by white women in the United States and Europe, black women in the NCNW were seen not just as African American women but also a voice for or connection to women of color internationally. At certain times, the NCNW not only encouraged that perspective, but also spoke from it, and yet, as Mason's letters suggest, they also understood the limits to that and wanted African women to be able to speak for themselves.

Mason and Bethune participated in the International Assembly conference, which was held in upstate New York in October 1946. At the opening banquet Bethune sat on the dais along with Eleanor Roosevelt, the guest of honor.[25] The Assembly did not have the connection to European communists that the Paris Congress did, yet participants nevertheless articulated support for progressive economic policies including full employment, strong government spending, a greater distribution of the goods, universal health care, and a vital place of labor unions, including of organized domestic workers, in the global economy.[26] Assembly attendees also advocated the idea of "world citizenship" and called for "racial tolerance and respect for human dignity." Finally, in their panels on politics, assembly attendees demanded that all citizens everywhere be granted an unrestricted right to vote without "literacy tests or a poll tax."[27] Not only did these international conferences and assemblies appreciate the importance of bringing women of color and white women together, they took a strong stand on issues that were critical to African Americans, as was evident in the above references, and to other people living in oppressive circumstances around the world.

Fighting for Human Rights—the NCNW and the United Nations

The NCNW maintained its commitment to U.S. struggles for racial and gender equality in the post-war period, but now they did so using the new institutions at their disposal, especially the UN. Bethune laid out the post-war challenges and opportunities in the letter she had penned to NCNW members during the San Francisco conference. Before the United States could legitimately engage in discussions of democratic ideals and human rights, she argued, it had to solve its own serious problems with racial discrimination. At the same time, she highlighted the exciting discussions that she, Walter White, and W.E.B. DuBois (the NAACP observers) were having with representatives from Africa. Positioning herself as a Pan-Africanist and assuming support of that perspective from her NCNW readers, Bethune wrote:

> There has been a conspicuous getting together by the people of darker races. A fellowship and brotherhood among them is being formulated which will mean much in the tomorrow...To the Negro people, the World Security Conference in San Francisco has but one meaning, that is how far democratic practices shall be stretched to embrace the rights of their brothers in the colonies as well as the American Negro's own security at home.[28]

Bethune believed that there was genuine potential in the UN's founding for "democratic practices" to be stretched to include the millions of black people living under colonialism as well as in Jim Crow America. Still, she knew it was only a possibility and that real change in economic and political institutions would require intense pressure that could now be brought through the UN. To that end, she urged Council women to get a hold of the UN documents and study them. They needed to be prepared for action.

NCNW leaders expressed hope that the United Nations could facilitate expansion of human rights, but they were not naïve. Executive Director, Eunice Hunton Carter, sister of Alphaeus Hunton, an avowed Communist and the education director of the CAA, wrote a detailed analysis of the UN's potential and its limitations, for the NCNW. At the conclusion of her studied assessment, she included recommendations for the NCNW to follow. Under the heading "Matters of Special Interest to Women And Minority Groups," she enumerated the articles of the UN Charter which supported "respect for human rights for all without distinction as to race, religion, language or sex." She also highlighted the UN's economic promises including its promotion of "higher standards of living, full employment, and conditions of economic and social progress and development."

And at a time when the vast majority of African Americans in the U.S. South were barred from voting and hundreds of millions of people lived under oppressive colonial rule, Carter explained that the Charter embraced the "right of self-determination." These important aspirations, Carter cautioned, were not matched by the Charter's mechanisms for implementation or enforcement. To buttress this point, Carter cited a CAA bulletin that focused on the failure of the UN to "establish the means for the UNO to insure the effective and rapid economic, social, and political advancement of colonial peoples throughout the world." As both her brother and Bethune were members of the left-leaning CAA, Carter had ready access to this salient critique. That she was willing to include it in an update to the NCNW membership spoke to complexity of the NCNW's politics and of the era more generally. Carter encouraged the NCNW to embrace and act on an assessment of the UN that far more radical organizations like the CAA, the NNC, and the CRC held. The goals set out in the UN Charter, she asserted, will only be met when people pressure their governments to take action. Carter recommended therefore that the NCNW members educate themselves to elect government representatives who were not only supportive of the Charter's ideals but also willing to support legislation to implement them. She also urged Council members to "establish contact with women of other minority groups and of dependent countries and unite with them in working for the ultimate goal of full citizenship for men and women everywhere."[29] Over the next few years, the NCNW strived to implement Carter's advice.

This organization of decidedly respectable, middle-class women fought for racial equality and full citizenship rights in the United States; at the same time they tied colonialism in Africa with racism in the United States and argued that "people of the darker races" had much in common and should make common cause. While the NCNW was considered a liberal organization committed to racial integration and to working through peaceful means to influence government policies, it was also capable of holding a more complex—at times even radical perspective—that critiqued the economic and political structures in the United States and in Africa.

The bold anti-colonial positions that NCNW leaders like Bethune, Carter, and Mason took brought them unwelcome attention from right-wing anti-communists, which not only impacted them personally, but also hurt the Council to the point where women in the South were afraid to join the organization.[30] Like more explicitly left-leaning activists and organizations, the NCNW felt the heavy hand of McCarthyism settle upon their shoulders. One way the organization fought back, or rather fought for its survival was by tacking right, just as many labor unions, other civil rights, and women's organizations did. A dramatic and telling example of the

NCNW's effort to take the political heat off played out on the global stage between the Council's executive director, Edith Sampson, and the world renowned performer, Josephine Baker.

When President Truman chose Sampson, a Chicago lawyer and NCNW board member, to serve as an alternate on the United States delegation to the UN General Assembly in 1950, the appointment was met with both excitement and concern. Whereas many Harlem luminaries including Congressman Adam Clayton Powell, Jr. and *Amsterdam News* columnist Gerri Major feted the new UN appointee at a huge party, others suggested that Sampson's selection "was made in an attempt to discredit Soviet propaganda regarding the treatment of Negroes in the United States."[31] In the Cold War era, U.S. foreign policy advisors worried justifiably about how manifestations of racist hatred in the United States played out in international newspapers. With stories of black men in military uniform, pregnant women, and fourteen-year-old children being brutally lynched in the South, there was plenty for anti-U.S. forces to use against it in the battle for hearts and minds.[32] Acting Secretary of State Dean Acheson stated the crisis succinctly in his warning to President Truman. "The existence of discrimination against minority groups in this country has an adverse effect upon our relations with other countries."[33] The administration tried to minimize the fallout from racist violence any way it could. One of its most successful strategies was sending ardently patriotic African Americans on international speaking tours to tout American democracy.[34] As it turns out, Edith Sampson was one of the most effective weapons of defense the United States wielded in this chapter of the propaganda war.

The year prior to her UN appointment, Sampson had participated in the "Round-the-World Town Meeting," a pro-American speaking tour that visited over twenty countries. Organized by radio host George Denny and encouraged by the State Department, it was designed to counter verbal attacks against the nation made by left-leaning African Americans like Paul Robeson, W.E.B. Du Bois, and Josephine Baker. These outspoken activists charged that discrimination in the United States was on par with colonial oppression overseas (a position that the NCNW had recently, frequently, and publicly espoused.) Although Sampson enthusiastically defended the United States, her reasons for participating in the tour were as much about the NCNW trying to defend itself against red-baiting, as they were about her own anti-communist beliefs. NCNW president Dorothy Height recalled in an interview years later that Sampson had gone on the world tour because Mary McLeod Bethune assigned her to it.[35] Bethune, who was under intense scrutiny by the FBI and congressional cold warriors, was likely happy to have Sampson dampen suspicion of the Council and by extension of her.

Sampson used the podium to speak positively about U.S. democracy, but she also challenged the government and her audiences to do more to advance civil rights at home. At a presentation in 1950, she claimed that the United States' failure to "grant full equality and full freedom to some of our citizens undermines our integrity in the United Nations and abroad." In one sentence she simultaneously encouraged a change in U.S. domestic policy on race relations and gave a Cold War justification for doing so. She suggested that the nation conduct a self-evaluation on the annual anniversary of the signing of the Declaration of Human Rights to "take inventory on the question of 'Rights' here in our own backyards."[36] Her critics as well as her enthusiasts could find something in Sampson's speeches to justify their appraisals.

Tension between Cold War liberals and U.S. critics boiled over in early 1952. American-born Josephine Baker held a French passport and had settled in Paris after World War II, claiming she felt much more at home there than in the United States. She opposed U.S. foreign policy and she deplored racism in America. During her tours in Europe and later in South America, she said as much.[37] Sampson refused to let Baker's accusations go unchallenged. She lashed out, insisting that, "[Baker] should stop and consider what France is doing to some 45,000,000 Negroes in its colonies. French colonialism is a blot on the world conscience...These people suffer much more than Miss Baker in Atlanta or New York." Sampson wanted to make sure Baker, and any Baker sympathizers got her point, so she went on, "When France tries to do one-tenth as much for its colonials, I will be willing to listen to Josephine Baker's complaints."[38] Sampson played a role in the Cold War drama in which the State Department could only rejoice.

Not only did she denounce Baker, but that same year, Sampson toured Scandinavia to challenge allegations made against the United States in the *We Charge Genocide* petition. Submitted to the UN by leftist activist/performer, Paul Robeson and Communist secretary of CRC, William Patterson, the petition accused the U.S. government of intentionally trying to destroy African Americans.[39] While Sampson "privately agreed with the petition," she was one of a number of African American liberals who spoke against it publically. Her exuberant speeches effectively denied the social, political, and economic realities that many African Americans lived under, and as historian Carol Anderson has argued, they "betray[ed] the cause of black equality."[40]

Even as Sampson toured the world defending the United States, the NCNW continued to embrace the UN as a vitally important place to learn about global struggles for justice including the fight against colonialism and for women's rights. They actively participated in its programs despite growing hostility towards the UN among conservative Americans.[41] In

1952, the American Association for the United Nations (AAUN), of which Eleanor Roosevelt was a founding and active member, asked Dorothy Ferebee, who had assumed the presidency of the NCNW when Bethune retired in 1949, to speak about the vital role women could play in developing support for the UN. With domestic hostility towards the UN escalating dramatically under the orchestration of conservative isolationists like Senator John Bricker of Ohio, the AAUN struggled to fight back by focusing its conference on "Our Faith in the United Nations."[42] What was clear by this point was that in the United States the UN needed defending. Many Americans feared it was a tool of the Soviet Union. The NCNW in contrast remained very committed to the institution and played a leading role in its defense.

But then in the spring of 1953, the United Nations as a functioning entity in the battle for human rights was dealt a staggering blow. As he settled into his new role as president of the United States, Dwight Eisenhower and his foreign policy team came under further assault by Bricker and his isolationist contingent. Insisting that the UN undermined U.S. sovereignty and that it was a Soviet front, Bricker tried in effect to denude the president of the capacity to engage in meaningful foreign policy. To preserve that ability, the Eisenhower administration abandoned commitments to all UN Conventions, including most remarkably, the Genocide Convention.[43]

Even still, the NCNW stayed committed to the UN throughout the 1950s and maintained its focus on anti-colonial struggles in Africa. Marian Croson, the Council's official UN observer, wrote updates in her column in *Telefact*, the NCNW's monthly newsletter. She kept the organization's membership abreast of African people's struggles for independence and at the same time highlighted similarities between the abuses of colonial power in Africa and racism in the United States. "As I listen in these subtle stormy sessions," she wrote, "I recognize the same old refrain echoed in defense of segregation here at home. 'Not ready yet, it will take many, many years.'"[44] Urging the NCNW's 800,000 members to take action, Croson spoke from an anti-colonial, Pan-Africanist perspective, not an easy feat by in the mid-1950s. Women from the black feminist Left including the Sojourners for Truth and Justice had long ago been forced into silence or in the case of Claudia Jones, deported.[45] Because the NCNW was considered a liberal organization (and understood itself as such) with a strong commitment to the promise of American democracy and racial integration, and because women like Edith Sampson had done so much for the Cold War effort, they could publically articulate such a position without raising politically deadly suspicions.

While anti-colonial movements were escalating, women around the world seized the opportunities created by the UN to advocate for their political, economic, and cultural rights. Just as she did with anti-colonial updates, Croson wrote about the efforts being made to secure women's human rights and legal standing. Of particular importance, she emphasized that the UN Charter and the Universal Declaration of Human Rights codified that "Women have equal rights to those of men without discrimination—*Equal pay for equal work—Equal rights in education—Equal political rights and Equal rights in marriage and divorce.*"[46] Black women had to look no further than the their immediate surroundings to know that the United States was not living up to its commitments when it came to women's human rights, especially the rights of poor women and women of color. Stressing that the United Nations was a powerful platform from which women could now make their voices heard, Croson suggested to her readers that these promises of gender equality would come only when women themselves made sure they were secured.[47] In the mid-1950s, however, most American women were not ready to take on this fight.

The steady reports about anti-colonial movements and updates about women's rights were perhaps some of the boldest aspects of the NCNW's international agenda by the mid-1950s. In 1957 Dorothy Height assumed the presidency of the NCNW. Under Height's leadership the organization continued to engage in various UN-related activities, but there was a marked shift in their substance and tone, similar to that of labor organizations that had purged leftist leaders and the NAACP, which distanced itself from vocal political critics like W.E.B. Du Bois, Paul Robeson, and Claudia Jones. An exchange between Stanley Rumbough, chairman of the U.S. Committee for the United Nations, and Height in June 1958 demonstrates that despite its continued interest in and support of the UN, the Cold War climate had very much settled upon the NCNW and affected the way it engaged the international body. Rather than hosting conferences encouraging "one world" themes, focusing on economic issues, and human rights as the AAUN did in the early 1950s, the U.S. Committee for the United Nations advised members like the NCNW on how to "make UN Day ... an exciting, pleasant and educational experience for all members of the family." In his letter to Height, Rumbough suggested that they sponsor an international family dinner where the children could make table decorations and flags of various countries, and they could don "headdresses or costumes." Adults (read *mothers*) should, of course, prepare new foods for the celebration. "[I]n this setting, where pleasure is derived from the knowledge of another way of life, parents could explain to the children the purpose of the United Nations," Rumbough closed. In a letter that underscored the NCNW's complicity with this slide into Cold War conformity, Height responded that the Council "deeply appreciates your stimulating proposal for a Round-the-World Dinner in honor of the 13th birthday of the United Nations. We think it is an excellent idea and will cooperate with you."[48] As a sign of the dramatic change, just six years earlier the NCNW participated in activities that demonstrated its belief or at least hope in the United Nations as a vehicle for serious, structural change in the world. Now it seemed that it had given up that expectation, or at least buried it beneath the trappings of superficial educational events.

Conclusion

In the wake of World War II, Mary McLeod Bethune and members of the NCNW Executive Committee, especially Vivian Carter Mason, Eunice Hunton Carter, Dorothy Ferebee, and Edith Sampson, understood that there could be no lasting peace in the world until there was real and meaningful justice. And that justice could not be attained, they suggested through their various international endeavors, until the people of the world who had lived under the forces of oppression, especially the women, had a say in making the world whole. Under Bethune's expert direction, the NCNW effectively fought for black women's participation in global discussions about peace and justice and for leadership roles in new organizations like the United Nations. At times, these women made appeals to the U.S. State Department, to the UN divisions, and to other women's organizations based on their concerns as women of color. At other times they astutely employed the language of universal rights.

While theirs were uphill battles, the NCNW secured an integral role in the Committee on Women in World Affairs, and despite its complex motivations, a position on the U.S. delegation to the UN. They also helped advance race relations within U.S. women's organizations by reminding white women that they had to consider the concerns of women of color and include them in policy and advocacy discussions. Finally, they made important contributions to building relationships with women in Africa, Asia, South America, and Europe. Together these efforts suggest why the NCNW's history deserves to be more fully integrated into post-World War II women's histories and simultaneously why it helps to undermine the dominant framework within which those histories are analyzed, particularly the waves narrative.

Finally, the NCNW's activities in this post-war period clarify the scale of the lost opportunity that transpired when the United States not only abandoned but also significantly weakened the United Nations as a vehicle for bringing about the full flowering of human rights. The women of the NCNW held out great hope and aggressively worked for the emergence of a new world order premised on full equality and true justice in the wake of World War II's horrors. That they were forced to narrow their expectations and curtail their activism in order to survive, as many other organizations like the powerful labor union, the Congress of Industrial Organizations (CIO) and the NAACP had to, is one more example of the price of domestic political repression in the 1950s. At the same time, that they were to able to publish articles in their newsletter all the way through the 1950s about anti-colonial efforts in Asia and Africa, and about the guarantees of women's rights, as posited in the UN Charter and the Universal Declaration of Human Rights, suggests that the NCNW leadership had cautiously but effectively crafted a strategic position for the organization. This position enabled them to remain engaged in conversations about human rights and though to a lesser extent, about U.S. foreign policy, as the African liberation struggles began to yield fruit with the independence of Ghana in 1957. It also created a space for them to serve as leaders and to gain a singularly important voice for black women when the U.S. civil rights struggle reached a mass movement level in the mid-1950s and when the U.S. government directed its focus to the status of women in American society in 1961 with the formation of President John F. Kennedy's Commission on the Status of Women.

Notes

1. Mary McLeod Bethune to NCNW, 10 May 1945, Series 5, Folder 6, Box 34, National Council of Negro Women Papers, National Park Service–Mary McLeod Bethune Council House NHS, Washington, D.C. Hereafter cited as NCNW Papers.
2. Penny Von Eschen, *Race Against Empire: Black Americans and Anticolonialism, 1937–1957* (Ithaca, NY: Cornell University Press, 1997), Brenda Gayle Plummer, *Rising Wind: Black Americans and U.S. Foreign Affairs, 1935–1960* (Chapel Hill: University of North Carolina Press, 1996), Gerald Horne, *Race Woman: The Lives of Shirley Graham Du Bois* (New York: New York University Press, 2000), Carol Anderson, *Eyes Off the Prize: The United Nations and the African American Struggle for Human Rights, 1944–1955* (New York: Cambridge University Press, 2003), Erik McDuffie, "A 'New Freedom Movement of Negro Women': Sojourning for Truth, Justice, and Human Rights During the Early Cold War," in *Radical History Review*, no. 101 (Spring 2008), 81–106; Jacqueline Castledine, " 'In a Solid Bond of Unity': Anticolonial Feminism in the Cold War Era," in *Journal of Women's History*, 20, no. 4 (Winter 2008), 57–81.
3. For a discussion of Communist-led protests in the 1930s, see Mark Naison, *Communists in Harlem* (New York: Grove Press, 1985). For an excellent treatment of the 1930s and 1940s Popular Front, which focused especially on cultural production, see Michael Denning, *The Cultural Front: The Laboring of American Culture in the Twentieth Century* (New York: Verso, 1996). For a discussion of broader-based battles for racial equality during the 1930s see Cheryl Lynn Greenberg, *Or Does It Explode?: Black Harlem in the Great Depression* (New York: Oxford University Press, 1997), Gail Lumet Buckley, *The Hornes: An American Family* (New York: Alfred Knopf, 1986). On Height's participation in Popular Front activities see Barbara Ransby, *Ella Baker & the Freedom Movement: A Radical Democratic Vision* (Chapel Hill: University of North Carolina Press, 2005), Dorothy Height, interviewed by Polly Cowan, in Ruth Edmonds Hill, ed., *The Black Women Oral History Project: From the Arthur and Elizabeth Schlesinger Library on the History of Women in America, Radcliffe*

College, vol. 5, (Westport, CT: Meckler, 1991), Dorothy Height, *Open Wide the Freedom Gates* (New York: Perseus Books Group, 2003).

4. Leila Rupp and Verta Taylor, *Survival in the Doldrums: The American Women's Rights Movement, 1945 to the 1960s* (New York: Oxford University Press, 1987), 155–58; Helen Laville, *Cold War Women: The International Activities of American Women's Organizations* (New York: Manchester University Press, 2002), 24–25.

5. Emily Hickman, Chairman of Committee on Women in World Affairs to Members and Guests, 18 January 1946. Series 5, Folder 1, Box 8, NCNW Papers. The CWWA was originally called the Committee on the Participation of Women in Post War Planning (CPWPWP). Member organizations included: the National Woman's Party, Women's International League for Peace and Freedom, the NCNW as well as women's business, religious, labor and civic organizations.

6. Emily Hickman to Members and Guests, 18 January 1946. Series 5, NCNW Papers, Folder 1, Box 8.

7. Judy Barett Litoff and David C. Smith, eds. *What Kind of World Do We Want? American Women Plan for Peace* (Wilmington, DE: Scholarly Resources 2000), 141–50, 165–74.

8. Bethune to Spruille Braden at State Department, 19 February 1946; Bethune to President Truman, 19 February 1946; Bethune to Burton, 26 February 1946; Bethune to Hickman, 13 March 1946. Series 5, Folder 1, Box 8, NCNW Papers.

9. There were no women appointed to the Dumbarton Oakes meetings, Litoff, 17. Mabel Newcomer, head of the Economics Department at Vassar College, was the only woman appointed to the U.S. delegation at the Bretton Woods Conference. See *New York Times*, 4 July 1944, 20.

10. The five women's groups invited to send representatives to San Francisco were: the American Association of University Women, the General Federation of Women's Clubs, the League of Women Voters, the Business and Professional Women's Clubs, and the Women's Action Committee for Victory and Lasting Peace. See Litoff and Smith, *What Kind of World Do We Want?*, 21.

11. Executive Secretary Jeanetta Welch Brown to Secretary of State Edward Stettinius, 11 April 1945, Series 5, Folder 6, Box 34, NCNW Papers.

12. Bettye Collier Thomas, *N.C.N.W. 1935–1980* (Washington, D.C.: NCNW), 6.

13. Bethune to Sue Bailey Thurman, 11 April 1945, Series 5, Folder 6, Box 34; Jeanetta Welch Brown to Edward Stettinius, Jr., 11 April 1945, Series 5, Folder 6, Box 34, Folder 6, NCNW Papers.

14. Frieda Miller, Director of Women's Bureau, to Mary McLeod Bethune, 26 March 1946, Series 5, Folder 9, Box 34, NCNW Papers.

15. Notes written by Constance Williams for Bethune from Meeting called by Frieda Miller's office, 29 March 1946, Series 5, Folder 9, Box 34, NCNW Papers.

16. Ibid.

17. Bethune to Lyman White, Liaison Economic and Social Council, 21 March 1947, Series 5, Folder 6, Box 34, NCNW Papers.

18. For a discussion of the significant transformation that the YWCA and the AFSC underwent in their commitments to racial integration and to racial equality in the 1940s see Susan Lynn, *Progressive Women in Conservative Times: Racial Justice, Peace, and Feminism, 1945 to the 1960s* (New Brunswick, NJ: Rutgers University Press, 1992).

19. Nicole de Barry to NCNW, 11 October 1945; Telegram from DeBarry to NCNW, n.d. Series 5, Folder 10, Box 8, NCNW Papers.

20. CAW Letterhead, Series 5, Folder 11, Box 8, NCNW Papers. See also Amy Swerdlow, "The Congress of American Women: Left-Feminist Peace Politics in the Cold War," in *U.S. History as Women's History: New Feminist Essays*, eds. Linda Kerber, Alice Kessler-Harris, and Kathryn Kish-Sklar (Chapel Hill: University of North Carolina Press, 1995), 297, 300, 307.

21. Zelda Berlin to Mason, 4 April 1946; Ruth Russ of the National Council of American-Soviet Friendship to Bethune, 1 March 1946; NCNW to President of the United States, 3 March 1946. All in Series 5, Box 8, Folder 11, NCNW Papers.

22. Mason, NCNW Exec. Director to Dorothy Bellanca, 30 January 1946, Series 5, Folder 13, Box 18, NCNW Papers.

23. Mason to Mrs. Ollie Okala, 20 February 1946; Okala to Mason, 26 February 1946, Series 5, Folder 13, Box 18, NCNW Papers.

24. Schain to Bethune, 8 February 1946, Series 5, Folder 13, Box 18, NCNW Papers.

25. Dais listing, see Series 5, Folder 13, Box 18, NCNW Papers.

26. "What Kind of An Economic World Are We Living In? A Summary of Panel Discussions," 13, October 1946, International Assembly 5/18/13, NCNW Papers.

27. Ibid.

28. Bethune to NCNW 10 May 1945, Series 5, Folder 6, Box 34, NCNW Papers.

29. Eunice H. Carter, "Brief Analysis of San Francisco Conference, United Nations Charter and Related Problems for the National Council of Negro Women," n.d. Series 5, Folder 6, Box 34, NCNW Papers.

30. Plummer, *Rising Wind*, 212.

31. "Mrs. Sampson Assigned to Complaint on Reds," *New York Amsterdam News*, 23 September 1950, 2; "Citizens' Planning Council Honors U.N. Delegate at Dinner Party in Waldorf," *New York Amsterdam News*, 21 October 1950, 4.

32. Anderson, *Eyes Off the Prize*, 12–13, 27–28, McDuffie, 89–90.

33. *To Secure These Rights: The Report of the U.S. President's Committee on Civil Rights* (Washington, D.C: United States Government Printing Office, 1947), 146.

34. See for example Mary Dudziak, *Cold War Civil Rights: Race and the Image of American Democracy* (Princeton, NJ: Princeton University Press, 2000), passim; Thomas Borstelmann, *The Cold War and the Color Line: American Race Relations in the Global Arena* (Cambridge, MA: Harvard University Press, 2001), 74–84; Michael Krenn, *Black Diplomacy: African Americans and the State Department, 1945–1969* (Armonk, NY: M.E. Sharpe, 1999), 5.

35. Dorothy Height, interviewed by Polly Cowan, Hill, ed., *The Black Women Oral History Project*, vol. 5, 138.

36. "Sampson Warns U.S. on Jim Crow," *New York Amsterdam News*, 11 November 1950, 18.

37. Mary Dudziak, "Josephine Baker, Racial Protest, and the Cold War," in *The Journal of American History* 81, Issue 2 (Sept. 1994), 543–70.

38. Edith Sampson Blasts Miss Baker During Paris Visit," *New York Amsterdam News*, 5 January 1952, 5.

39. Because his passport was denied, Robeson delivered a copy to the United Nations Secretariat in New York, and Patterson delivered it to the UN meeting in Paris. Civil Rights Congress, *We Charge Genocide: The Historic Petition to the United Nations for Relief of a Crime by the U.S. Government Against the Negro People*, (New York: International Publishers, 1970), 3; Anderson, 180–95.

40. See Plummer, *Rising Wind*, on Sampson's private support of the petition. See Anderson, *Eyes Off the Prize*, for extensive coverage of the speeches given in Scandinavia, 203–07. Scholars disagree in their assessments of Sampson's activities. For a generally sympathetic treatment of Edith Sampson's overseas work, see: and Helen Laville, *Cold War Women*, and Scott Lucas, "The American Way: Edith Sampson, the NAACP, and African American Identity in the Cold War," in *Diplomatic History* 20, no. 4 (Fall 1996), 565–90. For critical assessments of Sampson's international activities, see: Horne's, Von Eschen's, and Plummer's commentaries in the same issue as well as Anderson, 203–07.

41. Caroline Pruden, Conditional Partners: Eisenhower, the United Nations, and the Search for a Permanent Peace (Baton Rouge: Louisiana State University Press, 1998), 37, 199–203.

42. H. Bowen Smith of the American Association for the United Nations, Inc. to Dorothy

Ferebee. Series 7, F 11, Box 15; Clark Eichelberger, Director of the American Association for the United Nations, 17 January 1952. Series 7 F 12, Box 15, NCNW Papers.

43. Pruden, *Conditional Partners*, 198–203; Anderson, *Eyes Off the Prize*, 218–33.

44. *Telefact*, March, 1955, "With the United Nations," by Marian Croson, 5, Wilhelmina Adams Papers, Folder 1, Box 5. Schomburg Center for Research in Black Culture, New York Public Library, New York, New York. Hereafter cited as Adams Papers.

45. McDuffie, "A 'New Freedom Movement of Negro Women,'" 95–97; Castledine, " 'In a Solid Bond of Unity,'" 72–73.

46. *Telefact*, August, 1955, 3, Folder 1, Box 5, Adams Papers. Emphasis in the original.

47. *Telefact*, August, 1955. WA Papers, Folder 1, Box 5, Schomburg.

48. Stanley Rumbough to Dorothy Height, 19 June 1958; Height to Rumbough, 20. June 1958, Folder 12, Box 15, Series 7, NCNW Papers.

CHAPTER 6

From Ladies' Aid to NGO

Transformations in Methodist Women's Organizing in Postwar America

A. LANETHEA MATHEWS-GARDNER

Scholars rarely look to religious women in mapping the terrain of feminism and the development of women's movement organizations, particularly over the second half of the twentieth century. This omission is both a cause and consequence of the abiding pull of the wave metaphor to describe and explain the development and emergence of modern feminism. Thinking about women's activism as a series of successive waves detracts from the notion that there are historical antecedents in the forms, identities, and strategies of any women's organization, and that women's movements intersect with other movements across space and time in a complex web of gendered politics.[1] The waves metaphor suggests a profound breaking from the past. Scholars are left with little understanding of *why* women's organizations embodied *particular* forms, identities, and strategies at particular moments.

In this chapter I introduce the Woman's Division of Christian Service (WDCS)—predecessor to today's United Methodist Women (UMW)—as a critical organization in the development of both feminism and women's organizations in postwar America. I am less interested in the WDCS's effectiveness per se (although their accomplishments are impressive) than in understanding what its postwar development reveals about the broader conditions that fostered particular kinds of women's organizing in the

1940s, 1950s, and 1960s. Drawing loosely on notions of political opportunity structures,[2] I suggest that the emergence of the United Nations in 1945 fundamentally altered available identities, strategies, and forms of organization from which women's organizations could adopt. Churchwomen in particular were well-poised to embrace new opportunities that accompanied the development of the UN. In turn, they helped to pioneer global strategies that blended the language of human rights with the pursuit of women's interests, and began a process of transformation from a civic organization reminiscent of women's clubs of the Progressive era into a non-governmental organization (NGO) instrumental to the international gender order and emergent modern feminism.

It is particularly surprising that scholars of the women's movement and feminism have not given greater attention to churchwomen and their political significance, especially because gender clearly informs patterns of religious involvement.[3] Arguments that religious institutions are incompatible with feminism rest on a narrow definition of what counts as "feminist" and fail to historicize women's involvement with the church and within religiously affiliated civic groups.[4] Methodist churchwomen, for example, used their religion to make claims on the church and the state, arguing that "it is inherent in God's will that woman's rights—social, political, religious—should be equal with those of man."[5] I consider the WDCS to be a "women's organization" because it mobilized and sought to empower women around self-defined goals. The WDCS was also "feminist" insofar as it explicitly worked toward the elimination of gender, race, and class inequality and on behalf of democratic participation and the global erasure of disenfranchisement. Certainly, missionary work was central to the organizational identity of WDCS members, comprising over 90 percent of the entire WDCS's operating budget through the early 1950s. Similar to other organizations born of the "women's era" of organizing, the WDCS related both spiritual and political causes to a complex maternalist rhetoric—what Susan Dye calls "evangelical domesticity"[6]—claiming the moral best interest of society and legitimizing women's activism through public education and nonpartisan political mobilization.[7] Maternalism rarely produced a pure expression of womanhood but, instead, generated and reflected conflicting messages about women's role in home, society, and politics. In 1949, one WDCS leader characterized the Division as "part of the movement to improve the status of minority social, economic, and racial groups," "rather than a feminist movement."[8] More important than debating the extent to which the WDCS was or is "feminist," is recognizing their part in multiple struggles over the appropriate roles, responsibilities, and opportunities available to women and their organizations in the mid-twentieth century.

Growing rapidly after its formation in 1939,[9] by the mid-1950s, the WDCS was the largest national organization of Protestant women in the United States with more than 1.8 million women—easily surpassing 1 percent of the entire U.S. adult female population.[10] Members of the WDCS were organized into two inter-related groups, the Woman's Society and the Wesleyn Service Guild, the latter of which, designed to meet the specific needs and interests of working women, saw a six-fold membership increase immediately after World War II. Organizational growth, coupled with changes in the realities of women's lives—continued increased labor force participation and higher levels of educational attainment, for example— were important factors that compelled WDCS leaders to experiment with new structures and strategies after World War II. The Methodist Church's growing visibility in emergent civil rights struggles was another.[11] Clubwomen in the WDCS participated in boycotts and sit-ins in the late 1940s, for example, and regional leaders of the Division coordinated state-by-state campaigns to compel states and localities to enforce civil rights laws and, when possible, to pass anti-segregation legislation. Institutional affiliation with other church-based groups, most importantly the Federal (later National) Council of Churches and the United Church Women, encouraged WDCS leaders to adopt modern organizational strategies, such as filing *amicus curiae* briefs, maintaining legislative roll-call voting records, and forming a full-scale legislative lobby in Washington, D.C. Ultimately, the WDCS would eliminate "Ladies' Aid" from its administrative leadership thereby expanding notions of the social gospel to embrace political action as a legitimate activity of churchwomen.[12] These developments both reflected and reinforced the changing institutional context of challenges to prevailing gender (and race and class) relations.

An additional factor that contributed to transformations in the mission and structure of the WDCS was the formation of the United Nations in 1945. The development of the UN was a critical change in the political opportunity structure for all U.S. organizations—it was the first inter-governmental institution in history to formally recognize the participation of citizen groups and NGOs—but it provided unique opportunities to mid-twentieth century women's organizations making little headway with domestic reform efforts, and to religious organizations already linked across the globe in complex webs of international coordinating councils. The particular blend of strategy, identity, and structure that worked so well for Progressive era women's organizations, including the WDCS, had met significant challenges during the New Deal, when key political and bureaucratic allies were no longer receptive to maternalist reform.[13] By the mid-twentieth century, women's associations had lost much of their historical policy authority in social policy domains and could no longer count on long-standing routes to political influence. The UN opened up new possibilities for legitimizing churchwomen's work without having to rely on American national political institutions or political elites.

Likewise, the WDCS was well positioned to benefit from the development of the UN because it was connected to an international, interdenominational network of religious women across the globe through their participation the World Federation of Methodist Women (WFMW) and through ties to the United Council of Church Women (later Church Women United).[14] International networks were further bolstered by the formation of the World Council of Churches (WCC) in 1948, the National Council of Churches (NCC) in 1950 (formerly the Federal Council of Churches, 1908), and the World Methodist Council in 1951.[15] Each of these marked a general movement among Protestant churches to find new ways of cooperating and a greater voice in policymaking that had been underway since the early 1940s. It is no coincidence that international consolidation among Protestant religious groups overlapped with the formation of the UN in 1945.

The WDCS's response to changing opportunities provides greater insight into how the institutional legacies of the postwar era mattered to the particular ways that modern feminism and modern women's organizations emerged in later decades. Besides challenging the notion that the postwar era was a period of quiescence for women's organizing, the WDCS's postwar development marks important precursors to new understandings of feminist activism, feminist structures, and feminist goals that would become commonplace by the 1970s.

The Intersection of the National & the International: The WDCS & the UN

Congruent with the conventionally defined cusp between the second and third wave women's movements, an international feminist movement rose to global prominence following the UN International Women's Decade of 1975–85.[16] Yet, the origins of the globalization of modern feminism remain clouded by assumptions that the UN Decade for Women represented a profound break from the past.[17] At the time of the UN's formation in 1945, there were at least twenty-five international women's associations, not to mention countless national women's groups with global connections.[18] In the first four years of the UN's existence, seventeen women's organizations were granted "Level B" Consultative Status,[19] a designation marking them with a "special competency" in areas related to the UN's purposes and one which gave organizational leaders important rights of participation at UN meetings and access to UN documentation.

The UN was both a "push" and a "pull" factor in the changing terrain of WDCS activism. On the "push" side, the UN provided resources, incentives, and benefits for the Woman's Division that aided them in the recruitment of members; it provided the institutional space for the Division to form stronger international ties on behalf of Methodist womanhood; and it created a position from which the Division could pursue its policy goals and greater opportunities for women without having to depend on American national political institutions or U.S. political elites. On the "pull" side, opportunities created by the formation of the UN fundamentally changed the ways that the WDCS related to government and politics, and redefined their public work. Because the Woman's Division was connected to an international infrastructure of Woman's Societies and missionaries throughout the globe, it was not difficult for leaders to divert their attention and their resources to international issues—a pre-existing international network made it easier to send members to international meetings, for example. In addition, the National Council of Churches and the World Council of Churches were important connections, setting in place the prerequisites for liaison relationships with offices of the UN. Cooperation with the NCC and WCC gave the Woman's Division a stronger and more visible position from which to speak on behalf of women's rights to the international and U.S. communities. Similarly, the WDCS's affiliation with the United Council of Church Women (UCCW), newly formed in 1941, drew Methodist churchwomen into international events such as the International Assembly of Women called by peace organizations in 1946.[20] The UCCW became a department of the male-dominated NCC in 1950, giving women an institutional niche—however small—from which to carve out their own voice in religious and political affairs.

The UN—itself called "the town meeting of the world"[21]—brought Methodist churchwomen in touch with millions of women in Western European nations. Leaders were eager to become "world citizens." "Our domestic problems are international too," they declared.[22] "Present conditions," a leader of the Wesleyan Service Guild argued in 1945, "challenge woman to make the sphere of her endeavor and activity the 'world household'."[23] The programs of the UN and its agencies became a major focal point for the Woman's Division by the late 1940s. Local woman's societies distributed hundreds of thousands of leaflets and later, in conjunction with the Methodist Church, collected more than one million signatures on behalf of the United Nations. John Foster Dulles, who helped to draft the UN Charter, served as a three term U.S. delegate to the UN and later became the U.S. Secretary of State, credited this second accomplishment with pushing political leaders to act on the Charter.[24] Recognizing what they saw as "the urgent need for women to mold an intelligent public opinion favorable to the UN," the Woman's Division began directing the formation of "UN Information Centers" to be established by local groups for the purpose of providing information and tips for action to local citizens. Churchwomen were asked to write to the American Association for the United Nations,[25] to request pamphlets, posters, bumper stickers, and buttons that would publicize the promise of international cooperation; they were asked to encourage local store owners to display UN merchandise in shop windows.[26] Local churchwomen responded to these requests with enthusiasm, discussing UN programs in small circle meetings, speaking publicly in support of the UN in local newspapers and on local radio programs, and setting up "UN Councils" to further the work of the UN in local communities.[27] They put "UN We Believe" seals on letters and greeting cards, persuaded their local churches to fly UN flags, and distributed UN support cards to firms and businesses in their home communities in order to express their commitment to the institution.[28]

Leaders of the WDCS were not only concerned with the external effects of UN programs on world citizenship and peace. They were also intensely concerned with the role of women *within* the United Nations. Their efforts to increase women's representation in the UN were intermingled with similar efforts to increase women's policymaking and church representation in U.S.-based political institutions. Although there was a "sprinkling of women in the various delegations" to the General Assembly, one member argued in the late 1940s, there was "almost a complete scarcity of women in the membership of the various councils and commissions." Until women gained wider representation, they feared, "the men will likely continue their present failure to appreciate that women are part of international society."[29] In an effort to increase women's presence in the UN, *The Methodist Woman* printed updates and interviews with female UN delegates from around the globe, highlighting the impact of UN programs on women. Leaders also publicized their commitment to equal rights for women in the United States as a parallel to emergent debates within the UN about human rights, throwing their support behind Eleanor Roosevelt, chair of the 1948 Commission on for Human Rights, and the Universal Declaration of Human Rights.

In short, in the words of one WECS leader, the UN defined a "new role for women." Early on, the creation of the UN Committee on the Status of Women in 1945 heightened the resolve of the Woman's Division in seeking gender equality and gave their cause greater legitimacy within U.S. borders. "The status of women in any nation can well become a barometer of democracy in that nation," leaders argued.[30] The UN was the first international institution to formally recognize full legal equality for women and, as such, it brought with it rapid social and political change for women across the globe in the form of political rights, greater economic security, and new social programs. Between 1945, when the UN was formed, and 1960, thirty-eight countries took action to grant full or limited political rights to women. The "battle for principles has been won, at least in theory," *The Methodist Woman* noted after the passage of the UN International Declaration of Human Rights and the formation of the UN Commission on the Status of Women. Our task now, the article continued, "is to ensure the practical application of women's right to equality."[31]

In addition, the Universal Declaration of Human Rights and the UN Commission on the Status of Women created incentives among national organizations to collect information and data that could be used to compare and contrast human rights and social justice standards against international benchmarks. These became a "common standard of achievement," that not only heightened international awareness among churchwomen, but also encouraged leaders to begin measuring achievements on behalf of gender (and race and class) equality in new ways.[32] Leaders in the United Council of Church Women reflected further on the implications of U.S. membership in the UN: "it means exposure to international comparisons by generally accepted standards not only in economic matters, but in public health, literacy, social hygiene, human rights, the status of women and other fields." Because the UN had a "solid reputation for objectivity and accuracy," the UCC continued, it provided a "sound basis for constructive action in many fields."[33] Thus, in 1957, the Woman's Division adopted a "United Nations Credo," which affirmed their belief that the UN held the "best political potential for peace," and for working toward "social progress."[34]

If there was any lingering doubt that the formation of the United Nations defined and created new ways of organizing, it was dismissed with the creation of the Church Center for the United Nations (CCUN) in 1963. Methodist churchwomen themselves deserve some of the credit for the CCUN—the Woman's Division provided the financial backing for the center's construction and took out the mortgage on the building. A twelve-story complex located in the Carnegie Building across from the UN complex, the CCUN formalized the participation of religious groups in international relations and UN activities.[35] "Changing times have established the United Nations as the world's most important forum for political discussion and center of international planning," a Methodist publication read.[36] The purpose of the center was to enhance U.S. citizens' interest in the UN and to acquaint them with its programs and activities, holding an average of twelve hundred study programs per month and serving over twelve thousand church and lay people per year.[37] It would become a critical part of the policy machinery through which leaders and members of the WDCS struggled on behalf of gender equality and human rights in the late 1960s and 1970s and, as such, it further shaped the ways in which they formulated political arguments and strategies both internationally and within U.S. borders.

Simultaneous with growing internationalism, the WDCS undertook significant internal organizational change in the mid-twentieth century. These two factors—internationalism and organizational change—were both confluent and mutually constitutive. Leaders quickly realized that they would be unable to fully benefit from emergent political opportunities without significant internal reform. "Expanding and heavier future responsibilities," one postwar WDCS leader remarked, necessitates a "reappraisal of organizational patterns, relationships, and methods."[38] The development of the UN not only created new avenues for churchwomen's work on a global scale. It also provided leaders with an impetus for organizational experimentation, pushing the Division toward greater centralization, professionalization, and modernization. These were welcomed changes among a leadership facing increasing financial strain, a fatigued U.S. membership in steep decline by the mid-1960s, and changes in the prevailing gender order that further destabilized the rationale for much of churchwomen's work. Leader of the WDCS, Virginia Laskey, noted in 1962:

> As members of the Woman's Division we are frankly facing such facts as these: 1) Decrease in membership; 2) Giving reaching a plateau; 3) Employment of women; 4) Overlapping of church activities; 5) Widely diversified interest of women, a) community; b) church... Right now we are studying and asking: 1) Do we need to reexamine the purpose of the Woman's Society and Guild?; 2) Do we need more cooperation with the total church, its boards, agencies and commissions?; 3) Are there too many overlapping services?; 4) Should the whole area of program be reexamined?; 5) Is there too much inflexibility in our organization?[39]

An outside consulting firm hired to assess the assets and liabilities of the WDCS concluded that although the Woman's Division had a loyal and devoted membership and a well-structured organization, they could do more to strengthen administration and staff and to maximize coordination and planning.[40] Recommended changes included reducing administrative staff positions, reorganizing the Division around "sound management principles," and placing a "charismatic" leader in a general executive position to provide coordinated, centralized control. The WDCS implemented these and more drastic organizational changes over the following decade. Among the most telling changes, in 1968, the name of the WDCS was changed from Woman's Division to the Women's Division of Christian Service to better reflect current political meanings of gender. Then, in 1972, culminating a decade of organizational change and restructuring, the WDCS was reorganized as a "new inclusive organization" and renamed the United Methodist Women (UMW). The new configuration of organized Methodist womanhood, leaders argued, implied "a less rigid structure," described "not merely a meeting but a being," avoided "faddish terminology," and was "easily identifiable and descriptive."[41] At the time of its formation, the UMW claimed approximately 1.5 million members, employed a staff of twenty-six, operated a legislative affairs office in Washington, D.C., and was described by one leader as a "superstructure, a business organized for efficiency, doing bookkeeping, accounting, evaluation of program; setting goals and trying to solve problems."[42]

Leaders of the UMW increasingly embraced women's liberation as the twentieth century wore on—becoming, at one point, one of the most active religious organizations campaigning on behalf of the ERA according to Common Cause. A growing feminist consciousness is clearly evident in the papers of the UMW by the early 1970s. Leaders spoke about "male-dominated social structures," for example, and pointed to the ways in which the organization of the church reinforced and replicated women's subordinate role in society.[43] They pressured the Methodist Church to increase the number of women on governing boards—which they did through a quota system—and to amend male-oriented language in the *Book of Discipline*.[44] In 1963, 175 churchwomen participants in a national Woman's Division seminar were given copies of *The Feminine Mystique* to read for reflection, study, and discussion.[45] In 1970, the Division created a Committee on Churchwomen's Liberation, which recommended programs including the development of women's centers "where women could gather to discuss their own history and could find adequate resources to engage in discovery of…reflections on women"; a "counseling service…(on) abortion, child care, job problems and vocation direction"; the practice of "consciousness raising" among local Methodist churchwomen; and the development of strategies to work with non-church groups "toward full and equal participation of women in society."[46] In many of these areas, the UMW assumed an advocacy role, working on behalf of employed, single, young, poor, and minority women. Among the goals of "women in a new age,"[47] leaders of the UMW included "changes in attitudes and policies of the male dominated power structure," "positions at policy making and implementation" for women, the ERA, and careful study of the problems of "over population and planned parenthood."[48]

Internationally, the World Federation of Methodist Women emerged in the late 1960s as the central vehicle through which the UMW participated in the UN.[49] For decades, the WFMW had campaigned for its own accreditation with the UN, but was restricted to indirect participation through the World Council of Churches.[50] In the early 1980s, WFMW President, Elizabeth Kissack, wrote to Theressa Hoover, then Executive Secretary of the Women's Division, noting that "we have come to a sensitive stage in the development of the Federation." It is time for the Federation to measure up to "world sized problems" and to discard its "'cosy' [sic] image," Kissack argued. "The time has come to take a clearer line, to enable more women in Regions to understand the challenge and responsibilities for peace and development that women face today." "This would involve the Federation working towards N.G.O status at the UN," Kissack argued; "this is no departure from the programme, rather it is an unfolding of awareness, a stepping up of interest, and in that positive attitude we prepare to learn what is required of us."[51] Kissack sent a similar letter to the General Secretary of the World Council of Churches:

> The World Methodist Council has not yet sought NGO status at the UN, so the WCC has kindly extended its umbrella over us to take in the proceedings. For this we are most grateful...now we know that more women of the Federation need to be involved as many other world women's movements are. So, we plan to start procedures to become an NGO in our own right—no waiting for the World Methodist Council to do it for us.[52]

In response to Kissack's initiative, the WFMW hired a full-time staff devoted to achieving UN consultative status in the early 1980s. It would ultimately be granted in 1983.

Conclusion: Institutional Feminist and Organizational Legacies of the Postwar WDCS

The WDCS was not subsumed or replaced by budding women's organizations of the second and third waves. Rather, leaders of the Division took steps to transform their organizations from within and, in some cases, pioneered strategies that are most often associated with modern women's organizations and NGOs. The organizational changes undertaken by the WDCS are noteworthy. In three short decades, leaders transformed a decentralized organization focused primarily on missionary enterprise into a centralized, professionalized, and more politicized organization resembling a modern-day interest group possessing clear global dimensions—complete with its own lobby headquartered in D.C., and, through its international counterpart, an NGO formally accredited with the UN.

More than merely filling in gaps in the historical record (itself a worthy goal), the historical specificities of the WDCS's transformation bring empirical evidence to bear on the emergence of modern feminist organizational goals, methods, and collective gender identities.

The WDCS's experiences suggest that the political development of postwar women's organizations was driven in large part through responses to institutional change. At the same time that the UN created new opportunities for the WDCS internationally, it also pushed leaders toward a reappraisal of goals and tactics. An additional important lesson gleaned here is that the forms, structures, and strategies of modern feminism were both intentional *and* unanticipated consequences of leaders' steps in negotiating shifting opportunities that intersected with the pursuit of women's interests—emergent civil rights political strategies, for example, and a global stage legitimizing the language of human rights. Leaders and local members were not unanimous in a single pursuit of "feminism"—many disassociated from the concept entirely. Yet, there is a particular irony in the multiplicity of the Methodist WDCS's postwar political goals and strategies viewed in light of third-wave critiques that second-wave feminism failed to appreciate the diversity of women's identities across the lines of race, class, and nation. The historical narrative of the WDCS provides a clearer glimpse into the origins of the varied practices embodied in modern feminism. The experiences of the WDCS suggest that the landscape of women's organizations in the mid-to-late twentieth century did not profoundly break from the past between "waves" but instead slowly transformed from within in response to new national and international political opportunities.

Notes

1. Lee Ann Banaszak, "Women's Movements and Women in Movements: Influencing American Democracy from the 'Outside'?," in *Political Women and American Democracy*, eds. Christina Wolbrecht, Karen Beckwith, and Lisa Baldez (Cambridge University Press, 2008).
2. Banazkak, "Women's Movements and Women in Movements"; and Myra Marx Ferree, "Globalization and Feminism: Opportunities and Obstacles for Activism in the Global Arena," in *Global Feminism: Transnational Women's Activism, Organizing, and Human Rights*, eds. Myra Marx Ferree and Aili Mari Tripp (New York: New York University Press, 2006), 9.
3. Women are more likely than men to be attached to religious beliefs and practices, to read the Bible, and to attend church, for example. See Robert Wuthnow and William Lehrman, "Religion: Inhibitor or Facilitator of Political Involvement Among Women?," 300–22, in *Women, Politics, and Change*, eds. Louise A. Tilly and Patricia Gurin (New York: Russell Sage Foundation, 1992). See also Sidney Verba, Kay Lehman Schlozman, and Henry E. Brady, *Voice and Equality: Civic Voluntarism in American Politics* (Cambridge, MA: Harvard University Press, 1995), 520–21.

4. On similar arguments see Wuthnow and Lehrman, "Religion: Inhibitor or Facilitator of Political Involvement Among Women."

5. Mrs. L. M. Awtrey, "Status of Women," *The Methodist Woman* 10 (June 1950): 34.

6. Susan Dye Lee, "Evangelical Domesticity," and Carolyn DeSwarte Gifford, "For God and Home and Native Land," in *Women in New Worlds, Volume I, Historical Perspectives on the Wesleyan Tradition*, eds. Hilah F. Thomas and Rosemary Skinner Keller (Nashville, TN: Abingdon, 1981).

7. Paula Baker, "The Domestication of Politics: Women and American Political Society, 1780–1920," *American Historical Review* 89 (February-June 1984): 620–64; Elisabeth Clemens, "Organizational Repertoires and Institutional Change: Women's Groups and the Transformation of US Politics, 1890–1920," *American Journal of Sociology* 98 (January 1984): 755–98; Nancy F. Cott, *The Grounding of Modern Feminism* (New Haven, CT: Yale University Press, 1987); Anne F. Scott, *Natural Allies: Women's Associations in American History* (Urbana: University of Illinois Press, 1991); and Theda Skcopol, *Protecting Soldiers and Mothers: The Political Origins of Social Policy in the United States* (Princeton, NJ: Princeton University Press, 1992).

8. Journal of the Executive Committee, New York, NY, September 21, 1948, Records of the Women's Division of Christian Service of the General Board of Ministries, United Methodist Church Archives—General Commission on Archives and History, Madison, New Jersey (hereafter WDSCA).

9. The WDCS was formed through a unification of several pre-existing Methodist women's associations dating back to the mid-1880s.

10. "Goals for 1947, 'Thy Kingdom Come,': Suggestions for Help in Attaining These Goals," *The Methodist Woman* 7 (November 1946): 15. According to Theda Skocpol, among women's associations, only the Order of the Eastern Star (auxiliary to the Masons) and the Woman's Missionary Union also crossed the 1 percent mark in the mid-twentieth century. See Skocpol's *Diminished Democracy: From Membership to Management in American Civic Life* (Norman: University of Oklahoma Press, 2003).

11. For a brief review of the WDCS's involvement in civil rights, see "Political Development of Female Civic Engagement in Postwar America," *Politics & Gender* 1 (December 2005): 547–75.

12. Stevens, *Legacy for the Future.*

13. Suzanne Mettler, *Dividing Citizens: Gender and Federalism in New Deal Public Policy* (Ithaca, NY: Cornell University Press, 1998).

14. Denomme, "'To End This Day of Strife'," 3.

15. See Susan Hartmann, *The Other Feminists, Activists in the Liberal Establishment* (New Haven, CT: Yale University Press, 1998), 94–95; and Elizabeth M. Lee, "The National Council of the Churches of Christ in the USA," *The Methodist Woman* 11 (November 1950): 12–13.

16. Betty A. Reardon, *Women and Peace: Feminist Visions of Global Security* (State University of New York Press, 1993).

17. Myra Marx Ferree, "Globalization and Feminism: Opportunities and Obstalces for Activism in the Global Arena," in *Global Feminism: Transnational Women's Activism, Organizing, and Human Rights*, eds. Myra Marx Ferree and Aili Mari Tripp (New York: New York University Press, 2006).

18. Leila J. Rupp, "Constructing Internationalism: The Case of Transnational Women's Organizations, 1888–1945," *The American Historical Review* 99 (December 1994): 1571–1600. See also Aili Mari Tripp, "The Evolution of Transnational Feminism: Consensus, Conflict, and New Dynamics," in *Global Feminism* (see note 17).

19. Some of these groups simply "transferred" similar relationships from the League of Nations to the UN. Level B consultative status was granted to organizations possessing a "special competence" in areas of UN activities; it granted organizations the opportunity to observe

public meetings of the UN Council and to have limited communication with Council members. The seventeeb women's groups included: All India Conference, Associated Country Women of the World, International Alliance of Women for Equal Rights and Equal Responsibilities, International Bureau for the Suppression of Trafficking in Women and Children, International Co-Operative Women's Guild, International Council of Women, International Federation of Business and Professional Women, International Federation of Friends of Young Women, International Federation of University Women, International Union of Catholic Women's Organizations, Liaison Committee of Women's International Organizations, Women's International Democratic Federation, Women's International League or Peace and Freedom, World Association of Girl Guides and Girl Scouts, World Movement of Mothers, World's Woman's Christian Temperance Union, World's Young Women's Christian Association. See *Yearbook of the United Nations*, 1946–7; and "List of NGOs Granted Consultative Status by ECOSOC as of October 1949," working paper transmitted by the Interim Committee on Consultative Non-Governmental Organizations, United Nations Studies.

20. Josephine Schain, "The International Assembly of Women," *The Methodist Woman* 7 (May 1947), 12–13, 31.

21. Women's Division of Christian Service of the Board of Missions and Church Extension of the Methodist Church, *Seventh Annual Report*, 1947–1948, Records of the Women's Division, GCAH.

22. Thelma Stevens, Eleanor Neff, and Dorothy Weber, "Advance in the New Quadrennium," *The Methodist Woman* 8 (May 1948): 29.

23. Wesleyan Service Guild, "Untitled," *The Methodist Woman* 5 (April 1945): 26.

24. *Sixth Annual Report*, 172; Stevens, *Legacy for the Future*; John Foster Dulles, "A First Step in World-Cooperation," *The Methodist Woman* 5 (March 1945): 5.

25. The American Association for the United Nations was founded in 1943 under the leadership of Eleanor Roosevelt. It united several civic organizations and sought to educate Americans about the UN and important international issues.

26. Mrs. Clifford A. Bender, "Advance Without Loss," *The Methodist Woman* 11 (October 1950): 17.

27. Journal of the Executive Committee, Buck Hill Falls, PA, June 14, 1949, GCAH.

28. "UN We Believe" [booklet], United Nations CCUN—Folder One, Women's Division, Records of the Women's Division, GCAH.

29. Josephine Schain, "The Commission on the Status of Women," *The Methodist Woman* 8 (November 1947): 13.

30. *Seventh Annual Report*, 190.

31. "Women's Position in the World Today," *The Methodist Woman* 9 (November 1948): 16.

32. In Thelma Stevens, "Universal Declaration of Human Rights: A Community Action Worksheet," *The Methodist Woman* October 1962: 27–30.

33. United Church Women of the National Council of Churches, "The New Nations, Women and the Church, 1959–1960 [booklet], Women Folder 1, 1956–1958, Records of the Women's Division, GCAH.

34. Stevens, *Legacy for the Future*, 124.

35. "The Church Center for the United Nations" [booklet], United Nations CCUN—Folder One, Records of the Women's Division, GCAH.

36. "The Methodist Office at the Church Center for the United Nations," May 25, 1964, United Nations CCUN—Folder Four, Records of the Women's Division, GCAH.

37. "The Church Center for the United Nations."

38. Ibid.

39. Virginia Laskey to Mrs. John L. Mitchell, March 23, 1962, Virginia Laskey—Correspondence 1962–1963, Records of the Women's Division, GCAH.

40. General Administrative Study of the WDCS 1959.

41. Background Papers: Reports—"One New Inclusive Organization" 1971, Records of the Women's Division, GCAH.

42. Barbara E. Campbell, *In the Middle of Tomorrow* (New York: Women's Division, Board of Global Ministries, United Methodist Church, 1975), 15, 19.

43. "Seminar on International Women's Year, 1975" [booklet], United Nations, 1952–1984, Women's Division, Records of the Women's Division, GCAH.

44. Campbell, *In the Middle of Tomorrow*, 48.

45. Stevens, *Legacy for the Future*, 89–90.

46. Ibid., 116–18.

47. Campbell, *In the Middle of Tomorrow*, 50–51, 90.

48. "Seminar on International Women's Year, 1975."

49. World Federation of Methodist Women, 1938–1986, "Handbook of the World Federation of Methodist Women, 1961–1966," Records of the Women's Division, GCAH.

50. According to the records of the Women's Division, the WFMW's appeals for consultative status were thwarted in part by the opposition of Dr. O. Frederick Nolde, World Council of Churches Executive Director of the Commission of Churches on International Affairs. Nolde worried that accrediting the WFMW would result in "confusion" on the part of Protestant organizations and open the floodgates to accreditation. Memo regarding the World Federation of Methodist Women and the United Nations, United Nations, May 10, 1966, Records of the Women's Division, GCAH.

51. Kissack to Hoover, September 4, 1980, United Nations 1952–1984, Records of the Women's Division, GCAH.

52. Kissack to Dr. Philip Potter, September 2, 1980, United Nations 1952–1984, Records of the Women's Division, GCAH.

PART **III**

The Politics of Location

The Consumers' Protective Committee

Women's Activism in Postwar Harlem

JULIA SANDY-BAILEY

In October 1947, the Consumers' Protective Committee made plans for a massive protest rally on 125th street, Harlem's main retail district. The Committee (CPC) had formed only two months earlier when a group of middle-class African American women met at the YWCA to discuss rising postwar prices and the sometimes dishonest practices of Harlem merchants. Their rally was one piece of a wide-ranging campaign, which grew to include boycotts, picketing, political lobbying, and negotiations with the Uptown Chamber of Commerce. Declaring themselves activist housewives, the CPC's actions drew support from many in the community and one person underscored its popularity when he declared, "The campaign not only has attracted civic and religious groups but has brought a quick response from individual women, who do most of the shopping and therefore are closest to the price situation."[1] In the local press many of Harlem's women echoed this assessment and one headline proclaimed they were "Shoppers Ready for the Signal" to join in the Committee's fight.

In organizing the CPC, activists built on a long history of female-led protests that cast women as natural experts on consumer issues. Historians such as Dana Frank, Annelise Orleck, Lizabeth Cohen, and Meg Jacobs have shown how women turned their domestic duty as the primary family shopper into a civic responsibility wielded for the public good, and into numerous consumer campaigns waged throughout the twentieth century. Unlike white activists, black women, including CPC members, exposed the ways in which *race* uniquely shaped consumer issues, arguing that in black neighborhoods high prices and cheating merchants were as much about racial discrimination as they were about consumer exploitation. Although men often supported and even encouraged women in these activities, at times tensions arose in communities where women engaged in such public work. Harlem was no exception. Before the rally could take place, the Committee found itself fighting not only high prices but also Harlem's male leaders who came to regard its work as a threat to the community. The CPC refused to end its campaign and would go on to become one of the most active consumer rights organizations in postwar Harlem.[2]

Throughout its existence the work of the CPC brought important resources and new allies to the struggle for consumer rights in Harlem. Committee activists believed these rights were vitally important to the well-being of their community and fought to achieve economic justice for black New Yorkers. They did so by engaging in very visible work and utilizing a variety of tactics—from public protests, picketing, and boycotts, to retail investigations, consumer education programs, and testifying before state and federal government committees. Their work helps challenge the "waves" metaphor that often masks women's activism in the twentieth century. Joanne Meyerowitz's now classic *Not June Cleaver: Women and Gender in Postwar America, 1945–1960* brought to light women's organizing between the so-called first and second waves, and more recent books by Daniel Horowitz, Anne Enke, and Judith Ezekiel, among others, have also helped question the usefulness of the waves metaphor. Despite this work, the idea of waves—crests of activism which emerged out of lulls or even backlashes against women's organizing—still persists in much of the scholarship and teaching of women's history. The CPC's history demonstrates that women did not abandon public activism between the first and second waves.[3]

The history of the Consumers' Protective Committee challenges another persistent stereotype in historical research and teaching—that the leadership of the black freedom movement was the exclusive purview of African American men. In the past decade scholars have begun to address the lack of attention paid to black female activists in this movement. However, with the exception of such high-profile women as Ella Baker and Fannie Lou Hamer, in most of these studies women did not assume formal leadership positions but instead remained "bridge leaders," to use the term coined by sociologist Belinda Robnett. As bridge leaders black women were rank-and-file activists who organized communities and campaigns. They might take on leadership positions in moments of crisis, but when the crisis passed they turned organizational control over to black men. By contrast, even though men were a part of the CPC from its founding, the leadership and identity of the group remained in the hands of its women. Its public persona as a group of housewives gave the CPC legitimacy in the community, an identity it would maintain throughout the postwar era. That the group included many working professionals with a history of activism, as well as many men, failed to diminish its reputation as a housewives' organization. To build and sustain their public role, CPC activists drew on gendered assumptions about consumption and argued that as women they were uniquely qualified to understand and fight for consumer rights. As such their work both affirmed and challenged traditional gender roles; exploring their history sheds light on women's work and gender dynamics within the postwar black freedom movement.[4]

Origins of the CPC

Like their white counterparts, African American women's consumer activism became organized and public during the Great Depression. Their work was part of a growing national movement that sought increased government regulation to counteract price fixing, ensure honest product labeling, and support consumer education initiatives. Historian Lizabeth Cohen terms these activists "citizen consumers" who thought of themselves "as responsible for safeguarding the general good of the nation, in particular for prodding government to protect the rights, safety, and fair treatment of individual consumers."[5] Cohen also argues that consumer activism became a new avenue into the public arena for groups formerly denied access to political and economic power, especially for women and African Americans. In Harlem, black women joined in the consumer protection fight through organizations such as the Harlem Housewives League, the Consolidated Housewives League, and Consumers' Unit No. 1. These groups investigated members' complaints against local stores, educated women on how to identify unfair and dishonest practices, and negotiated for better treatment from store clerks.

During World War II, women's consumer work became part of America's total war effort. Activities such as supporting recycling drives, adhering to price and rationing restrictions, planting Victory Gardens, and reporting on black marketers were all part of one's patriotic duty. In this context a woman's consumer function was important not only to her family but to the vitality of the nation. Throughout the war much of women's consumer work took place with the help of the Office of Price Administration (OPA), set up by the federal government in June 1941. The creation of the OPA signaled the importance of consumer issues to the war effort and through it the government intervened into the relationship between shoppers and merchants to an unprecedented extent. Black women worked with Harlem's OPA in much the same ways white women did with their neighborhood OPA offices, and the two groups shared many goals and strategies. Both taught consumer education workshops, investigated prices and practices of merchants, distributed ration books, and lobbied legislators for increased consumer protections. In so doing they not only fulfilled their domestic and public consumer responsibilities they also gained influence and experience as community activists.[6]

During the Great Depression and WWII, black women, including those in Harlem, connected consumer rights to the black freedom movement by consistently arguing that racial discrimination was at the root of the dishonest business practices in their neighborhoods. They had good reason to do so, as surveys of New York City stores always confirmed that black New Yorkers paid more money for inferior goods. Harlemites faced deceitful selling practices such as short changing, short weighing, and "pulling-in," a system whereby stores paid people to stand outside their businesses and aggressively pull shoppers inside. Even OPA officials acknowledged the racial discrimination black consumers faced, and when it opened the local branch admitted, "there are unusual economic pressures in Harlem. Item for item, food prices are higher there, and we want an office in that section that can act."[7] At the end of the war, the situation became even more critical when Congress failed to renew the OPA and black New Yorkers lost an important ally in their consumer struggles. Costs rose dramatically, and Harlem's housewives complained about the impact of soaring prices on their family budgets. The black press was full of stories about women who made long treks downtown to take advantage of significantly lower prices.[8]

In the summer of 1947, the Uptown Chamber of Commerce (UCC), an organization of mostly white merchants in Harlem, responded to these charges by launching a public relations campaign to attract shoppers back to neighborhood stores. The campaign, titled "Prices are Down, Uptown," kicked off with a dance at the Apollo Theater where, signaling women's identification with shopping, a Miss 125th Street was crowned. The dance was followed the next day by a parade and a special week-long "Bargain Jubilee," billed as "the mightiest Sale in 125th Street History."[9] Two local black newspapers, the *People's Voice* and the *New York Age*, participated in the campaign and ran ads from the UCC and local businesses highlighting their sales. Many UCC ads portrayed the organization as a consumer champion, with headlines such as "We Lead the Fight to Bring Prices Down." All ads and flyers contained the slogan, "Save Time, Save Money, Save Fare."[10]

However, many Harlemites were not swayed by the UCC campaign, and in August a group of women met at the Harlem YWCA to discuss rising postwar prices and the business practices of Harlem merchants. Out of this meeting emerged the Consumers' Protective Committee, an organization of mostly middle-class African American women. CPC members ranged in age from their mid-twenties to their late fifties and included married and single women. The co-chairs were Walton Pryor and Aloncita Flood. Walton, whose unusual first name was sometimes mistakenly listed in the press as Walter, was a thirty-eight-year-old accountant—as was her husband, Christopher. Flood was the Activities Director of the Young Women's Christian Association (YWCA) in Harlem. Her husband, Roger Flood, was an architect and manager of the Harlem River Houses, the only housing development in Harlem run by African Americans. Gladys Mangum, the CPC treasurer, was a graduate of New York University and enrolled in Columbia's Teacher College. She was recently married and her husband was a police officer and law student. Other founding CPC members included Mrs. Joseph Wells, whose husband owned a popular restaurant in Harlem, Blanche Eckles, a dressmaker and locally celebrated soprano whose husband was a school teacher, and the nationally famous contralto Carol Brice who served as a member of the education committee.[11]

Most CPC activists were also prominent in Harlem's social circles. Throughout the 1930s and 1940s, they hosted parties and other gatherings, and future CPC activists met one another through these social functions. They often received notice in the local black press and even in the *Chicago Defender* and *Pittsburgh Courier*. Gladys Mangum's 1947 marriage was billed as "one of Harlem's largest society weddings."[12] The Pryors frequently made the society section of Harlem's newspapers, including the announcement of their 1942 marriage, which was officiated by the Rev. Adam Clayton Powell, Jr. Powell was the charismatic head of Harlem's Abyssinian Baptist Church and the first African American councilman in New York City history. In 1944 Powell would be elected to the U.S. House of Representatives, and he remained a popular and prominent leader in Harlem throughout the postwar era. Christopher Pryor belonged to the Kappa Alpha Psi fraternity and Walton was a member of that fraternity's "sweethearts" auxiliary organization where she attended parties given by Myrtle Martin, who would be on the CPC Board of Directors. Aloncita Flood was a leading member of the Alpha Kappa Alpha sorority, and in the early 1940s helped establish a local chapter with Irma Wilson, one of the Committee's first vice-chairs. At wedding showers, charity balls, bridge tournaments, and other parties around Harlem, CPC women developed social networks which would serve them well in their organizing.[13]

Prior to the organization's founding, CPC activists had also worked together in Harlem's vibrant and diverse civic groups, including both mixed-sex and women's groups, where they gained experience in political organizing and fighting racial discrimination. In the 1920s Eva Parks helped organize the Ladies' Auxiliary of the New York Urban League, where she was joined over the years by many other future CPC members. Parks was also a member of the Harlem Housewives League and in the 1930s worked on employment and consumer campaigns. CPC activists belonged to the National Association for the Advancement of Colored People (NAACP), including Aloncita Flood who chaired the organization's 1949 membership drive. Pryor and Flood were also members of the Harlem Chapter of the Committee on Discrimination in Education, and several CPC women belonged to Harlem's district committee of the Community Service Society, an organization which worked to eradicate poverty in New York City. There were Republicans and Democrats in the CPC ranks. In the spring of 1947, Walton was the Executive Director of the People's Committee, the political organization started by the Democrat Adam Clayton Powell, Jr. Ruth Bushong, on the other hand, was the Assistant Recording Secretary of the Lincoln Republican Club and, in 1958, was a Bronx delegate to the New York State Republican Convention. Though it formed working relationships with Democratic administrations in the postwar era, the CPC's bipartisan makeup continued throughout its existence.[14]

The formation of the CPC arose from these social and organizational networks of women with a history of local activism. They brought to the Committee extensive experience, skills, connections, and status in the community. Yet, the CPC was not exclusively a women's organization, and a number of men were involved with the early formation of the group. Neil Scott, for example, was a founder and the vice chair in charge of public relations. Scott was the husband of CPC member Carol Brice and owned his own public relations firm.[15] Men were also shown in newspaper photos as participants in street rallies and picket lines. Despite the presence of men in the organization, and the fact that many CPC activists worked outside the home and were leaders in local organizations, the CPC presented itself publicly as a group of housewives who had been spurred to action by injustices to Harlem's consumers. Many identified themselves only by their husbands' names, including Aloncita Flood, who was usually identified as "Mrs. Roger Flood." Newspaper articles failed to mention their employment or political activism and instead repeatedly characterized the CPC as a group of housewives who represented "the average woman shopper on West 125th Street."[16] Undoubtedly, some CPC activists were housewives, but identifying themselves solely as such highlighted their middle-class status and gave them legitimacy as consumer experts.

Directing their attacks against both the Uptown Chamber of Commerce and white-owned businesses, CPC activists charged local merchants with committing a variety of offenses against black New Yorkers. The most common complaints were about high prices, inferior quality, and high-pressure selling techniques. To these they added that white-owned merchants gave nothing back to the community in that they failed to support civic organizations or employ African Americans in adequate numbers. Additionally, they argued that "through some process of collusion, it is impossible for Negro businesses to be established on [125th] Street."[17] Their arguments helped highlight the importance of consumer issues for Harlemites and helped connect those issues to the larger black freedom movement. Their fall campaign integrated a variety of techniques: they lodged complaints with the Uptown Chamber of Commerce, conducted shoppers' surveys, staged rallies, and picketed individual stores. In late October they threatened a community-wide boycott and planned a massive rally set for mid-November.[18]

Local leaders and groups initially endorsed the CPC campaign. Support came, especially, from ministers' organizations. This endorsement was hardly surprising given the number of CPC women who were active in area churches. The CPC also understood the influence wielded by Harlem's religious leaders, a traditional power base in the community, and specifically sought their support. They urged ministers to "help Harlem and its collective pocketbook" by leading their congregations to CPC meetings and demonstrations.[19] In early November the New York Baptist Ministers' Conference appeared in a photo on the front page of the *Amsterdam News*; in the photo dozens of ministers were shown shouting "Down With Prices in Harlem" to signify their endorsement of the CPC. The ministers pledged their assistance in staging the November rally, which the *Amsterdam News* hyperbolically proclaimed would be, "the most gigantic demonstration ever attempted by any group of people in a fight to improve their economic welfare."[20] Days before the rally took place, however, merchants invited both the CPC and ministers to a conference to discuss the growing campaign. While ministers agreed to the meeting, CPC activists refused to attend or cancel their street protests. It was at this point that the CPC and ministers publicly parted ways. As historian Martha Biondi argues, black male leaders turned against the CPC for a variety of reasons. They feared their own loss of control over the protests, and also believed that a large-scale boycott would hurt local stores which employed African Americans and made financial contributions to their own organizations.[21]

Harlem's three newspapers chose sides in the dispute, with the *People's Voice* and the *Age* backing the ministers and the *Amsterdam News* supporting the CPC. The *Age* was the oldest African American weekly paper in Harlem, founded in 1887 by the civil rights leader and journalist T. Thomas Fortune; the youngest of the papers, the *People's Voice*, was founded by Adam Clayton Powell, Jr. in 1942. Billing itself as a political, leftist, and crusading publication, in 1946 the *People's Voice* had a circulation of twenty-eight thousand. The third paper, the *Amsterdam News*, far outpaced the popularity of the other two with a 1947 circulation of over 100,000. Founded in 1909, during the Great Depression prominent Harlem physicians C.B. Powell and Philip M.H. Savory bought the paper as an economic investment. Powell, no relation to the Rev. Powell, was a leading figure in Republican politics in Harlem. The two Powells often used their newspapers to publicly attack the motives and political views of one another, which may be one reason they chose opposing sides in the CPC dispute. Given Pryor's close relationship with Rev. Powell, and his paper's reputation as a radical voice in Harlem, it is more difficult to discern the motivations of the *People's Voice*. Not only did this paper attack the CPC, Rev. Powell charged in the *Age* that C.B. Powell would withdraw his support for the Committee if stores increased their advertisements in the *Amsterdam News*.[22]

Throughout November and December, a bitter struggle ensued as the CPC and ministers fought over goals and tactics, and over which group could legitimately claim leadership of Harlem's consumer rights activism. The conflict was expressed by both sides in highly gendered terms and crystallized around competing conceptions of women's acceptable public role. Having originally supported the CPC as a group of activist housewives, the ministers now set out to discredit them by ignoring their claims to consumer expertise and employing negative gender stereotypes. In the *Age* and the *People's Voice*, CPC activists were no longer referred to as "the housewives" but were instead "the women," and were characterized as unreasonable, unruly, and unsafe. The adjective "hysterical" was repeatedly used to describe their activities. Street demonstrations, which had a few weeks earlier been supported by the ministers, were now portrayed as a dangerous activity. The *Age* warned that "the CPC's threat of mass picketing is irresponsible in that it can cause serious results—such as possible rioting, straining of racial tensions, and dismissals of Negro workers, not only on 125th street, but also throughout the city, in the case of chain stores which employ Negroes in other areas."[23] Instead of being the natural protectors of the home and Harlem's consumers, the CPC now threatened the community's stability and economic vitality and also jeopardized interracial relations.[24]

The CPC's refusal to negotiate with the merchants was especially criticized, and portrayed as the response of irrational women. In an article titled "125th St. Merchants Invited Women to Conference *Twice*," Reverend John Johnson told the *Age*, "there ought to be negotiation and all the facts ought to be learned before anyone goes off half-cocked. Every possible step should be taken to work the thing out reasonably."[25] Ministers and the men who joined them were, by contrast, depicted as Harlem's true leaders, and although they opposed high prices and cheating merchants, they supposedly took more sensible steps to bring about a solution to these problems. They petitioned the city to open a public market in Harlem, lodged complaints about high prices with local business associations, and lobbied President Harry Truman and Congress to reestablish wartime price controls. In late November the ministers met with the Uptown Chamber of Commerce without the CPC and negotiated an agreement requiring local stores to clearly mark prices, stop their "pulling-in" techniques, and display all policies on refunds, exchanges, and lay-away plans. The agreement also set up a Shopper's Mediation Board with representatives from the Uptown Chamber of Commerce and the black community to act as an intermediary in disputes between shoppers and merchants.[26]

For their part, CPC activists were unwilling to concede their leadership to the community's black male leaders, and they, too, waged their campaign on gendered grounds. Although they drew on their status as housewives, theirs was not a maternalist argument and instead highlighted the gendered knowledge and experience they drew on as women and housewives. As Flood explained to the *Amsterdam News*, "No one knows better than the women of Harlem that prices generally are high." She further asserted CPC leadership over the traditional male power base when she claimed, "what is happening in Harlem is not merely high prices as are evident elsewhere, but downright cheating and stealing. Any Harlem leader who doesn't know this, is unfit to lead whether he heads a church organization or a social club." She continued, "It is hardly conceivable that in the face of admissions from the merchants themselves that many of the stores operate two-price policies, certain Harlemites have sought to obstruct our program."[27]

The CPC defended its refusal to negotiate with the Uptown Chamber of Commerce, calling arbitration a "political solution," which would not produce any real change in the community. Referring to previously broken promises, one activist argued, "We don't intend to permit our program to become bogged down in any series of discussions and studies. We remember too well the 1935 Report of Conditions in Harlem, which the late Mayor LaGuardia pigeonholed."[28] Instead, the CPC gave endorsements to those individual shops they felt treated customers fairly. Tappin's Jewelry Store, for example, ran ads in the black press with the headline, "You can Buy With Confidence at Tappin's," along with an endorsement by the CPC. The *Amsterdam News* remained an important ally to the CPC and conducted numerous woman-on-the street interviews about the CPC campaign, reporting that all Harlem women were tired of negotiations and meetings. Those interviewed did not view the boycott and public demonstrations as threats but instead urged the CPC to move forward with their plans; "the sooner it starts, the better," was their frequent response.[29]

Indeed, CPC protests became more radical as the fall wore on. In December they rented a sound truck for use in street meetings. Initially granted a permit for the truck, the police department quickly revoked it, and CPC activists complained that the police were intervening on the side of the UCC. Rumors circulated that "subversive elements in the community" were using the CPC to create tensions in Harlem, but the organization refused to capitulate.[30] As it became apparent the CPC was not going to end its direct action protests, the city government decided to intervene through the Mayor's Committee on Unity (MCU). The MCU, first organized in 1944, included white and black New Yorkers and was the mayor's organization for investigating and managing the city's racial issues. MCU members were initially reluctant to accept the CPC's complaints and argued that Harlem consumers were themselves responsible for whether or not they were cheated. Edith Alexander, the African American Associate Director of the mayor's committee, told the *New York Times*, "persons trained to know quality and to look for it were no worse off in Harlem than elsewhere."[31] In its initial report to Mayor O'Dwyer, the MCU sought to downplay any racial aspect to the high prices, arguing repeatedly, "the issues are not basically interracial," and that Harlemites paid more because they weren't discerning shoppers and because more women worked outside the home, leaving little time for "selective shopping."[32]

But the mayor's committee knew it needed to act and, in late December, succeeded in persuading the CPC to meet with the Uptown Chamber of Commerce and ministers in a series of conferences. The women activists continued their public demonstrations even as they negotiated, arguing, "we intend to continue our siege until we get results."[33] Out of the conferences all parties agreed to a nine-point program. Merchants pledged to conduct fair business practices such as clearly marking prices, identifying product quality, stopping the use of "pullers in," and, when applicable, discontinuing the practice of charging higher prices in Harlem than in their lower Manhattan stores. Additionally, businesses agreed to "cooperate with local—Harlem—newspapers," which meant they would increase their ads in the black press, and they also set up the Harlem Community Chest to funnel donations to civic and charitable groups.[34] Lastly, the negotiations established the Harlem Merchant-Consumer Arbitration Board as a place where shoppers could lodge complaints and receive a hearing. On the board were UCC representatives, community leaders, Pryor, and Edith Alexander of the mayor's committee, who would serve as an impartial chair.[35]

On the whole, the agreement was very similar to the one negotiated between the ministers and the merchants in November, and was the political solution that CPC members denigrated during their street protests.

By holding out, CPC activists pressured the city government into joining them at the negotiating table and guaranteeing a settlement. The CPC's initial reluctance to negotiate was, in part, a tactic designed to strengthen their own position and pressure the MCU to commit its own political capital to the outcome. Both in terms of its sponsorship of the conferences and, more importantly, its agreeing to chair the Harlem Merchant-Consumer Arbitration Board, the mayor's committee became a player in Harlem's consumer struggles. The arbitration board also took a much more active role in consumer issues than the one initially negotiated between the merchants and ministers. Instead of simply mediating problems between individual stores and shoppers, the board sought wider solutions to consumer and economic problems in Harlem. While it was a tremendous gamble, the CPC's willingness to stand up to both the UCC and the ministers also established their own leadership in the community.

Expansion of Consumer Activism

In the wake of their settlement with the MCU and merchants, the CPC once again secured the support of the ministers and for the next fifteen years remained at the forefront of consumer rights activism in Harlem. Throughout its existence the organization would continue as a volunteer group. By February 1948 the CPC reported it had 450 members, at which point it incorporated and set up offices at 217 West 125th Street, immediately launching a membership drive and electing officers. Although most founding members stayed with the group, Flood left in the spring of 1948. The CPC quickly established sub-committees to work on issues such as consumer education, merchant investigations, and consumer rights legislation. CPC members balked at an early suggestion that they merge with another organization such as the National Urban League, but they showed a willingness to work with groups across the political spectrum in Harlem. They worked with black nationalist leaders such as Carlos Cooks and Arthur Reid, the socialist Brotherhood of Sleeping Car Porters, the liberal NAACP, the Urban League, as well as numerous church groups and other civic organizations. That CPC activists or their spouses were often members of these groups made cross-organizational alliances a natural fit for the CPC.

Throughout the postwar era, CPC activists often turned to direct action campaigns to protest unfair selling practices, drive stores to the negotiating table, educate consumers, or support their political lobbying efforts. Their backgrounds as prominent middle-class women gave them social connections and status in the community, but did not prevent them from participating in radical and street-based campaigns. Although these types of protests had, during their founding campaign, left them vulnerable to gendered attacks as dangerous and hysterical women, similar charges were not leveled at them during subsequent direct action efforts. Instead, the CPC was consistently portrayed as an organization of housewives fighting for economic and racial justice for Harlemites. Their willingness to use these direct action tactics demonstrated a comfort with the types of radical protests often avoided by black middle-class women. In her recent study of black women's activism in Durham, North Carolina, historian Christina Greene finds that middle-class women in that community most often left more radical forms of protest to their poor and working-class sisters. In groups such as the United Organizations for Community Improvement, poor black women in Durham organized picket lines, mass meetings, and public demonstrations in their fight for the rights of black tenants, while middle-class women preferred to operate behind the scenes or with less confrontational tactics such as information gathering and negotiation.[36]

In contrast, women were not just rank-and-file activists in CPC protests but organized and led them. Walton Pryor remained the organization's chair and women were most often its public face. Men were part of the organization from its founding, and more joined the CPC in the 1950s and 1960s, working on sub-committees and participating in various consumer rights efforts. Even so, women did not relinquish their dominance or control of the group and assumed most of the public and leadership positions in the organization. In this way the CPC anticipated women's public leadership in civil rights organizing in the 1950s and 1960s. It was not until the mid-1950s that women such as those in the Women's Political Council helped launch and sustain the historical boycott against busing segregation in Montgomery, Alabama. Even then, women's work was visible at all levels of the year-long boycott. Yet, the group to emerge out of this action was the male-dominated Montgomery Improvement Association, led by Dr. Martin Luther King, Jr. As historian Barbara Ransby argues, while African American women had always taken part in radical protests alongside men, it was not until the 1960s, within the Student Nonviolent Coordinating Committee, that women were embraced "as key participants in mass protests and as leaders at the center of the struggle."[37]

Despite their public leadership roles, CPC activists did not call themselves feminist and did not organize specifically on behalf of women's rights. They understood consumption in gendered terms as an area in which women were natural experts, indeed they relied on this assumption to support their public work in the community. They did not, however, consider consumption a women's issue but instead fought for consumer rights in order to achieve economic justice for all black New Yorkers. Although they were not feminist organizers, the public nature of their ongoing fight for consumer rights created a role for themselves as leaders in Harlem's black freedom movement, which places them within the ideology of womanist consciousness described by Alice Walker and Elsa Barkley Brown, among others. In Brown's words, womanism "negates, for black women at least, the public/private dichotomy," and argues that "an expanded role for black women within the black community itself [is] an essential step in the community's fight to overcome the limitations imposed upon the community by the larger society." [38] In this argument black men have the affirmative responsibility to support and encourage women's public work on behalf of the community. When Harlem's ministers failed to do so in 1947, CPC activists demonstrated they would hold men to this standard. So while they drew on a traditional set of assumptions about women's natural expertise as shoppers, they did so to support a non-traditional public leadership role for women.

An important focus for the CPC was its consumer education program, and activists believed knowledgeable shoppers were a key component in maintaining fair business practices for Harlem. The Committee held public events with a wide variety of speakers, such as Sylvia Purrington of the New York State Department of Adult Education, and Sidney Margolis, the consumer editor of the leftist newspaper *P.M.*, who spoke on a study his paper made of consumer problems in Harlem. The CPC also published a bulletin called "Dollar Wise," and arranged for a series of evening consumer education courses held at local high schools. Course topics included "Wise Buying," "Making Over of Old Clothing," and numerous cooking workshops. To support their consumer education programs, the Committee held a large fundraiser each year in the form of a tea and fashion show. This event, which underscored their status as socially prominent middle-class women, was enormously popular and often described as one of the top social events of the seasons. Notices of it ran even in the *Chicago Defender* and *Pittsburgh Courier.*[39]

The CPC's consumer education goals were sometimes aided by street-based demonstrations. In the summer of 1951, the group led a fight against short-weighting, a practice where merchants weighed food products on faulty scales, resulting in overpricing. The CPC set up a scale on 125th street and weighed shoppers' purchases—finding 90 percent of the customers had been short-weighted. Group volunteers distributed leaflets with tips on fraud prevention and Office of Price Stabilization regulations. The following summer CPC activists returned to the streets to again protest short-weighting, and brought with them an inspector from the City Department of Markets to test scales in local grocery stores. Merchants whose scales were inaccurate were issued a summons by the inspector.[40]

The CPC proved particularly adept at working with state and local government agencies. Perhaps because of their success with the Mayor's Committee on Unity, the CPC often turned to government and legal channels for help with consumer issues. During the 1950s, members of its legislative committee testified at government hearings and helped write consumer legislation. CPC activists, especially Pryor, frequently worked with Dr. Persia Campbell, Consumer Counsel to New York's Governor Averell Harriman and a member of his cabinet. Under Campbell's sponsorship, CPC members participated in state-wide conferences and legislative hearings about consumer issues. In 1957 Pryor and Campbell testified before a U.S. Congressional committee about high food prices in Harlem. In that same year, Pryor was named to the New York Attorney General's Division of Consumer Protection, where she helped A.G. Lefkowitz devise his consumer protection legislative agenda.[41]

In 1957 CPC members were the only civic group invited to Governor Harriman's signing of the Retail Installment Sales Act, also known as the All Goods Bill. It was designed to prevent fraud against consumers purchasing on installment plans. The act, which was reported to have been originally drafted by civil rights attorney and CPC member Paul Zuber, set up regulations requiring the full disclosure of all terms and conditions of credit and installment programs. Pryor, Zuber, and William Bowe participated in the legislative hearings and meetings about the issue. Bowe, who would become one of the CPC vice chairs in the 1960s, was also a member of the executive committee of the Brotherhood of Sleeping Car Porters. Upon passage of the All Goods Bill the CPC held street meetings throughout Harlem to educate shoppers about the new law.[42]

The CPC's ability to use direct action protests and political lobbying can be seen in one of its most significant achievements—the campaign to establish a public market in Harlem. For decades individuals and groups had pushed for this market, supporters included Congressman Adam Clayton Powell, New York City Councilman and communist activist Benjamin Davis, and the Urban League of Greater New York. Harlemites wanted the market because it would replace the unregulated and often unsanitary vendor push-carts, which dotted Harlem's streets. Merchants in the public market would be closely monitored by the New York Department of Markets. The CPC, like activists before them, considered the public market a strong step toward ensuring better quality, prices, and shopping conditions for Harlem consumers. Throughout the late 1940s and early 1950s, Mayors William O'Dwyer and Vincent Impelliterri, the City Department of Markets, the Board of Estimate, and the City Planning Commission all failed to deliver on their promises of a market in Harlem. During this time the city repeatedly set aside funds for the land and building but delayed actual construction of the building. In 1948, after its successful founding campaign, the CPC turned its attention to the public market. In 1950 it established a special committee to work for the market, which was spearheaded by Pryor and CPC member Glester Hinds. Hinds was a well-known local activist and the head of the Harlem People's Civic and Welfare Association. He and Pryor worked closely with the Mayor's Committee on Unity (MCU) to ensure creation of the market.[43]

In December 1952 the city government was reportedly ready to again approve a site and funds for the market. However, at the Board of Estimate meeting the United Real Estate Owners Association made a last-minute attempt to block it. Samuel Schachter, the Association's leader, argued that erecting a new building was unnecessary and the city could instead use an existing building at the proposed location. Although Schachter did not argue against a public market to Harlemites, his proposal meant that the original plan was being delayed and altered, and his proposal raised enough questions that the Board of Estimate tabled the vote until January. The *Amsterdam News* argued, "to say that a market should be set up in the old building now on the market site is to reveal that [Schachter] believes that 'any old thing is good enough for Harlem.'... No makeshift will do. Neither should this community lose a modern market because some interests would prefer collecting rent from the city than having the city construct its own building."[44] The Board's decision to postpone its vote outraged black New Yorkers who had for decades endured these types of delays.

The CPC, Mayor's Committee, Urban League of Greater New York, and other local organizations sent representatives to the January 15 meeting of the Board of Estimate. On that day the CPC held a public demonstration and led a police-escorted bus caravan to the Board meeting, where Pryor gave an impassioned speech. She outlined the familiar reasons for wanting a market in Harlem and to these she added what she termed a "by product" of the market: "There is one factor which cannot be measured in dollars. This is the indisputable fact that the market will further race relations and establishing good will in the community since it will be interracial in character."[45] The Board agreed to allocate $500,000 for the market. Unlike previous allocations, this one was carried out and on September 5, 1955, the public market opened on 142nd street and 8th Avenue. The market housed over one hundred stands, which were supervised by the Division of Markets. Mayor Wagner presided over a ribbon-cutting ceremony attended by over 3,000 people. Speakers at the event included city officials and CPC representatives Pryor and Hinds. So while the women-led CPC joined forces with other male-led organizations, they did not give up leadership of the issue, and were publicly acknowledged as the group responsible for the market's establishment.[46]

In addition to education programs and government protection, the CPC never lost sight of its initial mission—monitoring the practices of Harlem's stores. Even after the establishment of the Harlem Merchant-Consumer Arbitration Board in 1948, the CPC knew consumer issues required constant vigilance. When Harlemites had complaints about specific merchants, they could lodge their grievances with the CPC, whose volunteers would then conduct investigations of these issues. In 1953, for example, the organization received numerous complaints about a common business practice in some local appliance stores, referred to as the "blank sales contract racket." Unsuspecting customers would sign a blank conditional sales contract and, after installation of their appliance, find that they had been charged up to 30 percent more for their purchase. The CPC met with local legislators about the practice and worked to publicize the names of guilty companies in order to warn consumers. Throughout the 1950s and 1960s, the organization launched numerous other investigations about practices ranging from grocery store sanitation to discriminatory interest rates charged by General Motors. [47]

In the wake of investigations, the CPC frequently returned to the streets to publicize and protest unscrupulous practices in area stores. In 1949 the CPC accused the Bishop Dress Shop of charging higher prices than advertised, using pullers in, and offering shoddy merchandise. Members picketed and staged a rally outside the store. Referring to the MCU-negotiated settlement of the previous year, Pryor told the press this was the "first phase of our direct action program to force Harlem merchants to our nine-point program."[48] Sometimes the CPC even pushed businesses to go beyond those guarantees. In August 1949 it staged a demonstration in front of the Michigan Furniture Company, one of the largest furniture stores in Harlem. After months of protests and negotiations, the company agreed not only to sign the nine-point pledge, it also lowered service charges for installment purchases and hired an African American accountant, reported to be the first black accountant employed by a white Harlem retailer. In September 1963, the CPC picketed an A&P grocery store on 110th street for "undesirable quality meat, lack of brand name products and vegetables poor in quality and variety."[49] Within the first day of picketing, A&P officials reported a 95 percent drop in business, and they quickly took action to remedy the store's problems. By December CPC activists told the press A&P had improved, "90 per cent. The other 10 per cent we will take care of in due time."[50] Throughout their campaigns, whether based in consumer education, government protection, or direct action protests, they continued to make connections between consumer rights and black equality. In 1961, in language reminiscent of the CPC's founding era, Pryor wrote an open letter in the *Amsterdam News* in which she issued a stern warning to area merchants: "Our organization hopes that it will not ever be necessary again for the women of Harlem to 'hit the bricks' in the cause of economic justice and decency on 125th street. But we just wanted…the merchants of 125th street to know that if such a time comes, we are ready."[51] Having established the legitimacy of their public activism in the late 1940s, the CPC continued to assert this role in throughout the postwar era.[52]

Their activities endeared them to the community, and in 1949 and 1953 Pryor was chosen one of the most popular black New Yorkers in an *Amsterdam News* poll. In 1953 the paper noted that her selection as the sixth "leading Harlemite" was due to her inexhaustible work on local consumer issues.[53] Pryor and other CPC members were also invited to work with local organizations on a variety of issues, a testament to their standing in the community. In 1951 representatives from the CPC were invited to join in a jobs campaign with other area organizations, including the Urban League of Greater New York, the People's Civic and Welfare Association, the Harlem Branches of the YMCA and the YWCA, and the *Amsterdam News*. In so doing, they demonstrated the importance of consumer rights in the lives of black New Yorkers and the extent to which they had effectively wedded those rights with the black freedom movement.

In spite of their popularity and status, by the mid-1960s news of CPC activities waned and after 1966 it fell off the pages of the black press—though it would be mentioned in connection with Walton Pryor and Glester Hinds into the late 1970s. In the 1960s several other consumer rights groups emerged in Harlem, including the Harlem Consumer Education Council run by another local woman. As the Consumers' Protective Committee had replaced local housewives leagues as the prominent consumer rights organization, the Harlem Consumer Education Council may have pushed the CPC out of the public eye. Certainly, by this time, the era's other black freedom movement protests garnered much press and community attention. Whatever the reason for their public decline, CPC activists left a legacy of successful direct action protests, strong female leadership, and the use of consumer activism for achieving economic justice for black New Yorkers.

Notes

Sections of this chapter appeared in earlier form in conference papers and in "The 'Negro Market' and the Black Freedom Movement in New York City, 1930–1965," (Ph.D. dissertation, University of Massachusetts at Amherst, 2006), 188–99. I would like to thank those who commented thoughtfully on these earlier drafts, especially Kathy Peiss, Ula Taylor, Karen Mahar, and June Patton.

1. "Shoppers Ready for the Signal," *New York Amsterdam News*, 15 November 1947, 1.
2. See Dana Frank, *Purchasing Power: Consumer Organizing, Gender, and the Seattle Labor*

Movement, 1919–1929 (Cambridge: Cambridge University Press, 1994); Annelise Orleck, *Common Sense and a Little Fire: Women and Working-Class Politics in the United States, 1900–1965* (Chapel Hill: University of North Carolina Press, 1995); Lizabeth Cohen, *A Consumers' Republic: The Politics of Mass Consumption in Postwar America* (New York: Vintage Books, 1994); Meg Jacobs, *Pocketbook Politics: Economic Citizenship in Twentieth-Century America* (Princeton, NJ: Princeton University Press, 2005).

3. Joanne Meyerowitz, ed., *Not June Cleaver: Women and Gender in Postwar America, 1945–1960* (Philadelphia: Temple University Press, 1994); Daniel Horowitz, *Betty Friedan and the Making of "The Feminine Mystique": The American Left, the Cold War, and Modern Feminism* (Amherst: University of Massachusetts Press, 2000); Anne Enke, *Finding the Movement: Sexuality, Contested Space, and Feminist Activism* (Durham: Duke University Press, 2007); Judith Ezekiel, *Feminism in the Heartland* (Columbus: Ohio State University Press, 2002).

4. Belinda Robnett, *How Long, How Long, African American Women in the Struggle for Civil Rights* (Oxford University Press, 1997). For other works exploring African American women's activism in the black freedom movement see: Pamela E. Brooks, *Boycotts, Buses, and Passes: Black Women's Resistance in the U.S. South and South Africa* (Amherst: University of Massachusetts Press, 2008); Bettye Collier-Thomas and V.P. Franklin, eds., *Sisters in the Struggle: African American Women in the Civil Rights-Black Power Movement* (New York: New York University Press, 2001); Vicki Crawford, Jacqueline Rouse, and Barbara Woods, eds., *Women in the Civil Rights Movement: Trailblazers and Torch Bearers, 1941–1965* (Bloomington: Indiana University Press, 1990); Christina Greene, *Our Separate Ways: Women and the Black Freedom Movement in Durham, North Carolina* (Chapel Hill: The University of North Carolina Press, 2005); Peter J. Ling and Sharon Monteith, *Gender and the Civil Rights Movement* (New York: Garland, 1999); Lynne Olson, *Freedom's Daughters: The Unsung Heroines of the Civil Rights Movement from 1830–1970* (New York: Scribner, 2001); Jeanne Theoharis, Komozi Woodard, Dayo Gore, eds., *Want to Start a Revolution?: Radical Women in the Black Freedom Struggle* (New York: New York University Press, 2009).

5. Cohen, *A Consumers' Republic*, 18.

6. Julius J. Adams, "OPA Opens Harlem Branch to 'Police' Food Prices," *New York Amsterdam News*, 14 August 1942, 11; Office of Price Administration press release, 9 August 1943, Clippings File, Schomburg Center for Research in Black Culture, New York Public Library, New York, New York. Hereafter Schomburg.

7. Adams, 11.

8. Numerous surveys were conducted in Harlem in the 1940s by organizations including the NAACP, National Urban League, and Negro Women, Inc.

9. Uptown Chamber of Commerce Advertisement, *People's Voice*, 14 June 1947, 25.

10. Ads ran in both the *People's Voice* and the *New York Age* throughout the summer of 1947. For more on the UCC campaign see, "125th Street Moving into High Gear in Campaign to Send Values Up, Prices Down," *New York Age*, 14 June 1947; "'Miss 125th Street' And Her Running Mates on the Apollo Stage," *New York Age*, 21 June 1947, 1.

11. "Harlem Women Fight High Prices," *New York Amsterdam News*, 22 October 1947; "Urban League Housing Management Planned," *Chicago Defender*, 18 December 1943; "John and Blanche Eckles Live 'A Happy Song'," *New York Amsterdam News*, 23 April 1966, E-3; "Popular Deb on Honeymoon," *New York Amsterdam News* 1 March 1947, 8.

12. "The Mangums Divorced, Calloways Separated," *Pittsburgh Courier*, 23 October 1965, 1.

13. "Formulate Plans to Fight Education Bias," *New York Amsterdam News*, 17 May 1947; Photo Standalone, *New York Amsterdam News*, 11 July 1942; "Silhouettes in Gay Xmas Program," *New York Amsterdam News* 21 December 1946; "A.K.A.'s Hold Gayest Formal," *New York Amsterdam News* 15 February 1940.

14. "Chinese Disease Toll Put at 10,000,000 in '47," *New York Amsterdam News*, 21 April

1947, 17; photo caption in *Chicago Defender*, 11 June 1949, 18; "Negro Job Watch is Set on Radio-TV," *New York Times*, 19 January 1955, 16; "Committee Pushes Crusade for Jobs," *New York Amsterdam News* 29 January 1930, 11; "Urban League Auxiliary Installs New Officers," *New York Amsterdam News*, 9 April 1930, 4; "Ruth Bushong Installs New Officers, Board," *New York Amsterdam News*, 29 January 1949, 15; "Women's Action and People's Committee to Enlist 10,000," *New York Amsterdam News*, 1 March 1947, 9; "Formulate Plans to Fight Education Bias, *New York Amsterdam News,* 17 May 1947, 20.

15. "Shoppers Hit 'Disservices' of W. 125th," *New York Amsterdam News*, 1 November 1947; "Harlem Stores Picketed," *New York Times*, 23 November 1947.

16. "Shoppers Hit 'Disservices' of W. 125th."

17. Neil Scott to Mayor William F. O'Dwyer, 29 November 1947, Mayor's Committee on Unity Papers, Folder Correspondence Uptown Chamber of Commerce, Box 1613, Municipal Archives, New York, New York. Hereafter MCU Papers.

18. "Mayor's Committee on Unity Report on the 125th Street Controversy," 16 January 1948, City Hall Library, New York, New York; Dan W. Dodson to William O'Dwyer, 25 November 1947, Folder Uptown Chamber of Commerce Correspondence, MCU Papers; Edith Alexander to Dan W. Dodson, 18 December 1947, Folder UCC Correspondence, MCU Papers; "Open Letter to…Consumers Protective Committee," *New York Amsterdam News* 18 October 18, 1947; "Women Demand New Policy in Harlem Stores," *New York Amsterdam News,* 25 October 1947.

19. Consumers' Protective Committee to Dear Reverend, 31 October 1947, Folder Correspondence Uptown Chamber of Commerce, MCU Papers.

20. "Eder Recommends Driving Unfair 125th St. Stores Out of Business," *New York Amsterdam News*, 8 November 1947, 21.

21. "'Down With High Prices': Battle Cry of N.Y. Ministers," *New York Amsterdam News,* 8 November 1947; "Eder Recommends," 1; Edith Alexander to Dan W. Dodson, 22 November 1947, Folder Correspondence Uptown Chamber of Commerce, MCU Papers. Also see, Martha Biondi, *To Stand and Fight: The Struggle for Civil Rights in Postwar New York City* (Cambridge, MA: Harvard University Press, 2003), 89–91; Julie Gallagher, "Women of Action, In Action: The New Politics of Black Women in New York City, 1944–1972" (Ph.D. diss, University of Massachusetts at Amherst, 2003), 37–42. Biondi notes that the CPC employed black nationalist rhetoric in this early stage of the CPC. Carlos Cooks and Arthur Reid also took part in one of the CPC's fall demonstrations, which may have further worried the ministers. Their inclusion, however, is more reflective of the CPC's willingness to work with groups across the political spectrum and not an indication of their own nationalist beliefs. CPC activists had not participated in black nationalist work before their founding campaign, nor did they partner with black nationalist groups in later work.

22. "Powell Denounced 125th Street Picket Campaign As Phony; Plans Own Fight; Endorses Eisenhower," *New York Age*, 10 January 1948, 1. For information on Harlem's three weekly newspapers see Charles Simmons, *The African American Press* (Jefferson, NC: McFarland & Company, 1998); Armistead S. Pride and Clint C. Wilson, *A History of the Black Press* (Washington, D.C.: Howard University Press, 1997); Roland Wolseley, *The Black Press, U.S.A,* 2nd ed. (Ames: Iowa State University Press, 1990); Vishnu Oak, *The Negro Entrepreneur* (Yellow Springs, OH: Antioch Press, 1948).

23. "Leading Citizens Express Views on Consumers Protective Comm. Plans; Warns Against Picketing," *New York Age*, 15 November 1947, 1.

24. Ibid.; "Ministers Rescind Endorsement of CPC, Name Own Committee to Meet with 125th St. Merchants," *New York Age*, 15 November 15 1947.

25. "Leading Citizens Express Views."

26. "Harlem Business Men Ask Price Control," *People's Voice*, 15 November 1947; "Harlem Committee Gets Promise of Probe in High Prices at Uptown Launderettes," *New York Age,*

22 November 1947; "Uptown C of C Sets Up Board for Mediation," *People's Voice*, 6 December 1947; "Merchants Adopt Code of Ethics After Meeting With Ministers; Mayor Orders 2 Depts to Act," *New York Age*, 29 November 1947, 1.

27. "Some Stores Rival Hall's 40 Thieves in Grab for Money," *New York Amsterdam News*, 22 November 1947, 1.

28. "Newspaper Ad Exposes 125th Street Merchant," *New York Amsterdam News*, 29 November 1947, 1.

29. "Shoppers Ready for the Signal." Tappin's advertisement appeared in the *New York Amsterdam News* beginning December 13.

30. Edith Alexander to Dan W. Dodson, 22 November 1947.

31. "Harlem Store Row Goes to City Body," *New York Times*, 24 December 1947, 9.

32. Edith Alexander to Dan W. Dodson, 22 November 1947, MCU Papers; "Mayor's Committee on Unity Report on 125th Street Controversy."

33. "'Confession' Puts Gyp Stores on Spot," *New York Amsterdam News*, 27 December 1947, 1.

34. "Ethics Code Set Up By Harlem Stores," *New York Times*, 28 January 1948, 39.

35. "'Confession' Puts Gyp Stores on Spot," "Harlem Merchants Will Get Emblems," *New York Amsterdam News*, 26 June 1948.

36. "Harlem Consumers Group Incorporated," *Pittsburgh Courier*, 20 March 1948; Mayor's Committee on Unity Meeting Minutes, 9 February 1948, MCU Papers, Folder Notices of Meetings; Walton Pryor to Edith Alexander, 4 June 1948, MCU Papers, Folder Correspondence Uptown Chamber of Commerce. For further discussions of class and black women's activism see Greene, *Our Separate Ways*; Brooks, *Boycotts, Buses, and Passes*.

37. Barbara Ransby, *Ella Baker and the Black Freedom Movement: A Radical Democratic Vision* (Chapel Hill: University of North Carolina Press, 2003), 292. For a recent examination of the Women's Political Council in Montgomery see Brooks, *Boycotts, Buses, and Passes*.

38. Elsa Barkley Brown, "Womanist Consciousness: Maggie Lena Walker and the Independent Order of Saint Luke," *Signs* (Spring 1989): 610–33. On black women's feminism also see Pamela E. Brooks; Patricia Hill Collins, *Black Feminist Thought: Knowledge, Consciousness, and the Politics of Empowerment*, (New York: Routledge, 1991); Ula Y. Taylor, *The Veiled Garvey: The Life and Times of Amy Jacques Garvey* (North Carolina: University of North Carolina Press, 2002); Anne M. Valk, *Radical Sisters: Second-Wave Feminism and Black Liberation in Washington, D.C.* (Urbana: University of Illinois Press, 2008); Theoharis, Woodard, and Gore.

39. "Consumers Group Launches Organizational Campaign, Elects First Officers and Board," *New York Amsterdam News*, 27 March 1948; "Buyer Group Hears Consumer Specialist," *New York Amsterdam News*, 15 May 1948; "Consumers' Protective Committee to Hold Annual Tea and Beauty Show," *New York Amsterdam News*, 25 September 1948; "Top Models Will Spotlight CPC Show at Riviera Terrace," *New Pittsburgh Courier*, 20 October 1962.

40. "Find Weight Cheats Still Rob Shoppers," *New York Amsterdam News*, 28 July 1951; "Big Harlem 'Gyps'!," *New York Amsterdam News*, 28 July 1951; "Try Scales for Weight," *New York Amsterdam News*, 31 May 1952.

41. Persia Campbell to Miss Jean Blackwell, 14 November 1957, Schomburg Clippings File, Consumer Market: 1955–1957; House Subcommittee on Consumers of the Committee on Agriculture, *Food Marketing Costs*, 85th Congress, 1st session, 1957, 8 and 9 October 1957, 3–17; "Lefkowitz names 16," *New York Times*, 17 December 1957; "Harlem Consumers, Businessmen to Meet," *New York Amsterdam News*, 4 October 1958; "Consumer Group Meeting Friday," *New York Amsterdam News*, 20 December 1958; "Consumer Conference to Be Held," *New York Amsterdam News*, 30 December 1961. Like the progressive-era African American women studied by Glenda Gilmore, CPC activists were "ambassadors" to the government on behalf of the black community. Unlike the women in Gilmore's study, however, they did not do so in a context of political disfranchisement for black men. See

Glenda Gilmore, *Gender and Jim Crow: Women and the Politics of White Supremacy in North Carolina, 1896 – 1920* (Chapel Hill: University of North Carolina Press, 1996)

42. "Consumers Group Sees Bill Signed," *New York Amsterdam News,* 18 May 1957; "Harlem Learns About Sales Act," *New York Amsterdam News,* 16 November 1957; "CPC Prepares Program on Consumer Education," *New York Amsterdam News,* 1 March 1958.

43. "Harlem Gets Ready for Market Fight," *New York Amsterdam News,* 10 January 1953.

44. "Public Market a Must," *New York Amsterdam News,* 27 December 1952, 14.

45. Consumers' Protective Committee Press Release, 15 January 1953, Folder Public Market, MCU Papers.

46. "Harlem Gets Ready for Market Fight"; "Harlem Market Opened by Mayor," *New York Times,* 8 September 1955.

47. "Launch Campaign Against Unfair Appliance Co.'s," *New York Amsterdam News,* 12 February 1955; "Sweet Talk and Fast Money," *New York Amsterdam News,* 12 February 1955; "Solon to Address Consumer Group," *New York Amsterdam News,* 12 February 1955; "GM Story Stirs Consumers Probe," *New York Amsterdam News,* 21 November 1953; "Charge Auto Loan Rates are Illegal," *New York Amsterdam News,* 28 November 1953.

48. "CPC Pickets Store for Its 'Pulling' Act," *New York Amsterdam News,* 23 April 1949, 1.

49. "Ex-Pickets of A&P Say: Store Improved 90%," *New Pittsburgh Courier,* 7 December 1963.

50. Ibid.

51. "Mrs. Pryor Hits 125th St. Merchants," *New York Amsterdam News,* 16 April 1961.

52. Carl Lawrence, "Merchants Rob Harlemites: Rotten Food, High Prices Take Huge Weekly Toll," *New York Amsterdam News,* 25 November 1950; "Consumer Committee Gets New Agreement," *New York Amsterdam News,* 7 January 1950.

53. "Willie Bryant Again Wins Leaders' Poll — Glester Hinds Second," *New York Amsterdam News,* 31 January 1953.

CHAPTER 8

"Pregnant? Need Help? Call Jane"

Service as Radical Action in the Abortion Underground in Chicago

REBECCA M. KLUCHIN

"Pregnant? Need Help? Call Jane. 643-3844." Chicago women saw this cryptic advertisement in underground newspapers in the late 1960s and early 1970s. Jane was the code name for a feminist underground service that performed over 11,000 illegal abortions between 1969 and 1973.[1] Group members were housewives, teachers, students, secretaries, social workers, and community organizers between roughly twenty and forty years old. They were not doctors or nurses. They had no formal medical training whatsoever.

Criminalized in the late nineteenth century, abortion went underground for most of the twentieth until the Supreme Court legalized the procedure (in the first two trimesters) with the landmark decision *Roe v. Wade* in 1973. Criminalizing abortion did not stop women from having abortions; it simply made it more difficult and dangerous for them to do so. In the 1960s, feminists rallied together to demand the legalization of the controversial procedure. Some lobbied state legislatures, others filed lawsuits and staged protests. A few established their own underground referral services. Jane began as part of this last trend, but evolved into an independent abortion provider. In the process, it developed a distinct type of activism premised upon the provision of service and specific to the abortion underground.

Like other radical activists of the era, including those involved in the Student Non-Violent Coordinating Committee (SNCC), the Black Panther Party (BPP), and the Chicago Women's Liberation Union (CWLU), Jane members strove to instigate social change through direct action tactics and service programs, the latter of which often involved the creation of alternative institutions. Direct action was a founding tenet of the civil rights movement and the New Left. SNCC, the BPP, and the CWLU paired direct action with the creation of alternative institutions in communities in which they organized. SNCC, for example, created Freedom Schools in the summer of 1964 to replace shoddy public schools in poor black Mississippi communities, and to empower those it served to confront the institutions and laws that denied them citizenship rights.

Most radical activists of the era viewed direct action and service as complementary and tended to value the former over the latter. This value was often gendered. Men in the civil rights and New Left movements celebrated the dangers direct action tactics carried and used their masculinity to claim these assignments. During SNCC's Freedom Summer, for example, women disproportionately assumed service roles as teachers in Freedom Schools, community librarians, and office workers, and often were excluded from more dangerous activities like driving.[2] When the women's liberation movement emerged from the civil rights and New Left movements, many feminists continued to value direct action over service. The CWLU described its direct action programs as designed "to make *concrete changes* [emphasis added] in the institutions that affect our everyday lives," and its service programs as designed "to make women's lives better by *helping to meet their needs now* [emphasis added]."[3] This preference for direct action over service reflected activists' participation in the civil rights movement as well as a long history of women's exclusion from leadership roles in social movements, and their struggle to gain rights when they lacked access to major political institutions. Historically, much of women's activism has involved service and charity. Denied citizenship rights, early American women activists developed voluntary organizations that did not upset conventional gender norms.[4] Throughout the nineteenth century, women involved in moral reform, temperance and abolitionism drew upon gender specific ideas of "morality and compassion" to advance their causes, deliberately separating themselves from male activists when they entered the political arena in an effort to shield themselves from criticism.[5] The beginning of the suffrage movement in 1848 brought the "woman question" into public debate, but many suffragists continued to couch their demands for political rights in the language of maternalism and women's inherent difference from men.[6] Forty years after winning the right to vote, feminists rejected the politics of maternalism and sought equality with men on their own terms. They were not interested in subverting gender norms as their predecessors had, they wanted to destroy them. In this context, for many feminists, service activism absent direct action represented the constraints of sexism and marked women as caretakers and charity workers whose labor improved the lives of those they served but lacked the ability to challenge the structures that created inequality.

Jane was a workgroup of the CWLU, but its members did not agree with the distinction between direct action and service because for them, direct action and service were inseparable. Women came to Jane pregnant and left not pregnant.[7] Through the provision of safe, affordable abortions, Jane changed thousands of women's lives and raised the consciousness of many in the process. Jane members took direct action by providing a service.

Service activism fit the goals of Jane and the specific issues it addressed. Unwanted pregnancies require immediate intervention. A woman carrying an unwanted pregnancy in 1969 could not wait for the Supreme Court to legalize abortion in 1973 (nor would she have known that this decision would come down when it did). A sit-in or demonstration could call attention to the problem of unwanted pregnancies and the risks associated with underground abortions, but it could not resolve a woman's problem like an abortion could. Hundreds of thousands of women disobeyed the law every year and sought underground abortions while an untold number of others tried to induce their own abortions. All did so at great risk to their lives and health. Jane, or the Service as its members called it, responded to an immediate need by creating an alternative medical system in the abortion underground that provided women with safe, affordable abortions.[8]

The Service functioned as part of the larger women's health movement, which aimed to educate women about their bodies, redistribute the power between physicians and women, and establish woman-centered health care institutions.[9] But the clandestine nature of its work combined with its members' preference for action over ideology set Jane apart from other feminist health activists of the era. Through its mobile abortion clinic, the Service subverted and undermined the existing medical model by seizing control of abortion from physicians, the only experts actually licensed to perform the surgery, and returning the practice of abortion to lay women trained outside of organized medicine. This model rejected contemporary healthcare practices, sliced away hierarchies, and placed women undergoing abortion at the center of the system. Some Janes saw their work as harkening back to an earlier era when women relied on midwives to practice reproductive medicine in homes rather than hospitals and clinics.[10]

The illegal nature of abortion provision pre-*Roe* was critical to this radical reconstruction of health care. Operating outside the law, the Service was not subject to health codes, institutional protocol, or other mechanisms of medical control or legal regulation. The criminal nature of abortion care granted Service members unprecedented freedom to develop a feminist health care institution on their own terms. Notably, the system they created was guided by a service provision rather than a specific political philosophy. Jane members' politics ranged from moderately liberal to very radical, but the lack of a shared political perspective rarely caused conflict within the group because of its emphasis on action. "No matter how much people had different politics...it could never matter because ultimately you had to do the abortion," one Jane recalled.[11]

Other reproductive rights activists established illegal clinics, most notably Margaret Sanger in the 1910s and Estelle Griswold in the 1960s, but Jane was distinct in that it intended to provide reproductive healthcare alongside organized medicine whereas other activists opened clinics in order to challenge reproductive policies. When Sanger opened her first clinic in 1916, for example, she did not supply women with the diaphragms with which she fit them. Service members were not interested in changing public policy because they believed that legalization of abortion would not make the procedure available to all women, nor would it fundamentally change the practice of reproductive medicine in America. Like Sanger, Service members believed that women could not achieve equality until they gained control over their reproductive decisions.[12] Unlike Sanger and Griswold, Service members refused to work within the medical and legal systems that they believed perpetuated racial, sexual, and socioeconomic inequalities. Instead of lobbing, suing, and demonstrating, they created their own medical system and provided abortions on their own terms.

The Association to Repeal Abortion Laws (ARAL) created by Patricia Maginnis in 1966, is perhaps the closest organization to Jane. Maginnis and ARAL ran an abortion referral service in California that openly circulated a list of illegal providers in Mexico. Historian Leslie J. Reagan argues that ARAL "was a forerunner of the women's health movement" that developed a philosophy of reproductive freedom which subsequent activists, including Jane members, adopted.[13] Like the Service, ARAL created an alternative institution in the underground. Although it did not perform abortions, it referred thousands of women to safe providers. ARAL members inspected the clinics on their list, "licensed" those of which they approved, and instructed women seeking abortions to request to view these certifications before agreeing to the transaction.[14] ARAL and Jane employed similar tactics to reduce the cost of abortions; they offered abortionists a high volume of patients in exchange for a reduction of the price of each procedure. Both groups understood that in order to ensure the safety of women who relied on them for referrals, they had to regulate the abortionists they used. They conducted follow-up interviews with the women they served and stopped referring women to providers who received poor reviews. Yet Jane went one step further than ARAL and seized control of the abortion process.

Some CWLU members doubted Jane's potential to create social change and referred to the Service as a "Band-Aid" organization, suggesting that members constituted a collective of charity workers who "patched up" some problems, but lacked the ability to solve them.[15] Service members disagreed with this criticism on the grounds that the service they provided fundamentally changed the lives of thousands of women.[16] Not only did they help these women terminate their pregnancies safely, they also specifically intended for the alternative medical system they created to raise women's consciousness and encourage them to demand that their legitimate medical providers grant them the same power and respect that the Service did. Jane redefined the abortion experience by demedicalizing the space in which abortions occurred, allowing women to control the pace of the procedure, and reducing the cost of abortion to whatever a woman could pay. Service members hoped that women who experienced woman-centered healthcare would demand the same treatment from their legitimate providers and in this way, instigate grassroots social change.

Early Years

The Service has a two-part history. In its first phase, between 1965 and 1969, Heather Tobis Booth, a white student at the University of Chicago, provided an informal abortion referral service to students on campus. A veteran of SNCC's Freedom Summer, Booth became involved in abortion referral after a fellow activist's sister asked for her help locating an abortionist. Using her movement contacts, Booth found a black physician and civil rights activist, Dr. T.R.M. Howard, on Chicago's South Side willing to perform the surgery.[17] Gradually, word of her contact spread beyond the campus and throughout the Midwest, and Booth began to include a brief counseling session along with her referral. By 1968, women's requests for referrals increased to several a week. This was more than Booth could balance with her recent marriage, pregnancy, new commitment to graduate school, and existing commitment to the civil rights, New Left, and feminist movements. Unwilling to abandon her project, but also unable to continue it herself, Booth recruited women from organizations in which she was already involved to continue her work. She led discussions about the relationship between abortion and feminism, shared her counseling techniques, passed on her doctor contacts, and left the group.[18] Early in 1969, four women formally established Jane, or the Abortion Counseling Service. This began the second phase of the Service's history, which ran from 1969 to the 1973, when *Roe v. Wade* was decided. The Service grew to include about twenty to thirty active members by fall 1970 and membership stayed constant around this level through 1973.[19]

Chicago was a center of feminist organizing during the 1960s and 1970s. The city hosted a myriad of feminist groups, including chapters of the National Organization for Women (NOW) and women's liberation groups like the CWLU. Betty Friedan, founder of NOW, and her colleagues practiced what scholars refer to as a liberal feminism, meaning that they sought to include women within existing institutions and claim equality this way. They did not challenge political, economic, and social systems themselves; instead, they sought equal access to them. Liberal feminists tended to be older and more conservative than women's liberationists, whose movement for sexual equality grew out of their experiences with the civil rights and New Left movements.[20] Women's liberationists insisted that the existing systems perpetuated racial, sexual, and socioeconomic inequality and therefore had to be overturned before women could experience true equality with men. They developed two distinct political philosophies: radical feminism and socialist feminism. Radical feminists placed sex above race and class when they analyzed women's roles in society, viewing economic and racial structures as products of patriarchy, which they deemed the most oppressive system in American society. In contrast, socialist feminists believed that sexual equality needed to be understood in the context of American capitalism and race relations.[21] Liberal, radical and socialist feminists participated in the women's health movement, a movement within the feminist movement that challenged male medical authority over women's health care, especially reproductive health issues.[22]

Action-oriented Jane culled members from all three feminist perspectives. Its founder, Heather Tobis Booth, situated herself at the forefront of Chicago's women's liberation movement. Not long after she began to provide abortion referrals, she helped to form Women's Radical Action Project (WRAP), a women's group at the University of Chicago, and a few years later became a founding member of the Westside Group, one of the nation's first women's liberation groups.[23] Booth was also a founding member of the CWLU, established over Halloween weekend in 1969. Notable for its size, ambition, and socialist feminist politics, the CWLU was an umbrella organization of more than two hundred dues paying members that was premised upon the notion that the combination of service, direct action, and education could instigate social change.[24] The CWLU addressed a range of feminist issues including education, women's health, lesbian rights, and employment rights and contained a graphics collective, rape crisis hotline, a legal aid clinic, pregnancy testing center, a monthly newsletter, and a liberation school.[25] A Jane member attended the CWLU inaugural retreat and the Service became loosely affiliated with the CWLU, which in turn became an important source of referrals.[26]

The legalization of abortion was one of the first issues that white feminists of all politics tackled, but they were not the first abortion rights activists. Efforts to reform abortion laws began in the 1950s when a minority of physicians and other public health professionals began to question hospital restrictions on therapeutic (medically indicated) abortions. At a 1955 conference organized by Planned Parenthood, these professionals discussed reforming hospital abortion policies in order "to free physicians from the restrictions of laws and committees and to eliminate the sense that providing therapeutic abortions was a shady, disreputable business."[27] In 1959, legal professionals entered the debate when the American Law Institute (ALI) proposed a model abortion law that liberalized restrictive hospital abortion policies by expanding indications for surgery to include physical and mental health issues, fetal complications, and pregnancies that resulted from rape and incest. Notably, neither group attempted to increase women's ability to choose abortion. Instead, they strove to establish physicians' ability to perform therapeutic abortions without controversy.[28] In the subsequent decade, population controllers and feminists added their voices to national conversations about the reform of abortion laws. Among population control groups, Zero Population Growth (ZPG) was especially active. Chicago hosted at least ten local ZPG chapters, most of which were based in universities.[29]

Chicago's vibrant feminist culture caused the city to become a hub of abortion rights organizing. In addition to the CWLU, Jane, and ZPG, the National Abortion Rights Action League (NARAL) was founded in the city in 1969 at a conference organized by abortion rights activists Lawrence Lader and Lonny Myers, and attended by Betty Friedan. Chicago clergy led by Rev. Spencer Parsons, Dean of the University of Chicago's Rockefeller Chapel, also involved themselves in abortion referral. Parsons formed the Chicago Clergy Consultation Service (CCS) in 1969, part of a national network of clergy that provided abortion referrals for women who could travel to England, Japan, Mexico, and Puerto Rico, where abortion was legal and/or available.[30] Parsons "used the Jane service quite a bit" between 1966 and 1969, before formally establishing his own referral program.[31] He continued to use Jane after founding the Chicago CCS when women who contacted him lacked the financial resources to travel abroad.[32]

The CWLU articulated its support for the repeal of laws criminalizing abortion in a position paper titled, "Free Abortion is Every Woman's Right" in which it declared that women could not gain equal rights until they gained access to safe, legal abortions.[33] CWLU activists employed direct action tactics to reinforce this point and to make clear that they believed that "one of woman's most basic freedoms is her right to control her own body and to determine if she bears a child."[34] They held speak-outs, in which women shared their experiences with illegal abortion publically in order to remove the shame associated with abortion and expose the dangers illegal abortions held. They also staged protests and demonstrations and participated in street theater.[35]

In the only public document the Service produced, a pamphlet titled, "Abortion: A Woman's Decision, A Woman's Right," the group insisted on a common feminist theme: women's liberation depended upon reproductive freedom. "Women should have the right to control their own bodies and lives. Only a woman who is pregnant can determine whether she has enough resources—economic, physical and emotional—at a given time to bear and rear a child," it maintained. It then urged women to free themselves by challenging the laws and norms that demeaned and debased women and uniting to create change. "It is time for women to get together to change the male-made laws and to aid their sisters caught in the bind of legal restrictions and social stigma," the Service declared.[36]

The Service was in its referral form when it published this pamphlet—no Service member had considered performing an abortion herself when writing it—and yet the idea that women must work together to transform institutions of oppression undergirds this document. Although Jane began as a referral service, from the beginning, its members aimed to upend existing medical and legal practices that prevented women from making their own reproductive decisions.[37] This reflects the radical nature of the organization. Notably, this document identified the ways in which abortion affected women of color and poor women differently than it did their white middle-class sisters, something that many other white abortion rights activists took a few more years to recognize.[38]

Although the Service developed in the context of existing abortion rights organizations, it existed on the margins of organized feminism. This outsider status played a critical role in the development of its distinct service activism by immunizing the group from feminist conflicts over tactics, strategies, and politics, and leaving its members free to develop an independent service organization without ideological constraints. Women from across the Left joined Jane because it was action-oriented. "Politics doesn't matter," a Service member declared, "what matters is action and service."[39]

Despite the diversity of political perspectives, most Janes were white, college-educated wives and mothers living on the South Side of Chicago. Half were between twenty and thirty years old, and they ranged in socioeconomic status from poor to upper-middle class.[40] Their roles as wives and mothers shaped their perspective on feminist issues and distinguished them from other feminists, many of who were single and childless. These Janes understood what it meant to be a mother and the consequences of an unplanned pregnancy. These understandings drew them to the Service.

One Jane had become pregnant at age twenty and was rushed into marriage by her family. "I think that for me was a very radicalizing thing to be forced into motherhood," she explained.[41] Another Jane struggled with infertility and her efforts to become a mother shaped her abortion politics. "I identified with those on the other side who didn't want to be pregnant," she stated. "I felt they should have the same control over their bodies that I needed."[42] Some Service members' own experience with underground abortion motivated them to join the group and to provide other women with the safety, affordability, and dignity they and their friends had been denied.[43] When the Service began to provide abortions, it found that some women who came through the Service were so moved by their experiences that they joined the group.

Many women joined Jane because the work accommodated their childcare responsibilities in a way that other feminist activities did not.[44] Members counseled women at their own homes while they cared for their children, folded the laundry, and prepared dinner. As the Service expanded, the demographics of the group changed; more younger, childless women became counselors and a few became directly involved in abortion provision. When the Service began to pay its most active members, some childless women quit their day jobs and began working full time alongside the mothers.[45] Yet, even as membership changed to accommodate younger activists, Jane remained a group led by mothers and shaped by the politics of their experiences in this role.

As the women Booth recruited assumed responsibility of the Service and grew more experienced negotiating with underground abortionists, they determined that in order to really change women's abortion experience they needed to gain control over the physicians they employed. Service member Laura Kaplan recalls in her collective memoir of the group, "It wasn't enough to locate and refer women to competent doctors willing to perform abortions. The group had to be able to call the shots and make demands."[46] Underground abortion entailed numerous risks including botched procedures that caused hemorrhage, organ perforation, and infection, among other things. Some abortions failed, others were faked by con artists; women lacked recourse in both instances. Those who sought medical assistance for injuries caused by illegal abortions faced harsh interrogation and threats of non-treatment if they did not reveal the name of their abortionist. Not surprisingly, most women avoided doctors and hospitals whenever possible, and sometimes those who sought admittance did so too late to receive the medical attention they desperately needed. Jane experienced one such fatality. A woman came to them severely infected as a result of previous abortion attempts. The Janes who attended her told her that she was very sick and needed immediate medical attention and refused to perform her scheduled abortion. One day later she went to the hospital, but it was too late. She died from complications of an abortion that pre-dated her visit to Jane by at least a week.[47]

Some abortionists demanded payment and sexual favors from clients. One of the few black women active in Jane recalled accompanying her roommate to an illegal abortion. The abortionist was drinking when they arrived, demanded sex from one or both of the women before he began the procedure, and prevented them from leaving when they refused. This Jane called the police—a bold move given her illegal activity—but when the police arrived the abortionist paid the officers to leave. Luckily, the women managed to escape during this transaction.[48] In contrast to these underground nightmares, the Service intended to connect women with competent abortionists who treated them respectfully and provided safe procedures. They persuaded one of their regular contacts to allow a few members to observe his work and later assist him. Access to the abortion process gave the group the control it sought, but it also created a hierarchy of knowledge and power.

The Service developed two types of members: those who counseled women and those who participated in abortion provision. The few women who participated in abortions held more knowledge and thus more power in the group and constituted what Kaplan refers to as the "inner circle."[49] When women in the inner circle entered the abortion room, they learned that one abortionist was not a doctor as he had claimed. Seeking profit, this man's brother had apprenticed him to a physician who taught him to perform safe abortions, and he began his own practice in the underground that generated income for himself, his brother, and his brother's girlfriend. Most members of the inner circle were not bothered by the abortionist's lack of official medical credentials. Their underground dealings taught them that the best abortionists were those with the most experience, which ruled out most physicians.[50] One Jane explained, "Doctors didn't know how to do abortions, because they were illegal. They never did them. The only people who did them and really perfected the skill... as a medical specialty, were the illegal abortionists."[51] The revelation that their primary abortionist was not a physician empowered those in the inner circle to enter the realm of abortion provision themselves.[52] "If he can do abortions," one Service member realized, "we can do abortions."[53] The male abortionist trained one Service member to perform abortions, and she taught four other members the same skill. By early 1972, Jane had transformed from an abortion referral service dependent upon male abortionists to a self-sufficient, women-run abortion clinic that provided between sixty and ninety abortions per week.[54]

The Service did not want to perpetuate the trend in organized medicine and the underground that granted women with financial resources greater reproductive freedom than those without. Once in control of the abortion process, the Service lowered the price from $500 to $100, but because it accepted whatever a woman could pay, the average cost of a Jane abortion was $50.[55] Here again, Jane did more than "just" provide a service; it created what it believed to be a fair and equitable healthcare system that did not discriminate against poor women and women of color as the existing medical system did. In the 1960s, some states liberalized their therapeutic abortion policies to allow these procedures in cases when pregnancy threatened a woman's physical and/or mental health. These new laws increased white middle- and upper-class women's access to surgery, as these women had the resources and connections to locate a psychiatrist willing to declare them mentally unstable and unable to carry a pregnancy to term, but they did not increase poor women's (especially women of color) access to abortion.[56] Changes to therapeutic abortion laws further reproduced the inequities of reproductive medicine as women with resources gained greater access to safer, legal surgeries while poor women remained dependent upon the underground.

In 1970, New York State legalized abortion, making access to the procedure more equitable for local women, but repeating the same inequities for those who needed to travel to the state to receive care. Women from Chicago (and other states) could fly to New York and undergo a legal abortion, but the total cost of the trip and surgery equaled the cost of an underground procedure, making it accessible to women with financial resources but not those without them. Jane's clientele changed considerably after New York changed its abortion policy. Increasingly, Jane clients were poor women, especially women of color, who lacked the resources necessary to travel to New York to undergo a legal abortion and who also lacked the funds to purchase a full price black market abortion in Chicago.[57] By reducing the cost of abortion dramatically and accepting whatever women could pay—including jars of coins—Jane equalized the cost of abortion and granted poor women the same access to the procedure as middle and upper-class women.[58] In 1972, the Service evaluated its safety record using data collected by a friendly physician who performed free follow-up exams the group. The results indicated that Jane had the same low complication rate as legal clinics in New York.[59]

Creating an Alternative Institution in the Abortion Underground

The Service viewed itself as an alternative to the medical system and its members as pioneers of a new type of medical industry governed by laywomen and emphasizing patient participation. A Jane explained, "The contrast was not a back alley. The contrast was regular meds…We were an alternative to the medical system which was not providing the health services that women need."[60] Jane's alternative medical system went beyond providing abortions to include preventative care. Counselors offered birth control advice, abortionists took pap smears, and members of the inner circle created a formal follow-up program whereby the Service paid a sympathetic physician to perform post-abortion exams for its patients.[61]

The need to maintain secrecy led Service members to develop a mobile abortion clinic, the location of which changed each of the three days a week it operated. Women waiting for abortions, along with their supportive friends and relatives, and sometimes children, congregated at what was called the Front, usually a Jane member's living room or dorm room. The Front was run by a least one, often two, Jane counselors who were responsible for checking women in, reviewing aftercare information, and informally counseling women who had concerns and questions about their abortions. They provided childcare for Jane clients and counseled women's husbands and boyfriends while they waited anxiously for their loved ones to return from their procedures. The Front functioned as a security system that created a "barrier between the police and the abortionists."[62] Every clinic day, the inner circle designated a driver to transport four to five women at a time from the Front to the Place, which was the apartment or home where abortions were performed. The driver collected money during this transition. Both the Front and the Place changed daily, so as not to attract attention.[63]

Jane purposefully constructed Fronts and Places against traditional medical spaces. Instead of barren white waiting rooms with hard chairs and boring magazines, the Front was someone's home. People at the Front watched television, ate cookies, drank tea and coffee, read magazines and books, and if they were children, played with donated toys. Service members tried to create a comfortable environment that put women at ease before their surgery. Kaplan writes that Jane members "hoped the Front would be different from a doctor's waiting room where people felt isolated from each other. They wanted the people at the Front to understand that they were active participants, not passive receivers of a service."[64] Service members reinforced this interdependence through their language. They talked about women "coming through" the Service rather than "to" it and referred to the women who sought them out as counselees rather than clients or patients. The first Service member to perform an abortion rejected the term "patient" because she believed it objectified women. Instead, she viewed the women whose abortions she performed as "partners in political activities—partners in crime, to be exact."[65] She and other abortionists referred to themselves and to assistants as "paramedics," deliberately classifying these positions as equal in order to undermine any sort of hierarchy that could be built based upon medical knowledge.[66] Abortionists and assistants shared the work during each procedure in order to "break down impressions of individual status." The abortionist held the woman's hand while the assistant prepared her for the abortion. The Janes switched places when the abortion began and the assistant comforted the patient while the abortionist worked.[67]

The Service rented apartments to use as Places. Seeking to replace physicians' sterile operating rooms with a warm alternative, Service members decorated these apartments with women's liberation posters, donated furniture, and furniture they bought at thrift stores.[68] At the Place, two abortionists and two assistants concurrently performed abortions in separate bedrooms decorated with loud, colorful sheets and Indian print bedspreads.[69] Abortionists and assistants wore jeans and t-shirts, signaling the informality of their clinic space and their lack of legitimate medical expertise. While many women seeking abortions accepted these signals, others felt unnerved by them. In an interview decades after her abortion with Jane, one woman remained upset that her abortionist did not wear a nurse's uniform. (Note that she expected the female abortionist to be a nurse, not a doctor.) Instead, her abortionist wore a flannel shirt and jeans and did not tie her long hair back in a ponytail when she performed the procedure. The lack of a legitimate medical atmosphere unnerved this woman, but made other women feel comfortable.[70]

While Jane rejected traditional medical spaces and provider/patient dynamics, it generally followed established medical protocol, with the exception of wearing surgical scrubs, as noted above. Abortionists and assistants sterilized all their surgical equipment, changed and cleaned the bedding between patients. When operating, Jane abortionists used Xylocaine to numb the cervix, Ergotrate to prevent bleeding, and sent women home with a week's supply of tetracycline to prevent infection, just as legal physicians did. Jane obtained these drugs from a sympathetic pharmacist who agreed to supply the group with the drugs it needed as long as it promised to "soak the labels off the bottles so they could not be traced back to him."[71] Posing as physicians, Service members purchased the other medical supplies they used including, curettes, forceps, dilators, sponges, gauze, and sterilizing trays, from local medical supply companies.[72]

Education played a critical role in the Service's agenda for social change. Service members believed that educating women about their bodies empowered them to challenge medical and legal restrictions on their reproductive decision-making. "Women educated about their bodies could," Kaplan maintains, "ask intelligent questions, demand answers, and refuse treatment. They were less likely to be mistreated by the medical profession."[73] Counselors distributed copies of *The Birth Control Handbook* and *Our Bodies, Ourselves* and offered women extra copies to give to their friends so that they could share knowledge about their bodies with other women. Service members hoped that after making an informed decision about abortion, the women who came through Jane would make other similar decisions and that, collectively, these decisions could change medical practice.

In most formal medical relationships, patients depended upon physicians and submitted themselves to their professional authority. In Jane, the relationship between abortionists and their partners was far more interdependent and fluid; women who came through the Service worked in tandem with their abortionists. Jane abortionists required women take an active role in their procedures. They insisted that women remain awake during their surgeries and administered only local anesthesia. In part this reflected a concern about the possibility of drug allergies and drug interactions, but it also reflected the group's belief that women should be in control of their bodies during the procedure.[74]

Patients controlled the pace of the surgery. Those who wanted the abortionist to pause for a few minutes need only ask. Those who wanted to stand up and stretch their legs in the middle of the procedure could do so, which was possible because Jane did no use gynecological stirrups. The only things women could not do during their abortion were scream, because this would draw attention to the clandestine clinic, and squirm, as this could compromise the surgery.[75] Abortionists and assistants insisted on explaining the abortion procedure to women while it was occurring. Sometimes women told Jane members that they did not want to know what was happening. Their requests were refused. One Jane explained, "Those women who said they didn't want to know what was happening were told why it is important to know, why it is important not to detach oneself from one's body or to submit to anyone else, even to someone who is 'helping,' even to us."[76] This attitude, however, illuminates a contradiction between Jane's philosophy of respect for women's reproductive choices and its practice of overruling women's decisions to forgo the explanation. In this rare instance, Jane abortionists insisted that the women they serve experience abortion on Jane's terms rather than their own.

The Services' ability to maintain its alternative medical system rested upon its members' ability to trust their "partners in crime" with their secret.[77] Historically, law enforcement punished both abortionists and women who had abortions, but only abortionists faced criminal penalties. Women who had abortions were punished through humiliating interrogation tactics and public exposure, but rarely prosecuted for their crime.[78]

Most illegal providers went to great lengths to hide their identities and scare women into keeping silent. Jane did not. Its members operated (literally) without masks on their faces or blindfolds covering the faces of their patients. They also counseled women in their own homes, with their children visible, and sometimes involved.

In May 1972, Chicago Police busted the Front and Place, arresting seven Service members and charging them with three counts each of abortion and conspiracy to commit abortion.[79] The arrest was a fluke. Jane members had been under police surveillance for years, but as long as they practiced abortion safely, the police left them alone.[80] Still, Jane members lived with the fear of arrest constantly and made plans to deal with such an event if it occurred. Initially, they intended to politicize an arrest, but revised this position after they became directly involved in abortion provision and the population they served became increasingly poor. Service members determined that "the importance of the alternative service Jane provided became even more important than the political statement we might make if we were arrested…our position became that our first responsibility in case of arrest was to protect the service and keep it functioning."[81] This is exactly what the Service did after the May bust.[82] It continued to work until *Roe v. Wade* legalized abortion the following year. On March 7, 1973, the state of Illinois dropped all charges against the Abortion 7. The Service continued to operate for a few months after *Roe*, until legal clinics could be established in Chicago, and then closed forever.

Following the model set by civil rights activists, black nationalists, and women's liberationists, Jane created an alternative medical institution in the abortion underground designed to challenge the existing medical model that Service members believed disrespected women and rendered them powerless over their own bodies and reproductive decisions. While other activists paired direct action tactics with service (and sometimes education) programs, women in Jane took direct action by providing abortions and teaching women about their bodies. Some in the CWLU characterized Jane as a "Band-Aid" group that provided a needed service, but lacked the ability to change the larger healthcare system. Jane members believed otherwise. They insisted that the alternative institution they created held the potential to create broader social change, to do more than "just" provide women with safe, affordable abortions, which in and of themselves could be life changing. By educating women about their bodies and asking them to participate actively in the abortion process, Service members aimed to empower women to take control of their bodies and their lives and to challenge the medical and legal restrictions that regulated their reproduction.

Jane's service activism pushes scholars to reconsider service as a feminist action and to look beyond organized feminism to activists at the margins of the women's movement. Jane was led by mothers, a group of activists often overlooked by scholars of feminism and feminists themselves. These women's experiences with pregnancy profoundly shaped their feminist politics and contributed to their preference for action over political ideology. The outcome of their work—ending over 11,000 unwanted pregnancies—transformed the lives of thousands of women, some of whom had their consciousnesses raised in the process. Jane's service activism functioned at the most grassroots level, woman by woman. The Service helps to break the wave theory by illuminating the radical potential of service activism and the non-traditional activists who practiced it. Its history pushes scholars, activists, and students to expand their understanding of where and how social change occurs as well as their understanding of feminist politics and philosophies. Much of the history of second-wave feminism involves conflicts between activists, yet Jane's story offers an example of feminists with different politics uniting to create an alternative medical system in the abortion underground with the power to fundamentally change the lives and consciousness of the women who came through it. The service activism Jane practiced continued a tradition of women's activism that began during the American Revolution and evolved over two centuries to become increasingly radical and transformative.

Notes

1. Laura Kaplan, *The Story of Jane: The Legendary Underground Feminist Abortion Service* (Chicago: University of Chicago Press, 1995), 280.
2. Sara Evans, *Personal Politics: The Roots of Women's Liberation in the Civil Rights Movement and the New Left* (New York: Vintage Books, 1979), 77.
3. Margaret Strobel, "Organizational Learning in the Chicago Women's Liberation Union," in *Feminist Organizations: Harvest of the New Women's Movement*, eds. Myra Marx Ferree and Patricia Yancey Martin (Philadelphia: Temple University Press, 1994), 146–47; CWLU, "The Chicago Women's Liberation Union," 1, Chicago Historical Society, Chicago, folder CWLU Background—The History of the CWLU, 1968–76, Box 1, CWLU Records (hereafter Records-CWLU).
4. Anne Firor Scott, *Natural Allies: Women's Associations in American History* (Urbana: University of Illinois Press, 1993), 2; Anne M. Boylan, *The Origins of Women's Activism: New York and Boston, 1797–1840* (Chapel Hill: University of North Carolina Press, 2002).
5. Scott, *Natural Allies*, 51–52.
6. Mary P. Ryan, *Mysteries of Sex: Tracing Women and Men through American History* (Chapel Hill: University of North Carolina Press, 2006), 179.
7. Pauline B. Bart, "Seizing the Means of Reproduction: An Illegal Feminist Abortion Collective, How and Why It Worked," *Qualitative Sociology* 10 (Winter 1987), 347.
8. Jane members referred to their group as the Service not Jane. Although it is more accurate to refer to Jane as the Service, to do so here, in an article about service activism, is sometimes confusing. For this reason, I will use both Jane and the Service in reference to the group.
9. See Carol S. Weisman, *Women's Healthcare: Activist Traditions and Institutional Change*

(Baltimore, MD: Johns Hopkins University Press, 1998), 74; Helen Marieskind, "The Women's Health Movement," *International Journal of Health Services*, 5 no. 2 (1975), 217–23; Sheryl Burt Ruzek, *The Women's Health Movement: Feminist Alternatives to Medical Control* (New York: Praeger, 1978); Mary K. Zimmerman, "The Women's Health Movement: A Critique of Medical Enterprise and the Position of Women," in *Analyzing Gender: A Handbook of Social Science Research*, eds. Beth B. Hess and Myra Marx Ferree (Newbury Park, CA: Sage, 1987), 442–72.

10. Paula Kamen interview with Judith Arcana, September 8, 1992, Northwestern University, Charles Deering McCormick Library of Special Collections; Johnson, "Something Real," 8–9.

11. Bart, "Seizing the Means of Reproduction," 346, 347.

12. Ibid., 20–22; Ellen Chesler, *Woman of Valor: Margaret Sanger and the Birth Control Movement in America* (New York: Simon and Schuster, 1992), 11, 14, 192.

13. Leslie J. Reagan, "Crossing the Border for Abortions: California Activists, Mexican Clinics, and the Creation of a Feminist Health Agency in the 1960s," *Feminist Studies* 26 (Summer 2000), 324; The National Association for the Repeal of Abortion Laws (NARAL), established in 1969 and in existence today, was named after Maginnis' group.

14. Ibid., 332–333.

15. Kaplan, *The Story of Jane*, 45; Jane, "The Most Remarkable Abortion Story Ever Told, Part II" *Hyde Park-Kenwood Voices*, July 1973, 2, folder Jane, Northwestern University, Charles Deering McCormick Library of Special Collections, Women's Ephemera Collection (WEF) (hereafter WEF)

16. Strobel, "Organizational Learning in the Chicago Women's Liberation Union," 156.

17. David T. Beito and Linda Royster Beito, *Black Maverick: T.R.M. Howard's Fight for Civil Rights and Economic Power* (Urbana: University of Illinois Press, 2009), 204.

18. Heather Booth interview with Rebecca Kluchin, September 7, 1999; Amy Kesslman with Heather Booth, Vivian Rothstein, and Naomi Weisstein, "Our Gang of Four," in *The Feminist Memoir Project: Voices from Women's Liberation*, eds. Rachel Blau DuPlessis and Ann Snitow (New York: Three Rivers Press, 1998), 27.

19. Kaplan, *The Story of Jane*, 103.

20. Evans, *Personal Politics*.

21. Ryan, *Mysteries of Sex*, 258–61; Barbara Ehrenreich, "What is Socialist Feminism?" Retrieved July 28, 2009, from http://www.cwluherstory.org/what-is-socialist-feminism. html; Elizabeth Fee, "Women and Health Care: A Comparison of Theories," in *The Politics of Sex in Medicine*, ed. Elizabeth Fee (Farmingdale, NY: Baywood, 1982).

22. Weisman, *Women's Health Care*, 72; Fee, "Women and Health Care."

23. Heather Booth interview with Rebecca Kluchin, September 7, 1999; Kessleman et al., "Our Gang of Four: Friendship and Women's Liberation," 28, 38; Evans, *Personal Politics*, 186, 195–201.

24. Chicago Women's Liberation Union, "The Chicago Women's Liberation Union," 1; Kesselman et al., "Our Gang of Four," 38; Strobel, "Organizational Learning in the Chicago Women's Liberation Union," 156.

25. CWLU untitled document, folder CWLU background—history of the CWLU 1968–76, Box 1, CWLU Records.

26. Kaplan, *The Story of Jane*, 44–46.

27. Leslie J. Reagan, When Abortion Was a Crime: Women, Medicine, and the Law in the United States, 1867–1973 (Berkeley: University of California Press, 1997), 219–20.

28. Ibid., 220–21.

29. Suzanne Staggenborg, *The Pro-Choice Movement: Organization and Activism in the Abortion Conflict* (New York: Oxford University Press, 1991), 18–19.

30. "A View from the Loop: The Women's Health Movement in Chicago," draft, 3, folder 10, Box 6, Jenny Knauss Papers, Northwestern University, Charles Deering McCormick Spe-

cial Collections, Evanston (hereafter Knauss Papers); Staggenborg, *The Pro-Choice Movement*, 23–24; David P. Cline, *Creating Choice: A Community Responds to the Need for Abortion and Birth Control, 1961–1973* (New York: Palgrave MacMillan, 2006), 113–15; Arlene Carmen and Howard Moody, *Abortion Counseling and Social Change: From Illegal Act to Medical Practice* (Valley Forge, PA: Judson Press, 1973).

31. Paula Kamen interview with Rev. E. Spencer Parsons, October 9, 1992, 1, Northwestern University, Charles Deering McCormick Library of Special Collections, Evanston.
32. Kaplan, *The Story of Jane*, 61–65, 204.
33. Strobel, "Organizational Learning in the Chicago Women's Liberation Union," 146–47; Chicago Women's Liberation Union, "Free Abortion is Every Woman's Right," 1, folder abortion—Chicago Women's Liberation Union WEF.
34. CWLU, "Free Abortion is Every Woman's Right," 2.
35. See for example, "Speak Out for Safe, Legal Abortion," Knauss Papers, folder 1 Box 4; "A View from the Loop: The Women's Health Movement in Chicago" (draft), 7, Knauss Papers, folder 10, Box 4.
36. Abortion Counseling Service, "Abortion: A Woman's Decision, A Woman's Right." Retrieved July 1, 2009, from http://www.cwluherstory.org/abortion-a-womans-decision-a-womans-right-2.html
37. "Abortion Counseling Service, "Abortion: A Woman's Decision, A Woman's Right."
38. Jennifer Nelson, *Women of Color and the Reproductive Rights Movement* (New York: New York University Press, 2003).
39. Kaplan, *The Story of Jane*, 71.
40. Paula Kamen interview with Anonymous Jane and husband, September 21, 1992, 1, Northwestern University, Charles Deering Library of Special Collections; Bart, "Seizing the Means of Reproduction," 349.
41. Kate Kirtz and Nell Lundy, *Jane: An Underground Abortion Service*, Women Make Movies, 1995.
42 Kaplan, *The Story of Jane*, 18.
43. See for example, Kamen interview with anonymous Jane and husband, 4; Kaplan, *The Story of Jane*, 52, 168; Jane, "The Most Remarkable Abortion Story Ever Told, part I,"1.
44. Kaplan, *The Story of Jane*, 89.
45. Bart, "Seizing the Means of Reproduction," 345, 348.
46. Kaplan, *The Story of Jane*, 38.
47. Ibid., 182.
48. Kamen interview with anonymous Jane and husband, 1; Micki Leaner interview with Paula Kamen, May 22, 1999, 7–8, Northwestern University, Charles Deering McCormick Library of Special Collections; Ellen Messer, *Back Rooms: Voices from the Illegal Abortion Era* (New York: Prometheus Books, 1994).
49. Kaplan, *The Story of Jane*, 161.
50. Ibid., 110–11.
51. Kamen interview with anonymous Jane and husband, 2.
52. The knowledge that Jane's primary abortionist was not a doctor led some women to leave the group. Kaplan, *The Story of Jane*, 112–13.
53. Johnson, "Something Real," 15.
54. Kaplan, *The Story of Jane*, 203–04.
55. Kamen interview with Anonymous Jane and husband, 2–3; Kaplan, *The Story* of Jane, 43, 75; "The Most Remarkable Abortion Story Ever Told, Part V," 4; Laura Kaplan, "Beyond Safe and Legal: The Lessons of Jane," in *Abortion Wars: A Half Century of Struggle, 1950–2000*, ed. Rickie Solinger (Berkeley: University of California Press, 1998), 35; Bart, "Seizing the Means of Reproduction," 348.
56. Kristin Luker, *Abortion and the Politics of Motherhood* (Berkeley: University of California Press, 1984), 67–91.

57. Kaplan, *The Story of Jane*, 90–91, 176; Bart, "Seizing the Means of Reproduction," 341.
58. Rebecca Kluchin interview with Jeanne Galatzer-Levy, September 17, 1999.
59. Kaplan, *The Story of Jane*, 267.
60. Kamen interview with Arcana, 5.
61. Kaplan, *The Story of Jane*, 176–77, 264.
62. "The Most Remarkable Abortion Story Ever Told, Part VI," *Hyde Park-Kenwood Voices*, November 1973, 4, WEF, folder Jane.
63. Kluchin interview with Galatzer-Levy.
64. Kaplan, *The Story of Jane*, 107.
65. Ibid., 107–08.
66. Ibid., 179.
67. Jane, "The Most Remarkable Abortion Story Ever Told, Part V" *Hyde Park-Kenwood Voices*, October 1973, 4, WEF, folder Jane.
68. Kaplan, *The Story of Jane*, 122.
69. Ibid., 124.
70. Paula Kamen interview with Lory, November 22, 1992, 3–5, 7. Northwestern University, Charles Deering McCormick Library of Special Collections.
71. http://www.cwluherstory.org/on-the-job-with-jane-2.html;"Jane by Jane," 20; Kaplan, *The Story of Jane*, 115–16; Johnson, "Something Real," 17.
72. Ibid., 115; Johnson, "Something Real," 18; "'Jane,' by Jane, Printed in Voices, June-November, 1973. Reprinted and excerpted with permission of author," 20–21. Northwestern University, Charles Deering McCormick Library of Special Collections, Jenny Knauss Collection.
73. Kaplan, *The Story of Jane*, 138–39.
74. Kaplan, "Beyond Safe and Legal," 37.
75. Kaplan, *The Story of Jane*, 128–29; Johnson "Something Real," 18.
76. Johnson, "Something Real," 19.
77. Kaplan, *The Story of Jane*, 251.
78. Reagan, *When Abortion Was a Crime*, 114.
79. "Excerpts from Daily News Article, May 4, 1972 by Phil Blake," Knauss Papers, folder 5, Box 6; Chicago Women's Liberation Union, "Dear Sister," May 30, 1972, Knauss Papers, folder 5, Box 6.
80. Kamen interview with Arcana, 7; Bart, "Seizing the Means of Reproduction," 346; Jane, "The Most Remarkable Abortion Story Ever Told, part VI," *Hyde Park-Kenwood Voices*, November 1973, 3 folder Jane, WEF.
81. Jane, "The Most Remarkable Abortion Story ever Told, part VI," 3.
82. Kaplan, *The Story of Jane*, 232–42.

CHAPTER 9

Feminizing Portland, Oregon
A History of the League of Women Voters in the Postwar Era, 1950–1975

JENNIFER A. STEVENS

In December 1960, members of Portland, Oregon's League of Women Voters gathered to celebrate the holidays and reflect on a truly notable year. The previous twelve months had been marked by the publication of, and widespread praise for, *A Tale of Three Counties*, the culminating report of an intensive two-year study about the state of urban affairs in Portland. The Christmas gathering was an opportunity to continue discussion of various urban concerns together in a social setting, as the women joined their voices to sing these new lyrics to the tune of *White Christmas*:

> I'm dreaming, too, of conservation; of water resources so pure;
> Where the streams and rivers, Run clear and sparkling; a supply
> that always will endure. I'm dreaming of urban renewal; To make
> our city grand and new; With a council manager, and civil service;
> and all that's best for me and you.[1]

The specially created lyrics pointed to the League's wide range of interests in the 1950s and early 1960s, and particularly to the women's conceptual linking of environmental and urban causes. The event itself points to an important and overlooked part of women's history between the so-called first and second waves of feminism, when women were not only active in the public realm, but shaping significant urban policy debates in the West.

By 1960, League of Women Voters (LWV) members already had a history of making major contributions to the democratic process, particularly on the local level. Their demographic profile points to a particularly privileged group who had the means and influence to contribute to society.[2] In the 1950s, women who joined the League on a national level were mostly married, past their child-bearing years, relatively well educated, and had an income of more than twice the national median family income.[3] Portland-area membership was similar in profile, with one additional characteristic that informed their activism—a propensity to have migrated from other places outside of Portland. The somewhat common trait of having "adopted" Portland as home gave these women some very strong beliefs on how Portland was when they arrived and how it should continue to be.

Historians who have attempted to link the first and second wave feminist eras have often oversimplified matters as they relate to women's approach to public affairs. A study of postwar life in western urban centers—starting with Portland—suggests that a more nuanced hypothesis is in order.[4] As the clearest language to identify, many have looked to maternalist politics—the idea that women's role as caretakers justified their presence in social policy debates—as the strain of continuity that sustained women's presence in public life from Progressive Era politics through the 1970s. While it is important that we not overlook that rhetoric, my research shows that at some point between the two waves there were scores of women's groups across the West, including the Portland League of Women Voters, who took up important urban environmental work that was not directly related to domestic issues or their role as public housekeepers.[5] Their work, undertaken without the mantle of maternalism and with only a pointed and strategic use of domesticity, represented what I call a "cautious feminism." It ventured beyond the safety of maternalist politics by advancing women's public lives on more equal footing with men's. And, by taking up distinctly urban issues, the women actively resisted the physical extension of domestic containment: suburbia.

Western women's revolt against suburbia and their defense of denser cities tells a unique story. With different tensions than those long-standing racial and ethnic strains that existed east of the Mississippi, the West experienced urbanization and urban renewal differently than the East, facing some of these issues for the first time. As such, women in the West had a distinctive relationship with their cities and with the open spaces that surrounded them. One historian wrote in 1988 that, "with the exception of avant-garde intellectuals and a small number of politically active feminists, few Americans articulated viable alternatives to the suburban lifestyle."[6] But this chapter, which briefly analyzes the League's impact on postwar development in Portland, Oregon, should cause scholars of women's history to question these assumptions about the era between the close of World War II and the so-called second wave of feminism. The Portland League was only one of many women-led groups across the West that advocated and offered a very distinct vision for urban living, using this critical postwar policy issue to create a new space for women in public life in a younger part of the United States where lines of local politics were not so clearly drawn.

Portland is a city where women's ideals for city life in the postwar period shaped how the modern city developed. Throughout the 1950s and 1960s, the women studying urban issues in Portland aimed to affect real, lasting urban change and create a city whose legacy would stand in contrast to the old industrialized cities in the eastern United States. Hundreds of western women in the League and other groups led public debates about city centers, urban revitalization, and environmental protection, and advocated for regional planning and the protection of open space.[7] Their cautious brand of feminism respected the mores of the time, yet relied on more gender-neutral terms than women in the so-called "first wave" of feminism to justify their activism in the public space. Their activism had a subtle but powerful impact on the history of feminism, and their stories represent an important, unexplored moment in the budding environmental movement and pre-second wave feminism. These western women defied the domestic suburban trend, promoting and creating great cities and launching a critical space for women in public life. Although men, such as iconic governor Tom McCall, frequently receive the credit for creating policies that fostered Oregon's modern-day quality of life, scholars must also give due credit to the women in the League of Women Voters who guided leaders to develop the policies and laws that have made Portland what it is today.

To those familiar with contemporary city planning issues, modern Portland conjures up images of ample green space surrounding a clean, well-maintained, lively central city. A well-used light rail runs quietly through the city's downtown core, neighborhoods of historic homes have been preserved and maintained, warehouse districts have been sensitively revitalized and brought many residents back into the city limits, and wild, untamed and unlandscaped open space is walking distance from many points within the city. The city of Portland spreads majestically across both sides of the bustling Willamette River, and the city is framed by a snow-capped Mt. Hood to the city's East. Portland itself lies in Multnomah County, but the larger metropolitan area straddles two other counties as well. The Tri-County region, as it is called today, comprises Portland's original streetcar suburbs such as the city's well-known northwest neighborhood, as well as post-World War II suburbs such as Beaverton.[8] Neighborhood groups are so involved in city issues that an entire staff at City Hall is devoted to serving these non-professional citizen groups. How did Portland create such a unique urban space?

By the middle of the twentieth century Oregon as a whole found itself at an environmental crossroads, and the state's largest city, Portland, was the poster child for the problems. Portland lies at the north end of the Willamette Valley, a narrow swath of land whose fertile soil and mild climate drew many settlers over the decades, but whose natural limits eventually forced the population to contend with difficult choices on issues of growth and identity. As in other cities across the West, wartime urban growth and urban sprawl in the Portland area had consequences that transcended political boundaries and created uncertainty and chaos for many of the city's residents. Traffic congestion did not respect city lines or the three county lines that that city straddled, and the disappearance of open space impacted more people than simply those living within the municipal boundaries that failed to protect it. The provision of clean and adequate water supply, clear air, plentiful open space, and sufficient sewage lines all became concerns associated with the tremendous growth that the Portland area experienced during and after World War II. By 1955, Portland seemed to be a mess. If you fast forward almost sixty years to today's Portland, however, a person might feel as city expert Jane Jacobs did just before her 2006 death, when she called modern Portland "a place that gives me great hope."[9]

Today's Portland, in essence, is a woman's city, representing distinctly feminine ideas about urban space that grew out of a revolt against the suburbanization of the 1950s and 1960s. Portland-area League of Women Voters (LWV) played a critical role in this transformation. The League of Women Voters was founded by Carrie Chapman Catt toward the end of the 1910s suffrage movement and evolved into an issues-based advocacy group during the course of the twentieth century. At its inception, the League was concerned with governmental efficiency and with creating well-informed voters. As it became a serious study group for women, the League soon took up important issues of the day—primarily revolving around women and children—and lobbied local officials for changes to related policies. Oregon's chapters were no different, and beginning in 1954, the local groups collectively pursued the *Know Your Community* studies, aimed at a traditional League goal—learning in-depth information about a community in order to be a better citizen.

In the *Know Your Community* studies that began in 1954, the women in the state's urban chapters discovered that Portland's growing postwar population had caused an explosion of special districts, agencies, and boards, which taken together resulted in an increase in the cost of basic services such as garbage and sewer due to a lack of efficiency, and rapidly disappearing open space thanks to poor (or nonexistent) zoning policies. The lack of efficiency and accountability sparked a fight in the group that lasted through 1973, as the seemingly innocuous topic of community studies spawned a major change in focus for the Portland chapters, and the women embarked on a prolonged effort to change urban governance and create better cities.

Before the studies commenced in 1954, the local League had only limited influence over issues unrelated to women and children, and continued to justify their activism on other issues, such as poverty, via their domestic expertise and maternalism.[10] But these women, many of whom had chosen Portland as home after being reared in and educated at prestigious institutions in the East or Midwest, felt that they had a stake in the community's growth.[11] The League's success in effecting urban change may be attributed in part to the commonalities that the women found in each other's company and the common perceptions fostered by such unity, eventually creating an alternative to the suburban lifestyle being thrust upon them by the cold war culture of the postwar United States. While they maintained the appearance of being socially benign, thereby remaining publicly acceptable, the League did make distinctions between itself and traditional women's organizations that served primarily social ends, and in this simple way pushed up against the domestic roles that conservative times foisted upon them. In one membership appeal, the Portland League insisted that it was "*not* just another social group," making the point that they wanted women who wanted to make a substantial difference in their world.[12]

The results of the *Community* studies compelled the women in the Portland League to fight the postwar urban decline they had identified, for government reform would be critical in addressing the city's needs. Portland was like many West-coast cities during the war years—booming with new industry such as the Kaiser shipyards (which, incidentally, had employed women in large numbers), and flooded with fresh residents. But the shipyards closed or downsized after the war ended, and Portland's postwar landscape was riddled with new, complicated problems. Housing needs, for one, were critical. And Portland's economy and its ability to employ the new residents in the wake of peace were uncertain, despite great optimism. In Portland, as in other cities around the country, a great debate over local government ensued in the postwar years. Oregon county government had only limited powers, as they were initially designed to serve the needs of rural populations. But much of Portland's wartime growth had occurred in unincorporated areas of heretofore rural fringe areas of the Portland area's three counties, where no zoning existed to restrain builders or control growth.[13] Weak county governments had necessitated the creation of the many special service districts. In 1942, there had been about 40 such districts in Portland; by 1963, the Portland metropolitan area contained between 218 and 330 of them.[14] The complete lack of coordination between these entities had contributed to an environmental mess and inefficient governing in metropolitan Portland. Local government needed a major overhaul.

While governmental efficiency had been the League's calling card since the late 1920s, efficiency in the cold war era took on new meaning. The famous 1959 Kitchen Debate between President Richard Nixon and Soviet Premier Nikita Khrushchev highlighted the laborsaving inventions from the latest generation of American entrepreneurs. The "debate" represented the quintessential American boasting from the era, which saw everyone from President Nixon down to popular literature bragging about new appliances and their impact on the *efficiency* of America's housewives. The underlying argument was clear: that the United States was superior to the Soviet Union in domesticity even while it lagged in space age technology. It followed that only capitalism could produce the benefits of suburban bliss. And when women spoke about efficiency, well, people—men—listened. The League women do not seem to have had any conscious awareness of the impact of the language of efficiency, but they embraced it to promote land use planning just the same.[15] Co-optation of this cold war language was one way that the League of Women Voters gained a level of acceptance in this policy debate without having to go the direction of maternalism. The women's solution to the lack of efficiency, which caused declining open space and polluted air and water, was metropolitan planning. But in the 1950s, government was not set up to take on this massive task. The League women, who felt genuine passion over the cause, also found that they were able to fill the vacuum of leadership in government and provide guidance to officials whose focus had been elsewhere.

The *Know Your Community* studies collectively served to identify sprawl as a serious problem in the Portland area, and the women felt that a citizens committee should start advocating for a regional master plan to be developed for the metropolitan area. They began efforts, such as visiting community clubs, to arouse interest.[16] At a meeting held in early 1955, LWV member Francis Samuels argued for the importance of Portland to the larger region:

> We hope to show that while we must plan for our city and metropolitan area, we cannot lose sight of the fact that we are also involved in a great regional development and must be prepared to meet it."[17]

A master plan, Mrs. Howard Kemper argued, should use zoning to establish a land use plan for the "entire metropolitan area." It should designate land use for industry, housing, recreation, public reservations of land, and "areas which are open space." At a membership meeting, Kemper outlined the region's history of local planning efforts, such as visits to the city from John Olmsted in 1903 and Lewis Mumford in 1938, the city's outdated (1924) zoning law, its 1939 Parks and Recreation Plan, and Multnomah County's creation of a planning commission in 1951. But Portland zoning had only been done on a limited basis within the city, and in the women's minds efficient coordinated planning was the key to a long-term vision for Portland. The League vowed to continue its fight for regional planning by voting to keep the item on its annual agenda, and began turning up the publicity through events such as radio shows and old fashioned door knocking.[18]

A look at Portland's zoning history and the League's push for comprehensive zoning is not without its problems. As Lizabeth Cohen points out in *A Consumer's Republic*, zoning and urban renewal in the postwar period was often used to segregate a growing minority population out of the more desirable parts of a city or metropolitan area.[19] But in Portland, where the African American population made up a small percentage of the total (4.2 percent of Portland's total in 1950) and racial tension was relatively low, the League's concerns appear to be genuinely related to efficiency and a concern for the natural environment.[20] It is nonetheless true—although nothing obvious stands out in the record—that the majority of League women were middle-class white women who may have been driven, in some regard, by their desire to retain the status quo.[21] Their intuitive and learned understanding of the metropolitan nature of Portland's problems caused the League to widen the scope of their studies to "fringe areas" beginning in 1956, as they gradually watched their friends and neighbors move out of the city and into the newly developing country.[22] They invited representatives from such fringe areas (not yet referred to as suburbs) as Beaverton, Milwaukie, and Oak Grove to give reports on the lack of planning in their own areas. To better reflect the expansion, the Portland League changed the name of its *Know Your Community* committee to "Metropolitan Area Committee" in February 1956, and passed, after "considerable discussion," a new agenda item called Promotion of Orderly Metropolitan Planning.[23]

Although desire for efficient government and service delivery was a prime consideration for women taking up this cause, the changes being wrought by sprawl also had visible impacts on the women's individual lives. The lack of efficiency was clearly troubling for these women, and perhaps it was due to their accepted role as household organizers that their couching of the urban problem in the language of efficiency also made their expertise on this issue acceptable. Their use of this language no doubt impacted the public's perception of their legitimacy. But at a more basic level, women in the League recognized the problem of sprawl earlier than most because it affected their individual lives through the loss of open space, increased service rates, and the decline of the businesses that they frequented.

In March 1957, the Portland chapter issued a memo entitled "The Mess We Are In," which summarized the problems associated with this sprawl. They noted that before World War II, Portland had been a "reasonably self-contained city." But the war brought with it industrial expansion and new population, and the "family automobile was making possible the growth of residential developments miles from the city center." Of course the businesses followed the houses, and "urban sprawl has grown up without benefit of planning, control or adequate services." They argued that the lack of a jurisdictional entity to rule the growing metropolitan area was the crux of the issue. Without a single governmental unit in charge of land use, the city suffered from loss of business in the downtown core and a lowering of land values and tax base; poorly designed developments and a bad mix of rural and urban land use which increased the cost of services; higher expense to provide sewers and water service to outlying suburbs, which resulted in a loss of open space; and hundreds of special service and taxing districts due to unregulated growth. It was inefficient and confusing, and in their estimation, resulted in decreased citizen interest in local government.[24]

In the wake of the memo, League members opted to promote a new unit of government with wide ranging powers, referring to their brainchild as Metro, a new governmental entity that would include the city of Portland together with the urban populations in Multnomah, Clackamas, and Washington Counties.[25] While the new entity would not replace any existing county or town, they hoped it would in effect get rid of the special districts that had proliferated. Metro would have "planning for long-range areawide [sic] development" as one of its functions, the power to raise money by taxation and bond issues, and would conduct its affairs through a policy/legislative body. Finally, they hoped that the government of Metro "would be simple in structure, representative of the people in the area and responsible to them for its performance."[26] The League hoped that orderly metropolitan development could be advanced through the creation of an entity with implementation powers.

In spite of their sharply focused ideas for the Metro entity, the women continued to study the problem, providing community for the women involved. The suburban women were officially brought into the fold in 1957 when the Tri-County Metropolitan Government Committee of the LWV decided that the Portland, Oswego, Beaverton, and Milwaukie League chapters would operate as a single unit on this issue.[27] The cooperation of

League chapters across the Portland area promoted community for women during a period that could have been quite isolating. They met regularly, discussed the impacts of growth on their immediate environment, and collaborated to find solutions, empowering these women to be at the forefront of an issue critical to local, state, and national citizens.

The Tri-County Metro Committee spent the next two years huddled over plans and laws, trying to come up with detailed plans and promotion schemes for the proposed Metro. During 1959, the committee looked at transit, health and welfare services, and air pollution. After extensive research, Portland League member Mrs. Charles McKinley, whose husband was a political science professor at Reed College and specialized in regional planning, reiterated that the traditional approaches to metropolitan problems—annexation, city-county consolidation or separation, functional consolidation, special districts—were "inapplicable or inadequate" to deal with Portland's problems. Instead, the League believed that a compact, efficient city that was governed as a region would improve things. The Tri-County Metro Committee concluded that "without some sort of unified governmental jurisdiction over the metropolitan area as a whole, plans for metropolitan development could never be effectively implemented."[28] The League's Metro proposal for a single agency embodied the efficiency the women desired, and accomplished planning for the region as well. Upon agreement by both city and suburban chapters, the committee began to promote a unified service district that could serve the entire area as well as providing area-wide planning.

The state League's organizing body, which had been content in the early years to allow the Portland-area chapters to take the *Know Your Community* issue to its logical extreme, soon realized that sprawl impacted all Oregon communities' environments, and in 1960 required all local chapters to place "Metropolitan Problems" on their study agendas.[29] Oregon State Item Chairman Virginia Campbell suggested some items for immediate reading that would demonstrate to members how tied the metropolitan governing problems were to the concern over preservation of open space and other environmental problems. Most importantly, she suggested a compilation of articles in a book called *The Exploding Metropolis*, one of which was Jane Jacobs' article, "Downtown Is For People." Jacobs articulated her disgust with national planners in the article, and with architects who were "deadening" national downtowns with their redevelopment projects. She lamented the ongoing national projects that were tearing down entire blocks and creating "open spaces with long vistas and lots and lots of elbowroom." She argued that "suburban amenity is not what people seek downtown." Jacobs was decidedly opposed to large institutional centers (such as performing arts centers) that would take away the street as a gathering place, instead favoring density, compactness and mixed uses in all forms, with large open spaces preserved at the *perimeter* of cities, not falsely created in their cores. Jacobs advocated for taking advantage of a city's natural environment where it already existed. Looking at Portland's downtown many years later, it is clear that much of Jacobs' advice was heeded, which explains her end-of-life comment on the hope of Portland. Thanks in large part to the lobbying efforts by the League of Women Voters—from the short city blocks to the incorporation of the waterfront, to the preservation of old buildings and a dense mix of uses—Portland has become what it is today. But it was not without a long and only somewhat successful fight against suburbanization.[30]

In addition to assigning Jacobs' writing on cities to the local chapters, Campbell also penned a telling poem that she included in her correspondence with them. She called her poem, "Saga of Suburbia":

> Is the sky as blue as it used to be; Is the air as pure and clean; Is the lake as near, or the stream as clear; Is the countryside as green? Are the taxes higher than you can take; Do the buses make you stand; Is the concrete ho[t], are the sewers not; Is the budget out of hand? Is the lovely view a rooftop now; Is the zoning in a mess; Is the parking nil; *ow that water bill*, Is your husband showing stress? Are the dozers working overtime; Is the traffic getting worse; Have the trees gone down; WHERE'S OUR LITTLE TOWN? It's ruined with your purse.[31]

The explosion of suburbia represented the junction of multiple issues to Campbell. Her comment, "it's ruined with your purse" points to the intersections of consumerism and gender that historians have argued were altered during this period of modern suburbanization, when shopping moved from central to peripheral districts and purchasing decisions became more of a "family" activity instead of one driven by, and empowering to women. Campbell wanted to draw her colleagues' attention to their consumerism and the problems she outlines in the rest of the poem, and asked them to question their own lifestyles and curb the suburban monster. Campbell called the women to action with this new study item, and hoped that Oregon's League women could provide help to the local and state governments to stem the tide.

That same year, the Portland area Leagues published *The Tale of Three Counties, One Metropolitan Community* to rave—if somewhat surprised—reviews. In Campbell's statewide announcement of the Portland study, she crowed: "we can congratulate ourselves upon our early recognition of this nationwide challenge and threat to our secure and pleasant ways of living. It has been deemed a problem second only to national defense in importance." Referring to the publication and the very significant way that the sprawl and overbuilding had affected each and every woman she addressed, she further noted: "it is a study that every League member can enjoy, because in every sense it has a personal application."[32]

A Tale of Three Counties was a study of what the League called "the widening spread of the metropolitan virus" in Oregon. In the publication, the women's foresight and conceptualization of the problem was truly remarkable.[33] The women provided a stunning indictment of suburbia, at a time in the country's history when middle-class women were believed to be enchanted with it, or at least being told they should be. In their introduction to the study, they noted the disappearance of valuable farm land through the "criss-cross of traffic arteries and the steel and concrete accompaniment that it requires." While they acknowledged the importance of the industrial potential of the area, they pleaded for an equal awareness of "the residential and recreational benefits of this unique setting...This also means that we must securely retain wide green belts of open land as farms with their attendant streams and lakes."[34] Alarmed by the rate of population growth in Portland's "suburban bedroom communities," the women wanted to bring attention to the problems such growth had wrought. The need to provide services to the "widely scattered suburban, residential and industrial developments" had resulted in higher sewer, water, and transit costs, and they remarked that "there is great risk of loss of the irreplaceable amenities of our beautiful countryside, as well as danger of substantial loss of taxable wealth to the area as a whole through the misuse of its basic currency—the land." They complained that county government "is no longer able to handle or control the myriad problems of the lusty suburbs," and that the thousands of new suburban residents, desperate for services, had "been impelled to organize a crazy-quilt of special districts to supply them."[35] The women's language here, was telling. Describing the suburbs as "lusty" assigned certain male characteristics to the suburban growth, and pointed to women's efforts in Portland to reclaim the central city as their own. They described the governmental chaos as harmful to their city and a threat to their quality of life, and put forth another vision, a vision of a revitalized downtown and a regional government that would bring back their central role as the maker of consumer choices, which they had been in the downtown landscape. Their embrace of the consumer role shows the Portland women's attempts to regain a certain power that had been theirs but which was gradually eroded with the growth of suburbs in the urban west.

A Tale illustrated the women's ability to conceptualize the entirety of the problem and link seemingly disparate issues, as well as their embrace of a vibrant downtown and their lament of its decline. For instance, when discussing public transit, they argued that "new freeways encourage the use of private automobiles which clog the downtown streets and slow down bus schedules, so business declines and the company raises fares which further cuts down the number of riders...a mass transit system is vital to the healthy development of any large metropolitan area, and especially to the preservation of its central core."[36] Fear of Portland's decline was evident throughout the document. And the references to Jane Jacobs' theories on cities were more than subtle. For instance, in describing the increasing wealth on the city's outskirts, the authors noted that "Portland would be impoverished were all these present and potential buyers and employees to be subtracted from its economy. Little by little this is presently being effected, as the movement of business to the suburbs accelerates."[37] Jacobs, in her advocacy for the downtown core, also knew that without a genuine mixture of uses and people, downtowns would die.[38] The League's study was also unique for its focus on "typical" female concerns such as parks, as well as more typical "male" concerns such as the business climate and the economy. Their willingness to address issues of economics was a new dimension to their political engagement, yet deferring to the experts and using the language of efficiency made such discussions acceptable. In this way, they appeared not to stretch too far from their prescribed roles, in spite of the unique voice they provided.

Ultimately, the women's biggest concern was sprawl and the consumption of land. They bemoaned the estimation that by 1975, only one-fifteenth of the projected population would live on farms, and were further despondent that fringe growth would be exacerbated by the federal highway system and what they called "automation," which would "[place] a premium on sprawling one story plants, [and] will send industry farther afield onto the hinterland." Alarm was apparent in the document, with predictions of the country evolving into fourteen gigantic "strip cities," and "destroying forever the old patterns of living."[39] They believed that the creation of a multipurpose metropolitan service district would "forestall repetition of uncontrolled fringe developments."[40] Such a district would draw *a line around development boundaries*, and provide jurisdiction over zoning and land use for some distance outside those boundaries, as well. The idea of a "growth boundary," though the term was not yet in use, was a novel and unique one, and these women were key to its genesis. No other similar organization or group was doing in-depth studies of the concept, not even the Oregon's Committee on Local Government. And no one but the League was proposing a regional solution.

The strength of the study did not escape notice, and eventually led to official posts for women in formal policy-making structures. Policy makers and elected officials were among the study's readership, as well as newspaper boards and quite likely many others.[41] Mrs. Paul Homer, sitting on the League's national board, wrote to the Tri-County Metro Committee that the Portland chapter women were "indeed pace setters in this field." In addition to the recent publication, she praised the women's success in getting the issue of metropolitan growth on the State of Oregon's agenda in the spring of 1959, with their earlier publication, *The State's Role in the Problems of Government in Metropolitan Areas.*[42] A local newspaper with a predominantly (if not all) male board also characterized the women's efforts as "one of the leading forces in the critical analysis of governmental problems and the general enlightenment of the public regarding these problems." Clearly, these women in Portland were perceived as more than just children tenders, and were being taken seriously on an issue unrelated to their domestic roles. Their input on this important policy problem was valued and respected. In spite of this, the same editorial concluded with a call to action specifically for *men*:

> Now that the ladies have pointed out the needs and the possible approaches to their fulfillment, perhaps enough men will be stirred to action to insure that metropolitan area problems will be met effectively before they get out of hand. For the men it's fast becoming a choice between proving their competence as responsible citizens [read: as men], or, as suggested above, finding some means of passing the membership tests of the League of Women Voters. [43]

Although these editors wanted their male readership to step up to the plate, the women's hard work, rigorous studies, and ambitious solutions would bring them into the formal policy making fold over the next three years, providing them a degree of influence in formal policy making. The LWV became a path into the committee rooms and onto the committees that shaped Portland's urban policy for decades to come. When the Legislature passed the bill that created the Portland Metropolitan Study Commission in 1963 and charged it with the study of six key issues, women from the League of Women Voters were appointed to chair three of those six committees. This step marked success in setting the agenda and influencing the public discussion.

The women's work continued for the next decade, culminating in the passage of Oregon's famous Senate Bill 100, a land-use bill that placed planning control in the hands of the state's thirty-six counties,[44] created the Land Conservation and Development Commission, and mandated Urban Growth Boundaries for every incorporated city in Oregon.[45] The League remained involved until the end, and saw the implementation of many of the solutions they proposed. Governing Portland regionally finally became a reality. The League of Women Voters persisted in their dream of efficiency and decreased sprawl.[46] The city is well recognized today for urban planning solutions that originated in the committee meetings of the Portland area League of Women Voters.

There is no better city than Portland to illustrate the cross-section of issues between the trend of western urbanization and the natural environment during the postwar period, nor a better location to demonstrate the impact that women had on the development of western metropolitan areas. The women belonging to the Portland area chapters of the League of Women Voters acquired the best understanding of the connections between these issues of any group of people in the West. The readings they assigned themselves, which included essays by authors like Jane Jacobs, helped them interpret the ongoing national planning debate as well as the national impacts of urban decline. They simultaneously analyzed the visible effects of sprawl on their own area, such as polluted air and water, faltering businesses, and snarled highways. The myriad impacts of suburban growth on their individual lives helped women comprehend the convergence of the urban and environmental issues.

These women, few of whom worked outside the home, utilized their educations and their ample free daylight hours to take advantage of the long-standing national respect for the League of Women Voters to impact local and state leaders' decision making. Suburban flight contributed to the decline in the Portland League's membership, and as the fringe-area chapters increased their own membership rolls, the need for cooperation between city and suburb was not lost on the city women. Their conception of the area as a region, and their ability to look beyond potential jurisdictional squabbles for the greater good of democracy, made them a unique voice in metropolitan planning efforts. They emerged with arguably the most innovative urban growth policy ideas in the entire country, policies that created a city widely credited with doing one of the best jobs in the United States of preserving open space and a green perimeter.

Until the issue of metropolitan planning was undertaken, the League historically had focused its attention almost exclusively on woman- and child-centered policy concerns. As they moved without hesitation into a less obviously gendered issue, they tested their ability to engage a largely male profession with their ideas, independent of maternalist rhetoric. In this way, they were testing the waters for engagement in other policy debates that were also outside the historic realm of their acceptability as women. Their concerns in Portland were maintaining a quality of life and the protection of the natural environment as well as a continuing concern with efficiency. Both of those goals were met by contending with urban policy issues.

The League's involvement setting the agenda for significant urban policy debates and the organization's guidance toward solutions led directly to the implementation of today's Metro, the regional planning agency for the Portland area that sets growth boundaries for the urban vicinity. Although frequently embroiled in controversy, many would argue that Metro has been the most successful tool conceived of yet to handle issues of urban growth. The policies it implements and the values it embodies are in large part thanks to those articulated by the League of Women Voters in the 1950s and 1960s, when middle-class white women are perceived to have been doing little more than fulfilling their domestic responsibilities.

Their involvement in the issue of metropolitan planning shows that they were not only active outside their homes, but that there was a shift in American political culture that was allowing women into policy debates unrelated to their domestic roles. Such a shift is widely perceived to have occurred much later, as second-wave feminism rocketed onto the scene later in the 1960s. But in Portland, women played a significant role in the wartime economy of Portland shipyards, and a woman served as mayor as early as the late 1940s. While the League was active in some of Portland's urban renewal battles that resulted in the destruction of minority neighborhoods (primarily Jewish and Italian), the overall impact of urban renewal in this city was significantly less than in other big cities. Thus, a space for urban planning was opened up much earlier in Portland, allowing women there to begin a new march toward equality on the American political scene.

Notes

1. White Christmas, December 1960, Portland: Committee Reports 1954–1967, Box 32, League of Women Voters of Oregon, Record Group Bx 173 (hereafter cited as Bx 173), University of Oregon Special Collections.
2. Susan Ware, "American Women in the 1950s: Nonpartisan Politics and Women's Politicization," in Louise A. Tilly and Patricia Gurin, eds., *Women, Politics, and Change* (New York: Russell Sage Foundation, 1990): 282.
3. Ware, "American Women in the 1950s," 284.
4. Many books and essays have addressed women's activism during this era. See Susan Lynn, "Gender and Progressive Politics: A Bridge to Social Activism of the 1960s," in Joanne Meyerowitz, ed., *Not June Cleaver: Women and Gender in Postwar America, 1945–1960* (Philadelphia: Temple University Press, 1994), 103–27; Dee Garrison, "'Our Skirts Gave Them Courage': The Civil Defense Protest Movement in New York City, 1955–1961," in Meyerowitz, 201–26. Amy Swerdlow also examines how motherhood impacted female activism in the later postwar period in *Women Strike for Peace: Traditional Motherhood and Radical Politics in the 1960s* (Chicago: University of Chicago Press, 1993). Susan Ware examines the demographic makeup of the national League of Women Voters' organization

in, "American Women in the 1950s: Nonpartisan Politics and Women's Politicization," in
Louise A. Tilly and Patricia Gurin, eds., *Women, Politics, and Change* (New York: Russell
Sage Foundation, 1990): 281. Finally, Joanne Meyerowitz looks at cold war rhetoric as a lens
through which to view female activism in, "Sex, Gender, and the Cold War Language of
Reform," in Peter J. Kuznick and James Gilbert, eds., *Rethinking Cold War Culture* (Wash-
ington, D.C.: Smithsonian Institution Press, 2001): 106–23.

5. The Boise, Idaho, chapter of the League was also quite active in these issues, as well as local
Los Angeles neighborhood groups such as the Federation for Hillside and Canyon Associations whose most active members were women. Additionally, in the San Francisco area,
Dorothy Erskine organized a group she called Citizens for Regional Recreation and Parks,
or CRRP, in 1958, which eventually became the very successful non-profit Greenbelt Alliance. There are many other examples of western women leading local organizations to save
open space and improve central cities. See Jennifer Stevens, "Feminizing the Urban West:
Green Cities and Open Space in the Postwar Era, 1950–2000" (Ph.D. diss., University of
California, Davis, 2008).

6. Elaine Tyler May, *Homeward Bound: American Families in the Cold War Era* (New York:
Basic Books, 1988): 174.

7. Stevens, "Feminizing the Urban West."

8. Locals refer to Portland neighborhoods by quadrants—northwest, northeast, southeast,
and southwest. Burnside Avenue separates the north from the south halves, while the Willamette River does the same for the east and west halves.

9. Jeff Joslin, letter to the editor, *The Wall Street Journal*, 2006.

10. Melissa Estes Blair, "Women's Organizations and Grassroots Politics: Denver, Durham,
and Indianapolis 1960–1975" (Ph.D. diss., University of Georgia, forthcoming).

11. *The League Alert*, Volume IV, No. 16, December, 1967; *The League Alert*, Volume IV, No. 17,
January, 1968; *The League Alert*, Volume IV, No. 19, March, 1968; *The League Alert*, Vol-
ume IV, No. 15, November, 1967; *The League Alert*, Volume IV, No. 13, August, 1967; *The
League Alert*, Volume IV, No. 16, December, 1967; *The League Alert*, Volume V, No. 2, Sep-
tember, 1968, *The League Alert*, Volume IV, No. 15, November, 1967, all in folder "Portland
Bulletins 1967–69," Box 32; "Meet the Metro Chairman!," *The League Alert*, March, 1968,
"Local League Annual Reports: 1967–1968, III," Box 6; "Meet the New Law Enforcement
Chairman," *The League Alert*, February, 1968, "Local League Annual Reports: 1967–1968,
III," Box 6; all in League of Women Voters of Oregon, Bx 173, University of Oregon Special
Collections.

12. Let's Talk About the League of Women Voters, Local Leagues Annual Reports: 1963–
1964, I, Box 5, League of Women Voters of Oregon, Bx 173, University of Oregon Special
Collections.

13. Subscription Service, Tri-County Metropolitan Government, February 1961, Current
Agenda Item, 1960–61—Beaverton, Milwaukie, Oswego, Portland, Tri-County Metro
Comm., Box 34, League of Women Voters of Oregon, Bx 173, University of Oregon Special
Collections.

14. "Metropolitan Commission Mulled in Legislature," by James Lattie, *The Oregonian*, February 10, 1963, in Urban Growth and Crises: 1959–1963, Box 16; Portland Metropolitan
Study Commission (hereafter PMSC), Water Supply Committee Interim Report, September 18, 1964, Portland Metropolitan Study Commission: 1964–1966, Box 16, both in
League of Women Voters of Oregon, Bx 173, University of Oregon Special Collections.

15. Joanne Meyerowitz also argues that women utilized cold war rhetoric to their advantage in
order to gain greater footholds in public life. Meyerowitz, "Sex, Gender and the Cold War
Language of Reform."

16. LWV, Portland Board of Director Minutes, August 16, 1954, Portland: Minutes (Board)
1951–1959, Box 31, League of Women Voters of Oregon, Bx 173, University of Oregon Special Collections.

17. LWV, Portland Board of Director Minutes, January 5, 1955, Portland: Minutes (Board) 1951–1959, Box 31, League of Women Voters of Oregon, Bx 173, University of Oregon Special Collections.

18. LWV, Portland Board of Director Minutes, Feb. 2, 1955, Portland: Minutes (Board) 1951–1959; LWV, Portland Board of Director Minutes, March 2, 1955, Portland: Minutes (Board) 1951–1959, Box 31, League of Women Voters of Oregon, Bx 173, University of Oregon Special Collections.

19. Lizabeth Cohen, *A Consumer's Republic: The Politics of Mass Consumption in Postwar America* (New York: Alfred A. Knopf, 2003). See especially chapter 5, "Residence: Inequality in Mass Suburbia."

20. Craig Wollner, John Provo, Julie Schablitsky, *A Brief History of Urban Renewal in Portland, Oregon*, published by the Portland Development Commission, August 2001, 3.

21. There is evidence that the League was actively seeking African American members.

22. LWV, Portland Board of Director Minutes, June 1, 1955, Portland: Minutes (Board) 1951–1959, Box 31, League of Women Voters of Oregon, Bx 173, University of Oregon Special Collections.

23. LWV, Portland Board of Director Minutes, Dec. 7, 1955; February 1, 1956; March 7, 1956, Portland: Minutes (Board) 1951–1959, Box 31, League of Women Voters of Oregon, Bx 173, University of Oregon Special Collections.

24. "The Mess We Are In," by Metropolitan Planning Committee, Portland: Committee Reports 1954–1967, Box 32, League of Women Voters of Oregon, Bx 173, University of Oregon Special Collections.

25. Metro was the name ultimately adopted by the regional government that emerged in the 1970s, though no credit was given to the women! Annual Report, Portland, 1956–1957, Local Leagues Annual Reports: 1956/57, 5, League of Women Voters, Bx 173, University of Oregon Special Collections.

26. Study of Tri-County Metropolitan Government, LWV of Portland, December 1957, Portland Bulletins 1971–73, Box 32, League of Women Voters of Oregon, Bx 173, University of Oregon Special Collections.

27. LWV, Portland Board of Director Minutes, December 4, 1957, Portland: Minutes (Board) 1951–1959, Box 31, League of Women Voters of Oregon, Bx 173, University of Oregon Special Collections.

28. Summary of the Joint Study Committee on Metropolitan Government: Portland Tri-County Area, June 1, 1959, Tri-County Metropolitan Government - Growth: 1957–1967, Box 16, League of Women Voters of Oregon, Bx 173, University of Oregon Special Collections.

29. Colorado and Michigan followed in 1961. Subscription Service, Tri-County Metropolitan Government, February 1961, Current Agenda Item, 1960–61 – Beaverton, Milwaukie, Oswego, Portland, Tri-County Metro Comm., Box 34, League of Women Voters of Oregon, Bx 173, University of Oregon Special Collections.

30. Jane Jacobs, "Downtown Is For People," in *Exploding Metropolis: A Study of the Assault on Urbanism and How Our Cities Can Resist It* (Garden City, New York: Doubleday Anchor Books, 1958), 140–68, quotes at 141, 142, 143, 164.

31. Mrs. C. Herald Campbell to Local Chairman, State Item II - Metropolitan Problems, January 29, 1960, Urban Growth and Crises: 1959–1963, Box 16, League of Women Voters of Oregon, Bx 173, University of Oregon Special Collections.

32. Mrs. C. Herald Campbell, State Item Chairman, to Local Chairman, State Item II-Metropolitan Problems, January 29, 1960, folder Urban Growth and Crisis: 1959–1963, Box 16, League of Women Voters of Oregon, Bx 173, University of Oregon Special Collections.

33. *A Tale of Three Counties, One Metropolitan Community*, by League of Women Voters of Beaverton, Milwaukie, Oswego, Portland, p. 3 Multnomah County Library.

34. Ibid, 4.

35. Ibid, 4–5.
36. Ibid, 8–9.
37 Ibid, 11.
38. Jacobs, *The Death and Life of Great American Cities.*
39. *A Tale of Three Counties*, 13.
40. Ibid, 27.
41. This is evidenced by local newspaper editorials that discussed the League's work, as well as the wide circulation of the League's various publications, which appear in many related correspondence files in the state. Memorandum, October 7, 1966, to Planning and Boundary Review Committee, from AMR (A. Mackay Rich), Intergovernmental Cooperation Commission Planning + Zoning 1965–1966, Box 4 of 4, Portland Metropolitan Study Commission, RG P16, Oregon State Archives.
42. *A Tale of Three Counties*, 3.
43. "The Ladies Report on 'Metro' Problems," *Eugene Register Guard,* Urban Growth and Crisis: 1959–1963, Box 16, League of Women Voters of Oregon, Bx 173, University of Oregon Special Collections.
44. With the exception that in areas with cities in excess of 300,000, such as Portland, where the cities themselves or a regional planning agency would assume this control.
45. Enrolled Senate Bill 100, Oregon Legislative Assembly—1973 Regular Session, Sponsored by Senators Macpherson and Hallock.
46. Brent Walth, *Fire at Eden's Gate: Tom McCall and the Oregon Story* (Portland: Oregon Historical Society, 1994): 351–54; May 8, 1973, Statement on Eng.-Re-Engrossed SB100 before House Committee on Environment and Land Use, League Testimony 1961–1973, Box 13, League of Women Voters of Oregon, Bx 173, University of Oregon Special Collections.

CHAPTER **10**

Barrio Women
Community and Coalition in the Heartland

JANET WEAVER

Between 1945 and 1975, Mexican American women in the United States pressed for the rights of economic citizenship. They challenged gender and racial inequity through coalition building, community organizing, and union and political activism. In the eastern Iowa towns of Davenport and Muscatine, their activism traversed a broad spectrum of progressive reform from fundraising for educational scholarships to picketing local factories and supermarkets. Collectively and individually—often in partnership with men—they chipped away at the structures that contributed to gender and racial discrimination.[1] Yet these Mexicana mothers, daughters, breadwinners, and nuns rarely identified themselves as feminists.[2]

In this they were by no means unique. Concurrently on the west coast, Dolores Huerta engaged in community organizing, co-founded the United Farm Workers union, led its national grape boycott campaign and by 1975, had become its chief lobbyist for the landmark California Agricultural Labor Relations Act. Her work on behalf of agricultural laborers improved the lives of countless women and children. Still, when asked in a recent interview to what extent she had identified with the women's movement during those years, Huerta responded, "I have to confess that I didn't."[3]

Because the community activism of these Mexican American women mirrors the work of many who did identify themselves as feminists, their experience invites us to examine, expand, and enrich our understanding of the history of feminist activism, questioning the narrowly defined parameters of its persistent "waves" metaphor.[4]

Since the 1980s, scholarship on feminist activism in the Southwest has challenged us to contemplate the intersection of race and gender as we move away from a predominantly white, Euro-centric interpretation of feminism.[5] But the agency of Mexicanas in the Midwest remains obscure—a significant omission given that, by 1970, over 500,000 individuals of Mexican descent lived in the ten-state area between Kansas and Ohio, half of them women.[6] Despite substantial efforts to collect and interpret this history, much remains to be done.[7] Like their sisters in the Southwest, Mexicanas in the heartland were part of a complex cast of historical actors who shaped change. Our ability to understand and interpret their agency affects how we describe and define feminist history.

In the Iowa Mississippi River town of Davenport, barrio women established early patterns of activism in response to immediate needs of family, community, and employment. Mexicanas formed the backbone of tight-knit communities like the Cook's Point barrio in southwestern Davenport. From the 1920s to 1952, this two-acre site with its frame houses, boxcars, and boathouses was home to approximately 270 residents, the majority of whom were Mexican nationals and their U.S.-born children. Subject to regular flooding, the settlement's streets went unpaved and its homes never had running water, electricity, or sanitary facilities. A city dump was located close by.[8]

Children raised in Cook's Point benefited from strong female role models provided by women like Mary Ramirez Terronez. Born in 1918 in the Mexican state of San Luis Potosí, Terronez had lived at Cook's Point since she was five years old. She married in 1936, raising five of her six children in the barrio. Like many women at "the Point," Mary supplemented the family income with seasonal work in the onion fields of nearby Pleasant Valley. Yet, in other respects she was unusual among the women of her generation. She drove a truck, worked in a poultry processing factory, and developed the practice of engaging individual onion growers in informal wage negotiations on behalf of barrio field workers. By the 1940s, her fearless and outspoken nature had established the young, bilingual Terronez as a community leader and activist.[9]

During World War II, over half a million Mexican Americans entered the armed forces, where they were disproportionately represented in comparison to all other ethnic and minority groups.[10] On the homefront, comparatively high numbers of Mexicanas filled nontraditional jobs in war production industries. After the war, as was true for all women, their newly acquired skills did not translate to ongoing economic opportunities and the majority of Cook's Point families remained in the barrio.[11] What kept them there was a combination of poverty, prejudice, and a sense of place so strong that it would reunite its former residents every year, even fifty years after the Point was closed.[12]

During the twenty-nine years that Mary Terronez lived at Cook's Point, from 1923 to 1952, the settlement remained largely invisible to most Davenport residents. In January 1952, it drew local attention when its owner issued evacuation notices to residents, to make way for a factory to be built on the site. He gave barrio residents just six months to find alternative housing. Despite her status as a Mexican national, Terronez stepped forward to help her community deal with the impending housing crisis, working with a cross-section of community activists and local government officials.[13] Along with other Cook's Point residents, she attended a gathering of around 150 community members and made what was, by all accounts, a remarkable speech, in which she refuted accusations that Mexicans liked the poor living conditions of Cook's Point. She concluded, "We want our children to grow up in as good an environment as your children."[14] While Terronez's appeal was consistent with traditional women's issues of family and community, her willingness to speak out defines her as an activist and early feminist in the tradition of "community feminism" described by Ula Taylor.[15]

The closing of Cook's Point marked a turning point for a cadre of Mexican and Mexican American men and women. Through their community work, Terronez and others became acquainted with members of the League for Social Justice, a Davenport organization that promoted racial equality through grassroots organizing, propelled by an enthusiastic cross-class, multicultural, and interfaith membership. The League was inspired by former students of activist priests on the faculty of St. Ambrose College in Davenport.[16] One such student was Charles Toney, an African American Roman Catholic activist and welder at John Deere Plow. His wife, Ann Toney, was a beautician. Aside from being members of the League for Social Justice, the Toneys were also leaders of the Davenport NAACP and veterans of the local civil rights movement. In 1945, they had won a landmark suit in Iowa district court against a Davenport resident who refused to serve them at a local ice cream parlor. Looking back, Ann Toney remarked, "After the ice cream parlor, I knew that we were headed to try to make life a lot better for everybody. No one said it, but we knew that something had to be done."[17]

Seven years later, in 1952, Ann Toney and other League members turned their attention to the residents of Cook's Point. Toney went door-to-door conducting a survey of the barrio while other members of the League for Social Justice assisted in locating affordable housing for the soon-to-be displaced residents of Cook's Point. Some League members quite literally moved Cook's Point houses to a new area on Highway 22, where the Ramirez family had purchased land. Shortly after the barrio was closed, the Toneys became godparents to Mary Terronez's nephew.[18] This early experience of community organizing based on coalition building and multi-cultural friendship and cooperation provided a strong foundation for future activism.

In the years after the closing of Cook's Point, the children of barrio women carried their tradition of activism into new neighborhoods and organizations. In the late 1950s, former barrio residents founded local chapters of two Mexican American organizations—the American GI Forum and the League of United Latin American Citizens (LULAC). Founded in Texas in 1948 to uphold the rights of Mexican American World War II veterans, the Forum supported a wide range of civil rights issues. Nationally, women were active partners and sometimes leaders in the affairs of the Forum. At its first annual conference in 1956, women successfully lobbied for recognition of a women's auxiliary; the next year they sponsored a women's leadership conference. Mary Vasquez Olvera—a former Cook's Point resident whose two brothers were killed during World War II—worked closely with her husband to form an Iowa chapter of the Forum in 1958. She took a lead role in managing its affairs as well as its women's auxiliary, whose members were active in politics, education, and civil rights. By creating and demanding opportunities in leadership and political activism, Forum women nurtured and passed on to their children an activist consciousness firmly rooted in their cultural heritage and identity.[19]

As Cynthia Orozco has pointed out, prior to the 1970s, Mexican American women did not belong to any national organizations specifically for women, and their participation in voluntary organizations composed of both men and women is "a history largely untold." Orozco notes that when LULAC, the oldest Mexican American civil rights organization in the United States, was founded in Texas in 1929, it was distinctly patriarchal. In 1933, it created women-only chapters known as "Ladies LULAC" councils, which were discontinued in 1960, after which all LULAC councils were composed of men and women.[20] Of Iowa's five LULAC councils, the only Ladies LULAC was Council No. 308 in Des Moines, which was chartered in 1958. The next year, LULAC Council No. 10 was formed in Davenport.[21]

From its inception in 1959, Council 10 included both men and women. Reflecting on an early effort to form a Ladies LULAC Council in Davenport, one "LULACker" recalled, "The guys didn't want us to. They wanted us to stay with the men."[22] Perhaps the male members foresaw the pivotal role the women would play in Council 10, which immediately pushed forward a strong civil rights agenda, establishing a reputation as "Iowa's most active council."[23] In 1960, Estefanía Rodriguez—the daughter of Norberto Rodriguez, a Mexican railroad worker, and of "Muggie" Adams Rodriguez, an African American woman from Alabama—held the office of secretary of LULAC Council 10. In that capacity, she worked with her younger brother, Ernest, to publish a Spanish-language newspaper, *El Reportero*. While the council's predominantly male leadership served on the Davenport Human Relations Commission and local civil rights organizations, its women proved indispensable to the day-to-day running of the council, supporting community projects, preserving cultural traditions, and fighting racial discrimination.[24] Operating under the radar, these midwestern Mexicanas maneuvered deftly between family and community to uphold their rights in a largely patriarchal world.

Working through LULAC and the GI Forum, women demanded rights of economic citizenship as they quietly and strategically integrated neighborhoods and school districts. After buying a home in an Anglo neighborhood in 1963, stay-at-home mom Lucy Vargas—whose husband was a laborer at John Deere Plow, president of LULAC Council 10, and a member of the Davenport Human Relations Commission—responded with wit and steely determination to neighbors' concerns: "I had neighbors come over here and ask me, 'Oh, we hear that you're a family with fourteen kids.'... I says, 'No, there's seven but they make enough noise for fourteen.'" By upholding her right to live in an Anglo neighborhood, Vargas asserted the right for her children to be educated in the Anglo school. Nor did she allow the chilly reception she received at local PTA meetings to deter her from planning for the educational future of her children.[25]

Rather than work through unresponsive PTAs, Mexican American women used the networks and resources of LULAC and the American GI Forum. They coordinated chili suppers and raffle ticket sales for annual fiestas and queen competitions to raise money to support educational scholarships for Mexican American students. A 1961 Council 10 newsletter reflects the traditional role of the women in those early fundraising drives: "ATTENTION ALL WOMEN DONATING CHILI: Here is the recipe to follow so all the Chili will be uniform." LULAC Council 10's extraordinary success in fundraising for its educational scholarship program, which each year brought in between five and twenty-five thousand dollars, illustrates how women used traditional roles to achieve far-reaching objectives.[26]

The strong tradition of women's activism, handed down through barrio families, became increasingly visible over time. During the 1960s, women battled for opportunities embedded in the civil rights legislation of the day, moving outside Mexican American organizations to participate in community coalitions and fill leadership positions in local, state, and regional organizations. As a result, we can begin to discern the agency of midwestern Mexicanas in the type of labor feminism described by Dorothy Sue Cobble and Dennis Deslippe.[27]

In the decade that followed the passage of the Civil Rights Act of 1964, LULAC Council 10 worked with the Davenport Catholic Interracial Council (the successor to the League for Social Justice). The interracial cooperation fostered since the 1950s brought hard-earned victories in the form of a fair housing ordinance and a paid, full-time director for the Davenport Human Relations Commission funded by the City of Davenport. Building on their historical experience of community-based feminist activism, Mexicanas from Iowa and Illinois expanded their activism to employment rights in the 1960s and 1970s. An important catalyst to this development came when local concern for the rights of migrant workers in Iowa fused with the national issues raised by the Delano, California, grape strike that had been underway since 1965.[28]

The farmworker movement for justice, led by Cesar Chavez and Dolores Huerta, had a profound impact in Iowa, where a core group of activists simultaneously supported the rights of grape pickers in California and of migrant workers in Iowa's agricultural industry. National publicity on the Delano grape strike helped Iowa activists draw attention to conditions endured by the roughly three thousand migrant workers and their families who arrived each year to work in the fields of Iowa and southern Minnesota. Many Iowans, previously unaware that migrant workers were employed in their state, now identified farm labor in Iowa with the powerful 1960 CBS documentary *Harvest of Shame,* which had brought to light the deplorable condition of migrant workers employed in Florida's agricultural industry.[29]

The children of barrio women led the grape boycott campaign in Iowa. Mary Terronez's son, John, born in Cook's Point in 1938, was the state director of Iowa LULAC when he formed the Quad City Grape Boycott Committee in 1968. His committee co-chair, Ernest Rodriguez, born in boxcar No. 8 in Holy City in 1928, was the son of Muggie Adams Rodriguez, and brother of LULAC secretary Estafanía Rodriguez. These and other former barrio residents, who had worked together on civil rights issues for many years, now turned their attention to the rights of grape pickers in California. LULAC Council 10 led the coalition to support the grape boycott campaign in Davenport. Through their involvement in that campaign, Davenport Mexicanas gained activist skills picketing local supermarkets, preparing mailings, attending meetings, and coordinating rallies. During the dedication of a World War II monument on Hero Street in nearby Silvis, Illinois, Mary Terronez's daughter climbed to the top of the monument to hold high a "Boycott Grapes" poster.[30]

Between 1967 and 1970, "settled-out" migrant workers and Mexicana activist nuns turned to the Iowa struggle, where high-profile battles in the Iowa legislature were waged for the rights of migrant workers.[31] Mexican Americans and their Anglo allies supported bills to establish a minimum age for the employment of migrant children on Iowa farms and to establish health and safety standards for migrant worker housing. In 1967, Irene Guzman voiced her support for the migrant child labor bill at a joint hearing before the Iowa House and Senate committees on human and industrial relations. She refuted the claim of Iowa canning companies that migrant workers themselves pressured employers to allow children to work in the fields, arguing instead that she and her husband felt "very strongly that we have a right to give [our children] the education we didn't have."[32]

The legislative struggle for the rights of Iowa migrant workers also engaged Mexican American women in Muscatine, a major center for migrant labor twenty-five miles downstream from Davenport on the Mississippi River. Each year approximately one thousand agricultural laborers, predominantly U.S. citizens of Mexican descent from Texas, came to work in the tomato fields around Muscatine where the H. J. Heinz Company operated a large canning facility. In 1969, leaders of the 150-member Muscatine Community Effort Organization (CEO) helped expose the shameful conditions endured by migrant workers and their children on some Iowa farms. Inspired by the national grape boycott campaign, CEO members proclaimed in their flyer: "RAZA, apoyenos para ganar nuestros DERECHOS en beneficio de todos nostros y sobre todo nuestros hijos" (Raza, let's lift ourselves up to gain our rights for the benefit of us all and especially of our children).[33] Members of the Muscatine CEO and Quad City Grape Boycott Committee joined forces to work with organized labor and Iowa House Representative John Tapscott to plan the official start of a boycott of H. J. Heinz Company products.[34]

In southeastern Iowa, Mexican American activist nuns Irene, Molly, and Lucinda Muñoz led the fight in the fields. They earned a reputation as "trouble-shooters on the front lines."[35] The biological sisters, who were bilingual, were the children of first- and second-generation Mexican immigrants. They grew up in a working-class, ethnically and racially diverse neighborhood in West Des Moines, Iowa. Irene Muñoz trained as a public health nurse and joined the order of the Congregation of the Humility of Mary (CHM) in Davenport. Responding to principles set forth by the Second Vatican Council, Sister Irene sought and received permission to go out into the community where she felt she could be of greater service to others.[36]

In 1967, Sister Irene arrived in Muscatine, where she would spend the next fifteen years providing health services to migrant workers. Working for the Muscatine Migrant Committee in cooperation with doctors from the University of Iowa, she helped organize the free medical clinic that served patients each Friday evening in the basement of a local church.[37] In 1973, with funding from the Department of Health, Education, and Welfare, Sister Irene and her sister, Sister Molly Muñoz, opened the doors of the modest but welcoming Muscatine Migrant Clinic. Staffing the clinic with the assistance of two University of Iowa medical students, the sisters provided free medical care to migrant workers. Within four years of its opening, the clinic was serving over 2,500 migrant workers annually in 32 labor camps in six counties along the Iowa and Illinois border.[38]

Over time, some Muscatine growers grew increasingly hostile toward the sisters. "Rabble rousers, they called us," Sister Irene remembered. "I think about when we first arrived, my sister and I, they called us the good nuns and then when we left, they called us the damned nuns."[39] Because of their status in the church, the nuns were initially given some latitude, but that waned as they became a potential threat to farmers' profits. Growers did not always welcome the sisters' regular visits to the homes of migrant workers living temporarily on their property, as it afforded an opportunity for the nuns to inspect the camps and report violations of Iowa's migrant housing law. Sister Irene had "run-ins" with the farmers, and one farmer kept a shotgun to "throw her off." On one occasion, Sister Molly was arrested for "criminal trespassing" on private property.[40]

Looking back on her years in Muscatine, Sister Irene Muñoz noted, "We really pushed for a lot of changes in the state of Iowa."[41] In 1969, she testified at a public meeting in Davenport called by the Iowa State Advisory Committee to the U.S. Commission on Civil Rights. Her testimony helped lay the groundwork for the creation of the Iowa Spanish Speaking Peoples Task Force, which led to the formation of the Iowa Spanish Speaking Peoples Commission in 1976, on which Sister Irene served.[42] She was elected to represent Iowa on a steering committee charged with the formation of a Midwest Council of La Raza in 1970.[43] During this period, like Dolores Huerta, Sister Irene Muñoz identified with *el Movimiento Chicano* rather than the organizations of predominantly white, middle-class feminist movements. Yet by 1977, when the National Women's Conference convened in Houston, Sister Irene was the only Mexican American delegate from Iowa to attend.[44]

Between 1968 and 1975, the momentum generated by the grape boycott campaign and nurtured by the social justice ideology of a liberal clergy was captured in a wave of grassroots organizations in Davenport. One such organization was the Minority Coalition, known as MIN-CO. Formed in the spring of 1970, it drew representatives from the NAACP, LULAC, the local grape boycott campaign, and neighborhood committees. Although women did not hold leadership positions in MIN-CO, they supported its demands to strengthen educational opportunities for minority students, which had long been an objective of LULAC and GI Forum women. Foremost among MIN-CO's demands was that the Davenport School District hire 150 African American teachers and 50 bilingual Mexican American teachers. (Two years earlier, just 10 of the district's 973 teachers were African American, and only 1 was Latino.) By the start of the 1970 school year, the number of minority teachers employed by the Davenport School District had risen to 30 as it bowed to pressure from local activist coalitions and the Iowa Civil Rights Commission.[45]

In addition to improving educational opportunities for minority students in Davenport, activists sought to change local employment practices that prevented many Mexican Americans from attaining economic citizenship. Former Cook's Point resident Dolores Carrillo understood that, for Mexican Americans, even a high school diploma did not guarantee union jobs with living wages such as those available to employees at the Oscar Mayer packinghouse in Davenport.[46] A second-generation Mexican American, Carrillo had studied for the GED to encourage her daughters to stay in school. She became discouraged when, despite their educational accomplishment, her daughters were unsuccessful in gaining entry to better-paying blue-collar jobs. In 1970, the thirty-six-year-old Carrillo saw the issue in terms of race and gender-based discrimination.[47]

That year Carrillo organized a boycott of the Oscar Mayer plant to draw attention to the company's discriminatory hiring practices. She understood the power of public protest from her experience in the local grape boycott campaign. "That's what I learned from that—fight for your rights," she explained. "You have the same right as anybody else. Fight for it. If you don't get it…you can picket until you do get it."[48] An experienced factory worker, Carrillo had expected to be hired by the Davenport Oscar Mayer company on each of the numerous occasions that she submitted her employment application. She suspected discrimination because, although the company stated that it was not hiring, Ernest Rodriguez—employed inside the plant at that time and also a member of the Davenport HRC—confirmed that Anglos were being hired.[49]

Carrillo worked with Ernest Rodriguez and Mary Terronez to coordinate the protest, bringing together Mexican American women from Davenport and Muscatine to picket the plant. A welfare mother herself at that time, Carrillo gathered other Aid to Families with Dependent Children (AFDC) mothers as well as African American women and men to stand picket duty outside the plant. Their signs proclaimed, "Brown is Beautiful," "Boycott Oscar Mayer" and "1970—Year of the Chicano." Their action received little attention from the Davenport media. However, an Iowa City feminist press with national circulation, *Ain't I A Woman?*, covered the story under the headline: "Not Everybody Loves an Oscar Mayer Wiener." This front-page coverage by a feminist publication commending the agency of Mexicana picketers supports the argument that, indeed, these women did the work of feminism.[50]

The Oscar Mayer boycott illustrates the multi-faceted approaches adopted by working-class Mexicanas as they confronted the dual oppression of race and gender discrimination. The women collaborated with Ernest Rodriguez to back up their action by filing a complaint with the Davenport HRC. The commission found that the Oscar Mayer Company was using a culturally biased test, known as the Bendix Dexterity Test, in its hiring procedure. The test, administered to women who applied to work at Oscar Mayer, was designed to measure the quickness of the applicant's fingers and involved reading and carrying out a series of written English-language instructions. As a result of the women's protest, the company discontinued its use of the Bendix test.[51]

In 1970, the Diocese of Davenport established the Area Board for Migrants (ABFM) to provide a community-based organization to tackle racial discrimination. With additional funding and support from the Dioceses of Rockford and Peoria in Illinois, the ABFM served as liaison between the Spanish-speaking community, public officials, and institutions.[52] In November 1970, Ernest Rodriguez left his packinghouse job for a full-time position as director of the ABFM. Working out of its Davenport store-front office, he filed civil rights complaints, edited the Spanish-language newsletter, *Columnus,* and initiated an immigration counseling service and a job placement program known as Trabajo.[53] He hired Mary Terronez as a job developer for the Davenport Trabajo program, where she worked with residents, employers, and welfare agencies, tracking hiring procedures and the retention of Spanish-speaking employees to see that their rights were upheld. Terronez often accompanied Latinos to job interviews, working directly with plant managers to ensure that they hired qualified minority applicants. Looking back, Rodriguez noted, "sometimes I wondered who was directing whom. She [Mary] kept me on track that the purpose of our program was to serve the needs of La Raza."[54]

As members and leaders of neighborhood associations, women used traditional community-based approaches to achieve far-reaching goals. Working with MIN-CO and the ABFM, residents addressed housing, education, police-community relations, and welfare rights. On the east side of town, Estefanía Rodriguez organized the Community Active Mothers and was well known in her neighborhood for the often repeated words of encouragement that had been passed down to her in the Mexican barrio by her African American mother: "Look up my young American, stand firmly on the earth. Noble deeds and mental powers give title over birth."[55]

In 1971, members of the Eastside Neighborhood Assembly organized a workshop for AFDC mothers led by Erma Gray, an African American leader of the Chicago-based welfare rights organization, Mothers' Power. Gray encouraged Davenport AFDC mothers to stand up for their rights and, if necessary, take their children and even sit in at the welfare office.[56]

Maria Aguilera, the sister of Dolores Carrillo and a long-time acquaintance of Mary Terronez, was an elected officer of the West Neighborhood Committee in 1970. She had participated in the local grape boycott campaign and also supported her sister by picketing Oscar Mayer.[57] Aguilera's experience in community organizing and protest prepared her to stand her ground in the workplace. A factory worker with many years of experience in Chicago plants, she set her sights on a good-paying union job at International Harvester Farmall in Rock Island, Illinois, where her husband was employed. In 1973, after her application was rejected on the basis that Mexican women were too short to work on Farmall's assembly line, she questioned the company policy. She explained to the hiring officer, "Nobody's ever told me I was too short to work." Aguilera remained outside the personnel office all day, returning each day for five days until she received an interview with the personnel manager. She was finally hired to work on the assembly line, a job she held for many years.[58]

Ongoing concern over discriminatory employment practices prompted fifty Mexican Americans to picket the Farmall plant in the fall of 1975. Production came to a halt when the union, United Auto Workers (UAW) Local 1309, honored the Latino picket line.[59] Aguilera's experience and that of other Mexican Americans, led LULAC Council 10 to file a complaint with the Department of Defense (DOD) against International Harvester Company Farmall Works. The DOD responded to their complaint in 1976 when it warned Farmall against continuing discriminatory practices in hiring, job retention, and termination. Its investigation found that "Latino women [sic] who applied for unskilled and semi-skilled jobs when compared to all other applicants, all female applicants and Black female applicants, were adversely affected." The report identified the use of height and weight requirements as a partial cause for the adverse screening out of Latino women prior to interviewing.[60]

Like Aguilera and Carrillo, Eva Savala applied for a nontraditional, blue-collar job, less as an expression of her feminist sensibilities than because it paid significantly more than the traditional women's jobs available in the region. The job involved manufacturing truck parts for Mack semi trucks in East Moline, Illinois. In 1973, the McLaughlin Body Company hired Savala to fulfill its requirement to employ more women. She joined the union—UAW Local 1414—and entered a male-dominated workforce with only three women working in the plant. Her job involved cleaning and hoisting truck parts after they came out of the press. The first few days were an unwelcome shock to Savala: "It was rough. I had never worked in a factory...and I almost walked out the first night—almost—because it was not very clean. The language!... I was not happy. I would come home and be dirty from head to toe. I couldn't eat."[61]

Apart from the physically demanding work she did, Savala was routinely subjected to degrading sexual remarks from co-workers. As she pursued avenues for addressing her sexual harassment grievance, she read the union contract to consider her options and decided to run against her union steward in the next election. With just three months seniority at the plant, Savala was elected to the position of union steward in UAW Local 1414, becoming the first woman and the first Mexican American to hold an office in that local.[62]

Eva Savala won the respect of her co-workers, who re-elected her to represent them as their union steward for the next twelve years. She spearheaded local programs to uphold the voting rights of minority populations, gaining experience in community service and political action through the union. As she prepared to leave the plant and go on staff as the first Latina international representative for UAW Region 4, the personnel manager remarked to Savala, "If I was ever in a bargaining position, I would want you to represent me."[63]

The road to economic citizenship taken by second-generation Mexican American women like Vargas, Carrillo, and Savala forged its way through the complex intersection of race, class, and gender. Iowa Mexican American women hailed from a rich tradition of women's activism exemplified by their mothers and other strong female role models in the barrios. Their activism was informed by their grassroots experience in civil rights organizing and their involvement in the farmworker movement for justice during the 1960s and 1970s. Mexicanas in the heartland identified with La Raza and *el Movimiento* Chicano, and their contributions to feminist advances took place in part through the labor movement. As a result of their community, labor, and civil rights activism from the 1940s through the 1960s, Mexicanas from Iowa and Illinois were able to demand, and in many cases secure, rights as workers and as U.S. citizens during the 1970s. Their identities as mothers, housewives, breadwinners, and nuns informed their approach to community organizing and workplace advocacy. By bridging the period between "waves," the activism of these midwestern Mexicanas challenges the notion that there was a lull in feminist activism. Their early and little-noted contributions to the women's movement demand a more expansive interpretation of feminist history, one that encompasses family and faith, idealism and bread and butter issues.

Notes

For their insightful comments on earlier drafts of this chapter, I wish to thank Marvin Bergman, Jacqueline Castledine, Karissa Haugeberg, Linda K. Kerber, Sharon Lake, Kathleen Laughlin, Bernard Sherman, Roberta Till-Retz, and Omar Valerio-Jiménez.

1. Janet Weaver, "From Barrio to '¡Boicoteo!': The Emergence of Mexican American Activism in Davenport, Iowa, 1917–1970," *Annals of Iowa* 68 (2009): 215–54.
2. *Feminist Coalitions: Historical Perspectives on Second-Wave Feminism in the United States*, ed. Stephanie Gilmore (Urbana: University of Illinois Press, 2008), 3.
3. Dolores Huerta, interview with author, "Relevant or Irrelevant," #49, KALA radio, St. Ambrose University, Davenport, Iowa, 24 June 2009. Richard A. Garcia, "Dolores Huerta: Woman, Organizer, and Symbol," *California History*, 72 (1993): 56–71; Margaret Rose, "Traditional and Nontraditional Patterns of Female Activism in the United Farm Workers of America, 1962–1980," *Frontiers: A Journal of Women's Studies*, 11 (1990): 26–32.
4. For a perspective on why Mexicanas did not identify as "feminists," see Alma M. Garcia, "The Development of Chicana Feminist Discourse, 1970–1980," *Gender and Society*, Vol. 3, No. 2 (1989): 217–38.
5. Vicki L. Ruiz, *From Out of the Shadows: Mexican Women in Twentieth-Century America* (New York: Oxford University Press, [1998] 2008); Benita Roth, *Separate Roads to Feminism: Black, Chicana, and White Feminist Movements in America's Second Wave* (New York: Cambridge University Press, 2004), 129–77; Cynthia E. Orozco, *No Mexicans, Women, or Dogs Allowed: The Rise of the Mexican American Civil Rights Movement* (Austin: University of Texas Press, 2009).
6. Dionicio Nodín Valdés, *Barrios Norteños: St. Paul and Midwestern Mexican Communities in the Twentieth Century* (Austin: University of Texas Press, 2000), 129.
7. Valdés, *Barrios Norteños*; idem, *Al Norte: Agricultural Workers in the Great Lakes Region, 1917–1970* (Austin: University of Texas Press, 1991); Richard Santillán, "Midwestern Mexican American Women and the Study for Gender Equality: A Historical Overview: 1920s–1970s," *Perspectives in Mexican American Studies* 5 (1995): 79–119; Zaragosa Vargas, *Proletarians of the North: A History of Mexican Industrial Workers in Detroit and the Midwest, 1917–1933* (Berkeley: University of California Press, 1993).
8. "Cook's Point Economic Survey: Tabulation of Results," 1949, Rev. William T. O'Connor Collection, St. Ambrose University Library Archives, Davenport, Iowa.
9. Biographical information, Mary Terronez Papers, Iowa Women's Archives, University of Iowa Libraries, Iowa City (hereafter cited as IWA); Mary Terronez, interview with Kären Mason, Davenport, Iowa, 30 December 2003, IWA.
10. Michelle Hall Kells, *Hector P. García: Everyday Rhetoric and Mexican American Civil Rights* (Carbondale: Southern Illinois University Press, 2006); Mary Vasquez Olvera, interview with author, Davenport, 7 November 2006, IWA.
11. Richard Santillán, "Rosita the Riveter: Midwest Mexican American Women During World War II, 1941–1945," *Perspectives in Mexican American Studies*, 2 (1989): 115–47; Estefanía Rodriguez, interview with Iskra Nuñez, Davenport, 11 August 2005, IWA; *Quad-City Times*, 31 August 2004; Mary Olvera interview.
12. Maria Aguilera Papers, IWA; Valdés, *Barrios Norteños*, 149; Weaver, "Barrio to '¡Boicoteo!'": 235.
13. Mary Terronez became a US citizen in 1963, Mary Terronez Papers; "Racial Injustice in Iowa," *Labor*, Vol. 26, No. 15 (October 1963), Rev. William T. O'Connor Collection.
14. "Racial Injustice in Iowa"; George William McDaniel, "Catholic Action in Davenport: St. Ambrose College and the League for Social Justice," *Annals of Iowa* 55 (1996): 262–65.
15. Ula Y. Taylor, *The Veiled Garvey: The Life & Times of Amy Jacques Garvey* (Chapel Hill: University of North Carolina Press, 2002), 64.

16. McDaniel, "Catholic Action in Davenport"; Weaver, "Barrio to '¡Boicoteo!'": 226–29.
17. Ann Toney, interview with author, Davenport, 22 May 2008, author's files; George William McDaniel, "Trying Iowa's Civil Rights Act in Davenport: The Case of Charles and Ann Toney," *Annals of Iowa* 60 (2001): 231–43.
18. McDaniel, "Catholic Action in Davenport"; Weaver, "Barrio to '¡Boicoteo!'": 226–29; Carmella and Perry Ramirez, interview with author, Davenport, 16 August 2007, IWA.
19. Teresa Paloma Acosta and Ruthe Winegarten, *Las Tejanas: 300 Years of History* (Austin: University of Texas Press, 2003), 217–18; Mary Olvera interview; Richard Santillán, "Latino Politics in the Midwestern United States: 1915–1986," in *Latinos and the Political System,* ed. F. Chris Garcia (Notre Dame, IN: University of Notre Dame Press, 1988), 99–124.
20. Cynthia E. Orozco, "Alice Dickerson Montemayor: Feminism and Mexican American Politics in the 1930s" in *Writing the Range: Race, Class and Culture in the Women's West,* eds. Elizabeth Jameson and Susan Armitage (Norman: University of Oklahoma Press, 1997), 435–56; idem, "Regionalism, Politics, and Gender in Southwest History: The League of United Latin American Citizens' Expansion into New Mexico from Texas, 1929–1945," *Western History Quarterly* 29 (1998): 459–83.
21. Jesse Mosqueda and Felix Sanchez, "Iowa LULAC History, 1957–1972," 3 June 1972, LULAC Council 10 records, IWA. Weaver, "Barrio to '¡Boicoteo!'": 229–33, 237–38.
22. Estefanía Rodriguez interview.
23. "Iowa LULAC History, 1957–1972."
24. Estefanía Rodriguez interview; minutes, 26 April 1960, LULAC Council 10 Records; LULAC Council 10 newsletter, 21 October 1998, idem; *Quad-City Times,* 31 August 2004. Born in 1923, Rodriguez grew up in Holy City, a predominantly Mexican settlement on the Mississippi in Bettendorf, Iowa, just three miles from Cook's Point. During the 1910s, her mother, "Muggie" Adams Rodriguez, managed a boarding house in the coal mining town of Buxton in southcentral Iowa. There Adams met and married Norberto Rodriguez, who had been a lodger at her boarding house. (Family history, Ernest Rodriguez Papers, IWA; Department of Commerce and Labor, *Thirteenth Census of the United States: 1910 – Population,* Buxton Town, Monroe County, Iowa.) The 1910 census records Margarita Adams as Muggie (her nickname) Glenn (the name of her first husband Adolphus Glenn).
25. Lucy Vargas, interview with author, Davenport, 3 October 2006, IWA.
26. LULAC Council 10 newsletter, April 1961, LULAC Council 10 Records; "scholarship program" folders, Box 4, idem; Salvador Lopez, interview with author, Davenport, 21 May 2007, IWA.
27. Dorothy Sue Cobble, *The Other Women's Movement: Workplace Justice and Social Rights in Modern America* (Princeton, NJ: Princeton University Press, 2004); For the role of rank-and-file women in legitimizing the demands of middle-class feminist organizations, see Dennis Deslippe, *Rights, Not Roses: Unions and the Rise of Working-Class Feminism, 1945–1980* (Urbana: University of Illinois Press, 2000).
28. Weaver, "Barrio to '¡Boicoteo!'": 235–53.
29. Ibid; *¿A donde vamos ahora? (Where are we going now?)* A Report of the Problems of the Spanish Surnamed and Migrant Population in Iowa prepared by the Iowa State Advisory Committee to the US Commission on Civil Rights, September 1970, LULAC Council 10 Records.
30. Quad-City Grape Boycott Committee newsletter, 18 April 1969, LULAC Council 10 records; *Times-Democrat,* 26 February 1969; film of Hero Street ceremony, possession of Mary Terronez.
31. The term "settled-out" describes former migrant agricultural laborers who had settled out of the migrant stream to live permanently in an area where they had previously worked seasonally.
32. "Ask Schools, Not Fields for Migrants," *Des Moines Register,* 28 February 1967; Irene Guzman, interview with Teresa García, Des Moines, 12 July 2007, IWA.

33. CEO letter, 24 April 1969, Muscatine Migrant Committee (MMC) Records, IWA; Gloria Casas, interview with Iskra Nuñez, Muscatine, Iowa, 16 June 2005, IWA. On the use of the term "La Raza" by Mexican American civil rights organizations, see David G. Gutiérrez, *Walls and Mirrors: Mexican Americans, Mexican Immigrants, and the Politics of Ethnicity* (Berkeley: University of California Press, 1995), 35–36.

34. "Migrants Set Heinz Boycott," *Davenport Catholic Messenger*, 10 April 1969; Weaver, "Barrio to '¡Boicoteo!'": 195–201.

35. "Sister Irene and Sister Molly: Nightingales for Migrant Workers," *Des Moines Register*, 20 November 1977.

36. Sister Irene Muñoz, interview with Iskra Nuñez and author, Ottumwa, Iowa, 3 August 2005, IWA.

37. MMC annual report, 1969, 38, University of Iowa Libraries; board of directors minutes, 28 March 1967, 27 June 1967, 5 July 1967, MMC records, IWA.

38 *Des Moines Register*, 20 November 1977.

39. Irene Muñoz interview.

40. Juanita and Ernest Rodriguez, interview with Iskra Nuñez and author, 6 August 2005, IWA; court intake record, Milan, Iowa, for Sister Molly Muñoz, arrested in Buffalo Prairie, Iowa, 22 August 1978, Sister Molly Muñoz folder, IWA.

41. Irene Muñoz interview.

42. *LULAC Glances*, October 1969, LULAC Council 10 Records; *¿A donde vamos ahora?*

43. "Davenport LULACs to Mexican American Midwest Conference," *LULAC Glances*, 26 May 1970; Registration for Urban Studies Mexican American Conference, University of Notre Dame, 17–18 April 1970; *Columnas*, Davenport, 28 May 1970, Ernest Rodriguez Papers.

44. *LULAC Glances*, 26 May 1970; "$624,000 asked by Midwest Council of La Raza," *Columnas*, 1970 (p. 8), Ernest Rodriguez Papers; *Los Desarraigados*, Notre Dame, IN, Vol. 1, No. 2, Junio 1973, Sister Irene Muñoz folder, IWA; *The Spirit of Houston, the First National Women's Conference* (National Commission on the Observance of International Women's Year, Washington D.C, March 1978), 280.

45. "MIN-CO Demand," *Friendly News*, Davenport, July 1970, LULAC Council 10 records; "Public Meeting MIN-CO," May 1970, idem; "30 Total in Davenport - Minority Teachers Hiked," *Times-Democrat*, 21 July 1970; "Profile Davenport Schools," 19 July 1968, report of the Iowa Civil Rights Commission, Merle Fleming papers, IWA.

46. "Not Everybody Loves An Oscar Mayer Weiner," *Ain't I a Woman? A Midwest Newspaper of Women's Liberation* Vol. 1, No. 4, 21 August 1970, IWA.

47. Ibid.

48. Ibid; *Times-Democrat*, 12 August 1970; *Times-Democrat*, 13 August 1970; Dolores [Carrillo] Garcia, interview with author, Davenport, 22 September 2005, IWA.

49. Dolores [Carrillo] Garcia, interviews with author, Davenport, 22 September 2005 and 26 September 2006; Ernest Rodriguez to author, 2 March 2006, author's files.

50. Mary Terronez, interview with author, Davenport, 10 October 2006, IWA; Dolores Garcia interviews; Maria Mercedes Aguilera interviews with author, Davenport, 22 September 2005 and 19 September 2006, IWA; *Ain't I A Woman?* 21 August, 1970.

51. *Ain't I A Woman*; Rodriguez to author. The Bendix Dexterity Test, given to women applicants at Oscar Mayer, was designed for female-designated jobs on the sliced meat line.

52. *Times-Democrat*, 27 February 1971; *Catholic Messenger*, 15 October 1970; Untitled history of the Area Board for Migrants (ABFM), ca. 1974, ABFM folder, MMC Records.

53. Untitled history of the ABFM.

54. Ernest Rodriguez, eulogy for Mary Terronez, 9 September, 2009, Mary Terronez papers; Mary Terronez resumé, ibid; Mary Terronez interview, 10 October 2006; Dolores [Carrillo] Garcia interview, 26 September 2006; ABFM folder, LULAC Council 10 Records.

55. LULAC Council 10 newsletter, 21 October 1998; *Quad-City Times*, 31 August 2004; *Quad-City Times*, 23 May 1999; Estefanía Rodriguez interview. The words passed down from

mother to daughter come from a poem by Caroline Howard Gilman published in *Stories and Poems by Mother and Daughter* (Boston: Lee and Shephard, 1872).

56. *The Eastside Story*, Davenport, January 1971, LULAC Council 10 Records; *Times-Democrat*, 30 January 1971; *Chicago Daily Defender*, 14 August 1969; Anne M. Valk, "'Mother Power': The Movement for Welfare Rights in Washington D. C., 1966–1972," *Journal of Women's History* Vol. 11, No. 4 (Winter 2000): 34–58.

57. *Friendly News*, Davenport, July 1970, Box 9, LULAC Council 10 records.

58. Maria Aguilera interviews.

59. "Farmall Workers Honor Picket," *Hard Times, the Workers' Newspaper*, Davenport, 5 November 1975, LULAC Council 10 Records; *Quad-City Times*, 4 November 1975; Henry Vargas, interview with author, Davenport, 26 September 2006, IWA.

60. From William D. Faughnan, Department of Defense, to Henry P. Vargas, president LULAC Council 10, 20 August 1976, LULAC Council 10 Records. The Department of Defense was the federal agency that oversaw contract compliance with federal employment regulations.

61. Eva Savala, interview with author, East Moline, Illinois, 27 September 2005, IWA; Savala resumé, IWA. Richard Santillán references Eva Savala, spelled "Zavala," in "Midwestern Mexican-American Women and the Struggle for Gender Equality," 104, and fn. 59 and 67.

62. Eva Savala interview.

63. Ibid.

PART **IV**

Feminist Consciousness and Movement Persistence

"Stop That Rambo Shit… This Is Feminist Softball"
Reconsidering Women's Organizing in the Reagan Era and Beyond

JACQUELINE L. CASTLEDINE AND JULIA SANDY-BAILEY

In 1992 the *National Enquirer* trained its tabloid lens on the small city of Northampton, Massachusetts, branding it "the strange town where men aren't wanted." According to the magazine, Northampton had become the home of "10,000 cuddling, kissing lesbians."[1] A flurry of mainstream media attention—rarely as colorful—followed the *Enquirer*'s article on the transformation of this former mill town into a lesbian haven. While some reporting followed the sensationalistic approach of the *Enquirer*, the liberal press portrayed the city and its lesbian population as models of tolerance in a period of heated culture wars. With such titles as "A Town Like No Other," (*Newsweek*), "Women Who Love Women" (*20/20*) and "Village People" (*London Independent*), both U.S. and overseas media expressed fascination with the visibility of these "out" lesbians.[2] Even in sympathetic coverage, their sheer numbers remained a focus of attention; *20/20* reported with awe, "There are enough of them to make up the majority of 16 teams in a women's softball league."[3]

By the early 1990s Northampton was both a center of feminist activism and the cultural heartbeat of the Pioneer Valley of Western Massachusetts. Progressive politics fueled by social justice causes had for centuries been a hallmark of this politically active community located in the lower

Connecticut River basin. The town's reformist politics was inextricably linked with Smith College alum Betty Friedan and her groundbreaking 1963 manifesto *The Feminine Mystique*; more recently, freedom of sexual expression, like issues of women's equality, peace, and civil rights had become prominent in Valley political organizing. As one scholar writes of the period, "the Valley, and particularly Northampton, was 'out' territory in terms of visibility, community activity and organization."[4] Nowhere was this intersection of space, visibility, and community activism more evident in the Valley than in the play and the politics of the Mary Vazquez Softball League.

While their sexuality was closely scrutinized by the *Enquirer*, the politics of Valley lesbians remained unexamined by the tabloid. Indeed, national media coverage of women's activism during this period nearly always highlighted a much discussed "backlash" against feminism, which some argued had crippled the movement. Few seemed to notice that depictions of Northampton's lesbians, including their softball league, suggested the healthy pulse of a feminist movement that many scholars and social critics had already declared dead. A recent community oral history project documenting the evolution of what would become the Mary V. Softball League, still active today, suggests a revision of long-standing paradigms central to U.S. women's social movement history may be in order.[5]

Scholars have already begun to question early analyses of "second wave" feminism that describe a post-suffrage movement fallen stagnant in the early 1920s until white, heterosexual, middle-class women were called to arms by the publication of Friedan's *Feminine Mystique*. Important studies on women's social movements have challenged this paradigm, weakening wave theory—that is, the theory that evolved to support the wave metaphor—by locating feminism in earlier decades and examining the activism of women of color and lesbians. Books by Joanne Meyerowitz, Kate Weigand, Daniel Horowitz, Dorothy Sue Cobble, Judith Ezekiel, Anne Enke, Kimberly Springer, Becky Thompson, and Stephanie Gilmore, among others, have broadened our understanding, and, in some cases the definition, of feminism. Still largely unchallenged in these studies, however, is the notion that since the mid-1980s feminism in the United States is a movement in decline. According to social critics, feminists facing backlash now focused their attention only on maintaining rights they won in the hard-fought battles of the late 1960s and the 1970s.[6]

A look beyond large national organizations to grassroots, local movements suggests that this may not be the case. Although neither extend beyond the 1980s, Enke's study of Minneapolis/St. Paul feminism, *Finding the Movement* and Ezekiel's of Ohio's National Organization for Women, *Feminism in the Heartland* help us to conceptualize new understandings of feminist activism by foregrounding the voices of local activists. As the history of Minneapolis/St. Paul is for Enke's study, and Ohio is for Ezekiel's, understanding the unique social and political history of "the Valley," and particularly the cities of Amherst and Northampton, is essential to understanding how social movement history in this area challenges current hegemonic theories about the perceived demise of modern feminism. Interviews with members of the Mary V. League about their activism in the 1990s and beyond map the league's competing and evolving feminisms, revealing the political, philosophical, and emotional struggles of women activists throughout the latter decades of the twentieth century. Moreover, these interviews illustrate the passionate debates surrounding the role that competition should play in feminist sport.

Women interviewed about their play in the Mary V. League recall an organization that provided members a supportive lesbian feminist community at the same time that it created the opportunity to discuss political issues—on the ball field, during practice, over drinks after games—as they explored how the "personal is political." Even some who had no history of prior political activism joined protests, including the unfurling of a banner across the Statue of Liberty demanding an end to discrimination based on race, gender, and sexual orientation.[7] As one player recalls, "even if you didn't have [a feminist sensibility] in the beginning, which some folks didn't, you got it."[8]

The Pioneer Valley Becomes "The Valley"

As early as the nineteenth century, the city of Northampton was a site of utopian political thought, serving as the home to such communities as the Northampton Association of Education and Industry. Counting abolitionist and former slave Sojourner Truth as a member, historian Christopher Clark writes that not only did the utopian Association declare human equality in its constitution "without distinction of sex, color or condition, sect or religion," but a former female member claimed "'the question of equality of the sexes was never discussed'" at Northampton because "'it was accepted as one of our fundamental principles.'"[9] With the Shaker community of Hancock Village established just forty miles to the west of the city in the late eighteenth century, the egalitarian social and political thought of Shakerism was also familiar to the area. The *Enquirer*'s discovery aside, women had long been draw to Northampton's social and religious movements for gender equality.

Education has played an especially important role in the development of Valley women's movements. Despite the convention of the times, the antebellum Northampton Association educated girls and boys using the same curriculum. In the decade following the Civil War, Smith College, one of the seven sister colleges, began admitting students. Sarah Gordon writes of Smith's early years, "the community was organized with a view to dissolving distinctions of wealth and status," and argues that for its students, "this attempted utopia created a valuable memory."[10] In the neighboring town of South Hadley, Mount Holyoke Seminary, founded in 1837, began in the mid-1880s its transition to an all-women college. Since their founding, these two elite women's institutions have continued to attract students who following graduation choose to make the Valley their home. Nearby Amherst and Hampshire colleges, along with the University of Massachusetts, join Smith and Mount Holyoke to form the Five College Consortium, providing solid support for women's movements.

This long tradition of Valley women's activism continued well into the twentieth century and included the 1969 formation of Amherst Women's Liberation, which within a year boasted one hundred members and a newly opened Valley Women's Center (VWC) offering study groups, welfare advocacy, and counseling. Clearly influenced by a vital national movement, in 1971 and 1972 local college organizations hosted talks by such high-profile feminist activists as Robin Morgan, Kate Millet, and Gloria Steinem. Following a now legendary 1971 commencement address at her alma mater Smith College—in which she famously accused President Richard Nixon of warmongering and called for the liberalization of abortion laws—Steinem paid a visit to Amherst's fledgling Women's Center.[11]

In important ways, the area's colleges and universities also helped lay the groundwork for a Valley women's softball league; its two founding teams, the Hot Flashes and Common Womon, began in local college communities. The former grew out of informal softball games organized by Jean Grossholtz, a professor in the Mount Holyoke Women's Studies department and a well-known leftist activist. At first the softball games organized by Grossholtz were little more than casual meetings of adults and children playing together on Sunday afternoons. These games drew wider participation when in 1976 Jean placed a classified advertisement in the alternative weekly the *Valley Advocate*, inviting anyone interested in playing softball to meet at a local school on Saturday mornings. Sociologist Martha Acklesburg remembers hearing about these freewheeling games when she was a newly hired faculty member at Smith College. As she recalls, the pick-up games slowly evolved into a more formal all-female team, with a decidedly feminist and lesbian composition. For the first few years after it was formed, the Hot Flashes, defiantly named by Jean for the symptoms she was experiencing in menopause, played against local church and community teams. Her lesbian household, which was a local hub of feminist and political activism, remained at the center of these early games.[12]

Grossholtz founded her team with an explicitly feminist philosophy that shared the vision of earlier utopian Valley movements.[13] As she explains, "We thought that we could build a new society that we could leave behind all of this male created social structure and make a different structure…so that we could deal with conflict, we could deal with each other, in a much different way…that's what we were trying to do with the softball league."[14] In tying social inequality to patriarchal capitalist values, her radical feminism expressed an expansive critique of capitalism and the role that competition for resources played in U.S. domestic and foreign policy.

At the same time that Grossholtz's team hoped to "expand the feminist community" in South Hadley, players on her team heard about another feminist team forming in nearby Amherst. Common Womon would become the long-running rival of the Hot Flashes. Founding team member Elaine Stewart remembers that the Amherst team grew out of the Southwest Women's Center at the University of Massachusetts.[15] Many of the players were UMass graduate students, who initially named their team the Lucy Stoners after the nineteenth-century suffragist. They soon changed the team's name to Common Womon in honor of a local restaurant best remembered not for its food, but for its strong support of women's causes.[16] For the first few years Common Womon played intramurals at the University of Massachusetts on whichever field they could appropriate and, like the Hot Flashes, played against community and church teams.[17] As the Hot Flashes and Common Womon began attracting more and more players, new lesbian-feminist teams grew out of them. The late 1970s brought the formation of half-a-dozen new teams. Though the exact date that these teams became a formalized league is disputed among players, most agree that by 1980 it was a lesbian-feminist softball league. Throughout the 1980s the league fielded between seven and fifteen teams, and in 1992 reached an all-time high of sixteen.

Lesbian Feminist Sport

As a growing women's liberation movement inspired women to challenge conventional gender roles in the early to mid-1970s, the Pioneer Valley was not the only home of lesbian feminist softball. Writing in 1976, activist Vicki Gabriner observed, "out-lesbian softball teams, both slow and fast pitch, have formed and entered City Leagues in Washington, DC, Lexington, Kentucky, San Francisco, California, Columbia, South Carolina, Athens, Georgia, to mention a few."[18] Anne Enke points out that for women involved in league play in the Midwest, "prior to the gay and lesbian liberation movement, softball provided a visible arena of lesbian community when other arenas were hidden, exclusive, or absent."[19] Valley players shared a great deal with their counterparts in other areas of the country who saw in softball the opportunity for healthy recreation and lesbian community building. The Mary V. League also shared a demographic make-up with other lesbian feminist teams and leagues that were largely white and middle class. Gabriner wrote of her team in Atlanta, for all of its earnest concern about diversity and its efforts to promote women's leadership, their movement "has been criticized justly for its middle class and white bias."[20] Unlike Atlanta, however, the demographics of the Mary V. League closely matched those of the area. Of the 824 Valley women identifying themselves as lesbians in the 1990 census, 99 percent were non-Hispanic white.[21]

In some ways the merging of Common Woman and Hot Flashes into a lesbian-feminist league was an ideal fit. As their names suggest, founders of these teams were deeply committed to women's issues, and feminist thought structured the rules and play of these early teams. The team philosophy of Common Woman mirrored the philosophy of Hot Flashes with its informal coaching and rules that, despite skill level, every member had the opportunity to play. As one Common Woman player recounts, "we were going to be very feminist" about including women who lacked playing experience, and that meant "you *had* to be encouraging."[22] The goal was to create a positive sports experience for women with little or no athletic background so they could gain new skills, build confidence, and learn teamwork. One Common Womon player remembers that "equality was the theme. So everyone had the opportunity, everyone got to play X amount of time. And [there was] lots of verbal support, emotional support, faith, confidence that women could do it, support to overcome whatever fears."[23] These and other collective memories of team members suggest that the community building fostered by league rules also helped to raise the feminist consciousness of league members.

Most importantly, the philosophy of non-competitive play was at the heart of both teams. Common Womon's team motto, "every ball missed helps another woman," expressed this idea entirely.[24] Even as it evolved from separate teams into a full-fledged league, players held onto a philosophy of non-competition established in this early era.[25] Indeed, the teams fielded on any given Sunday would not call balls and strikes or keep score, so that everyone batted until she got a hit. Jean Grossholtz remembers that when someone made a good play both teams would "stop playing and go hug that person.... [S]omebody would slide in and knock you over and... everybody would come over and hug the person who slid into you."[26] Gabriner's comment that Atlanta teams also, "downplayed the hard-line do-or-die fierce competition" and "sought to play in an atmosphere of positive support" suggests that the issue of non-competition was central to a developing lesbian feminist sports ethos.[27]

The spirit of non-competition defining the early years of the Mary V. League reflected political views of league leadership, and while some players remember the league as a strictly social experience, most considered it a place to be around politically likeminded women. Mary Ann Jennings remembers a fellow player who joined the league with "pretty much no awareness of feminism" who "constantly had her jaw drop at a conversation that some of us would be having about some such inequalities and unfairness."[28] League members were inspired by a variety of political causes, as illustrated by team names. Names like Common Womon, Womenrising, and Womynfire underscored a feminist philosophy. No Nukes of the North's play on the title "Nanook of the North" revealed both the light-hearted nature of its members and their identification with the antinuclear movement, while the Left Sox suggested an affiliation with leftist politics.

The very act of playing softball can be understood in feminist terms; many of the players who joined softball teams across the nation in the 1970s and early 1980s had never played sports as young women and "thought of sports as being a kind of unpleasant territory for women."[29] Included in the founding goals of the Mary V. League was the idea that women should learn athletic skills and gain experience working as a team, and that "every woman should have sort of success playing, because women had been excluded from sports."[30] One player remembers:

> I really loved wearing a uniform, I loved finding you could go to a sports store…and buy boys extra large baseball pants and wear 'em…. I loved getting sweaty, completely sweating to shreds t-shirts in a game. I loved getting dirty, [a]bove my cleats and at my ankles, sweating so much that clay caked up…. [This was] stuff you weren't supposed to do if you were a girl. [I] just loved it.[31]

For this player and others like her, softball was fun and confidence-building not in spite of the way it defied gender norms, but because of it.

Although it was not founded as an explicitly lesbian league, most Mary V. players were lesbian and understood the league as a safe space free of the hostility they encountered elsewhere. Ball fields in the Valley, as they did in communities across the nation, took on new meaning for women who in the past, if they considered it at all, thought of recreational public space as male territory. Enke writes that women exploring intersections of sport and sexuality were, "claiming new spaces, taking up space and moving aggressively within space: these were part and parcel of a new feminist and lesbian activism."[32] These two distinct social identities and the activism they inspired sometimes, but not always, converged in Mary V. League play. The feminism that resulted was defined by the belief that women were denied the social, political, and economic opportunities that men historically enjoyed—including participation in sport—and that through building an egalitarian feminist community, women could challenge and overcome gender inequality.

The intersection of social identities on ball fields often brought to light physical and emotional realities of lesbian life as well. Vicki Gabriner writes about her experiences, "Practice and games were a tremendous physical and psychic release for us after a day's work in the closet."[33] Some Mary V. League members believed the league was the *only* place where they could be "out." One player, Mary McClintock, worked in a conservative religious environment and felt she "had to be very closeted at work." She first heard about the league while an undergraduate at Mount Holyoke, but did not join a team until she returned to the area a few years after graduation. While she had played softball and other sports as a child, McClintock was attracted to the league as a way to "connect with other women and lesbians in the area." When she first began to play softball, she worked as a guide for outdoor activities and trips for kids in the neighboring communities of Agawam and Springfield. Yet, she found her work environment hostile to homosexuals, especially when her employer took sexual orientation *out* of its non-discrimination policy. Playing in the league offered McClintock a place to let down her guard and talk about her partner, also a teammate.[34]

As McClintock's experiences reveal, even for lesbians in Amherst and Northampton in the post-Stonewall years, the relative safety of the ball field was juxtaposed with the stark reality of homophobia still evident in areas of their communities. Linda Pisano played for New Attitude and also remembers meeting people through her work in the Northampton District Attorney's office who, despite the city's reputation as a bastion of progressivism, told homophobic jokes, and referred to homosexuals as "fags." For her, the softball league was an "incredibly safe place to go," providing the physical space and emotional support to be herself, and helping to balance the harsh realities of her professional life.[35] Therefore, while she felt safe on the field, a player might feel anxiety when her team would go out together after games. One interviewee remembered that while her teammates would loudly debate politics, feminism, and lesbianism in local restaurants and bars, she feared that straight colleagues may be within earshot, putting her job in jeopardy.[36]

Differing levels of political consciousness aligned in the Mary V. League with varying needs for social, professional, and interpersonal connections to create a lesbian feminist movement that was, like its teams, rarely static. One league event illustrates both the politically contested space of the softball field and the diversity of this grassroots activism. The Hot Flashes and Common Womon had a tradition of alternately hosting an extravaganza to mark their last contest of the playing season. In 1982 Common Womon performed a parody of the traditional "homecoming parade" before their game on a UMass field. With tongue in cheek, a baton twirling team member kicked off the parade, followed by a tiara-clad "parade queen" riding in the back seat of a convertible. With Meg Christian's anthem "Here Come the Lesbians" playing, the queen waved to those lining the route. Players marched behind the convertible, and at parade's end lined up to jump through a hoop reading, "Every Common Womon Needs a Hot Flash." Yet in sharp contradiction to the frivolity of the day, and perhaps because the parade was being filmed by a teammate, the player driving the queen's car sat behind a carnival mask, hiding from the larger community her membership in the league. Despite the opportunity to claim the right to public space as well as lesbian sexual and political identities, as many of her teammates did, this university employee chose to literally "mask" herself out of fear of losing her job. She was not alone in her concern about living an openly lesbian life, other players balked when an author proposing to write an article about the league sought to include team photos. "I can't be in that—nobody can take my picture—I'm a teacher, I'll get fired," one protested. [37] Seemingly unconcerned about being "out" on the softball diamond, these players did not believe that their concept of safe space extended beyond the confines of the ball field. Indeed, they believed that irrefutable documentation of their participation in a largely lesbian softball league threatened their financial well-being.

The ambivalence with which some players associated themselves with the league is best understood within the context of the history of the gay rights movement. Historian Richard Meyer argues that such radical organizations as the Gay Liberation Front of the early 1970s "positioned visibility—including the photographic visibility of its social gatherings and political demonstrations—as a key component of its broader mission." The camera, Meyers explains, functioned as "an active participant in, rather than a neutral recorder of, gay liberation." [38] As he suggests, photographs of events like the homecoming parade could potentially be used by both opponents of gay rights seeking to discredit the movement, and by supporters intending to promote it. Faced with this "double jeopardy," some league members went out of their way to avoid the camera's gaze.

Legal advances made by the national gay rights movement slowly helped to alleviate concerns among some about their visibility, and the 1980s marked a period of rising prominence for the Valley lesbian community. In a significant move toward greater collective visibility, Northampton's first Gay and Lesbian Pride parade took place in spring 1982. [39] Two years later the community rallied, albeit unsuccessfully, to protest Smith College's decision to close the lesbian dorm Hover House. In spring 1986 the University of Massachusetts established a Lesbian and Gay awareness week to bring attention to gay issues, and, by the end of the decade, a Lesbian and Gay Liberation March in Northampton attracted nearly two thousand supporters. In the early 1990s Mary Vazquez Softball League was named in appreciation for a member who took on the onerous task of organizing team play and scheduling ball fields. By this time it was more visible in the community and included such alumnae as openly lesbian Northampton city official Mary Clare Higgins. Indeed, no media report filed on the city in the mid-1990s was complete without mention of "its lesbian city councilor," now the mayor, or reference to the *National Enquirer*'s claim that Northampton was "Lesbianville, USA."

Lesbian Sport and Contested Values

As the league grew from two teams, to six, to fielding sixteen at its height, it became vitally important to expanding options for lesbian socializing in the Pioneer Valley. Jean Grossholtz explains that before the softball league the only place to meet other lesbians was at political meetings or bars. And unlike a bar scene, the softball league was:

> A place for people to get together and you didn't have to be drinking, or anything, or smoking, or anything like that. And you didn't have to be on the make… It took a lot of the pressure off of lesbian relationships, or lesbian[s] meeting and forming relationships.[40]

Teammates socialized after games, threw parties, and took vacations together. They saw each other through sicknesses, lost jobs, and the deaths of partners or other loved ones. UMass professor Pat Griffin remembers, "your team was your family."[41] Although league members' experiences mirrored those of other lesbian athletes—sports historian Susan Cahn writes that "From at least the 1940s on, sport provided space for lesbians to gather and build a shared culture"—the intensity of the bonds among league players is nonetheless notable.[42]

Yet, as the league grew in size, conflicts arose over its feminist philosophy. At issue was not whether feminist underpinnings would continue to guide league play, but rather what this feminism would look like. The most contentious debate was over the issue of competition in a feminist league. Common Woman quickly became one of the best and, to many, most competitive teams in the league. Their success raised questions about the role of competition in the league, whether it was compatible with feminist philosophy and, if it was, what feminist softball would then look like. Team co-founder Eileen Stewart remembers that in the early days some players so lacked skills that they ran away from the ball when it was hit near them. They "couldn't quite get the idea that you're supposed to catch [and] run toward the ball."[43] By 1980, however, the team had attracted several coaches from the University of Massachusetts as well as others with backgrounds in softball or other sports. These women questioned the assumption that competition and feminism were antithetical philosophies. Pat Griffin was one of those coaches who felt that competition and feminism went hand-in-hand. In the 1970s Griffin had come to UMass to pursue her Doctorate of Education. After completing her degree, she became a professor of Social Justice Education at the University. She would go on to become one of the leading experts in sports education and, in particular, heterosexism and homophobia in athletics. While an undergraduate at the University of Maryland, Griffin played basketball and field hockey, and in the late 1970s coached the University's swim team. Although softball "was never...one of my major sports," she decided to join Common Womon after attending games with friends. "Nobody ever said it was a lesbian league," remembers Griffin, but "it was pretty clear from the beginning that this was not going to be your average softball league."[44] With her strong athletic background she proved to be one of the league's better athletes.

Griffin had both an interest in sports and a commitment to feminism. "I defined my coaching style at UMass as feminist coaching," she remembers. "It really appealed to me, the ideas of having a place where women of all different...sports experience[s] and skill levels could come together and try to play a game hard and be competitive."[45] And Griffin was not the only woman for whom competition and feminism went hand-in-hand. Many league players felt empowered by the hard play they found on the field. As Common Womon co-founder Eileen Stewart summed it up: "I looked around and I said, 'listen, this is crazy to be saying we shouldn't be competitive. These women are *extremely* competitive, they are *extremely* achievement-oriented. And when they get up to bat, they want to get a hit.'"[46] For these women being competitive defied gender expectations and was a way to enjoy the game in a way usually reserved for men.

But many league members resented the competitiveness of some teams and believed that it violated the spirit of feminist sisterhood. "We CAN laugh about it now, but it hurt," recalls Stewart. "It was tough at the time. And that was a very central issue for feminism in this area, at least, about competition, and how you could be competitive." Could a feminist enjoy competition, or would embracing it signify "selling out" to destructive patriarchal principles? For Jean Grossholtz, the league represented an opportunity to expand her anti-poverty, gay rights, and feminist activism during a period of political repression. For lesbian feminists like Stewart, however, this too often looked like "the old kind of feminism where everything was a chore." In their view, focus on egalitarianism in team play too often led the league "to play to the lowest common denominator."[47] Even those who did not see their team play as feminist activism were influenced by the debates taking place.

These debates over competition occurred within a rapidly changing context surrounding women and athletics. Strenuous physical activity and competition had historically been associated with masculinity and seen as a threat both to women's health and to heterosexual norms. Historian Ellen Gerber points to the 1920s as a period when physical educators worked to end intercollegiate competition for women based, in part, on fears concerning the high levels of competition in varsity leagues.[48] Susan Cahn agrees, arguing that underlying concerns about women and competition was often the understanding that women's competitive sport was undesirable because it represented a challenge to U.S. manhood.[49] The issue of women's athletic competition gained new prominence with passage of Title IX in 1972. This act, which, among other provisions, prohibits gender discrimination in schools receiving federal funding, revolutionized women's participation in sports. Many women involved in sports before Title IX "shared a commitment to a more participation-oriented, less elitist approach to sports that differed fundamentally from the reining male model of sports which intertwined competition, winning, and commercialization."[50] As women's collegiate athletics grew, its management shifted from the female-led Commission on Intercollegiate Athletics for Women (CIAW) and Association for Intercollegiate Athletics for Women (AIAW) to the male-dominated National Collegiate Athletic Association (NCAA), an organization which governed most of men's college sports. As the NCAA took over more and more control of women's athletics, these women's organizations—along with female coaches and administrators—lost influence. With this shift, the traditional model for women's athletics gave way to a more competition oriented model. And while some women lamented this change, others embraced it as a way for women to challenge the gender norms of the past.[51]

The issue of competition surfaced continually within the Mary V. League. Linda Pisano believes that some considered her team, New Attitude, one of the more competitive teams in the league. This was especially apparent during a game when Jean Grossholtz chided one of her teammates for playing hard even though she had a bandaged leg. Pisano recalls Grossholtz yelling, "'Stop that Rambo shit' . . . This is feminist softball, you know, if you're hurt, sit down.'"[52] But even Jean believed that as the league formalized it was important that all players practice and learn basic skills, if only to avoid injury. Still, some members of the Hot Flashes thought this was being too competitive, and that "we were not living up to our own expectations."[53] A few members even left the league over its increasingly competitive nature.

Though different understandings of the role of competition in team play created tension, most chose to stay in the league and work to find a balance between egalitarian and competitive play, or what players referred to as the "sneakers vs. cleats" issue. Throughout the 1980s and early 1990s organizers struggled with the issue of how the league could accommodate both the utopian vision of its founding with the competitive philosophy of some players and teams who wanted to win but not "win the way that men do."[54] Drawing on existing models of feminism, the league resisted a hierarchical structure and instead sought common ground through egalitarian decision-making. The deliberative process of working through different understandings of competition took place mainly through yearly meetings of team representatives. At these meetings team reps would negotiate league rules, often establishing new ones based on problems they encountered the season before. Mary Ann Jennings, who was Common Woman's team representative at these meetings, remembers a sometimes bitter struggle over the idea of competition, that lasted "twenty years at least."[55] At meetings reps "went over the rules, and wept and gnashed our teeth over some things. There was always discussion over being competitive or non-competitive and it was endless, and it brought me to tears."[56] It was this very process, though, that embodied the spirit of feminism so important to the league.

Through this endless negotiation a delicate balance was struck over the issue of competition within a feminist league. What emerged was a set of rules designed to allow for competitive play while at the same time keeping the feminist philosophy of the league intact. Players had to be encouraging to everyone and could not heckle other teams. Everyone got to play in every game, and pitchers could be asked to slow their pitches to give all players a chance to hit. No standings were kept so there was no league champion. The "gracious sensitivity" rule, as some players called it, went into effect if one team was handily beating the other; the team winning would agree to changes to make the game more even. Thus, right-handed hitters batted left-handed, fielders played positions different from those they normally played, players forewent stealing bases or bunting, and some teams swapped players in the middle of games to even out playing levels. Perhaps most telling, the league created rules for a player who was wheelchair-bound, allowing her a pinch runner and forbidding players from stealing home when she was at bat.

Players also found less formal ways to deal with the issue of competition.

On some teams when a player was being too competitive her teammates would make her leave the field to cool down. Being "sent to the parking lot" was a sure sign someone needed to remember the spirit of the league and, policing their own behavior, players sometimes even took themselves out of the game.[57] Some of the best players also offered to attend other teams' practices to help them develop better skills. UMass softball coach Elaine Sortino gave clinics during the summer that were open to all players. During games she often stopped play to talk to opposing batters about how to best swing the bat.[58] An Incorrects teammate remembers that this spirit of helpfulness could sometimes be overwhelming: "I do remember standing at the plate one time and getting advice from fifteen people. I think they were all yelling at me [about] what I was doing—and I finally just keeled over because...I was so tangled up.... But it was all very friendly."[59] Players often celebrated a good play, even if that play was made by the other team. This happened, especially, when one of the less skilled league members got a big hit or made an exciting defensive play. A player interviewed remembers a woman who stayed in the league for years even though she had few athletic skills. When finally in one game she managed to catch a difficult fly ball, "both benches jumped up and screamed and yelled and clapped forever" because "It was just so cool to see her literally come from not being able to throw a ball to making this great play."[60]

For many, the focus on playing one's best—and seeing other women do the same—was the most important component of this lesbian-feminist league. Eileen Stewart describes herself as someone who, while an experienced softball player, at first had difficulty with the idea of competition in the Mary V. League. But, as time went on, she realized that the more skilled athletes "brought with [them] the possibility of playing [softball] beautifully, and *god*, I just wanted that so much.... I loved how the ball felt, I loved my glove, I loved to make a good play."[61] For Stewart and others the idea of healthy competition became central to what they took away from the league and helped to develop their feminist philosophy.

Mayor Mary Clare Higgins, who had little softball experience before joining the league, believes it was competitive in a "supportive way," and that learning to deal with competition was healthy for women. Higgins argues: "Men are really used to playing on sports teams and really competing and then walking away and being friendly with each other. Women are not used to doing that.... [The] league is a good way to separate that out...[the] idea of playing competition and then being able to walk away in a collaborative, convivial way."[62] Debates about competition were even a strength of the league for some. Pat Griffin argues this was "the essence of so much of what I enjoyed about the league...this managing all these contradictions.... [Not] taking any of them too seriously, but still, at the same time, trying to play this competitive game in a different way that was inclusive."[63] While probably not the feminism of founder Jeans Grossholtz, the league's philosophy by the mid-1990s was nonetheless still built upon a belief in gender equality and the potential of women's sport to help actualize it.

Conclusion

For many players the Mary V. League was a place where playing hard and being competitive gave them a new sense of self and of the possibilities for women. Eileen Stewart remembers an evening of practice when Elaine Sortino was pitching to Pat Griffin. The practice soon turned into a heated contest, as the two gifted athletes tried to better each other. "Elaine was just winging the ball and throwing it as fast as she could," remembers Eileen, and:

> Pat was up there, just swinging at everything, and trying...to put everything over the fence. And I can remember Elaine would... on her windup...throw *'huuht!'* like that, and Pat would take a big cut, *'unnnh!'* And this went on, the two of them, *'unnnh!' 'huuht!' 'unnh!' 'huuht!'* And I thought to myself, *'This is one of the first times I've actually see[n]—and been a part of— two women doing their athletic best, making no bones about it.'...* [It] was just this little flame of desire in both of them, and boy, it was just shining out. And I thought, *'Fabulous. Fabulous! This is me, this is what I want to be. I loved it.'*[64]

As Eileen's comments suggest, the league had a tremendous impact on the lives of many women, playing a significant role in transforming and then helping them to articulate their understanding of feminism. Mapping the competing and evolving feminisms of the Mary V. League reveals the political, philosophical, and emotional struggles of women activists throughout the latter decades of the twentieth century. Moreover, it suggests the vibrancy of this Valley movement as the oral histories of league players bring into question theories about the universality of the current "postfeminist" era. A paradigm shift that incorporates analysis of feminisms not traditionally examined in current literature, such as those evident in the histories of Mary V. League players, has the potential to provide a more comprehensive assessment of women's activism. In such a reassessment, scholars and other observers might start not with the question "does feminism survive in the twenty-first century," but rather with the question, "what does twenty-first century feminism look like?"

Notes

1. Laurie Loisel, "Features that Put Us on the Map," 27 October 2005, *Daily Hampshire Gazette*, http://www.gazettenet.com/2005/10/27/features-put-us-map?SESSa25b99270fe3 cc065395e9b3452635d0=gnews.
2. Barbara Kantrowitz, "A Town Like No Other," *Newsweek*, 21 June 1993, 56–57; "Women Who Love Women," *20/20 ABC News*, 23 October 1992 transcript; Jane Henriques, *Independent* (London), "Village People," 1 February 1997, 16–20.
3. "Women Who Love Women."
4. Ann Forsyth, "'Out' in the Valley," *International Journal of Urban and Regional Research* 21, no. 1, 57.
5. The oral histories quoted in this chapter are part of a project conducted by the Valley Women's History Collaborative (VWHC). The VWHC is a community-based organization in western Massachusetts made up of students, scholars, and community activists who collect and preserve the history of local women who are committed to social justice for women, including self-identified feminists, lesbians, womanists, and queers from the mid-1960s to the present. More information about the Collaborative is found at: http://www.vwhc.org. The authors are indebted to the VWHC students and volunteers who interviewed players from the Mary Vazquez Softball League. We also wish to thank those who graciously agreed to be interviewed for this project, including Lacey Johnston, whose documentary film *In League With US* was instrumental to our understanding of the league's history. See *In League With Us*, Northampton, MA: Elle Jay Productions, 2008, digital video disc, All interviews in this chapter are in possession of the authors.
6. See Elaine J. Hall and Marnie Salupo Rodriguez,"The Myth of Postfeminism," *Gender and Society* 17, no. 6 (2003): 878–902; Jacqueline Castledine, "Visions of a Future Seen Through the Past: Promise of Feminism in the Twenty-First Century," *Women's History Review* 13, no. 2 (2004): 303–10; Pamela Aronson, "Feminists or 'Postfeminists'?: Young Women's Attitudes Toward Feminism and Gender Relations," *Gender and Society* 17, no. 6 (2003): 903–22; Sue O'Sullivan, "What a Difference a Decade Makes: 'Coming to Power' and 'The Second Coming,'" *Feminist Review* no. 61 (1999): 97–126.
7. Sue Tyler, interview by Maria Abunnasr and Caterina Rost, digital recording, Belchertown, Massachusetts, 30 November 2006.
8. Maryann Jennings, interview by Laura Sandhusen, digital recording, Leeds, Massachusetts, 29 November 2007.
9. Christopher Clark, "A Mother and Her Daughters at the Northampton Community: New Evidence on Women in Utopia," *New England Quarterly* 75, no. 4 (Dec. 2002): 592.
10. Sarah H. Gordon, "Smith College Students: The First Ten Classes, 1879–1888," *History of Education Quarterly* 15, no. 2 (Summer, 1975): 148. For more on the history of the Pioneer Valley see Ann Forsyth, "'Out' in the Valley," *International Journal of Urban and Regional Research* 21, no. 1 (1997): 38–62; Tracy Kidder, *Home Town* (New York: Random House, 1999); Kerry W. Buckley, ed. *A Place Called Paradise: Culture and Community in Northampton, Massachusetts, 1654–2004* (Northampton: Historic Northampton Museum and Education Center, in association with University of Massachusetts Press, 2004); and the *Valley Women's History Collaborative Timeline*, http://www.umass.edu/vwhc/timeline.html.
11. Lisa Shawn Hogan, "Gloria Steinem," in *American Voices: An Encyclopedia of Contemporary Orators*, eds. Bernard K Duffy and Richard W. Leeman, (Westport, CT: Greenwood Press, 2005), 422–48. Also see "The Valley Women's Movement: A Herstorical Chronology 1968–1988" at the Valley Women's History Collaborative website, http://www.umass.edu/vwhc/timeline.html.
12. Martha Ackelsberg, interview by Jacqueline Castledine and Julia Sandy-Bailey, digital recording, Northampton, Massachusetts, 6 August 2007; *In League With Us*. Oral histori-

ans often confront with the issue of memory in their work, whether it is conflicting memories of interviewees or recollections that do not match existing historical records. We dealt with these issues throughout our oral history project, especially concerning memories of the founding of the league. Since no records were kept of the league's earliest years, we have relied on interviews to piece together the story of the league's founding. Most trace this to 1976, and the formation of the Hot Flashes and Common Womon. The best interviews for founding-era history are Jean Grossholtz, Maryann Jennings, Eileen Stewart, Sue Tyler, and Mary Vazquez. See also Lacey, *In League With Us*. For a discussion of oral history and memory see Michael Frisch, *A Shared Authority: Essays on the Craft and Meaning of Oral and Public History* (Albany: State University of New York Press, 1990); Ronald J. Grele, "Movement Without Aim: Methodological and Theoretical Problems in Oral History," in *The Oral History Reader*, eds. Robert Perks and Alistair Thomson (London: Routledge, 1998), 38–52. A. Portelli, *The Death of Luigi Trastulli: Form and Meaning in Oral History* (Albany: State University of New York Press, 1991), 1–26; Joan Sangster, "Telling Our Stories: Feminist Debates and the Use of Oral History," in Robert Perks and Alistair Thomson, *The Oral History Reader*: 87–100.

13. Jean Grossholtz, interview by Kristine Newhall, digital recording, Holyoke, Massachusetts, 16 March 2007.
14. Grossholtz interview.
15. Eileen Stewart, interview by Susan Tracy, transcript, Amherst, Massachusetts, 21 August 2000.
16. The restaurant's name was taken from a seven-part Judy Grahn poem "The Common Woman" (1969). The poem reads in part, "[T]he common woman is as common as the best of bread, and will rise, and will become strong." See *The Work of a Common Woman* (Trumansberg, NY: Crossing Press, 1978). We thank Susan Tracy for bringing this to our attention.
17. Pat Griffin, interview by Kristine Newhall, digital recording, Belchertown, Massachusetts, 23 February 2007.
18. Vicki Gabriner, "Come Out Slugging," *Quest: A Feminist Quarterly* 12, no. 3 (1976): 53.
19. Anne Enke, *Finding the Movement: Sexuality, Contested Space, and Feminist Activism* (Durham, NC: Duke University Press, 2007), 145.
20. Gabiner, *"Come Out Slugging,"* 53.
21. Forsythe, "'Out' in the Valley," 51.
22. Stewart interview. Emphasis in original.
23. Linda Marchesani, interview by Stephanie Aines, digital recorded, 10 May 2007.
24. Pat Griffin, interview by Kristine Newhall, digital recording, 13 February 2007.
25. Ackelsberg interview.
26. Grossholtz interview.
27. Gabriner, "Come Out Slugging." For more on the issue of sexuality in women's softball see James T. Sears, *Rebels, Rubyfruit, and Rhinestones: Queering Space in the Stonewall South* (New Brunswick, NJ: Rutgers University Press, 2001); Pat Griffin, "Diamonds, Dykes, and Double Plays," in *Sportsdykes*, Susan Fox Rogers, ed. (New York: St. Martin's, 1994), Yvonne Zipter, *Diamonds Are a Dyke's Best Friend: Reflections, Reminiscences, and Reports from the Field on the Lesbian National Pastime* (Ithaca, NY: Firebrand Books, 1988).
28. Mary Ann Jennings interview.
29. Stewart interview.
30. Ibid.
31. Jennings interview.
32. Enke, *Finding the Movement*, 159.
33. Gabriner, *"Come Out Slugging,"* 55.
34. Mary McClintock, interview by Caro Pinto, digital recording, Amherst, Massachusetts, 18 January 2007.

35. Linda Pisano, interview by Nick Rattner and Sandy Perot, digital recording, Amherst, Massachusetts, 16 October 2007.
36. Elaine Sortino, interview by Julia Sandy-Bailey and Jacqueline Castledine, digital recording, Amherst, Massachusetts, 11 December 2006. For more on homophobia in women's sports see Pat Griffin, *Strong Women, Deep Closets: Lesbians and Homophobia in Sport* (Champaign, IL: Human Kinetics, 1998).
37. Mary Vazquez, interview by Julia Sandy-Bailey and Jacqueline Castledine, digital recording, Northampton, Massachusetts, 27 July 2007.
38. Richard Meyer, "Gay Power Circa 1970: Visual Strategies for Sexual Revolution," *Gay and Lesbian Quarterly* 12, no. 3, 447.
39. Gay Pride parades evolved from New York City activists' commemoration of the one year anniversary of the 1969 Stonewall Riots and grew to include marches in cities and towns like Northampton throughout the country.
40. Grossholtz interview.
41. Griffin interview, 23 February 2007.
42. Susan K. Cahn, *Coming on Strong: Gender and Sexuality in Twentieth-Century Women's Sport* (New York: Free Press, 1994), 205.
43. Stewart interview.
44. Griffin interview, 13 February 2007.
45. Griffin interview, 23 February 2007.
46. Stewart interview.
47. Ibid.
48. Ellen Gerber, "The Controlled Development of Collegiate Sport for Women 1923–36," *Journal of Sport History* 2, Vol. 1 (Spring, 1975), 1–28.
49. Cahn, *Coming on Strong*, 209.
50. Susan Ware, *Title IX: A Brief History with Documents* (New York: Bedford St. Martins, 2006), 11.
51. For further discussion of the history of American women's athletics and the impact of Title IX, see Susan Cahn, *Coming on Strong*, Mary Jo Festle, *Playing Nice: Politics and Apologies in Women's Sports* (New York: Columbia University Press, 1996), and Ying Wushanley, *Playing Nice and Losing: The Struggle for Control of Women's Intercollegiate Athletics, 1960–2000* (Syracuse, NY: Syracuse University Press, 1994).
52. Pisano interview.
53. Grossholtz interview.
54. Stewart interview.
55. Jennings interview.
56. Ibid.
57. Sortino interview; Lacey, *In League With Us.*
58. Interviews with Lacey Johnston, Mary McClintock, Elaine Sortino, Eileen Stewart, and Sue Tyler. See also Johnston, *In League With Us.*
59. Mary Clare Higgins, interview by Jacqueline Castledine and Julia Sandy-Bailey, digital recording, Northampton, Massachusetts, 9 January 2007.
60. Jennings interview.
61. Stewart interview.
62. Higgins interview.
63. Griffin interview, 23 February 2007.
64. Stewart interview.

CHAPTER **12**

"It Would Be Stupendous for Us Girls"[1]
Campaigning for Women Judges Without Waving

SALLY J. KENNEY

When I began as a feminist scholar in the early 1980s, neither the terms "social feminism" nor "labor feminism" existed; only women who favored equal treatment and supported the Equal Rights Amendment could be feminists. Cobble labeled this narrow approach an "equal rights teleology."[2] Although I ultimately argued for an equal treatment position on protective legislation, my study of feminists in the United Kingdom, many of whom supported different treatment, as well as my historical analysis lead me to conclude that the issue was far more complicated than I had first believed.[3] Feminist theory neatly categorized feminists by ideological brands, sharply distinguishing radicals (younger women) from liberals (older women). Radical feminists separated themselves from the male-dominated institutions of government, political parties, labor unions, and churches. New York City was feminism's epicenter, if not its whole world. Second wave feminism of the 1960s and 1970s was a "tsunami,"[4] a massive rupture with a past where women were domestic and quiescent.[5] Happily, feminists have broadened their challenge to orthodox thinking from asking, "Where are the women?" to, "Where are the lesbians?" or, "Where are the midwestern women?" or, simply, "What were category x of women doing at this time?" challenging feminism's own generalizations as quickly as we established them. More recently, social historians have begun to rethink their disdain for the biographical as mere "great women" history and come to see how a careful examination of individual lives can help us to complicate historical narratives in important ways. [6]

By examining the lives of two women judges, this chapter joins the others in this volume in disrupting settled ideas about whether feminism had waves, who can be a feminist, and how to do women's history. Not all women retreated into domestic life between 1920 and 1968; rather, women were active in the professions, in clubs, and in international movements, working for peace, suffrage, and women's political power.[7] Women's liberationists were not first to call for women judges;[8] women's suffragists, housewives and professional women, first ladies,[9] and women lawyers preceded them. These women worked within the system in alliance with men while simultaneously creating a separate community of women partnered with other women, belying the characterization of distinct groups of radials and liberals that dominates accounts of feminism after 1968.[10] While both women judges self-identified as feminists, their participation in a male-dominated profession (law) and a male-dominated institution (the judiciary) rendered them at the very least liberal feminists. Women's liberationists' favored studying the most radical, the more separatist, and activists who focused on women's oppression to the exclusion of other causes. This chapter, and this volume, advocates a continued widening of the category of feminist as well as of the objects worthy of feminist inquiry. It challenges the idea of the doldrums and sees continuity not just rupture. By looking inside institutions, it challenges the utility of dichotomies such as radical versus liberal and attacks "bicoastal arrogance."[11] Taking to heart the maxim, "the personal is political," this chapter argues that careful attention to the biographical details of both women's lives, in particular, their sexuality, contributes to better social history.

Few women judges served before the 1970s, but we have much to learn from those who did. Not all of the early women judges or lawyers advocated for women's rights. Rather, some of these trailblazers saw themselves as lawyers first and women second and downplayed the relevance of their gender.[12] Nor did they all know one another. Despite their increasing numbers, women judges are still mostly invisible as is the issue of women's slow progress in integrating the judiciary. Unless the nomination of a woman to the U.S. Supreme Court piques media interest, scholars rarely discuss gender and the judiciary. Political scientists who study women and politics tend to ignore the judicial branch, just as organizations to increase women's political representation ignore judicial offices, despite the fact that many states elect their judges. Those who study the judiciary and judicial selection more generally usually leave gender out of their scholarship.

A careful look at the first women who sought federal and state judicial office, however, reveals a rich history of feminist activism, fought tenaciously with little social opprobrium, but feminist activism that was deep, wide, strategic, and well connected. Most of these women were alone or with only one or two other women in their law school classes until late into the 1970s, yet they founded women's bar associations. Both Florence Allen and Burnita Shelton Matthews, the first women federal judges, served the suffrage movement—Allen litigated in Ohio, Mathews served as counsel to the National Women's Party and picketed the White House with Alice Paul while in law school (a fact she kept from her classmates).[13] These women were joiners, connected to each other within broad networks of women social reformers. In fact, the first women on the state and federal bench were *more* likely to be networked feminists. Shirley Hufstedler, the first woman on the Ninth Circuit Court Appeals, was active in NOW and the National Women's Political Caucus, and Rosalie Wahl, the first woman on the Minnesota Supreme Court, was active in the DFL Feminist Caucus and Minnesota Women's Political Caucus, than the women who followed them. Connected to women inside government who pressed their case such as Molly Dewson and India Edwards, they waged impressive national campaigns to secure appointments for women, garnered significant media attention, and convinced presidents that women's votes turned on these, albeit token, appointments.

Women judges faced virulent opposition. It is no accident that the exclusion of women from juries was one of the last sex-based differentiations to survive constitutional scrutiny after the Court interpreted the equal protection clause as no longer allowed all sex-based classification.[14] Allowing women to sit in judgment of men transgresses a powerful taboo. The first women judges confronted a powerful backlash from men for their audacity in storming a citadel of male power. The backlash that continues against women judges and women judicial nominees, and the drop in the number of women appointed to the federal judiciary in the last eight years (from 28 percent to 22 percent),[15] reminds us that progress toward women's equality is neither steady, inevitable, nor irreversible. Rejecting the simple characterization of the doldrums as mere quiescence should dissuade us from the importance of understanding backlash.

Florence Allen

> Because Allen's primary relationship was not with a man, her private life—in particular her relationships with other women—has been ignored in Cleveland [Ohio] history, legal history, and social policy history. All are impoverished by this consistent refusal to deal with the significance of women's relationships.[16]

Florence Allen was the first woman in position to be considered for a seat on the U.S. Supreme Court. President Roosevelt appointed her from the

Ohio Supreme Court to the U.S. Court of Appeals for the Sixth Circuit, where she served from 1934–1959. Allen's father was the first Congressman from Utah, her mother the first student admitted to Smith College and an active club woman. Allen enrolled in the University of Chicago's Law School where she was the only woman in her class of 100[17] and ranked second in her first-year class.[18] After her first year, she leveraged connections with Hull House to land a position with Frances Kellor at the New York League for the Protection of Immigrants. Kellor and her life partner, Mary Dreier, formed part of Allen's lifelong social network and introduced her to a national network of social reformers. Allen then enrolled in New York University's law school, which she found more hospitable to women than Chicago, and graduated second in her class. The head of the College Equal Suffrage League Maud Wood Park chose Allen to be her secretary and "turned her life dramatically to the cause of woman suffrage."[19]

The Ohio Bar admitted Allen in 1914, but no law firm would hire her.[20] She joined the other three women practicing law in Ohio,[21] and threw herself into Democratic politics and suffrage work. She argued for municipal suffrage before the Ohio Supreme Court and campaigned for suffrage in every county in Ohio.[22] Like her mother, she was a club woman, and a joiner of associations generally, from the Daughters of the American Revolution to the Ohio Bar Association, and, when they let women join in 1918, the American Bar Association.[23] Dearer to her, however, was the National Association of Women Lawyers, formed in 1899 because the American Bar Association (ABA) would not permit women to be members.[24] She was also active in the General Federal of Women's Clubs, the Young Women's Christian Association, Business and Professional Women, the League of Women Voters, the National Association for the Advancement of Colored People, and the peace movement. She was appointed an assistant county prosecutor in 1919. After suffrage, she ran and won election to the common pleas court, making her the first woman on any general jurisdiction court in the United States. In 1922, she won election to the Ohio Supreme Court, making her the first woman on any state Supreme Court. Allen also aspired to a legislative career, but lost a bid for the U.S. Senate in 1926 and for Congress in 1932. Voters reelected her in 1928 to the Ohio Supreme Court by an even larger majority. Allen credited organized women with this victory. Tuve writes: "the election of Florence Allen…is one of the very rare examples of the power and possibilities of a united block of voting women."[25]

Allen's colleagues did not welcome her to her position—all had opposed her appointment. They had told background investigators for the FBI that she was "naturally unqualified" because of her sex.[26] The FBI's background check on Allen is infected with gender bias. Her colleagues labeled the possibility of her appointment "lamentable, laughable, disastrous," adding that it, "would make the Circuit Court appear ridiculous and would lower the high traditions of that bench."[27] Three judges failed to write a customary letter of congratulations. One judge took to his bed for several days.[28] The male judges regularly lunched together at an all-male club when they sat in Cincinnati; Allen swam, hiked, or lunched with women friends.[29]

She was merely acquainted with Eleanor Roosevelt,[30] but moved in the circles of women social reformers who were close to the first lady. Molly Dewson, the director of the Women's Division of the National Democratic Committee, led a large network of social feminists working within the National Consumers League, the Women's Trade Union League, and settlement houses, and, with the urging of Carrie Chapman Catt, worked for Allen's appointment to the Sixth Circuit,[31] the highest appointment a woman had ever achieved in the federal judiciary.[32] Dewson, like many social reformers, was fairly openly partnered with another woman, as was Allen. For twenty-five years, Allen was the highest ranking federal judge in the country, with no other women serving on the circuit courts.

Allen's most important decision, upholding the constitutionality of the Tennessee Valley Authority,[33] would have endeared her to Roosevelt's inner circle. Eleanor Roosevelt lobbied for her appointment to the U.S. Supreme Court in 1938 when Justice Sutherland retired—Franklin Roosevelt had four vacancies to fill between 1937 and 1939. Despite Eleanor's lobbying, and a full scale campaign from Allen's advocates that included a cover article of *Life Magazine*, President Roosevelt did not seriously consider her.[34] The National Association of Women Lawyers formed a Committee for the Advancement of Women Lawyers to High Judicial Office in 1941 and continued the letter writing campaign.[35] Allen's supporters held little hope that President Truman would appoint her; her chances diminished still further when Truman appointed an Ohioan, Harold Burton, in 1945.[36] India Edwards, executive director of the Women's Division of the Democratic National Convention, "begged" Truman to appoint Allen to one of the two vacancies in 1949. Truman consulted Chief Justice Vinson, who reported the justices solidly against appointing a woman because they could not meet informally without robes, shoes, and with shirt collars unbuttoned." And, most important, they could not figure out which restroom she could use.[37] A new generation of women, especially Business and Professional Women, worked to secure Allen an appointment on the International Court and, when that failed, to persuade President Eisenhower to appoint her to one of the two vacancies he filled on the U.S. Supreme Court. Despite their substantial efforts, age and party began to work against her.[38] Women's groups took up the cause again in 1965 and with each subsequent vacancy.[39]

Allen lived in two committed relationships with a woman,[40] but I had missed this fact about her until I read Faderman[41] and unearthed Joan Organ's unpublished dissertation.[42] Allen lived, worked, and traveled with Susan Rebhan, who managed Allen's campaign for the Ohio Supreme Court and later her U.S. Senate race and, when she became a judge, acted as her secretary from 1922 until Rebhan's death in 1935. (Rebhan earned a law degree and was elected to the city council while Allen served on the Ohio Supreme Court.) Until Allen died in 1966, she lived with Mary Pierce, a distant cousin, teacher, and director of Park School. Allen's biographer, historian Jeanette Tuve, describes the three as having "deep and enduring" commitments to each other, but characterizes them as housemates.[43] While she observes that Allen, Rebhan, and Pierce resisted the heterosexual imperative by not marrying, and describes Pierce and Allen's division of household labor as Pierce very much in the traditional wife's role, she never goes farther than calling them single and describing Pierce as companion and hostess.[44] The climate for lesbians became less tolerant over Allen's lifetime, and Allen's wide circle of women partnered with other women became more discreet.[45] Perhaps the strongest evidence about Allen's sexual identity comes from her correspondence with federal judge Marion Harron, who continued to press well into the 1950s for Allen's appointment to the U.S. Supreme Court. Harron was a federal judge on the Board of Tax Appeals and the Senate nearly failed to reappoint her in 1948 for being a suspected lesbian.[46] Allen wrote to her begging her to be anonymous and save them both from possible embarrassment or worse.[47] Unfortunately, Tuve has died, so I cannot ask her what she believed about Allen's sexual identity, and, if she did believe her to be a lesbian, why she erased that fact from her biography. Joan Organ reported Tuve told her that "she did not want to touch that subject."[48] In her insightful historical essay on the first women federal judges, Mary Clark documented the hostility of other judges to Allen's appointment to the Sixth Circuit to the U.S. Supreme Court, but does not consider whether Allen's sexual identity may have been a contributing factor. Clark described her as single and as having lived with her cousin who performed all domestic labor.[49]

I was, however, able to ask political scientist Beverly Blair Cook about Allen's sexual identity. Cook was the first political scientist to study women judges, she wrote several biographical essays on Allen, and she had considered writing Allen's biography. Her writings offered even fewer clues than Tuve to Allen's sexual identity. She merely alluded to Allen's unmarried status in explaining Sandra Day O'Connor's success in winning appointment to the Supreme Court and Allen's failure.[50] Yet Allen's network of women-identified women was clearly an important part of her identity and her success, and homophobia may have played a part in explaining her failure to reach the U.S. Supreme Court. Even if Cook did not want to identify Allen as a lesbian, a term we have no evidence Allen ever used for herself,[51] why did she not present the evidence and let the reader decide, rather than continue to erase the history of Allen's woman-identified social life? The answer is both that Cook doubted whether Allen was a lesbian and regarded mentioning the possibility as a terrible slur. She wrote to me in explanation:

> It is very hard to pin down the lesbian aspect despite her long-term living arrangements with two women, one of whom seemed to take an old-fashioned wife role. Since I went to Wellesley, I was familiar with the women professors in the 19c and 20c there who lived as couples, not in a sexual relationship but like sisters or cousins. So I didn't make any assumptions unless there was a reasonably direct statement in the sources.[52]

Cook is highly critical of Faderman. She criticized her for making it seem as though women could succeed with only the support, endorsement, and active campaigning of other women, and neglecting the way that they also needed the support of men and male-dominated groups like political parties. (Allen struggled to get the party's endorsement as a candidate for the U.S. Senate.) She claimed Faderman offered no citation for the most important piece of evidence, Allen's letter to Harron.[53] But Faderman cited Joan Ellen Organ's dissertation and Organ cited the letter.[54] Cook regarded labeling someone a lesbian as necessarily negative,[55] but she was also angry about the double standard:

> It was so necessary for women to stick together and to support and give publicity to the ambitious ones. It is interesting that men who did the same thing through their large variety of men's sports and social clubs did not have to deal with outsider's speculation on their sexuality.[56]

The evidence is clear that Allen lived in two loving committed relationships with women and moved in social circles of people who did the same. Since no women had ever served on the U.S. Supreme Court, sexism suffices to explain Allen's failure—one would not want to argue that but for homophobia, she would have been first. Moreover, Allen, unlike O'Connor, saw herself as a feminist and representing women.[57] But men from President Roosevelt to President Reagan may have preferred their women trailblazers to have impeccable heterosexual credentials.

As Freedman shows with her biography of prison reformer Miriam Van Waters,[58] if we erase the history of lesbians, or omit an understanding of lesbianism from our understanding of individual women's lives or intense social networks, we are eliminating a major factor in what kept women's activism vibrant between 1920 and 1968. Allen's story demonstrates that the suffrage coalition continued to be active after suffrage—it was not quiescent— and one of its activities was to press for women's appointment to the federal judiciary. It enjoyed some success. Although few women pursued a legal career, some did, and they were active in many cases.[59] Organ and Faderman demonstrated that lesbians lived openly and worked for social change actively post-suffrage, although they also demonstrated how social disapproval grew stronger with the onset of the Cold War. We cannot understand the history of women and women's activism without understanding the part sexual identity played in their intense social networks. Gordon estimated that 25 percent of these social reformers were lesbians.[60] Nor can we dismiss the relevance, post-1920, of suffragists, women professionals, women in the heartland states, such as Ohio, and, most importantly, lesbians. Though they may have spent weekends on what Allen called "a feminist retreat,"[61] these women who continued to be active after 1920 were insiders, not separatists. They included the first lady, the Secretary of Labor, the heads of the Women's and Children's Bureaus, women judges, women in political parties, and women in social clubs and political organizations. Feminism existed as a network of insiders and outsiders, and not exclusively as a group of radical outsiders.

Rosalie Wahl[62]

Feminists advocating for the first woman on the Minnesota Supreme Court in 1977 faced many of the same obstacles that Allen faced. In fact, Allen may have attended law school in a more hospitable climate, as the percentage of women attending law school actually declined after 1920. Wahl was one of two women in her class at William Mitchell College of Law night school.[63] Although women gained entry in increasing numbers into law schools in the 1970s, few made it to the bench. In 1977, no woman had served on the U.S. Supreme Court, only Florence Allen had sat on a federal appellate court, and only five other women served on state supreme courts.[64] The first woman to serve as a Minnesota trial court judge, Susanne C. Sedgwick, a Republican, acquired a seat on the Hennepin County court by running against an incumbent in 1970.[65] Like women social reformers after 1920, the nucleus of feminist supporters who lobbied for Wahl's appointment and campaigned for her election were a community of peace activists, members of women's professional associations, governmental insiders, lesbians, housewives, and women living in the heartland, in this case the Upper Midwest.[66] But they also included members drawn from group therapy and radicals, consistent with the political culture of the 1960s. Rosalie Wahl is a great example of how women did not neatly divide into two simple groups of either radical or liberal feminists. She was an older woman and a divorced mother of five, who worked on League of Women Voter-type issues like a local bookmobile. But she had lived in an intentional community collective and was virulently anti-racist and anti-war. Like Allen, she was the consummate founder, joiner, and organizer. She worked in groups. She may have looked, as Nadine Strossen said, "like everybody's favorite kindergarten teacher,"[67] but she participated in Catharine MacKinnon's and Andrea Dworkin's University of Minnesota Law School seminar on pornography, an experience that radicalized her on issues of sexuality as she had been radicalized on peace and civil rights. Wahl's colleagues were more receptive to her joining them than were Allen's, but her appointment created a backlash in the form of three male opponents in the next election who used gendered arguments to try to defeat her.

Wahl's first job out of law school was with the newly created state public defender's office. He was willing to employ women lawyers on a part-time basis—an important consideration for mothers of small children (Wahl divorced in 1972). Wahl defended the indigent and argued many times before the Minnesota Supreme Court, but never, in her 109 appellate cases, did she appear before a woman judge. William Mitchell College of Law hired her to help establish the criminal and civil law clinic in 1973. Wahl taught around sixty students a year in addition to an appellate law seminar. "Students stood in line all night before registration to be assured of a place in the clinic."[68] Wahl was a devoted mentor. William Mitchell students and graduates, public defenders, and those committed to social justice more generally joined feminists as her core supporters.

Like Allen, then, organized women and men committed to social reform catapulted Wahl to high judicial office. The National Women's Political Caucus had led the way on this issue in 1971 when Nixon had promised to "appoint the best man for the job" to the U.S. Supreme Court[69] and the Minnesota Chapter was very active. But the Democratic Farmer Labor Party's Feminist Caucus made perhaps the most important contribution by extracting from DFL Governor Rudy Perpich a promise to appoint a woman to the next court vacancy. *Minneapolis Star* reporters were present at the meeting and reported his promise. When the next vacancy occurred, those reporters reminded the governor of his promise, and he began his quest to find the best woman for the job.

Feminists in Minnesota were a highly visible group that came to be perceived as having more power, resources, and troops than they actually commanded. Rahn Westby, a young William Mitchell graduate and feminist activist, and her co-chair, Carol Connolly of the Ramsey County Women's Political Caucus, saw the appointment of a woman on the Minnesota Supreme Court as akin to blasting a woman astronaut into space—an event that would garner media attention and symbolize that things had changed for women, and that feminists were a force to be reckoned with. As with Nixon, who toyed with the idea of appointing Mildred Lillie to the U.S. Supreme Court,[70] and Reagan, who promised to appoint a woman to the U.S. Supreme Court once the gender gap emerged, women were an important constituency for Perpich. But Perpich was also more like President Carter and Governor Jerry Brown in his deep-seated commitment to appointing women to high political office and that included the judiciary. Moreover, Perpich, like Brown, was unconventional and savored the grand gesture.[71] Perpich announced his choice at a Hibbing High School Graduation, but timed it so that Minnesota Secretary of State Joan Growe could announce it the same day to a gathering of nearly 4,500 women meeting in St. Cloud, Minnesota, to hammer out a platform and choose delegates to the upcoming White House Conference on Women in Houston.

At a breakfast meeting of the women's legal fraternity, Phi Delta Delta, during her second year of law school, Wahl had met Esther Tomljanovich (the third woman appointed to the Minnesota Supreme Court in 1990) who had been a lawyer since the 1950s, as well as Phyllis Jones who was in the Ramsey County Attorney's office. Wahl recounts the transformative experience of finding others who were like her, "all of a sudden I realized I wasn't a duck. I was a swan."[72] When the organization merged with the male legal fraternity, Wahl and others founded Minnesota Women Lawyers in September of 1972 to "secure the full and equal participation of women in the legal profession and in a just society."[73] Along with the Minnesota Women's Political Caucus (whose national office was working on the appointment of women in the Carter administration), Minnesota Women Lawyers (MWL) was determined to overcome the problem of men elective officials who said they would appoint qualified women if only they could find them. MWL formed a committee to forward names of women qualified to serve on the bench. Wahl served on the committee that sent a questionnaire to all women lawyers asking if they would be willing to serve on boards or on the bench. It took Wahl two years to return her questionnaire.[74]

Wahl was on Minnesota Women Lawyers' list of seven names,[75] and on the lists the Minnesota Women's Political Caucus and the DFL Feminist Caucus gave Perpich.[76] Press reports featured pictures and biographical descriptions, reminiscent of speculation on vice presidential choices. Such open discussion of possible appointments was unprecedented in the history of judicial selection in Minnesota and more akin to current speculations about the U.S. Supreme Court.

Each state has its own system for choosing judges, few of which mirror the federal judiciary's procedure of executive appointment with legislative confirmation. Most have either partisan or nonpartisan elections or appointment with retention elections (the so-called Missouri Plan, or merit selection). Minnesota's system is a hybrid.[77] Formally, the state has nonpartisan elections with candidates identified only as incumbent or not, but in practice, sitting justices retire a year or more before the end of their terms and the governor nominates a replacement when the retirement is announced, allowing the governor's choice to run as an incumbent. If a justice was appointed more than a year before the next election, he or she had to stand in the next one, and then again every six years. As of 1977, only one member of the Minnesota Supreme Court had obtained his seat by election rather than appointment. The last incumbent unseated in an election was in 1900.

Perpich had clear goals in his appointments to the bench, but his primary concern with Wahl, or whomever he chose, was that she be able to win reelection. Ambitious lawyers who wanted to be judges would likely challenge any sitting judges perceived as easy to defeat, and the first woman appointed would automatically fall into that category. If Wahl failed to win reelection, Perpich would then have squandered the power to shape the bench. Connolly assured the governor that she could put her life on hold to manage Wahl's campaign, a campaign that had no shortage of devoted troops. The stakes were high. If Wahl lost, it would be a long time before feminists could persuade any governor to appoint another woman, nor would any woman be a credible candidate for challenging an incumbent. Among the candidates, Perpich thought Wahl best able to mount a state-wide campaign.

Rosalie Wahl became the tenth woman serving on a state supreme court in 1977.[78] As Perpich had predicted, for the first time in two decades, a seated Supreme Court Justice had a serious opponent, or rather in Wahl's case, three, meaning she would face a primary. Connolly always suspected that "the boys" were in cahoots to bring down Wahl. One day, for example, Marcia Fleur from TV station KSTP called Wahl to say she had received the confidential police file of Wahl's son, who had had a brush with the law. One of Wahl's opponents, former Attorney General Robert W. Mattson, had delivered the papers to the press himself, alleging Wahl had pulled strings on her son's behalf. Connolly went to pick up the file and that was the end of the matter, but Wahl thought, "I have to win; I cannot let Mattson become a Supreme Court justice."[79]

Wahl was the lead vote-getter with more than 231,000 votes to the next-highest vote-getter Mattson's 130,000. Plunkett had received 93,319 votes and Rochester District Court Judge Daniel Foley 104,610. If all those who had voted for Plunkett and Foley voted for Mattson, Wahl would lose her seat. The rival candidates had said Wahl lacked judicial experience. The general campaign turned even more negative. Mattson ran a series of negative ads claiming she had a poor win/loss record before the Supreme Court.

Another ad charged that "Ms. [sic] Wahl lets rapists loose." (She was the sole dissenter in *State v. Willis*, (269 N.W.2d [Minn. 1978]) a case of a rapist who had held his victim at knifepoint. Wahl had dissented because a trial court had suppressed evidence and the police had unlawfully searched the defendant's house.)

Wahl was the highest vote getter on the ballot in November 1978. Four important factors helped ensure Wahl's electoral success. First, Wahl enjoyed the support of her colleagues. Wahl used the long time after Perpich's announcement, and before MacLaughlin actually vacated the seat, to call on each of the justices individually to ask for his advice about the transition to becoming a Supreme Court Justice. Moreover, as the ninth and most junior justice she spoke last at conference. She did not find, as Florence Allen did, that the men would not look her in the eye or that they shunned her. She described them as well broken in by their wives and comfortable with strong women. In one short year, Wahl had earned the respect of her colleagues on the court. Chief Justice Sandy Keith who joined the court later wrote of her ability to get along with others.[80] Chief Justice Sheran had offered to reduce her caseload but she declined because she did not want to burden the other justices with extra cases.[81] Juergens comments:

> Life taught Wahl to take a punch, and that ability helped her be productive in situations where a less resilient and tolerant person would have fled in frustration. She appeared to be as comfortable with senior partners in the Manhattan boardroom at Sullivan & Cromwell as she was in southeastern Minnesota with a group of farm women. Her grace in working with those who did not necessarily share her ideals is one of her strongest qualities, and it allowed her to accomplish projects in the face of repeated setbacks.[82]

It may have been helpful that many of the judges currently on the bench shared Wahl's judicial philosophy. Judge Peterson, who also faced a challenger, could have distanced himself from Wahl and run separately but instead they campaigned together. By doing so, they could both draw on an existing fund called the Lawyers Committee to Retain Incumbent Justices, already in place from past elections. That fund gave them $10,000 as a base for the joint campaign and a chair already in place. Moreover, each justice found some quiet way to support Wahl's campaign—one by being absent and asking her to sit in his stead on an important bar committee, another by introducing her to an influential labor leader, a third by suggesting to a prominent lawyer friend that he write an editorial against Mattson.

Second, like Allen, Wahl actively campaigned and enjoyed widespread support in the newly mobilized women's community. Feminists such as

Westby and Connolly believed that if Wahl were to hold her seat, she needed more than to cultivate the high opinion of lawyers—she needed, instead, a political campaign that would excite women (and men) voters of both parties. They persuaded a reluctant Wahl to tour the state, glad-hand, issue buttons and bumper stickers, and even take out billboard ads. As Wahl recounted:

> the women were very crucial in this campaign because the women in the state knew that if I couldn't be elected, no governor would appoint a woman, because it would be just throwing an appointment away. So they really came together. Nieces were writing to their grandmothers.[83]

Carol Connolly and Bob Oliphant chaired the Citizens Committee to Retain Rosalie Wahl which ultimately raised about $29,000. Mary Pruitt, historian of second wave feminism in the Twin Cities, recalls the Wahl campaign as "the single moment everyone [in a very fractious feminist movement] worked together."[84]

The Citizens Committee organized fundraising events and pulled in allies from the Minnesota Women's Political Caucus and Minnesota Women Lawyers. The virtue of these two organizations is that they, like the League of Women Voters and the American Association of University Women, and unlike the DFL Feminist Caucus, could capitalize on their non-partisanship. Wahl's name would, after all, be on Republican and Democratic primary ballots, and she would not run on a party label but simply as an incumbent. Connolly recalls organizing a fundraising party kit that was kept in the trunk of her car—nametags, tablecloths, napkins, etc.—and dragged from one house to another.[85] On September 30th, at the Landmark Center, the Lawyer's Committee and the Citizens Committee held a huge event. Muriel Humphrey (widow of the vice president), Governor Perpich, and office holders from both parties joined local luminaries in endorsing Wahl's campaign. In her handwritten remarks thanking the Minnesota Women's Political Caucus for their efforts on her behalf and describing them as "magnificent" Wahl said, "Each contribution was indispensable. I understand better the story of the loaves and the fishes— where each of you reached out, there were five. The Governor's choice is an affirmation for each of us."[86]

The third factor was the quality of the candidate. Wahl was an experienced advocate—not from working for a downtown firm, but from defending the indigent as a public defender. Wahl had substantial experience arguing criminal law cases before the Supreme Court—appellate experience her challenger lacked. She had the support of her colleagues on the bench, the wider legal community, women, and the political establishment of both parties.

Plunkett's attempt to demean Wahl was counterproductive. He insulted and enraged the William Mitchell faculty and her former law students, who came to her defense. Not only was the candidate of a high quality, but she called upon a vast personal network that ranged far beyond the women's community to include those connected to William Mitchell College of Law, clinical law faculty from all institutions and their graduates more generally, and public defenders. Wahl put together a coalition of elites and grassroots organizers for social change, from feminists, to public interest lawyers, to Quakers, to the League of Women Voters.

Wahl was extremely well qualified legally, the architect of a powerful non-partisan coalition of elites and activists, she also proved to be an outstanding campaigner, and had the eloquence of a poet. Her sincerity, warmth, and down-home-folks style played well at backyard gatherings and house parties. And her passion for the underdog showed through. Moreover, Mattson's repetition of the lies in a debate before the Ramsey County Bar Association, combined with his efforts to smear her son in the press, further aroused Wahl's fighting spirit.[87] While trying conscientiously to serve as a justice on the Supreme Court, Wahl traversed the state, speaking to bar associations, women's groups, and other community organizations, such as churches and hospitals.

Fourth, Mattson's campaign backfired. The Minnesota State Bar Association, not a fan of judicial election and worried about the issue of judicial independence, came to Wahl's defense. Chief Justice Sheran talked to friends at the Bar Association and they wrote a letter to the paper denouncing Mattson's ads.[88] The *Minneapolis Tribune* editorialized against "Mattson's Injudicious Campaign" on October 22nd, saying his distortion of Wahl's office rendered him unfit for office. Wahl said she was lucky to face Mattson, in a way, "because a lot of lawyers did not think really highly of him."[89] Legal elites as a whole have never felt comfortable with Minnesota's election of judges and would prefer an appointive system or appointment with retention elections, the Missouri Plan favored by the American Judicature Society. Once Governor Perpich appointed Wahl, she became the elite insider, and Mattson the outsider. Wahl retained her seat easily without challenge in 1984. Until she retired in 1994, the Minnesota Supreme Court was the first state in history to have a majority (4 of 7) of women justices.[90]

Wahl had an enormous impact on the law, women's equality, the legal system, and legal education. She wrote 549 opinions over seventeen years. She looked at the judicial system from the bottom up, championing the underdog, the marginalized, or the outcast, such as criminal defendants. She believed that Minnesota's constitution held the government to a higher standard of rationality than the federal constitution did and argued for a more expansive interpretation of individual rights than under the U.S.

Constitution.[91] She wrote for the majority in holding that different penalties for crack and powder cocaine were unconstitutional in *State v. Russell* (477 N.W.2d 886 [Minn.1993]). Her opinions on race and sex discrimination were especially eloquent. She had what her former clerk, Jane Larson, called "her longest running struggle with other members of the supreme court" over how to interpret statutes allowing for the availability of permanent rather than rehabilitative maintenance for long-term homemaker spouses. Wahl would often say that she thought men had trouble understanding the experience of a midlife woman whose husband is divorcing her.[92]

She was a pivotal member of the National Association of Women Judges, which gave her its lifetime achievement award in 2004. She spearheaded and chaired the state taskforce on gender fairness and the courts; Minnesota was the sixth state to conduct such a study. She then went on to chair the racial bias taskforce. She was a long-time champion of the rights of the mentally ill. Her contributions to legal education had a national impact.[93] Wahl was the first woman to chair the American Bar Association's Accreditation Committee as well as the Section of Legal Education and Admissions to the Bar, where she shrewdly and skillfully put together the strategy for expanding clinical legal education. Minnesota Women Lawyers named its annual lecture in her honor.

Conclusion

Although President Roosevelt appointed the first woman, Florence Allen, to the federal bench in 1934, only seven other women served on federal courts until President Carter took office in 1976. President Carter appointed more women than all previous presidents combined; he appointed forty women to the federal bench (15.5 percent of his judges). A similar pattern existed on state courts—one or two women and then a breakthrough in the 1970s. Feminists campaigned hard for a woman on the U.S. Supreme Court and on local family courts, but met with little success until the late 1970s. Rosalie Wahl's appointment by a maverick governor in 1977 shows how fragile women's claim to judicial office was. Analyzing the unsuccessful efforts to elevate Florence Allen to the U.S. Supreme Court and Rosalie Wahl's successful election to the Minnesota Supreme Court shows feminist activists working strategically against the odds to advance the cause of women, occasionally with stunning success. Both fought the backlash against organized feminism.

At first glance, these facts fit within the conventional waves framework. Allen came out of the first wave, riding the legacy of the suffrage movement, and sat virtually alone among men on the bench in the doldrums until women swarmed law schools in the 1970s. Wahl ascended to the bench during the heyday of second wave feminism, but faced challengers immediately. As critics of the wave narrative argue, this storyline suppresses important information as well as reveals patterns. Boris argued that feminism's waves did not recede after suffrage nor did they come crashing back all of a sudden in the mid-1960s.[94] Allen's case is a reminder of the activity—albeit largely unsuccessful—that transpired in the interim among a vibrant network of women. And if one of the damning points of the wave narrative is that it focuses too much on middle-class white women in New York, Allen raises the interesting question of how to deal with sexuality. While never self-identifying as a lesbian, Allen's unmarried status and partnerships with women may have cost her the highest judicial office. Examining Ohio and Minnesota adds depth to New York-centered feminist histories.

Nadasen argued that the problem with the waves metaphor's focus on the surge is that it obscures the important day-to-day trench work outside the eye of the media.[95] By focusing on a particular starting point, such accounts minimize the political activism that preceded it. Wahl did not begin her career during the second wave. One activist emotionally said to Wahl in her appointment celebration, "thank you for being ready."[96] Many feminists stayed organized after suffrage and campaigned for women's issues, just as they did after the defeat of the ERA and the election of Ronald Reagan. To fully understand their success, we need to understand the work of feminists in the legal profession in the 1950s and 1960s when, according to the waves frame, they did not exist because they were all mired in domesticity, focused on "the problem with no name."[97]

To the extent to which historians and political scientists focus on women's political participation, they almost always neglect courts. The waves frame that relegates all activity between 1920 and 1968 to doldrums overlooks the role of women in the professions, in favor of a more radical feminism. Just as those who challenge the waves frame invite us to think of feminism more broadly to include multiple and intersectional identities, this chapter builds on the work of feminist scholars such as LeeAnn Banaszak,[98] Susan Hartmann,[99] and Mary Katzenstein,[100] who invite us to see feminists as working within institutions, too, whether they be unions, parties, or professions, and not just separate from them.

Notes

1. Wrote Molly Dewson to FDR advocating for Florence Allen's appointment to the U.S. Supreme Court in 1943. Beverly Blair Cook, "The First Woman Candidate for the Supreme Court—Florence Allen" in *Yearbook*, 19–35, 26. Thanks to Margot Canaday, Mary Clark, and Joan Organ for their helpful comments on this chapter and for research assistance from Lura Barber, Rachel Estroff, Rebecca Moskow, and Jacqueline Waddell-Boie.

2. Dorothy Sue Cobble, *The Other Women's Movement: Workplace Justice and Social Rights in Modern America* (Princeton, NJ: Princeton University Press), 7.
3. Sally J. Kenney, *Reproductive Hazards and Exclusionary Politics in the United States and Britain* (Ann Arbor: University of Michigan Press).
4. Sara M. Evans, *Tidal Wave: How Women Changed America at Century's End* (New York: Free Press, 2003).
5. Joanne Meyerowitz, "Women and Gender in Postwar America" in *Not June Cleaver: Women and Gender in Postwar America, 1945–1960*, ed. Joanne Meyerowitz (Philadelphia: Temple University Press, 1994), 1–16.
6. Estelle B. Freedman, *Maternal Justice: Miriam Van Waters and the Female Reform Tradition*, (Chicago: University of Chicago Press, 1996). Alice Kessler Harris, "Why Biography?" *American Historical Review* (June 2009): 625–30.
7. Leila J. Rupp and Verta Taylor, "Forging Feminist Identity in an International Movement: A Collective Identity Approach to Feminism." *Signs: Journal of Women in Culture and Society* 24 (Winter 1999): 363–86.
8. Sally J. Kenney, "Nixon Gaffe Sparks Era of Judicial Advance." Women's E-News, May 4, 2009. http://www.womensenews.org/article.cfm/dyn/aid/3999.
9. Eleanor Roosevelt worked actively for the president to appoint Florence Allen, and Betty Ford urged President Ford to appoint a woman. David M. O'Brien, "The Politics of Professionalism: President Gerald R. Ford's Appointment of Justice John Paul Stevens." *Presidential Studies Quarterly* 21(1) (1991): 103–26, 110. Shirley Hufstedler believed Lady Bird Johnson to have pressed her case for a female appointee to the Ninth Circuit; Mary L. Clark, "One Man's Token is Another Woman's Breakthrough? The Appointment of the First Women Federal Judges," *Villanova Law Review* 49 (2004): 487–550, 524.
10. Jo Freeman, *The Politics of Women's Liberation: A Case Study of an Emerging Social Movement and Its Relation to the Policy Process* (New York: Longman, 1975).
11. Term taken from the T-shirts for the 1984 National Women's Studies Association annual meeting in Columbus, Ohio, which read "stamp out bi-coastal arrogance."
12. Mossman, Mary Jane, *The First Women Lawyers: A Comparative Study of Gender, Law and the Legal Professions* (Portland, OR: Hart, 2006).
13. Clark, "One Man's Token," 504.
14. Linda Kerber, *No Constitutional Right to be Ladies: Women and the Obligations of Citizenship* (New York: Hill and Wang, 1998).
15. Jennifer Segal Diascro and Rorie Spill Solberg, "George W. Bush's Legacy on the Federal Bench: Policy in the Face of Diversity," *Judicature* 92 (2009): 289–301.
16. Joan Ellen Organ, "Sexuality as a Category of Historical Analysis: A Study of Judge Florence E. Allen, 1884–1966" (Ph.D. diss., Department of History, Case Western University, 1998), ii.
17. Clark, "One Man's Token," 494.
18. Jeanette E. Tuve, *First Lady of the Law: Florence Ellinwood Allen* (Boston: University Press of America, 1984), 22.
19. Ibid., 26.
20. Clark, "One Man's Token," 495.
21. Tuve, *First Lady of the Law*, 40.
22. Beverly Blair Cook, "Florence Allen," in *Notable American Women: The Modern Period—A Biographical Dictionary*, eds. Barbara Sicherman and Carol Hurd Green, (Cambridge, MA: Harvard University Press, 1980), 10–13.
23. Tuve, *First Lady of the Law*, 51.
24. Ibid.
25. Ibid, 67.
26. Clark, "One Man's Token," 499.
27. Ibid.

28. Florence Allen, *To Do Justly* (Cleveland, OH: Western Reserve University Press, 1965), 95.

29. Tuve, *First Lady of the Law*, 116, 135.

30. For a discussion of Eleanor Roosevelt's friendships with lesbian couples and her erotic relationships with women, see Blanche Wiesen Cook, *Eleanor Roosevelt, Volume One 1884–1933* (New York: Penguin, 1992), 13–15.

31. Lillian Faderman, *To Believe in Women: What Lesbians Have Done for America—a History* (Boston: Mariner, 2002), 92, 321.

32. Beverly Blair Cook, "Women as Supreme Court Candidates: From Florence Allen to Sandra O'Connor," *Judicature* 65 (1982): 314–26, 368.

33. *Tennessee Electric Power Company v. The Tennessee Valley Authority*, 21 F.Supp. 947 (1934).

34. A hostile newspaper reported that FDR had rejected Allen because her reversal rate was so high. Allen got other reporters to note that she had only been reversed twice. Cook, "The First Woman Candidate for the Supreme Court," 19–35, 28.

35. Ibid., 24.

36. Tuve, *First Lady of the Law*, 162.

37. India Edwards, *Pulling No Punches: Memoirs of a Woman in Politics* (New York: Putnam, 1974), 171–72.

38. Tuve, *First Lady of the Law*, 167–69.

39. Cook, "Women as Supreme Court Candidates," 314–26. 324.

40. For a discussion of when to apply the term lesbian historically, see Estelle B. Freedman, "The Burdening of Letters Continues: Elusive Identities and the Historical Construction of Sexuality," 159–74, in *Feminism, Sexuality, & Politics: Essays by Estelle B. Freedman* (Chapel Hill: University of North Carolina Press, 2006).

41. Ibid.

42. Ibid.

43. Ibid., 130.

44. Ibid., 131, 191.

45. Freedman, "The Burdening of Letters Continues"; David K Johnson, *The Lavender Scare: The Cold War Persecution of Gays and Lesbians in the Federal Government* (Chicago: University of Chicago Press, 2004).

46. Married women such as India Edwards saw Harron as an asexual spinster slandered by sexist male colleagues. But Harron's letters to Lorena Hickock, Eleanor Roosevelt's former lover, suggest otherwise, "Sexuality as a Category of Historical Analysis," 221–28.

47. Organ, "Sexuality as a Category of Historical Analysis."

48. Personal correspondence, July 13, 2009.

49. Clark, "One Man's Token," 536–37.

50. Cook, "Women as Supreme Court Candidates," 314–26.

51. Organ reported that Allen used this term in her diaries. Joan Ellen Organ, "Sexuality as a Category of Historical Analysis."

52. Beverly Blair Cook, personal correspondence with author, August 26, 2006. Sadly, Cook recently died of ovarian cancer.

53. As Cook's letter only includes one exclamation point, at the end, the punctuation in this passage reveals Cook's strong feelings. For Cook, a heterosexual woman, twice married with many children and stepchildren, and also a feminist, branding someone a lesbian is a slur, a form of silencing by targeting strong women, rather than a description.

54. Faderman cites Organ and Organ cites the correspondence in the Florence Allen papers which Cook apparently did not unearth. Organ credits Allen for alerting the network of social feminists (many partnered with women, including Eleanor Roosevelt) that turned the tide in the Senate Judiciary Committee back in favor of Harron in 1948. Organ, "Sexuality as a Category of Historical Analysis," 228. Organ cites the cautionary letter from Allen to Harron on page 242.

55. Cook appears to not only deny that Eleanor Roosevelt had a woman lover, but that she even knew that her social reformer friends were lesbians. "It is difficult to tell from the ER biographies to what extent she was knowledgeable or involved in the lesbian activity of her close friends." Ironically, Cook does seem to believe that Harron was a lesbian: "I think that Marion Harron's sexuality was pretty clear but I didn't have any documentation and so I just ignored it for the short bio" given Harron wrote love letters to Lorena Hickock, Eleanor Roosevelt's former lover.
56. Ibid.
57. Cook, "Women as Supreme Court Candidates," 314–26.
58. Ibid.
59. The erasure of sexual identity also occurs in accounts of Pauli Murray, the brilliant African American woman lawyer who linked sex and race discrimination, worked within the ACLU to challenge both forms of discrimination, and wrote powerful briefs advocating against women's exclusion from juries. Murray's own autobiography, *Pauli Murray: the Autobiography of a Black Activist, Feminist, Lawyer, Priest, and Poet,* (Knoxville: University of Tennessee Press, 1989), makes no mention of the fact that she sought psychiatric treatment for her sexuality. Darlene O'Dell, *Sites of Southern Memory: The Autobiographies of Katharine Du Pre Lumpkin, Lillian Smith, and Pauli Marray* (Charlottesville: University Press of Virginia, 2001), 146–47.
60. Linda Gordon, *Pitied but Not Entitled: Single Mothers and the History of Welfare.* (New York: Free Press, 1994), 78–79.
61. Organ, "Sexuality as a Category of Historical Analysis," 219.
62. For longer versions of Wahl's story, see Kenney 2001 and "Mobilizing Emotions to Elect Women: the symbolic meaning of Minnesota's first woman Supreme Court justice," under review, *Mobilization*.
63. Bonnie Watkins and Nina Rothchild, *In the Company of Women: Voices from the Women's Movement* (St. Paul: Minnesota Historical Society, 1996), 270–73.
64. Laura J. Cooper and Stacy Doepner-Hove, eds. "Transcript interview with Rosalie E. Wahl August 17, 1994" (St. Paul: Minnesota Historical Society, 2000).
65. Ibid., 36.
66. For accounts of women's feminism in the Midwest, see Arvonne Fraser, *She's No Lady: Politics, Family, and International Feminism* (Minneapolis, MN: Nodin Press, 2007); Patricia Gagne, *Battered Women's Justice: The Movement for Clemency and the Politics of Self Defense* (New York: Twayne, 1998); Louise Noun, *More Strong-Minded Women: Iowa Women Tell Their Stories* (Ames: Iowa State University Press, 1992), Judy Remington, *The Need to Thrive: Feminist Organizations in the Twin Cities* (Minneapolis: University of Minnesota Press, 1981); Margaret Strobel, "Organizational Learning in the Chicago Women's Liberation Union" in *Feminist Organizations: Harvest of the Women's Movement*, Myra Marx Ferre and Patricia Yancy Martin eds. (Philadelphia: Temple University Press, 1995); Nancy Whittier, *Feminist Generations: The Persistence of the Radical Women's Movement* (Philadelphia: Temple University Press, 1995).
67. Nadine Stossen, "The Leadership Role of the Legal Community in Promoting Both Civil Liberties and National Security Post 911," Minnesota Women Lawyers Meeting, Minneapolis, Minnesota, February 13, 2003.
68. Anne Juergens, "Essay Collection: Thirty Years of Clinical Legal Education at William Mitchell College of Law: Rosalie Wahl's Vision for Legal Education: Clinics at the Heart." *William Mitchell Law Review,* 30 (2003): 9–34.
69. Kenney, "Nixon Gaffe."
70. Dean, *The Rehnquist Choice*, 104–05, 113.
71. Laura K. Auerbach, *Worthy to Be Remembered: A Political History of the Minnesota Democratic-Farmer-Labor Party—1994–1984* (Minneapolis: Democratic-Farmer-Labor Party of Minnesota, 1984). Daniel, Elazar, Virginia Gray, and Wyman Spano, *Minnesota Politics*

(Lincoln: University of Nebraska Press, 1999). Betty Wilson, *Rudy! The People's Governor* (Minneapolis: Nodin Press, 2005).

72. Rosalie E. Wahl interview transcript, 26.
73. Karin A. Jacobs and Kim Buechel Mesun, "Minnesota Women Lawyers: Its Roots and its Future," *The Hennepin Lawyer*, 60 (1991): 26–29, 26.
74. Rosalie E. Wahl, interview transcript, 38.
75. Gwenyth Jones, "Women Lawyers Push Seven as Court Candidates," May 13, 1977, *Minneapolis Star-Tribune*, 11B.
76. Rosalie E. Wahl interview transcript, 47.
77. Phillip Kronebusch, "Minnesota Courts: Basic Structures, Processes, and Policies," 91–124, in *Perspectives on Minnesota Government and Politics*, eds. Steve Hoffman, Homer Williamson, and Kay Wolsborn (Boston: Burgess Publishing, 1998).
78. Beverly Blair Cook, "Women Judges: The End of Tokenism," 84–105, in *Women in the Courts*, eds. Winifred L. Hepperle and Laura Crites (Williamsburg, VA: National Center for State Courts, 1982).
79. Interview with author July 2006.
80. A. M. Keith, "A Tribute to Rosalie E. Wahl," *William Mitchell Law Review* 21 (1995): 1–4.
81. Jim Ramstad, "A Tribute to Rosalie Wahl." *William Mitchell Law Review* 21 (1995): 9.
82. Juergens, "Thirty Years of Clinical Legal Education at William Mitchell College of Law," 34.
83. Marvin R. Anderson, "Interview of Rosalie E. Wahl," in *The Social Justice, Legal and Judicial Career of Rosalie Erwin Wahl*, eds. Marvin Roger Anderson and Susan K. Larson (St. Paul: Minnesota State Law Library).
84. Mary Christine Pruitt, "*Women Unite! The Modern Women's Movement in Minnesota* (Ph.D. diss. University of Minnesota, 1987).
85. Interview with author 20 July 2000.
86. Rosalie Wahl Papers, Minnesota Historical Society, Saint Paul, Minnesota.
87. Gwenyth Jones, "Race Against Mattson Brings Out Defense Lawyer in Justice Wahl." *Minneapolis Star-Tribune*, November 3, 1978, A9.
88. Cooper, 68.
89. Ibid.
90. Carla E. Molette-Ogden, "Female Jurists: The Impact of Their Increased Presence on the Minnesota Supreme Court" (Ph.D. diss., Washington University, 1998).
91. Jane Larson, "The Jurisprudence of Justice Rosalie Wahl," in *The Social Justice, Legal and Judicial Career of Rosalie Erwin Wahl*, eds. Marvin Roger Anderson and Susan K. Larson (St. Paul: Minnesota State Law Library).
92. Watkins and Rothchild, *In the Company of Women*, 178.
93. Juergens, 10.
94. Eileen Boris, "Is it Time to Jump Ship": Rethinking the Waves Metaphor in Writing Feminist History," *Feminists Transformations* 22, no. 1 (spring 2010), 76–135.
95. Premilla Nadsen, "Is it Time to Jump Ship": Rethinking the Waves Metaphor in Writing Feminist History *National Women's Studies Association Journal* (forthcoming).
96. Justice Wahl repeatedly recounted this story in her public speeches, including at the Humphrey Institute in 1996.
97. Meyerowitz, *Not June Cleaver*, 3.
98. Lee Ann Banaszak, *The Women's Movement Inside and Outside the State* (New York: Cambridge University Press, 2009).
99. Susan Hartmann, *The Other Feminists: Activists in the Liberal Establishment* (New Haven, CT: Yale University Press, 1998).
100. Mary Katzenstein, *Faithful and Fearless: Moving Feminist Protest Inside the Church and the Military* (Princeton, NJ: Princeton University Press, 1999).

CHAPTER 13

Building Lesbian Studies in the 1970s and 1980s

SUSAN K. FREEMAN

In the late 1980s and early 1990s, as feminist and queer writers cast their gaze backward on lesbian feminists of the preceding decades, many found fault with their ideas and practices, cast crudely as depoliticized, essentialist, separatist, and prudish. Third wave and queer-identified thinkers highlighted their distinctiveness from earlier lesbians and feminists especially by asserting their embrace of sex radicalism and racial diversity. Yet, the lesbians presented as foils for a new generation's supposedly more progressive politics rarely derived from lesbian history or original texts.[1] Rather, through their overgeneralizations and reliance on unrepresentative historical figures, such thinkers demonstrated a lack of knowledge about lesbian communities from the 1970s and 1980s.

As one location where ideas about lesbian feminism were cultivated, the movement to create lesbian studies offers an opportunity to examine ideas and practices more closely. Early lesbian studies embodied, sometimes simultaneously, an inward-looking discovery and celebration of women's difference from men as well as a politicized, social constructionist, and, at times, anti-racist pursuit of sexual liberation and social justice for women. In fact, as an activist endeavor and a growing field of knowledge production, lesbian studies generated and circulated ideas about sexuality and diversity in the 1970s and 1980s that resonate with queer and third-wave ideologies. Such continuity encourages a reevaluation of the sharp contrast drawn between second and third wave in many discussions of feminism in the United States. This chapter demonstrates how building lesbian studies in the 1970s and 1980s—a collective process—contributed to innovations imagined by many to be distinctively third wave or queer.

Lesbian studies was made possible, to a great extent, by the existence of women's studies, which was being created by students and grassroots activists in the late 1960s and early 1970s. Both lesbian studies and women's studies struggled against similar contradictions in their earliest iterations, and the contradictions remain troubling for present-day teachers and students. On the one hand, classes and programs wanted autonomy and they wanted to revolutionize how learning occurred on campuses, prioritizing commitments to social justice and liberation over the academic agendas of straight male administrators. On the other hand, the creators of new curricula sought legitimacy for their subjects of study, which meant accepting and complying with academic expectations and institutional hierarchies. Although the latter approach—institutional legitimacy—came to prevail in both lesbian studies and women's studies, there remained during the 1970s and 1980s a liberationist impulse. Enthusiasm for expressing and delighting in lesbian sexuality in early lesbian studies classes, for example, competed with a dedication to making lesbian studies more intellectual, like other standard university courses.

Lesbian studies retained many of its initial priorities between 1969 and the late 1980s. Few classes or texts initially concerned themselves with the origins or causes of lesbian behavior, and most embraced the view that being a lesbian was a choice available to all women. The contention that claims about lesbians applied to all lesbians, however, was always problematic. Classes attended to gender, racial, and socioeconomic differences among women, and they especially considered the realities of lesbian mothers and older lesbians. But attention to differences was uneven, which then, as now, undermined the ability to attract diverse students, represent the range of lesbian lives, or fully appreciate the intersection of gender, sexuality, race, class, and other aspects of lesbian identities. During the 1970s and 1980s, women of color made significant contributions to lesbian studies; the majority of teachers and students, however, were white.

The process of building lesbian studies was, like most activist undertakings, sporadic and incomplete, with developments in different locations following various and often unpredictable trajectories. Nevertheless, as lesbian studies grew more formalized, with more publications from which to design a course and more academic expertise among its instructors, discussion of feminist scholarship was layered alongside the emphasis on collective knowledge production and personal transformation. Eventually, with a few notable exceptions, student-led courses and part-time teachers gave way to credentialed full-time faculty whose training and scholarship positioned them as experts in the field. Yet, students' self-examination, self-expression, and independent exploration of ideas about lesbians remained key features of the courses. Such foundations established the groundwork for the claims and questions posed by queer studies and third-wave feminists in subsequent decades.

Starting Points

Alternative learning environments, often called free universities, arose on college campuses during the 1960s and 1970s. They operated independent of university constraints, such as the requirement of a credentialed instructor or curriculum committee approval, to offer a peer-to-peer learning opportunity. Not surprisingly given its significance in the development of the free speech movement and other campus activism in the 1960s, the San Francisco Bay Area was a hub of alternative education, including classes with a gay focus. The only explicitly lesbian-focused course in the 1960s, however, took place at Seattle's Experimental College, a student-led effort affiliated with the University of Washington, in which students and community members gathered to mutually explore areas of interest. Jennifer Biehn led the course listed as Lesbianism in spring 1969. Catalogued as a "self-exploration" course or workshop, Lesbianism was offered alongside Group Dynamics, Vedic Literature, and Concept and Self-Concept, to name a few.[2]

As Biehn was not then a lesbian, Lesbianism was not exactly a course by, for, and about lesbians. It was, however, an opportunity to explore one of several themes that had been part of her experience of urban plunge. Later associated almost exclusively with introducing college students to homeless people and the problems of homelessness, the late 1960s urban plunge in Seattle acquainted students—primarily white liberal college students from suburbs or small towns—with a variety of urban communities and subcultures. Orchestrated by a progressive church, a group of student leaders studied racism together and then visited downtown Seattle bars and hangout spots. Biehn recalled being introduced to gay, African American, and transgendered people as a way to "open up our worlds." Also part of the "shock and jar" experience was viewing films that depicted a variety of explicit sexual acts, among them sodomy, and it was a time in Biehn's life when she was tentatively exploring her attraction to women. In 2009, she barely recalled having been part of, much less having led, the lesbian-themed experimental college course. But the connection to urban plunge brought back fuzzy memories of meeting on campus with others to talk about and with lesbians.[3]

Similar to many classes that would follow, discussion was the primary technique for learning and guest speakers from the community and film screenings were important. The catalogue announced that Wednesday afternoon meetings would "bring it out into the open! Through education and discussion the student will be brought to a better understanding of this seldom talked about subject." Also noted was the fact that class guests would "include lesbians themselves, urban plunge workers, and psychiatrists working directly with the situation." Finally, it mentioned there would be "films also."[4]

Nearly all the earliest lesbian studies courses, as Biehn's, were student-generated. They tended to adopt names including "liberation" and "revolution," signaling their connections to larger social movements of the day. In 1970–71, San Francisco's Breakaway Women's Liberation School offered The Gay Woman, Berkeley's Center for Participant Education offered Gay Women's Liberation, and a community college in Oakland offered Lesbianism: From Myth to Revolution.[5] Undergraduate students led the first attempt to institute a lesbian course at a four-year college, Sacramento State. The course was part of a successful though short-lived gay studies program developed by lesbian and gay students and faculty.[6] Feminist and recently out lesbian Shannon Hennigan developed and taught a class on a pass/no-credit basis in fall 1971 focused on lesbian sexuality.[7] Hennigan's course was listed through Experimental Studies, a unit on campus that offered interdisciplinary or innovative courses for academic credit.[8] Although modified and renamed, it retained a strong emphasis on sexuality. In the second and third offerings, it was co-taught with another student, Patricia Wallace, who had adopted the name Patty One Person.[9]

Even as lesbian and gay classes were joined together in Sacramento's gay studies program, the lesbian class was also indebted to the feminist movement and pursued a specific desire to teach women about their bodies and sexualities. Hennigan and One Person described the course as "primarily a sexual consciousness raising class for women"; it included lectures, required readings, and course projects, with lectures that would cover "basic sexuality and physiology."[10] Uncommonly explicit and playful discussions of sexuality were part of the classes, as Barbara Bryant noted from her recollections of being in all three. In addition to discussing sexuality openly and sharing personal experiences, which was optional, Bryant recalled watching in the class Holding, a short film that featured a lesbian couple having sex. Students in the class produced research or creative work, driven not by adherence to academic standards but more by student curiosity. Course projects, the 1972 course description noted, "can be anything dealing with women and sexuality." In previous classes, the instructors indicated that "films, tapes, journals, written fantasies and collages have been done."[11]

As explained in the Los Angeles-based periodical *Lesbian Tide*, "a small, but vociferous group of gay activists" were collaborating to create change in Sacramento. "'We must attack the universities…they are the heart of the body of misinformation about ourselves…' stated a member of Sacramento's lesbian-feminist group (a group that is centered on the campus, but is open to and serves the entire community)."[12] Misinformation about sexuality was one of several problems the class and related campus events addressed. During the course's second run, students brought Del Martin, Phyllis Lyon, Sally Gearhart, Rita Mae Brown, Joan Hand, Judy Grahn, and Pat Parker to campus for a symposium. The events concluded with a performance of Patty One Person and Cherie Gordon's play, *Homo Brontosaurus*, which featured lesbian brontosauruses dancing, singing, and, more than once in the play, making love.[13] Grahn and Parker both read their erotically charged poetry at the symposium, sharing work that highlighted working-class and African American perspectives. Brown's talk sparked deeper discussion of class, as Bryant explained, and more vocal expression by women's studies and gay studies participants from working-class backgrounds followed the symposium. At the outset of lesbian studies, activists paid attention to difference and sought to be inclusive of diverse lesbians.

Although Northern California and Washington State cultivated some of the earliest lesbian studies efforts, its development in the early 1970s was not confined to the West Coast. In the Midwest and Northeast, two courses were underway in fall 1972 at Kent State University in Ohio and the State University of New York, Buffalo. Similar to Hennigan, the instructors were active in feminist and gay circles, each becoming part of a newly formed lesbian feminist movement that mobilized around the concerns of women within the gay movement and lesbians within feminism. New York City's Radicalesbians, for example, had formed following the notorious purge of the "lavender menace" from the National Organization for Women. Joining various caucuses, rap groups, and wholly new organizations, lesbian feminists created separate space, yet many retained their other movement commitments.

A tenured English professor at Kent State, Dolores Noll began speaking on campus about gay issues in 1971; she had recently turned forty and was newly acquainted with the gay liberation movement. She made herself visible by coming out to administrators and serving as faculty advisor for Kent's Gay Liberation Front. Noll offered courses with a lesbian focus during the following year: she first taught Gay Womanhood in fall 1972, and she repeated the class in spring 1973. Her trajectory was somewhat similar to Hennigan's in Sacramento, only Noll was over a decade older and in a faculty position at the time. Her courses were offered through Experimental College and she was granted a course reduction to teach them.[14]

Educating students about the history and current status of lesbians and "help[ing] gay women taking the course to gain a greater understanding of and pride in themselves as women and as gays" were important aspects of Noll's class.[15] She encouraged self-exploration through two papers, to be submitted "one near the beginning and the other near the end—expressing your beliefs, attitudes, feelings, what-have-you, about gay womanhood." In the first quarter, the papers were not given grades.[16] In spring quarter, students who took the course as "Individual Investigation" (a non-controversial title of the course students could choose) completed a project with an oral presentation and written component.[17] Such aspects of the course made it very different from the English classes Noll ordinarily taught. She was a medievalist who had previously taught some classes on literature by women.[18]

Similar to the Sacramento class, Gay Womanhood was taught pass/fail. It attracted a mixture of students, some enrolling for credit and others attending out of interest. The fall and spring quarter courses enrolled women as well as a few men, some heterosexual or bisexual, though Noll indicated that the majority were lesbians. The spring class was co-taught with student activist Nancy Koch and open to student input: "the material to be discussed and the format of the class will be determined by both the instructor and the class as a whole. Much will depend on the interests of class members." Possible topics were closeted lesbians, subcultures, discrimination, religion, psychology, political action, and relationships with men, straight women, and other gay women. Within these topics were embedded a variety of issues that Noll enumerated, including bars, the law, parents, radical lesbianism, and butch-femme roles.[19] The updated version of the syllabus identified "meeting other gay women; one-night stands; maintaining long-lasting relationships; the 'open marriage'; handling rejection, possessiveness; sexual hang-ups" as indication of the scope of conversations about sexual relationships.[20]

In addition to texts and discussions, the course included films, speakers, excursions, and individual projects. The class viewed two short lesbian films, *Holding* and *Lavender*. The former, also screened in Sacramento, intermixed images of two women having sex with scenes of the couple outdoors in nature; the latter featured two lesbians discussing their lives. Additional films "about female and male homosexual love and sexual relationships were shown by a staff person from the Akron [Ohio] Forum." Moreover, the class went together to a lesbian bar in Akron, and afterward "reactions to this experience were discussed in class," as were "the past and present experiences" of "two women who had been in the lesbian subculture for some years."[21]

Simultaneously in upstate New York, Madeline Davis's Lesbianism had its first run in women's studies. Although women's studies would become an important home for lesbian studies in the 1980s, Buffalo was unique in putting forward a lesbian course in the early 1970s. Active in a local mixed-gender gay organization founded in 1969, Davis attended a Buffalo Radicalesbians meeting in 1971 and then joined Lesbians United, a group "formed for consciousness raising, study, and political action."[22] Davis credited graduate student Margaret Small as the catalyst for building a course. Small's socialist-feminist commitments had led her to value "organized study" as an essential aspect of social change work. The newly emerging women's studies program at Buffalo, with its strong presence of lesbians, welcomed the class, which Davis and Small developed by posing questions informally to lesbians, on and off campus, about what should be covered.

Although themes and topics were similar to Noll's, Davis's course design reflected the burgeoning sensibility of lesbian feminism: a week each was dedicated to "class differences," "the Black lesbian," "the lesbian mother," and "toward a women's culture," which featured "poems, music, art, submitted by class."[23] Unlike Gay Womanhood, no references to men or male-authored texts appeared on the Lesbianism syllabus. More firmly grounded in a historical approach and in lesbian-feminist thought, Lesbianism had students reading historical and contemporary novels as well as two lesbian-feminist texts that Noll also assigned, *Lesbian/Woman* and *Sappho Was a Right-On Woman*. Additional readings included essays, among them Radicalesbians' "Woman-Identified Woman," some pieces written by the Washington, D.C., lesbian collective the Furies, and a 1972 article on sexuality published in *The Ladder*, which was by then being published independent of Daughters of Bilitis.

The early 1970s was a period of discovery and personal development for many teachers as well as students. A musician and librarian long acquainted with Buffalo's lesbian community, Davis was newly returned to campus as a student in her thirties. She was the first openly lesbian Democratic National Convention delegate, urging adoption in Miami in 1972 of a gay rights plank.[24] Noll had become acquainted with new possibilities through her summer trips to Washington, D.C., and her involvement in the Modern Language Association's women's caucus; her then-lover, "a doctoral student in English," who was "more liberated than I, as well as a stronger feminist" and whose acquaintance she had made when the student came to see Noll about her Gay Womanhood class, was a significant influence.[25] Hennigan, too, was recently out as a lesbian and was raising a son from a previous relationship with a man while teaching her lesbian courses at Sacramento State.[26]

It was not until after all three instructors had offered their first courses that information about these and other classes began to circulate more widely. A fall 1972 story in the national gay magazine, the *Advocate,* described Sacramento's program. Proceedings of the 1973 Gay Academic Union meeting conveyed information to a far larger audience than was able to attend. *Gays on Campus,* published by the National Gay Student Center in 1975, included a handful of gay studies syllabi.[27] It would be a few years before lesbian studies—distinctive from gay and lesbian studies— would generate its own resources.

Present and Future Lesbian Studies, c. 1982

"Just as feminist courses were taught before books on women's studies were available, courses on lesbians have preceded a book titled *Lesbian Studies,*" wrote Peg Cruikshank in 1982 in her volume's introduction. "A new educational movement exists which ought now to be formally documented."[28] *Lesbian Studies* responded to the books and courses in women's studies that omitted lesbian lives and reflected the accomplishments of lesbian studies. By the late 1970s, more sites existed for networking among lesbian feminist teachers and scholars than ever before. The National Women's Studies Association was created in 1977, and Cruikshank's anthology was conceived at the inaugural 1979 meeting, a gathering of feminist teachers, researchers, and activists with a significant lesbian presence.[29] Connections fostered at the NWSA meeting helped make lesbian studies visible beyond the sporadic campuses where it was out in the open and not just tucked away into general women's studies courses. There was also a Lesbian-Feminist Study Clearinghouse out of Pittsburgh, collecting and distributing syllabi as well as published and unpublished manuscripts, and a "lesbian feminist research newsletter," *Matrices,* which began in fall 1977 and was by 1980 being sent from Lincoln, Nebraska, to over eight hundred subscribers.[30]

The dozens of lesbian studies courses offered between the mid-1970s and mid-1980s built on the precedent of earlier classes and the growing momentum of women's studies and lesbian publishing. During this time some of the earliest graduate students who had been part of the founding of women's studies were joining faculty, teaching part-time or full-time, sometimes in tenure-line jobs. From these positions, they designed courses explicitly to learn about lesbians—lesbian lives, lesbian writers, lesbian relationships, lesbian culture. Most proudly announced their lesbian emphasis. Alternative titles, some adopting the names of significant lesbian texts, arose in some women's and feminist studies programs in the 1980s: Women-Identified Women, Female Bonding: Women Loving Women, and Woman Plus Woman. Though perhaps euphemistic, such titles signaled a lesbian focus without using the L-word. The titles were thought to be more inviting to bisexual, closeted, or questioning women.

Many university instructors found it expedient to offer a lesbian-focused course using an existing course name/number, avoiding extra paperwork and levels of bureaucracy and scrutiny that could potentially stall or prevent the class from being offered. Some evidence indicates that the coded titles were more strategic yet. At the University of New Mexico in fall 1981, Trisha Franzen's flyer for Heterosexism and the Oppression of Women included immediately after the title and before the course number, in parenthesis, "The Lesbian Experience." A graphic of four women's symbols, although different from the common lesbian use of conjoined women's symbols, further marked the class as being about bonds among women. The course description on the flyer, however, refrained from mentioning the word lesbian until halfway through the last sentence; foregrounded was language about heterosexism, sex and gender roles, sexual preference, female friendships, matriarchy and patriarchy, and finally concluding with "legal, economic, and cultural institutions and practices which affect lesbians; the experience of lesbians of color; communication between lesbian and non-lesbian women; and the nature of lesbian culture and communities."[31] The course focus, it seems, was entirely about lesbians.[32]

Sensitive to those students reluctant to enroll in an explicitly titled course, most were willing to make alternative arrangements. It was not uncommon for students to attend but not enroll in courses. Student/teacher Barb Ryan was understanding and welcomed such students, typically numbering around ten, at her University of Oregon Lesbianism: Myth and Reality course in the early 1980s—students who wished to "prevent the course title from being indelibly inscribed in their transcripts."[33] At San Diego State University, students could opt for an independent study titled Alternative Lifestyles in Literature instead of Bonnie Zimmerman's Lesbian Life and Literature; in spring 1979, eight chose the covert option and twenty-eight registered under the regular title.[34] Similar to many other instructors, Zimmerman taught literature through women's studies. Although her Ph.D. from SUNY Buffalo was in English, her dedication to women's studies was nurtured in Buffalo, further developed in the nation's oldest women's studies program at San Diego State, and later exhibited in her service as president of NWSA in the 1990s.

The humanities were especially suited for discussing lesbian lives and lesbian feminist theories, and literature classes accounted for approximately half of the lesbian studies courses offered in the 1970s and 1980s. By the late 1970s, lesbian studies was, when not taught through interdisciplinary women's studies units, nearly always offered through a humanities discipline. Although there was less consciousness-raising activity around issues of sexuality in classes by the 1980s, sexuality remained a theme of importance, especially when poetry, fiction, or autobiography described or referenced lesbian eroticism.

A teacher and scholar of literature herself, Cruikshank's anthology demonstrated the significance of literature courses and literary texts in the compiled syllabi and accompanying essays. Literary criticism would later be central to the development of queer theory; well before the linguistic turn, *Lesbian Studies* presented literature as ripe for analysis of non-heterosexual realities. How literary texts were read in early lesbian studies classes varied based on the goals of the class and the inclinations of the instructor. Evidence suggests some blanket pronouncements about "the lesbian" were offered in classes, yet teachers avoided doing so. Sounding a note of caution about the misuses of literature, for example, professor and novelist Bertha Harris expressed reservations about teaching lesbian literature with an ideological agenda. At worst, Harris pointed out at the 1973 Gay Academic Union meeting, lesbian literature classes would be "'sociological' rather than literary—resulting in happier 'self-image,' but only for those disinterested in the rich variousness and complexity that informs both life and literature. In the service of political articulation, in the great rush for a piece of the action, our deathblow, if we are not careful, will be oversimplification in our work, and in our selves."[35]

As in all fields representing a minority group, there was a tension in lesbian studies between legitimizing the group and exposing its internal conflicts. In some versions of lesbian studies, instructors and students no doubt sought to represent lesbians as a whole, as a group of women united by their love of women; many more, however, acknowledged that they were sampling selected writings that illuminated some lesbian experiences. While women's studies began to eschew the concept of "woman," recognizing the plurality of women's experiences, a few lesbian studies courses persisted in using titles such as The Lesbian Experience or The Lesbian Woman. Yet, the phrase "the lesbian" was not always accompanied by an oversimplified understanding of lesbians. Joan Nestle's 1975 The Lesbian in Literature course shows how.

At Queens College in Flushing, New York, in 1975, teacher and Lesbian Herstory Archives founder Joan Nestle taught as an "honors tutorial" The Lesbian in Literature. The syllabus pointed students to bibliographies covering "all known novels, short stories, short novels, poetry, drama, non fiction work since 1907." The readings included selections by, among others, Rita Mae Brown, Pat Parker, Judy Grahn, Audre Lorde, Monique Wittig, Joanna Russ, and Ann Allen Shockley. Students in Nestle's class would make contributions to the Lesbian Herstory Archives—similar to other lesbian studies classes in the 1970s, their contributions would be a "gift to the future...in the form of tapes, poems, papers, bibliographies, graphics, photographs."[36] As an archivist of lesbian history, Nestle knew such materials would be of value to visitors, including the various lesbian studies and literature classes that regularly visited the archives.[37]

Recognizing that lesbians of color were greatly outnumbered by white authors and teachers of lesbian studies, Cruikshank sought to make perspectives of women of color prominent in *Lesbian Studies*. A bibliography of work by and about black lesbians before 1970 began the book's section on New Research/New Perspectives. Opening the compilation's appendix were the syllabi of two prominent lesbian authors and teachers of color, Barbara Smith and Cherríe Moraga, figures influential to third wave feminism. Furthermore, a dialogue between Smith and Moraga conveyed to readers the issues they faced in teaching their respective courses and expressed frustration over the whiteness of many lesbian-themed classes and texts.[38] Sentiments expressed in the anthology were not unique to lesbian studies, as feminists more generally were grappling with how to address white privilege and the marginalization of women of color in the movement.

Teachers of color were especially motivated to teach about lesbians marginalized by racism within the lesbian and feminist movements, but they were not alone in doing so. The Lesbianism course at SUNY Buffalo, as early as 1972, made space to talk about the distinctive experiences of lesbians of color. An anti-racist approach warranted both separate discussions about black experiences and racism, for example, and thoughtful attention to integrating black experiences and racism into all discussions of lesbian realities. In the introduction to *Lesbian Studies*, Cruikshank asserted that combating racism was one of the few agreed upon tenets of lesbian studies. She acknowledged her whiteness, that the whiteness of many of the field's visible spokespersons was a problem, and that well-meaning intentions did not make the work unbiased.[39]

Whether compelled or voluntary, some teachers sought to ensure that lesbians of color were represented throughout the class. Nestle's syllabus from 1975 succeeded in doing so, attributable to her anti-racist politics and also her access, through the archives, to a vast amount of material. Other instructors integrated material in varying degrees during the 1970s and 1980s. Evidence suggests that not only was difference a ubiquitous topic, but that power and privilege were also part of the discussion. At Sonoma State in the late 1970s, in a women's studies program virtually run by students, all courses, including those about lesbians, had to address on their syllabi what the women's studies committee (composed of students and one faculty director) called the "seven –isms": class, race, sexism, lesbianism, motherhood, age, and disability.[40]

Suggestions of lesbian homogeneity appear on syllabi from this era, but often the similarities of lesbian experience were called into question, and a number of classes made women of color a course's primary emphasis. Evelyn Beck's 1980 Lesbian Culture syllabus from the University of Wisconsin, Madison, for instance, opened with questions— "What is lesbian culture? By whom is it created? For whom?"—inviting a discussion of inclusivity and exclusivity in lesbian communities. Week one had as a central question "to what extent can we speak of a unified lesbian culture disregarding factors of race, class, religion, ethnicity, education, age, and other differentiations among lesbians?"[41] Among classes prioritizing the experiences of lesbians of color were Lesbian Literature and Invisible Woman in Literature, taught by Smith at Barnard and Boston, and Merle Woo and Cherríe Moraga's sections of Lesbian Literature at San Francisco State.[42]

When University of California, Berkeley students and allies formed the Multicultural Lesbian Gay Studies program in August 1982, they insisted that multicultural and multiracial perspectives belonged in the entirety of the program's curriculum: "all MLGS courses should use materials by and about Third World gays and lesbians," stated the handbook from 1984.[43] The genesis of the program came, in part, from students' frustration at the lack of diversity in an early 1980s gay sociology class; the founders also were part of a campus coalition of Third World student, feminist, and lesbian/gay groups.[44] MLGS grew out of student activism as had the early 1970s attempts to inaugurate lesbian and gay studies; unlike earlier efforts, Berkeley students succeeded in building a student-run program with longevity, significant campus funding, and a robust contingent of faculty allies by the end of the 1980s.

In its early days, an MLGS newsletter advertised the approach in their courses as one that "will try to present the diversity of our community from a multi-disciplinary approach." Courses were to be "truly multicultural, co-sexual, and community-based, at the same time they are academically rigorous."[45] Contradicting this agenda, individual MLGS courses were not necessarily "co-sexual," as two lesbian courses were offered in 1982–83: Lesbian Literature and Women Loving Women.[46] The co-sexual position was meant to discourage exclusion of women from gay-themed courses; it did not mandate that lesbian-focused courses include men. The multicultural position and links with the community were somewhat more important to the initial students involved in MLGS, who tirelessly sought connections with local resource persons and every publication that included perspectives of gay and lesbian people of color. They maintained a library and recommended contacts and material to instructors. Paula Gunn Allen and Woo, noted writers, teachers, and activists of color with ties to the university, were important mentors for the students and among the faculty sponsors of student-led courses.

Numerous new texts and teaching material made possible a more diverse portrait of lesbians during the 1970s, even though the most heralded texts—among them Gloria Anzaldúa and Moraga's *This Bridge Called My Back: Writings by Radical Women of Color* and Audre Lorde's *Zami*—were not published until after 1981. Syllabi show that many instructors taught poetry by Allen, Grahn, Parker, and others from the outset; they assigned the Furies's *Class and Feminism* and Brown's *Rubyfruit Jungle*. Judith Arnold's writing drew attention to aging and Maya Chumu's to bicultural experiences. New research about the lives of working-class lesbians in Buffalo was much discussed, and *Lesbians in Fiction*, a narrated slideshow presentation that included lesbian pulp fiction, was available for classes. A widely distributed documentary film, *Word Is Out: Stories of Some of Our Lives*, highlighted age, class, and ethnic diversity of lesbians. Though many syllabi did not incorporate all the above, it was a rare syllabus that did not make some gesture toward inclusiveness by the mid-1970s.

Whether as literature or in some other format, stories of lesbians were central to the development of lesbian studies. Most courses sought stories in different genres, from different time periods, and from women with different life experiences. In the quest to demonstrate that lesbians were everywhere, it was undesirable to marginalize women from diverse racial/ethnic or class backgrounds. What could be problematic, though, as Harris had earlier cautioned, was reading the stories of lesbians through an ideological lens—one that deemed certain kinds of sexual expression and life choices as "liberated" or feminist and others not. The righteous attitudes expressed in polemical early lesbian feminist tests—"Woman-Identified Woman" or the Furies's *Lesbians in the Women's Movement*—no doubt found expression in some lesbian studies classes. Yet, such views did not predominate and increasingly vocal was a perspective that cast doubt on monolithic views of lesbianism.

Conclusion

As an activist intervention into learning about women, lesbian studies in the 1970s and 1980s was in many ways an extension of the movement work lesbians did, on or off campus, to bring about social transformation. Classes aimed to erase the shame and stigma associated with lesbianism, correct the invisibility of lesbians, and create a lesbian-feminist space in which participants might feel pride as lesbians or lesbian allies. Whether in informal or formal academic settings, whether student-led or instructor-driven, the courses brought together self-identified lesbians and some who were not, though identities were often subject to change. Participants learned and taught from their life experience as well as from the first-hand perspectives of other lesbians.

During these decades little curiosity was directed toward the question of what makes a woman a lesbian, and hardly any energy was put into scientific or social scientific studies of lesbianism. From the point of view of contemporary lesbian feminist culture, lesbianism's foundations were not biological. Lesbian desire for companionship and affection of other women was thought to be a sexual preference, not a consequence of an innate sexual orientation. That some had felt their attraction to women from a young age and others only discovered it by becoming feminists was evidence of how lesbians were not all alike. Lesbian studies classes, like lesbian feminist art, music, and other cultural pursuits, were oriented toward sharing and creating, not commanding physical, psychoanalytical, or empirical evidence. Sharing and creating was a foundation for building a stronger, more visible lesbian presence in the world. Knowledge about lesbians past and present—and cross-culturally—enabled introspection and personal transformations, such as the courage to live openly as a lesbian and, at its best, the development of more nuanced lesbian feminist convictions.

As in other activist endeavors of this period, lesbian studies was a site of conflict over whose voices would be heard. Similar to sentiments expressed by Cruikshank in *Lesbian Studies*, Berkeley's Multicultural Lesbian Gay Studies exhibited a strong commitment to ensuring that lesbian and gay studies was not simply about white people. Yet the organizers of MLGS were not usually the teachers of the courses, and though they gave significant input to instructors on how to construct courses, especially by including Third World perspectives, the instructors retained many of their own priorities. Trudie Rogers, for example, translated her experience offering sexuality workshops to lesbians into the MLGS course Women Loving Women: An Exploration of Women's Intimacy. A thirty-five year old black lesbian, Rogers did not make race a central issue on her syllabus.[47] Rogers, similar to Hennigan in Sacramento, cared foremost about enabling women present in her workshop or classroom to experience and give sexual pleasure to one another.

Over time, Berkeley's MLGS gained institutional acceptance, and its student-led initiatives were replaced by regularized courses in the early 1990s.[48] At this point what was increasingly being called queer studies had grown, by some accounts, academically chic or even mainstream.[49] Retaining its ties to feminist activism, women's studies had also professionalized, such that fewer student-taught courses were available, and more part-time instructors without Ph.D.s lost opportunities to teach. The shift to lesbian courses taught by degreed professionals, increasingly with dissertations on lesbian topics, lent much credibility to the fields. When City College of San Francisco formed the first full-fledged Department of Gay and Lesbian Studies in 1989, however, it was sited at a two-year school where the attachment to respectability was less entrenched. As a tie to the past and as a consequence of significant student demand, a class on Lesbian Relationships that focused on personal growth was one bridge from the mid-1980s to the present.[50]

With the rise of lesbian, gay, bisexual, and transgender (LGBT) or queer studies since the late 1980s, lesbian studies has become somewhat rare as an independent undertaking. The mutability of sex and gender has especially captured the attention of queer and feminist theorists, and transgender identities and practices have become a significant line of inquiry. Increasingly, gender and women's studies offers introductory LGBT studies courses; less frequently, it appears, do lesbian-themed classes remain on the books. What Berkeley's MLGS once called the co-sexual position has come to predominate, and whereas before it worked to address the marginalization of women, now it seeks to remedy the exclusion of trans people and those who reject gender categorization. This seems to be one notable feature of the third wave; in the early twenty-first century gender divisions are suspect and separatism is rarely viewed as an acceptable strategy, as it is equated with enforcement of binary categories and intolerance of difference.

The creation of women-centered space and lesbian-specific curricula in lesbian studies was, to be sure, exclusionary. Yet, it was neither wholly exclusionary nor wholly essentialist. Students generally preferred to have women-only classes, and they sometimes insisted on it, but more than a few men and certainly a number of butch and gender ambiguous women participated. Men's ideas were mostly ignored, and in some cases, men themselves were subtly or not so subtly bullied out of classrooms. Women in lesbian circles of the 1970s and 1980s expressed gender in multifarious ways, with limits; many lesbians regarded drag queens as insulting to women, and lesbians who cross-dressed might be earnestly asked why they wanted to be men. But these were not the central issues that inspired students of lesbian studies. Rather, questions about sexual freedom, lesbian diversity, and liberating women from sexism and homophobia were core to building lesbian studies. Such questions remain vital to feminist and lesbian activists today, and the commonality has been obscured by the wave metaphor prevalent in discussions of U.S. feminism. Third-wave and queer feminism are a continuation of dialogue begun in the 1970s and 1980s, bringing fresh perspectives and approaches that need not diminish earlier efforts to merit attention.

Notes

1. See Astrid Henry, *Not My Mother's Sister: Generational Conflict and Third Wave Feminism* (Bloomington: Indiana University Press, 2004); Linda Garber, *Identity Poetics: Race, Class,*

and the Lesbian-Feminist Roots of Queer Theory (New York: Columbia University Press, 2001); 'Becca Cragin, "Post-Lesbian-Feminism: Documenting 'Those Cruddy Old Dykes of Yore,'" in *Carryin' on in the Lesbian and Gay South*, ed. John Howard (New York: New York University Press, 1997), 285–327; and Verta Taylor and Leila J. Rupp, "Women's Culture and Lesbian Feminist Activism: A Reconsideration of Cultural Feminism," *Signs* 19, no. 1 (1993): 32–61.

2. University of Washington, Experimental College [Catalogue], spring 1969, 13.
3. Jennifer Biehn, interview by author, Oakland, California, 18 September 2009.
4. U.W. Experimental College Catalogue, 13.
5. Carol Ahlum and Florence Howe, eds., *The New Guide to Current Female Studies* (Pittsburgh, PA: KNOW, 1971), 3, 5, 12.
6. Sasha Gregory, "Nation's First? Gay Studies Program Formed," *Advocate*, 16 (August 1972).
7. Barbara Bryant, interview by author, Berkeley, California, 23 September 2009.
8. Bryant's transcript lists the three classes as EXP 105 ALTERNATIVE LIFE, fall 1971; EXP 105 THE LESBIAN IN AMERICA, spring 1972; and EXP 050 THE LESBIAN + SOCIETY, spring 1973.
9. Gregory, "Nation's First"; Charles Moore, "Gay Studies Program," *Gay Sunshine*, no. 16 (January/February 1973), 15; and J. Lee Lehman, ed., *Gays on Campus* (Washington, D.C.: United States National Student Association, 1975), 61.
10. Lehman, *Gays on Campus*, 61.
11. Ibid.
12. "Can Gay Instructors Teach Gay Subjects to Gay Students in a California University? Sacramento Says YES!" *Lesbian Tide* (July 1972), 5–6. Ellipses in original.
13. Colloquium on Lesbian Women: Myth and Reality, 4–6 December 1972, program, carton 3, folder 9, Sally R. Wagner Papers, Department of Special Collections and University Archives, Library, California State University, Sacramento; and description of the play from Cherie Gordon Collection finding aid, p. 4, 29, Lavender Library, Sacramento.
14. Dolores Noll, "A Gay Feminist in Academia," *College English*, 36, no. 3 (1974): 312–15; and Dolores Noll, interview by author, Stow, Ohio, 20 November 2009.
15. Dolores L. Noll, "Teaching a Course on Gay Womanhood," abstract, n.d., Lesbian Studies folder, Lesbian Herstory Archives, Brooklyn (hereafter LHA).
16. Dolores Noll, Gay Womanhood syllabus, fall 1972, folder 13, Box 8, Gay Activists Alliance Records, 1970–1983, microfilm, New York Public Library.
17. Dolores Noll, Gay Womanhood annotated syllabus, 1972–73, Lesbian Studies folder, LHA.
18. Noll interview.
19. Noll, annotated 1972–73 syllabus; and Noll, 1972 syllabus.
20. Noll, annotated 1972–73 syllabus.
21. Ibid.
22. Madeline Davis, "Learning Through Teaching: A Lesbianism Course in 1972," in *Lesbian Studies: Present and Future*, ed. Margaret Cruikshank (Old Westbury, CT: Feminist Press, 1982), 93.
23. Cruikshank, *Lesbian Studies*, 231–32.
24. Elizabeth Lapovsky Kennedy and Madeline D. Davis, *Boots of Leather, Slippers of Gold: The History of a Lesbian Community* (New York: Routledge, 1993), preface; and Madeline Davis, http://en.wikipedia.org/wiki/Madeline_Davis, accessed 28 July 2009.
25. Noll interview; Angie DeRosa, "Founder of Kent LGBU Returns," *Daily Kent Stater*, 6 September 1976, 10; and Noll, "A Gay Feminist in Academia," quotation on 58.
26. Bryant interview.
27. Gregory, "Nation's First"; *The Universities and the Gay Experience: Proceedings of the Conference Sponsored by the Women and Men of the Gay Academic Union*, November 23 and 24, 1973 (New York: Gay Academic Union, 1974), 91–95; and Lehman, *Gays on Campus*.

28. Cruikshank, *Lesbian Studies*, xi.
29. *Matrices*, 3, no. 1 (October 1979), 5.
30. Lesbian-Feminist Study Clearinghouse brochure, n.d., Lesbian Studies file, LHA; and *Matrices*, 4, no. 1 (November 1980), 1, and 3, no. 2 (February 1980).
31. Flyer for Heterosexism and the Oppression of Women, Women's Studies: Issues, LHA.
32. Trisha Franzen, Heterosexism and the Oppression of Women syllabus, Women's Studies: Issues, LHA.
33. Debbie Howlett, "Class Explores Lesbianism," clipping, *Oregon Daily Emerald*, 9 April 1982, Overflow College and Universities, LHA.
34. Bonnie Zimmerman, "Lesbianism 101," *Radical Teacher* 17 (November 1980): 21.
35. Bertha Harris, "The Lesbian in Literature: Or, Is There Life on Mars?" in *Universities and the Gay Experience*, 51–52.
36. Cruikshank, *Lesbian Studies*, 228–29.
37. *Lesbian Herstory Archives Newsletter*, no. 8 (winter 1984).
38. Cruikshank, *Lesbian Studies*, 103–9, 55–65, 217–22.
39. Ibid., xii.
40. Ruth Mahaney, interview by David Reichard, San Francisco, 26 July 2006. Thanks to Dave Reichard for sharing this interview.
41. Cruikshank, *Lesbian Studies*, 229–31.
42. Ibid., 217–22; Barbara Smith, The Invisible Woman in Literature syllabus, Lesbian Studies folder, LHA; Merle Woo, interview by author, San Francisco, 23 September 2009; and Women's Studies Program, Schedule of Courses, San Francisco State University, fall 1986. Thanks to Dave Reichard for providing me with the 1986 document.
43. Multicultural Lesbian and Gay Studies: A Handbook for Faculty, April 1984, 6, Lesbian Studies folder, LHA.
44. Grahame Perry and Margaret Krouskoff, "Developing and Establishing a Multi-Cultural Lesbian Gay Studies Program at U.C. Berkeley," report, January 1983, 1, Box 1, Gay Studies Information folder, Records of the Harvard Gay & Lesbian Caucus, 1976–2000, Harvard University Archives, Cambridge, MA.
45. Announcement in *Matrices*, 8, no. 1 (January/February 1985): 19.
46. Multicultural Lesbian Gay Studies Program Newsletter, 22 March 1983, 1. A third class planned for that year, Lesbian Identity and Relationships, never materialized.
47. Trudie Rogers, Women Loving Women syllabus, folder 52, Box 3, and Krouskoff to Cherríe Moraga, 8 December 1982, folder 34, Box 2, both in Queer Resource Center Records, CU-486, University Archives, The Bancroft Library, University of California, Berkeley.
48. Alisa Klinger, "Moving the Pink Agenda into the Ivory Tower: The 'Berkeley Guide' to Institutionalizing Lesbian, Gay, and Bisexual Studies," in *Tilting the Tower: Lesbians Teaching Queer Subjects*, ed. Linda Garber (New York: Routledge, 1994), 186–97.
49. Liz McMillen, "From Margin to Mainstream: Books in Gay and Lesbian Studies," *Chronicle of Higher Education* (22 July 1992); A8–9, 13.
50. Lindy McKnight, interview by author, San Francisco, 22 September 2009, and Trinity Ordona, interview by author, San Francisco, 22 September 2009.

Conclusion
Looking Backward, Looking Forward

JACQUELINE L. CASTLEDINE

While still a graduate student studying women's and gender history, I presented a conference paper in spring 2004 that explored how the political work of postwar leftist women challenges our understanding of a dormant mid-twentieth century period for U.S. women's organizing. Given the panel topics, it is not surprising that the discussion at the end of our session centered on the efficacy of a "waves" metaphor that in a single word attempts to characterize over one hundred and fifty years of activism. Despite the improbability of agreeing on a more suitable metaphor, audience and panel members gamely proposed a series of evocative images that might better suggest the long history of women's work, while at the same time acknowledging the unique historical moments that have produced it. These included the suggestion that scholars consider how for centuries strands of women's organizing have wound together in rope-like fashion. This idea, and several like it, was rejected for not adequately reflecting the depth, breadth, continuities and discontinuities of women's lived experiences. Unfortunately, the panel session ended without answering the questions at the heart of our lengthy discussion: Is it time for us to disavow the waves metaphor? And, if so, would replacing it with another help us better understand and document U.S. women's history?

While recognizing that it has its limitations, some scholars have argued that the waves metaphor is not entirely without merit. In an especially eloquent defense of it, Cathryn Bailey points out that the metaphor is useful because it "captures the notion of continuity as well as discontinuity; waves are different from one another but are similar, too."[1] Bailey further reminds us that early second-wave feminists embraced the metaphor because they believed that associating their activism with that of successful "first wave" suffragists helped second wavers claim credibility at the same time that it inspired women to join their ranks. Despite general agreement that "there is something lovely about a wave," use of the metaphor continues to come under attack.[2]

One reason for the assault is that, not unlike ocean waves, the origin of women's activism—the winds of historical change that create the "crest" and the "trough" of social, cultural, or political movement—is too often invisible in wave rhetoric. Just as importantly, a focus on "crests" of activism created by large, centralized, national movements has marginalized smaller, regional, and local movements that quietly persist during seeming "troughs" of inactivity. By examining relationships between national, regional, and local activism, while mindful of their continuities and discontinuities with earlier and later movements and the complexity of their agendas and strategies, this volume documents a rich history of women's activism that persevered between 1945 and 1985. Not coincidentally, our time frame includes two notable interludes considered by many to be "doldrums" for women's organizing—the postwar period and the early 1980s.[3]

On no single issue has the shortcomings of the wave metaphor been more roundly attacked than in its marginalization of non-white, non-heterosexual women. Kimberly Springer writes that in reducing U.S. women's activism to the notion of a "first wave" for suffrage and "second wave" for women's liberation, "we effectively disregard the race-based movements before them that serve as precursors, or windows of political opportunity, for gender activism."[4] Julia Sandy-Bailey's discussion of postwar Harlem women's use of consumer activism to challenge the racial discrimination of neighborhood merchants, and the gender discrimination of male community leaders, vividly illustrates Springer's points about the nexus of race and gender in women's organizing. Julie Gallagher's research on the anticolonial work of the National Council of Negro Women demonstrates the importance of alliances forged not only across decades but also across continents in the mid-twentieth century, as she describes how African American women continued their work on a global agenda even in the face of harsh red baiting in the McCarthy era. This work, like Janet Weaver's chapter on Mexican American women's organizing in Iowa, suggests that throughout the twentieth century, whether or not they counted their activism as feminist, women of color continued with what many scholars and activists consider to be the work of feminism within single-sex and single-race, as well as mixed-sex and mixed-race, organizations.

Identifying discontinuities between first-, second-, and, eventually, third- wave agendas has become fundamental to how scholars map the chronology of generations of women's activism. Those who argue that generational differences help us to understand feminist movements describe second wavers as the first to make a demand for sexual equality central to their agenda, a sentiment they argue is typified in the second-wave mantra, "The Personal is Political." Leandra Zarnow's examination of the left-feminist origins of this powerful rallying cry, however, bears out that as early as 1950 Bella Abzug challenged U.S. courts to recognize women's legal right to sexual freedom. Marcia M. Gallo's examination of the Daughters of Bilitis further complicates the wave narrative of discontinuity by tracing the origins of its battle for lesbian rights not to social movements of the 1960s and 1970s, but rather to the efforts of women a decade earlier. Their work raises questions about whether generational overlap in agendas has been the rule rather than the exception in women's activism.

The notion of the 1980s as the decade in which significant advances resulting from women's organizing came to a dramatic halt is another assumption entrenched in wave theory. Like most theorists, Deborah Siegal defines the second wave as "the resurgence of women's organizing beginning in the mid-1960s and, in the United States, ending—or at least suffering major setbacks—with the defeat of the Equal Rights Amendment and the advent of the Reagan- Bush era."[5] The research of Sally J. Kenney, Susan K.Freeman, Jacqueline Castledine and Julia Sandy-Bailey suggests that the notion of the "doldrums" of the 1980s may be overstated. Kenny reminds us that women who successfully cracked the "glass ceiling" in the 1960s and 1970s continued to influence the legal system well into the 1980s and 1990s. At the same time that Rosie Wahl served on the Minnesota Supreme court, players in the Mary V. softball league in Western Massachusetts capitalized on such legal victories as passage of Title IX, using sport to expand their feminist activism. An argument for the significance of local and regional activism to women's history is further illustrated by Freeman's study of the origins and growth of lesbian studies programs. Student and faculty support for the Multicultural Lesbian/Gay Studies Program at the University of California in the late 1980s attests to the fact that sexuality, as it had for generations of women before the 1960s, remained an organizing issue after the official "death" of the second wave.

The idea of generational feminism becomes problematic not only when it ignores or minimizes the significance of agenda overlap, but also when it creates rivalries between activist cohorts. A look at current literature describing a third wave of women's activism rising from the ashes of the Reagan-Bush years reveals how closely wave metaphors and generational differences are associated—especially in the minds of those on each side of the presumed divides. Jennifer Purvis writes that common perception of third wave feminism holds that it "is the unique province of young women, often believed to have no uniting causes or feelings of collective political responsibility, but whose activities, vaguely organized around the issues of sexuality and identity."[6] As Purvis's observations suggest, the third wave does not have a dramatic origins story to rival that of the 1848 Seneca Falls convention or the 1966 founding of the National Organization for Women. This only adds to the ambiguity critics claim surrounds the movement.

Although others had used the term before, publication of Rebecca Walker's 1992 article in *Ms.*, "Becoming the Third Wave" is considered the most significant event in the founding of the third-wave movement. Her article sketched out the agenda of a new wave of young feminists, who defined themselves as much by what they did not stand for as for what they did. What these women were not, many surmised based on their reading of Walker and a host of authors who followed, were their second-wave mothers. Using new media including social networking sites and blogs to critique such issues as the representation of women's sexuality in popular culture, third wavers defined the term "activism" differently than many of their predecessors, who still associated sexuality with abortion rights and organizing with street demonstrations.

The entrenchment of a wave metaphor encouraged self-identified second and third wavers to emphasize discontinuities over the significant goals shared by cohorts of women active in both movements. The notion that second wavers were rigid and intolerant in their politics, and blind to issues of race and class privilege in their literature, pervades third-wave critiques. On the other hand, younger feminists are accused of advocating "a feminism lacking in empathy and imagination—a brave new feminism that trafficked in selfishness, maybe, but more likely, in false bravado."[7] Despite the gapping chasm portrayed by social commentators, one cannot help but be struck by the debt that this volume owes to some of the concepts espoused by the third wave—even if they did not originate in it. Most important to this discussion is the understanding that an expansive definition of such terms as "feminism" and "activism" allows us to more accurately document the breadth of women's experiences, encouraging us to consider the work of women previously consigned to the margins.

As third wavers argue, there is no rule book, nor should there be, defining who is or is not a feminist. Whether you admire Elizabeth Cady Stanton, Gloria Steinem, or Courtney Love, many scholars and activists now agree that the work of feminism across the generations has most often shared an agenda committed to gaining legal and social equality for women. This belief that activism comes in many forms, a cornerstone of third-wave theory, is evident in much of the work of individuals and organizations studied in this volume. Indeed, the activism of the League of Women Voters, Methodist Woman's Division of Christian Service, and

Minnesota Federation of Business and Professional Women's Clubs is often minimized because it did not include demands for a subversion of gender relations, a foundation of second-wave feminism.

Exploring the shared agendas of activist cohorts, often comprised of not one generation but several, does not mean that we should overlook the discontinuities between the movements studied in this volume and those who came before and after them. It is important to acknowledge that some women discussed here, especially in the earlier period, may have espoused racist viewpoints and worked to limit the opportunities of women of color. Their work demands critique from scholars and activists, not just third-wave or post-colonial theorists. It also demands debate about whether theirs was feminist work because, as chapters here demonstrate, not all women's activism *is* feminist. Placing women's organizing within a continuum is central to replacing the "crest" and "trough" framework of women's history currently under scrutiny.

Most recent attacks on the wave metaphor have come from younger activists less deferential to well-established historical frameworks. Editor of *Bitch* magazine, Lisa Jervis, claims that "What was at first a handy-dandy way to refer to feminism's history…has become shorthand that invites intellectual laziness." She goes so far as to conclude that "we've reached the end of wave terminology's usefulness."[8] Yet, others have proposed that still another wave—welcomed or not—is already underway. When asked by critic Deborah Soloman whether feminism has entered a fourth wave, founder of the blog Feminista.com, Jessica Valenti, suggested "maybe the fourth wave is online."[9] Although neither Valenti nor Jervis claims to find wave terminology useful, their observations concerning a third or even fourth wave raise important questions about the longevity of a metaphor that in the minds of many perpetuates the concept of monolithic waves of activism.

Whether thoughtful attention to a re-conceptualization of the waves metaphor that would incorporate Cathryn Bailey's notion of continuity can rehabilitate wave theory and help us to understand women's activism remains to be seen. How scholars, activists—and activist scholars—should move forward in the twenty-first century brings our discussion full circle. If not with the metaphor of the wave or a rope, what framework should we use to write the history of women's organizing? More important still is the question of how we should *teach* it.

An underappreciated consequence of presenting activism using the wave metaphor is the way in which it confines study of women's experiences to arbitrarily narrow periods of U.S. history. Survey classes routinely rely on a well-trod path from Susan B. Anthony, to Alice Paul, to Rosie the Riveter, to Betty Friedan, marking only the most dramatic moments in the history of a select group of women. The chapters in this volume help to suggest ways that waves may be replaced—or at the very least supplemented—by themes and periodizations that more fully demonstrate how women's economic, social, political, and sexual locations and *dis*locations within their cultures have informed their concepts of feminism and of activism.

Teaching U.S. women's history without "handy-dandy" shorthand, as we must when teaching other areas of history, requires recognition that important issues have united—and sometimes divided—women activists within and across generations. Concern for community welfare, freedom of sexual expression, workers' rights, and racial equality are a few of the issues that have since the mid-nineteenth century brought women into organizational alliances, a fact that deserves greater emphasis in the classroom. Indeed, as the chapters in this volume bear out, generational overlap in agendas pervades women's and feminist history. The contributors of this volume believe that a framework that incorporates this reality without diminishing the broad range of ideological thought within activist cohorts is the best guide for future scholarship.

Notes

1. Cathryn Bailey, "Making Waves and Drawing Lines: The Politics of Defining the Vicissitudes of Feminism," *Hypatia* 12, no. 3 (1997), 27.
2. Bailey, 17.
3. Leila Rupp and Verta J. Taylor, *Survival in the Doldrums: The American Women's Rights Movement, 1945 to the 1960s* (New York: Oxford University Press, 1987).
4. Kimberly Springer, "Third Wave Black Feminism," *Signs: Journal of Women in Culture and Society* 27, no. 4 (2002), 1061.
5. Deborah Siegel, *Sisterhood Interrupted: From Radical Women to Grrls Gone Wild* (New York: Palgrave Macmillan, 2007), 16.
6. Jennifer Purvis, "Grrls and Women Together in the Third Wave," Embracing the Challenges of Intergenerational Feminism(s), *National Women's Studies Journal* 16, no. 3, (2004), 96.
7. Siegel, *Sisterhood Interrupted*, 126.
8. Lisa Jervis, "Goodbye to Feminism's Generational Divide," in *We Don't Need Another Wave: Dispatches from the Next Generation of Feminists*, ed. Melody Berger (Emeryville, CA: Seal Press, 2006), 14.
9. Deborah Solomon, "Fourth-Wave Feminism," *New York Times*, 13 November 2009, http://www.nytimes.com/2009/11/15/magazine/15fob-q4-t.html.

Selected Bibliography

Women's Organizations and Organizing Before 1965

Books

Boylan, Anne M. *The Origins of Women's Activism: New York and Boston, 1797–1840.* Chapel Hill: University of North Carolina Press, 2002.

Cobble, Dorothy Sue. *The Other Women's Movement : Workplace Justice and Social Rights in Modern America.* Princeton, NJ: Princeton University Press, 2004.

Deslippe, Dennis A. *'Rights Not Roses': Unions and the Rise of Working-Class Feminism, 1945–1980.* Urbana: University of Illinois Press, 2000.

Feldstein, Ruth. *Motherhood in Black and White: Race and Sex in American Liberalism, 1930–1965.* Ithaca, NY: Cornell University Press, 2000.

Gabin, Nancy. *Feminism in the Labor Movement: Women in the United Auto Workers Union, 1935–1975.* Ithaca, NY: Cornell University Press, 1990.

Harrison, Cynthia. *On Account of Sex: Public Policies on Women's Issues, 1945–1970.* Berkeley: University of California Press, 1989.

Harvey, Anna L. *Votes Without Leverage: Women in American Electoral Politics,1920–1970.* New York: Cambridge University Press, 1998.

Horowitz, Daniel. *Betty Friedan and the Making of the Feminine Mystique.* Amherst: University of Massachusetts Press, 1998.

Kaplan, Laura. *The Story of Jane: The Legendary Underground Feminist Abortion Service.* Chicago: University of Chicago Press, 1995.

Kerber, Linda K. *No Constitutional Right to be Ladies: Women and the Obligations of Citizenship.* New York: Hill and Wang, 1998.

Laughlin, Kathleen A. *Women's Work and Public Policy: A History of the Women's Bureau, U.S. Department of Labor, 1945–1970.* Boston: Northeastern University Press, 2000.

Levine, Susan A. *Degrees of Equality: The American Association of University Women and the Challenge of American Feminism.* Philadelphia: Temple University Press, 1995.

Lynn, Susan. *Progressive Women in Conservative Times: Racial Justice, Peace, and Feminism, 1945 to the 1960s.* New Brunswick, NJ: Rutgers University Press, 1993.

McEnaney, Laura. *Civil Defense Begins at Home: Militarization Meets Everyday Life in the Fifties.* Princeton, NJ: Princeton University Press, 2000.

Messer, Ellen. *Back Rooms: Voices from the Illegal Abortion Era*. New York: Prometheus Books, 1994.

Meyerowitz, Joan, ed. *Not June Cleaver: Women and Gender in Postwar America, 1945–1960*. Philadelphia: Temple University Press, 1994.

Rymph, Catherine E. *Republican Women: Feminism and Conservatism From Suffrage Through the Rise of the New Right*. Chapel Hill: University of North Carolina Press, 2006.

Rupp, Leila J. and Verta Taylor. *Survival in the Doldrums: The American Women's Movement in America, 1945 to the 1960s*. New York: Oxford University Press, 1987.

Reagan, Leslie J. *When Abortion Was a Crime: Women, Medicine, and the Law in the United States, 1867–1973*. Berkeley: University of California Press, 1997.

Articles

Baker, Paula. "The Domestication of Politics: Women and American Political Society, 1780–1920." *American Historical Review* 89 (February-June 1984): 620–64.

Clemens, Elisabeth. "Organizational Repertoires and Institutional Change: Women's Groups and the Transformation of US Politics, 1890–1920." *American Journal of Sociology* 98 (January 1984): 755–98.

Meyerowitz, Joanne. "Sex, Gender, and the Cold War Language of Reform." In *Rethinking Cold War Culture*, edited by Peter J. Kuznick and James Gilbert, 106–23. Washington, D.C.: Smithsonian Institution Press, 2001.

Storrs, Landon. "Red Scare Politics and the Suppression of Popular Front Feminism: The Loyalty Investigation of Mary Dublin Keyserling." *Journal of American History* 90, no. 2 (2003): 491–524.

Ware, Susan. "American Women in the 1950s: Nonpartisan Politics and Women's Politicalization." In *Women, Politics and Change*, edited by Louise A. Tilly and Patricia Gurin, 281–99. New York: Russell Sage Foundation, second edition, 1992.

Diverse Issues, Communities, and Standpoints

Books

Berube, Allan. *Coming Out Under Fire: The History of Gay Men and Women in World War Two*. New York: The Free Press, 1990.

Boyd, Nan Alamilla. *Wide Open Town: A History of Queer San Francisco to 1965*. Berkeley: University of California Press, 2003.

Collins, Patricia Hill. *Black Feminist Thought: Knowledge, Consciousness, and the Politics of Empowerment*. New York: Routledge, 1991.

D'Emilio, John. *Sexual Politics, Sexual Communities: The Making of a Homosexual Minority in the United States, 1940–1970*. Chicago: University of Chicago Press, 1983.

Dudziak, Mary L. *Cold War Civil Rights: Race and the Image of American Democracy*. Princeton, NJ: Princeton University Press, 2000.

Enke, Anne. *Finding the Movement: Sexuality, Contested Space, and Feminist Activism*. Durham, NC: Duke University Press, 2007.

Garber, Linda. *Identity Poetics: Race, Class, and the Lesbian-Feminist Roots of Queer Theory*. New York: Columbia University Press, 2001.

Fosl, Catherine. *Subversive Southerner: Anne Braden and the Struggle for Racial Justice in the Cold War South*. New York: Palgrave Macmillan, 2002.

Horne, Gerald. *Race Woman: The Lives of Shirley Graham Du Bois*. New York: New York University Press, 2000.

Meeker, Martin. *Contacts Desired: Gay and Lesbian Communications and Community, 1940s–1970s*. Chicago: University of Chicago Press, 2006.

Orozco, Cynthia E. *No Mexicans, Women, or Dogs Allowed: The Rise of the Mexican American Civil Rights Movement*. Austin: University of Texas Press, 2009.

Ransby, Barbara. *Ella Baker and the Black Freedom Movement: A Radical Democratic Vision*. Chapel Hill: University of North Carolina Press, 2003.

Ruiz, Vicki L. *From Out of the Shadows: Mexican Women in Twentieth-Century America*. New York: Oxford University Press, 2008.

Debra Schultz. *Going South: Jewish Women in the Civil Rights Movement*. New York: New York University, 2001.

Taylor, Ula Y. *The Veiled Garvey: The Life and Times of Amy Jacques Garvey*. North Carolina: University of North Carolina Press, 2002.

Theoharis, Jeanne, Komozi Woodard, and Dayo Gore, eds. *Want to Start a Revolution?: Radical Women in the Black Freedom Struggle*. New York: New York University Press, 2009.

Valk, Ann. *Radical Sisters: Second-Wave Feminism and Black Liberation in Washington, D.C.* Urbana: University of Illinois Press, 2008.

Articles

Cragin, 'Becca. "Post-Lesbian-Feminism: Documenting 'Those Cruddy Old Dykes of Yore.'" In *Carryin' on in the Lesbian and Gay South*, edited by John Howard, 285–327. New York: New York University Press, 1997.

Garcia, Richard. A. "Dolores Huerta: Woman, Organizer, and Symbol." *California History*, 72 (1993).

Flood, Dawn Rae. "'They Didn't Treat Me Good': African American Rape Victims and Chicago Courtroom Strategies During the 1950s." *Journal of Women's History* 17, no. 1 (2005): 38–61.

McDuffie, Erik S. "A 'New Freedom Movement of Negro Women': Sojourning for Truth, Justice, and Human Rights during the Early Cold War." *Radical History Review* 101 (Spring 2008): 81–106.

McGuire, Danielle. "'It Was Like All of Us Had Been Raped': Sexual Violence, Community Mobilization, and the African American Freedom Struggle." *Journal of American History* 91, no. 3 (2004): 906–31.

Rose, Margaret. "Traditional and Nontraditional Patterns of Female Activism in the United Farm Workers of America, 1962–1980." *Frontiers: A Journal of Women's Studies*, 11 (1990): 26–32.

Feminist Movements and Activism

Books

Evans, Sara. *Tidal Wave: How Women Changed America at Century's End*. New York: Free Press, 2004.

Freedman, Estelle. *No Turning Back: The History of Feminism and the Future of Women*. New York: Ballantine Books, 2002.

Gilmore, Stephanie, ed. *Feminist Coalitions: Historical Perspectives on Second-Wave Feminism in the United States*. Urbana: University of Illinois Press, 2008.

Hartmann, Susan. *The Other Feminists: Activists in the Liberal Establishment*. New Haven, CT: Yale University Press, 1998.

Henry, Astrid. *Not My Mother's Sister: Generational Conflict and Third-Wave Feminism*. Bloomington: Indiana University Press, 2004.

Reger, Jo, ed. *Different Wavelengths: Studies of the Contemporary Women's Movement.* New York: Routledge, 2005.

Rosen, Ruth. *The World Split Open: How the Women's Movement Changed America.* New York: Viking, 2000.

Roth, Benita. *Separate Roads to Feminism: Black, Chicana, and White Feminist Movements in America's Second Wave.* New York: Cambridge University Press, 2004.

Siegel, Deborah. *Sisterhood Interrupted: From Radical Women to Grrls Gone Wild.* New York: Palgrave Macmillan, 2007.

Staggenborg, Suzanne. *The Pro-Choice Movement: Organization and Activism in the Abortion Conflict.* New York: Oxford University Press, 1991.

Weigand, Kate. *Red Feminism: American Communism and the Making of Women's Liberation.* Baltimore, MD: Johns Hopkins University Press, 2001.

Whittier, Nancy. *Feminist Generations: The Persistence of the Radical Women's Movement.* Philadelphia: Temple University Press, 1995.

Articles

Jervis, Lisa. "Goodbye to Feminism's Generational Divide." In *We Don't Need Another Wave: Dispatches from the Next Generation of Feminists*, ed. Melody Berger, 13–19. Emeryville, CA: Seal Press, 2006.

Purvis, Jennifer. "Grrls and Women Together in the Third Wave," Embracing the Challenges of Intergenerational Feminism(s)," *National Women's Studies Journal* 16, no. 3 (2004).

Scott, Joan W. "Conference Call," *differences* 2, no. 3 (1990): 52–108.

Springer, Kimberly, "Third Wave Black Feminism." *Signs: Journal of Women in Culture and Society* 27 (2002): 1059–1082.

Taylor , Verta and Leila J. Rupp, "Women's Culture and Lesbian Feminist Activism: A Reconsideration of Cultural Feminism." *Signs: Journal of Women in Culture and Society* 19 (1993): 32–61.

Internationalism and Foreign Affairs

Books

Anderson, Carol. *Eyes Off the Prize: The United Nations and the African American Struggle for Human Rights, 1944-1955.* New York: Cambridge University Press, 2003.

Laville, Helen. *Cold War Women: The International Activities of American Women's Organizations.* New York: Manchester University Press, 2002.

Plummer, Brenda Gail. *Rising Wind: Black Americans and U.S. Foreign Affairs, 1935-1960.* Chapel Hill: University of North Carolina Press, 1996.

Rupp, Leila, J. *Worlds of Women: The Making of an International Women's Movement.* Princeton, NJ: Princeton University Press, 1997.

Stoner, Lynn K. *From the House to the Streets: The Cuban Woman's Movement for Legal Reform, 1898-1940.* Durham, NC: Duke University Press, 1991.

Swedlow, Amy. *Women Strike for Peace: Traditional Motherhood and Radical Politics in the 1960s.* Chicago: University of Chicago Press, 1993.

Von Eschen, Penny. *Race Against Empire: Black Americans and Anticolonialism, 1937-1957.* Ithaca, NY: Cornell University Press, 1997.

Articles

Castledine, Jacqueline. "'In a Solid Bond of Unity': Anticolonial Feminism in the Cold War Era." *Journal of Women's History* 20, no. 4 (2009): 57–81.

Ehrick, Christine. "*Madrinas* and Missionaries: Uruguay and the Pan-American Women's Movement." *Gender and History* 10 (November 1998): 407–24.

Rupp, Leila J. and Verta Taylor. "Forging Feminist Identity in an International Movement: A Collective Identity Approach to Feminism." *Signs: A Journal of Women in Culture and Society* 24(1999): 363–86.

Contributors

Jacqueline L. Castledine, University Without Walls, University of Massachusetts-Amherst. As well as teaching interdisciplinary studies, Jacqueline is educational director for the Valley Women's History Collaborative, which documents radical women's activism in the Pioneer Valley of Massachusetts. Research interests include transnational women's social movements, the subject of several recent publications, and oral history. Her current project is a book manuscript, "Beyond McCarthyism: Progressive Women's Peace Politics, 1945–1975."

Susan K. Freeman, Associate Professor, Gender and Women's Studies, Minnesota State University, Mankato, Mankato, Minnesota. She is the author of *Sex Goes to School: Girls and Sex Education before the 1960s* (University of Illinois Press). Her current research focuses on college and community-based courses inspired by gay liberation and lesbian feminism between 1969 and 1989.

Julie A. Gallagher is Assistant Professor of History, Penn State University, Brandywine, Media, Pennsylvania. She has just completed a book manuscript titled, "Women of Action: A History of Black Women's Political Activism in New York City, 1915–1972." The study documents three generations of black women who engaged in politics starting in the 1910s in New York City and concludes with Shirley Chisholm's run for the U.S. presidency in 1972.

Marcia Gallo, Assistant Professor of History, University of Nevada, Las Vegas, is the author of *Different Daughters: A History of the Daughters of Bilitis and the Rise of the Lesbian Rights Movement* (Carroll & Graf, 2006), winner of a 2006 Lambda Literary Award. Her teaching ranges from the history of sexuality to oral history methodology; her research interests include these as well as gender, race, social movements, and urban history. Gallo's current project is a book manuscript that explores the impact of the 1964 murder of Catherine "Kitty" Genovese, entitled "Hidden in Plain Sight."

Susan M. Hartmann is Arts and Humanities Distinguished Professor of History at Ohio State University, Columbus, Ohio, where she has also served as director of women's studies. Her books include *The Home Front and Beyond: American Women in the 1940s*; *From Margin to Mainstream: American Women and Politics since 1960*; and *The Other Feminists: Activists in the Liberal Establishment*. She is a fellow of the Society of American Historians and has received fellowships from the Rockefeller Foundation, the National Endowment for the Humanities, the American Council of Learned Societies, and the Woodrow Wilson International Center for Scholars. Her current research deals with gender and the reshaping of U.S. politics and policy after World War II.

Sally J. Kenney, Executive Director, Newcomb College Institute, Newcomb College Endowed Chair, and Professor of Political Science, Tulane University, New Orleans, Louisiana. She is the author of *For Whose Protection? Reproductive Hazards and Exclusionary Policies in the United States and Britain*, and is the co-editor of *Politics and Feminist Standpoint Theories, and Constitutional Dialogues in Comparative Perspective*. She is currently completing a book entitled *Gender and Judging* to be published by Routledge and a book of case studies on women and public policy.

Rebecca M. Kluchin, Assistant Professor, Department of History, California State University, Sacramento, is the author of *Fit to Be Tied: Sterilization and Reproductive Rights in America, 1960–1980* (Rutgers University Press, 2009). Her current research examines pregnancy and the concept of fetal rights in America.

Kathleen A. Laughlin, Professor of History, Metropolitan State University, St. Paul, Minnesota. She is the author of *Women's Work and Public Policy: A History of the Women's Bureau, U.S. Department of Labor, 1945–1970* (Northeastern University Press, 2000). She is also project director of "Team Hillary/New England: A Study of Historic Campaign," an oral history project on Hillary Clinton's 2008 presidential campaign under the auspices of the Center for Women in Politics and Public Policy, University of Massachusetts-Boston.

A. Lanethea Mathews-Gardner, Associate Professor of Political Science, Director of the Center for Ethics, Muhlenberg College, Allentown, Pennsylvania. Her research and teaching interests center on the study of gender in American political development, and the study of gender in the discipline of Political Science. Her recent publications include the article, "The Transformation of the Black Women's Club Movement in Postwar America: The Intersection of Gender, Race, and American Political Development, 1940–1960," forthcoming in *Women, Politics and Policy* in December 2010.

Catherine E. Rymph, Associate Professor of History, University of Missouri, Columbia, Missouri, is the author of *Republican Women: Feminism and Conservatism from Suffrage through the Rise of the New Right* (University of North Carolina Press, 2006). Her current research examines care work and child welfare in the U.S. foster care system, 1935–1980.

Julia Sandy-Bailey, Assistant Professor of History, Shepherd University, Shepherdstown, West Virginia. Research interests include the northern black freedom movement, consumer culture, and public history. Her current project is a book manuscript, "Unsheathing the Consumer Sword: The 'Negro Market' and Consumer Activism in Black New York, 1930–1970."

Jennifer A. Stevens, Ph.D., Principal, Stevens Historical Research Associates, Boise, Idaho. Jennifer runs a small historical consulting firm that engages in public environmental history for a variety of clients. She is also currently working on turning her dissertation into a book manuscript entitled, "Feminizing the Urban West: Green Cities and Open Space in the Postwar Era, 1950–2000," a study of women's impact on the open space movement and western cities. In addition, Jennifer also teaches as an adjunct professor in the History Department at Boise State University and serves on Boise's Planning and Zoning Commission.

Janet Weaver, Assistant Curator, Iowa Women's Archives, University of Iowa Libraries, Iowa City. Over the past thirty years, she has worked on a variety of oral history and labor history projects including the Mujeres Latinas Project of the Iowa Women's Archives and the Iowa Labor History Oral Project (ILHOP) of the Iowa Federation of Labor, AFL-CIO. She is the author of "From Barrio to '¡Boicoteo!': the Emergence of Mexican American Activism in Davenport, 1917–1970," *Annals of Iowa* 68 (summer 2009).

Leandra Zarnow, Ph. D. candidate, Department of History, University of California, Santa Barbara. She is near completion of her dissertation, "Bella Abzug and the Promise of Progressive Change in the United States," and has published various articles related to past and contemporary feminisms.

Index

A

Abortion
  Chicago Women's Liberation Union, 137–151
  creating alternative institution, 146–151
  criminalizing, 136
  direct action, 137
  history, 136–137
  Jane, 136–151
  legalized, 146
Abzug, Bella, 5, 28–40
  feminism defined, 28
  Left lawyers, 28–40
    black-on-white rape case, 28–40
    blacks excluded from juries, 34
    challenge of sexual color line, 28, 33
    Civil Rights Congress, 30, 31
    civil rights law, 32
    Committee on Constitutional Liberties of
      Guild's New York Chapter, 32
    critique of rape law, 35–36
    link sexual autonomy to racial equality, 37
    southern lynching culture, 35–36
    southern rape law, 29
    "un-American" label, 32
    Witt & Cammer, 31
  McGee rape trials
    appeals, 34
    execution, 39
    final court maneuvers, 37–39
    finds lawyers for, 30
    sexual color line, 35
    threats, 37–38, 39
  Personal is Political, 36, 37
African American women
  Consumers' Protective Committee, 6, 115–132
  female-led protests, 115–116
  Great Depression, 117–118
  Harlem, NY, 115–132
  human rights, 80–95
  international politics, 5–6
  postwar era, 80–95, 115–132
    planning participation, 82–88
  World War II, 117–118
Allen, Florence, 211–216
  first women federal judges, 211
  judicial career, 7–8
  Roosevelt, Eleanor, 213
  sexual identity, 213–216
  U.S. Supreme Court, 211–212, 213
American Association for the U.N., 91–92
American Association of University Women,
  segregation, 82
American GI Forum, 176–177, 178
American women's organizations, *see also* Specific
  type
  Cold War, 66
  World War II, 66
Association to Repeal Abortion Laws, 138–139
  Jane, 138–139

B

Baker, Josephine, 90–91
Banning, Margaret Culkin, 11, 13
Barrio women, *See* Mexican American women
Bethune, Mary McLeod
  National Council of Negro Women, 80, 82,
    83–92
    women appointed to U.N., 83–85
Black-on-white rape cases, 28–40
  National Association for the Advancement of
    Colored People, 34
Booth, Heather Tobias, 140

C

Carrillo, Dolores, 181
Catholic Interracial Council, 178
Catt, Carrie Chapman, League of Women Voters,
  67, 68

Chicago, IL, underground, 136–151
Chicago Women's Liberation Union, 137
    abortion, 137–151
    direct action, 137
    Jane, 137–151
Church Center for the United Nations, 105–106
City planning, 157–158
Civic feminists, 11–24
    clubwomen, 12
Civil Rights Congress, 30, 31, 81
Cold War
    American women's organizations, 66
    Daughters of Bilitis, 51–52
    Left feminists, 29–30
        Left feminist lawyers' defense work, 29–30
    Minnesota Federation of Business and
        Professional Women's Clubs, 21
    National Council of Negro Women, 86
    National Lawyers Guild, 31
Collective action, autonomy, 3
Commission on the Status of Women, National
        Council of Negro Women, 84–85
Committee on Women in Post War Planning, 83
Committee on Women in World Affairs, 83
Communist purges, 32
Community activism, Mexican American women,
        173–184
Community-based service, 6
Congress of American Women, 81
Consensual inter-racial sexual relationships, 29
Consumers' Protective Committee
    African American women, 6, 115–132
    black male leaders, 121–123
    consumer education program, 127–128
    consumer rights activism, 115–132
    expansion of consumer activism, 125–131
    Harlem, NY, 6, 115–132
    Harlem Merchant-Consumer Arbitration
        Board, 130–131
    history, 115–132
    history of local activism, 119–120
    Mayor's Committee on Unity, 124
    media, 121–122
    origins, 116–125
    political lobbying, 123–125, 128–129
    postwar era, 115–132
    protests, 119–125
    public market, 128–129
    refusal to negotiate with merchants, 121–123
    Retail Installment Sales Act, 128
    Uptown Chamber of Commerce, 124–125
        agreement, 124–125
Council of African Affairs, 81

D
Daughters of Bilitis, 4–5, *See also* Lesbians
    late 1960s and early 1970s
    accomplishments, 48
    balancing visibility with privacy, 52
    Cold War, 51–52
    disbanded, 59
    dual activism as women and as members of
        sexual minority, 48–49
    feminist perspective, 48
    founding Daughters, 49
    founding history, 51
    gender equality, 49, 60
    greater militancy, 57–58
    The Ladder, 47, 48, 56–57, 57–58
        gender politics *vs.* gay politics, 58
    lesbians characterized, 47
    Los Angeles, CA, 54–55
        founding, 54
        national conferences, 55
        private space, 55
    Mattachine Society, 52
    National Organization for Women, 58–59
    New York, NY
        alliances with other East Coast gay groups, 56
        convention, 57
        founding, 56
        independence within Daughters of Bilitis, 56
        The Ladder, 56–57
        media coverage, 57
        organizing strategy, 51
    range of projects, 50
    remaking identity, 59–60
    San Francisco, CA, 50–54, 55–56
        female independence, 53
        office and meeting space, 52
        organizing, 50–54
        police raids, 50–51
        postwar feminism, 53
        private space, 53–54
        projects, 53–54
    social reform, 49, 60
    Stearn, Jess, 55–56
    structural model, 52
    tensions between West and East Coast, 56
    women moving freely in public sites
        independent of men, 50
Davenport, IA, Mexican American women, 6,
        174–175
    American GI Forum, 176–177, 178
    Catholic Interracial Council, 178
    Council 10, 176–177, 178
    farmworker movement for justice, 178–179
    League for Social Justice, 175–176
    League of United Latin American Citizens,
        176–177, 178
    rights of migrant workers, 178–179
    tradition of women's activism, 176–177
Democratic Farmer Labor Party, Minnesota
        Federation of Business and Professional
        Women's Clubs, 14–15, 20–21, 22
Direct action
    abortion, 137
    Chicago Women's Liberation Union, 137
    Jane, 137

E
Economic citizenship, Mexican American
        women, 173–184
Environmentalism, 158
Equal pay, Minnesota Federation of Business and
        Professional Women's Clubs, 22

Equal Rights Amendment, 49
  Minnesota Federation of Business and
    Professional Women's Clubs, 16, 18–19,
    21–22
  National Federation of Business and
    Professional Women's Clubs, 13, 18
  Operation Buttonhole, 20
  World War II, 11

F
Farmworker movement for justice, 178–179
Federal Employees Loyalty and Security Program,
  82
Federal government
  Federal Employees Loyalty and Security
    Program, 82
  homosexuality, dismissal of thousands of
    employees on suspicion, 52
  Office of Price Administration, 117–118
Feminism
  activism
    continuity, 7
    forms, 249–250
    longer view, 3
  categorized, 209–210, 249–250
  diversity, 2–3
  equal rights teleology, 209
  feminist lesbian organizing, 1950s, 47–60
  from feminist lesbians to lesbian feminists,
    59–60
  forms, 3–4
  visibility within institutions, 7
First wave feminism, 2
Flood, Aloncita, 119
Foreign policy
  League of Women Voters, 65–66, 68–77
  Methodist women, 101–108
  National Council of Negro Women, 84–92,
    88–92
  religious women, 101–108
  Woman's Division of Christian Service,
    101–108
Free universities, lesbian studies, 231–236
Friedan, Betty, "lavender menace" comment, 59

G
Gender, nation building, 65–77
Gender bias, women judges, 210–224
Gender equality
  Daughters of Bilitis, 49, 60
  international comparisons, 75
Gender oppression, Left feminists, 29
Gender relations, 7
General Federation of Women's Clubs,
  segregation, 82
Generational feminism, 248–250
  rivalries between activist cohorts, 248–249
Geo-political realignments, National Council of
  Negro Women, 85–87
German women
  democratic society, 65, 68
  League of Women Voters
    exchange programs, 65, 68–69

  relative gender equality, 74
  women's citizenship *vs.* political
    empowerment, 70–72
Governmental efficiency, 160
Great Depression, African American women,
  117–118
Griswold, Estelle, 138

H
Harlem, NY
  African American women, 115–132
  consumer rights activism, 115–132
  Consumers' Protective Committee, 6, 115–132
  postwar era, 115–132
  public market, 128–129
Harlem Merchant-Consumer Arbitration Board,
  Consumers' Protective Committee,
  130–131
Homophile movement
  male chauvinists, 59–60
  National Association for the Advancement of
    Colored People, parallels, 58
  North American Conference of Homophile
    Organizations, 59
Homosexuality, federal government, dismissal of
  thousands of employees on suspicion, 52
Huerta, Dolores, 173
Human rights
  African American women, 80–95
  National Council of Negro Women, 88–92
  postwar era, 80–95
  U.N., 88–92
  women's clubs, 5

I
Ideological continuity, 7
Illegal abortions, 136–151
  creating alternative institution, 146–151
I Love Lucy Show, 1
Institutional feminism
  Methodist women, 101–109
  religious women, 101–109
  Woman's Division of Christian Service,
    101–109
International Assembly conference, National
    Council of Negro Women, 87
International politics
  African American women, 5–6
  clubwomen, 5
  League of Women Voters, 5
  Methodist women, 5
  National Council of Negro Women, 5–6
Inter-racial sex, 29
  rape law, 36
Intersectionality, 32

J
Jacobs, Jane, 163–164
Jane
  abortion, 136–151
  access to abortion process, 145
  Association to Repeal Abortion Laws, 138–139
  Chicago Women's Liberation Union, 137–151

Jane (*continued*)
  control over physicians employed, 144–145
  creating alternative institution, 146–151
  demographics, 144
  direct action, 137
  early years, 140–145
  financial resources, 146
  history, 138
  members, 145
  public document, 143
  referral form, 140–144
  service activism, 138
Japanese women
  democratic society, 65, 68
  League of Women Voters
    exchange programs, 65, 68–69
    relative gender equality, 74
    slippage between "women" and "mothers,"
      73–75
    women's citizenship *vs.* political
      empowerment, 70–72
Juries
  blacks excluded from, 34
  women excluded from, 211

K
Know Your Community studies, 158–162

L
Labor movement, Taft-Hartley Act, 31
The Ladder
  apart from Daughters of Bilitis, 59–60
  Daughters of Bilitis, 47, 48, 56–57, 57–58
  gender politics *vs.* gay politics, 58
Land-use bill, 167–168
League for Social Justice, 175–176
League of United Latin American Citizens,
  176–177, 178
League of Women Voters
  Catt, Carrie Chapman, 67, 68
  contributions, 156
  democratic society, women's civic engagement,
    65–77
  demographic profile, 156
  disinterested commitment to general welfare,
    67, 6867
  evolution, 66
  foreign policy, 65–66, 68–77
  German women
    exchange programs, 65, 68–69
    relative gender equality, 74
    women's citizenship *vs.* political
      empowerment, 70–72
  goals, 66, 67
  history, 156
  international politics, 5
  Japanese women
    exchange programs, 65, 68–69
    relative gender equality, 74
    slippage between "women" and "mothers,"
      73–75
    women's citizenship *vs.* political
      empowerment, 70–72

joining organizations, 70
media, 72–75
middle-class womanhood, 70
as model of women's democratic citizenship, 68
Portland, OR, 6
  city planning, 157–158
  developed policies and laws, 157
  environmentalism, 158
  explosion of suburbia, 164–165
  governmental efficiency, 160
  how modern city developed, 157
  Know Your Community studies, 158–162
  land-use bill, 167–168
  Metro entity, 162
  metropolitan planning, 155–169
  planning control, 167–168
  Portland as women's city, 158
  public transit, 166
  sprawl, 160–163, 166
  study of state of urban affairs, 155
  *Tale of Three Counties, One Metropolitan
    Community,* 155, 164–167
  Tri-County Metropolitan Government
    Committee, 162–163
  Western women's revolt against suburbia,
    156–157
  wide range of interests, 155–156
  zoning history, 161–162
projects, 67?
rights *vs.* responsibilities of female citizenship,
  66–67
traditional associational life among American
  women, 74–75
wave metaphor, 66–67
Left feminist lawyers
  mixed-sex, multi-issue organizing, 32
  National Lawyers Guild, 31
    protests, 37
  ostracized, 32
Left feminists, 29
  Cold War, 29–30
  Left feminist lawyers' defense work, 29–30
  gender oppression, 29
  race oppression, 29
Left lawyers
  Abzug, Bella, 28–40
  black-on-white rape case, 28–40
  challenge of sexual color line, 28, 33
  Civil Rights Congress, 30, 31
  civil rights law, 32
  Committee on Constitutional Liberties of
    Guild's New York Chapter, 32
  critique of rape law, 35–36
  excluded blacks from juries, 34
  link sexual autonomy to racial equality, 37
  southern lynching culture, 35–36
  southern rape law, 29
  "un-American" label, 32
  Witt & Cammer, 31
McCarthy era, 29–31
Lesbian, gay, bisexual, and transgender studies,
  lesbian studies, relationship, 243
Lesbian feminists, remaking identity, 59–60

Lesbian feminist sports
  contested values, 200–205
  softball, 195–199
Lesbians, 4–5, *See also* Daughters of Bilitis
  from feminist lesbians to lesbian feminists,
    59–60
  Friedan, Betty, "lavender menace" comment, 59
  importance of cities, 49–50
  importance of history, 215–216
  media, 57
  National Organization for Women, 58–59
  Northampton, MA, 191–205
    ambivalence, 199–200
    competitiveness, 200–205
    contested values, 200–205
    history, 191–192, 193–195
    "sneakers *vs.* clients" issue, 200–205
    wave theory, 192–193
  police harassment, 50–51?
  softball, 191–205
    ambivalence, 199–200
    competitiveness, 200–205
    contested values, 200–205
    intersection of social identities, 198–200
    "sneakers *vs.* clients" issue, 200–205
    wave theory, 192–193
  women judges, 213–216
Lesbian studies, 229–243
  1970s and 1980s, 229–243
  coded titles, 237
  early, 229
  free universities, 231–236
  lesbian, gay, bisexual, and transgender studies,
    relationship, 243
  literature classes, 237–239
  present and future, 236–243
  programs, 7
  queer-identified thinkers, 229–230
  queer studies, relationship, 243
  racism, 239–240
  site of conflict, 242
  starting points, 231–236
  students reluctant to enroll, 237
  texts, 236–237, 238, 240–241
  third wave, 229–230
  trajectories, 230–231
  women of color, 239–240
  women's studies, relationship, 230, 236–237
Literature classes, lesbian studies, 237–239
Los Angeles, CA, Daughters of Bilitis, 54–55
  founding, 54
  national conferences, 55
  private space, 55
Lyon, Phyllis, 51

M
Martin, Del, 51, 59
Mary V. Softball League, 191–205
  contested values, 200–205
  founding, 194–199
Mason, Vivian Carter, National Council of Negro
  Women, 86–87
Mattachine Society, Daughters of Bilitis, 52

Matthews, Burnita Shelton, first women federal
  judges, 211
Mayor's Committee on Unity, Consumers'
  Protective Committee, 124
McGee, Willie, 28–29, 32–40
McCarthy era
  Left lawyers, 29–31
  National Council of Negro Women, 89–92
McGee rape trials, 28–40
  Abzug, Bella
    effects on Abzug, 39–40
    execution, 39
    final court maneuvers, 37–39
    finds lawyers for, 30
    sexual color line, 35
    threats, 37–38, 39
  first trial, 33
Media
  Consumers' Protective Committee, 121–122
  League of Women Voters, 72–75
  lesbians, 57
  Minnesota Federation of Business and
    Professional Women's Clubs, protests
    against stereotyping, 15–16
Methodist women
  foreign policy, 101–108
  history, 99–109
  institutional feminism, 101–109
  international politics, 5
  U.N., 101–108
Metropolitan planning, 155–169
Mexican Americans, World War II, 174–175
Mexican American women
  community activism, 173–184
  Davenport, IA, 6, 174–175
    American GI Forum, 176–177, 178
    Catholic Interracial Council, 178
    Council 10, 176–177, 178
    farmworker movement for justice, 178–179
    League for Social Justice, 175–176
    League of United Latin American Citizens,
      176–177, 178
    rights of migrant workers, 178–179
    tradition of women's activism, 176–177
  economic citizenship, 173–184
  Muscatine, IA, 179–180
    boycott of Oscar Mayer plant, 181–182
    dual oppression of race and gender
      discrimination, 182–185
    health services, 179–180
    Mexican American activist nuns, 179–180
    picket Farmall plant, 183
    sexual harassment, 184
    traditional community-based approach,
      182–183
Minnesota Commission on the Status of Women,
  23–24
Minnesota Federation of Business and
  Professional Women's Clubs, 4
  Cold War, 21
  culture, 12–24
  Democratic Farmer Labor Party, 14–15, 20–21,
    22

Minnesota Federation of Business and
   Professional Women's Clubs (*continued*)
   as educational and civic organization, 15–16
   equal pay, 22
   Equal Rights Amendment, 16, 18–19, 21–22
   Governor's Commission on the Status of
      Women, 22–23
   legislative action, 19
   media, protests against stereotyping, 15–16
   Minnesota Commission on the Status of
      Women, 23–24
   national security, 21
   National Woman's Party, 16
   Operation Buttonhole, 20, 21
   placing in policy-making posts, 19
   Political Alertness Project, 18, 19
   politics, 12–24
   protective labor legislation, 16–17, 20–21
   in state government, 14–15
   state legislative platforms during 1950s, 21
   World War II, 13–14
Multicultural Lesbian Gay Studies program,
   University of California, Berkeley, 240,
   242–243
Muscatine, IA, Mexican American women,
   179–180
   boycott of Oscar Mayer plant, 181–182
   dual oppression of race and gender
      discrimination, 182–185
   health services, 179–180
   Mexican American activist nuns, 179–180
   picket Farmall plant, 183
   sexual harassment, 184
   traditional community-based approach, 182–183

N
National Association for the Advancement of
   Colored People
   black-on-white rape cases, 34
   homophile movement, parallels, 58
National Association of Women Judges, 223
National Association of Women Lawyers,
   Committee for the Advancement of
   Women Lawyers to High Judicial Office,
   213
National Council of Churches, 102
National Council of Negro Women
   African American and white women in
      partnership, 82–84
   anti-colonial positions, 89–92
   Bethune, Mary McLeod, 80, 82, 83–92
      women appointed to U.N., 83–85
   Cold War, 86
   Commission on the Status of Women, 84–85
   fight for recognition, 85
   foreign policy, 84–92, 88–92
   geo-political realignments, 85–87
   history, 81–83
   International Assembly conference, 87
   international politics, 5–6
   Mason, Vivian Carter, 86–87
   McCarthyism, 89–92
   San Francisco conference, 84

U.N.
   human rights, 88–92
   non-governmental organization consultative
      status, 85
National Federation of Business and Professional
   Women's Clubs, 11
   1920s and 1930s forays into politics, 13
   1946 convention, 18
   Equal Rights Amendment, 13, 18
   segregation, 82
   World War II, 16, 17
National Lawyers Guild, 31
   Abzug, Bella, 31
   Cold War, 31
   Left feminist lawyers, 31
      protests, 37
   sex discrimination, 37
National Negro Congress, 81
National Organization for Women
   Daughters of Bilitis, 58–59
   lesbians, 58–59
National security, Minnesota Federation of
   Business and Professional Women's Clubs,
   21
National Woman's Party, 49
   Minnesota Federation of Business and
      Professional Women's Clubs, 16–17
   segregation, 82
Nation building, gender, 65–77
New York, NY, Daughters of Bilitis
   alliances with other East Coast gay groups, 56
   convention, 57
   founding, 56
   independence within Daughters of Bilitis, 56
   The Ladder, 56–57
   media coverage, 57
Non-governmental organizations, women's clubs,
   99–109
North American Conference of Homophile
   Organizations, 59
Northampton, MA, lesbians, 191–205
   ambivalence, 199–200
   competitiveness, 200–205
   contested values, 200–205
   history, 191–192, 193–195
   "sneakers *vs.* clients" issue, 200–205
   wave theory, 192–193

O
Office of Price Administration, federal
   government, 117–118
Okala, Ollie, 87

P
Paul, Alice, 49
Personal is Political, 28, 30, 40
   Abzug, Bella, 36, 37
Planning control, 167–168
Police harassment, lesbians, 50–51
Political life cycles of women, 7–8
Political lobbying, Consumers' Protective
   Committee, 123–125, 128–129
Politics of location, 6